W9-AQT-603

Zondervan Illustrated Bible Backgrounds Commentary

SOFTCOVER EDITION

Isaiah

David W. Baker

John H. Walton, *General Editor*

ZONDERVAN

ZONDERVAN.com/
AUTHORTRACKER
follow your favorite authors

ZONDERVAN

Isaiah
Copyright © 2009, 2013 by David W. Baker
Previously published in *Isaiah, Jeremiah, Lamentations, Ezekiel, Daniel*

Requests for information should be addressed to:

Zondervan, *Grand Rapids, Michigan 49530*

This edition: ISBN 978-0-310-49209-2

The Library of Congress has cataloged the complete volume as:

Isaiah, Jeremiah, Lamentations, Ezekiel, Daniel / John H. Walton, general editor.
p. cm. — (Zondervan illustrated Bible backgrounds commentary ; v. 4)
Includes bibliographical references and index.
ISBN 978-0-310-25576-5 (hardcover, printed)
1. Bible. O.T. Prophets — Commentaries. I. Walton, John H., 1952-
BS1505.53.I83 2009
224'.07 — dc22 2009009777

All Scripture quotations, unless otherwise indicated, are taken from The Holy Bible, *New International Version®, NIV®*. Copyright © 1973, 1978, 1984 by Biblica, Inc.™ Used by permission. All rights reserved worldwide.

Maps by International Mapping. Copyright © 2009 by Zondervan. All rights reserved.

Any Internet addresses (websites, blogs, etc.) and telephone numbers this book are offered as a resource. They are not intended in any way to be or imply an endorsement by Zondervan, nor does Zondervan vouch for the content of these sites and numbers for the life of this book.

All rights reserved. No part of this publication may be reproduced, stored in a retrieval system, or transmitted in any form or by any means — electronic, mechanical, photocopy, recording, or any other — except for brief quotations in printed reviews, without the prior permission of the publisher.

Interior design: Mark Sheeres

Printed in China

13 14 15 16 17 18 19 20 /GPC/ 20 19 18 17 16 15 14 13 12 11 10 9 8 7 6 5 4 3 2 1

Acknowledgments

We are grateful for so many who have provided us photographs, some at reduced prices and others free of charge, to help make this work a visual resource on the ancient world. Credits appear by each photograph, but we would especially recognize the following:

Wikimedia Commons makes photographs available through commons.wikimedia.org under a variety of licenses. We have benefited greatly from those that have been released into public domain and have sought out appropriate permission for those that have creative commons licensing (cc-by or cc-by-sa). These photographs are not copyright protected in this set but are available for use under the same terms that we used them.

In connection to Wikimedia, we have used a number of photographs from the Yorck Project, whose images are indicated as being in the public domain, but with compilation protected under the GNU Free Documentation License.

We would like especially to thank Marie-Lan Nguyen, who provided so many photos in public domain on Wikimedia, as well as Rama, who even went and took specific photos that we wanted. Others who provided numerous photographs through Wikimedia include Guillaume Blanchard and Keith Schengili-Roberts.

We are grateful to so many who posted their photographs on Flickr and made them available to us when we requested them. Lenka Peacock, Manfred Nader, and Peter White were particularly generous and gracious as they allowed us to use many of their photographs.

The Schøyen Collection supplied many photographs at no charge, and we are grateful to Elizabeth Sorenssen for her capable help.

Edward Loring, Research Fellow and Network Administrator Russian Academy of Sciences Centre for Egyptological Studies, Moscow (CESRAS), Russian Institute of Egyptology in Cairo (RIEC), provided photographs we could not have otherwise gotten.

Photography Suppliers were very helpful in our endless searches for photographs and we would especially like to acknowledge Todd Bolen (www.bibleplaces.com), Zev Radovan (www.biblelandpictures.com), Art Resource (www.artres.com, with thanks to Ann and Jennifer), Werner Forman (www.werner-forman-archive.com, with thanks to Themis), Jim Martin (see photo credits on page xxvii), Jack Hazut (www.israelimage.net), Richard Cleave (Rohr Productions), and Neal Bierling (www.phoenixdatasystems.com).

Thanks also to my colleagues who provided photographs: Fred Mabie, Steven Voth, John Monson, Jim Monson, Rami Arav, Scott Noegel, Aren Maier, Daniel Master, the Leon Levy Foundation, Alan Millard, Stephen Bourke, Constance Gane, and Randall Younker.

We are also grateful to those who supplied photographs from their personal collections: Michael Greenhalgh, Tim Bulkeley (eBibleTools.com/israel), Caryn Reeder,

Christina Beblavi, Lisa Jean Winbolt, Brian McMorrow, Kim Walton, David Hall, and the late Maurice Thompson (photographer of the Bible Scene Set), his sons Peter and Andrew, and Geoff Tucker, who scanned the slides for us.

Our gratitude also goes to Patti Ricotta, who provided helpful financing for Song of Songs pictures.

For artwork we are grateful to Susanna Vagt, Alva Steffler, and Jonathan Walton.

For help with the maps, we are most grateful to Carl Rasmussen, the author of the *Zondervan NIV Atlas of the Bible.*

Thanks also goes to Charlie Trimm for the preparation of the visuals index.

We would like to thank the always helpful staff at Zondervan whose hard work made this project possible: Katya Covrett, Verlyn Verbrugge, and Kim Tanner deserve special mention, as well as Jack Kuhatschek, who got the project started while he was still at Zondervan.

Finally, my entire family was involved in the project. Jill and Josh provided photos and Jonathan provided artwork. But far beyond those contributions, words cannot express the gratitude I owe to my wife, Kim, who for three years served as my research assistant in tracking down pictures with her consummate research skills. Without her perseverance, creativity, and companionship, the product here provided could not have been achieved. Through countless hours working by my side, going through the manuscript entry by entry to decide what visuals to provide and then painstakingly researching where they could be found, she became an expert in iconography and art from the ancient world. But more than that, she stepped into my world as a cherished partner in my work and ministry, making every day "a day for a daydream." To her these volumes are dedicated with love, respect, and admiration.

John H. Walton
General Editor

Abbreviations

AAA . . . . *Annals of Archaeology and Anthropology*
AASOR . . . . Annual of the American Schools of Oriental Research
AB . . . . Anchor Bible
AB . . . . *Assyriologische Bibliothek*
ABC . . . . *Assyrian and Babylonian Chronicles*. A. K. Grayson. TCS 5. Locust Valley, New York, 1975
ABD . . . . *Anchor Bible Dictionary*. D. N. Freedman. 6 vols. New York, 1992
ABL. . . . . *Assyrian and Babylonian Letters Belonging to the Kouyunjik Collections of the British Museum*. R. F. Harper. 14 vols. Chicago, 1892–1914
ABR. . . . . *Australian Biblical Review*
ABRL . . . . . . Anchor Bible Reference Library
AbrN . . . . *Abr-Nahrain*
ABS. . . . . Arab Background Series
ACCS . . . . . . Ancient Christian Commentary on Scripture
ACEBT . . . . . *Amsterdamse Cahiers voor Exegese en bijbelse Theologie*
ADD . . . . *Assyrian Deeds and Documents*. C. H. W. Johns. 4 vols. Cambridge, 1898–1923
AEL . . . . *Ancient Egyptian Literature*. M. Lichtheim. 3 vols. Berkeley, 1971–1980
AfO . . . . *Archiv für Orientforschung*
AfOB . . . . . . Archiv für Orientforschung: Beiheft
ÄgAbh. . . . . . Ägyptologische Abhandlungen
AHw . . . . *Akkadisches Handwörterbuch*. W. von Soden. 3 vols. Wiesbaden, 1965–81
AJA . . . . *American Journal of Archeology*
AJBA . . . . . . *Australian Journal of Biblical Archaeology*
AJSLL . . . . . . *American Journal of Semitic Languages and Literature*
AMD. . . . . . . Ancient Magic and Divination
AnBib . . . . . . Analecta biblica
ANEP . . . . . . *The Ancient Near East in Pictures Relating to the Old Testament*. J. B. Pritchard. Princeton, 1954
ANET . . . . . . *Ancient Near Eastern Texts Relating to the Old Testament*. J. B. Pritchard. 3rd ed. Princeton, 1969
ANF . . . . *Ante-Nicene Fathers*
AnOr . . . . . . Analecta orientalia
AnSt. . . . . *Anatolian Studies*
AO. . . . . Antiquités orientales
AO. . . . . *Der Alte Orient*
AOAT . . . . . . Alter Orient und Altes Testament
AOB . . . . *Altorientalische Bilder zum Alten Testament*
AOS . . . . American Oriental Series
AOTC. . . . . . Abingdon Old Testament Commentary
AOTS . . . . . . *Archaeology and Old Testament Study*. D. W. Thomas. Oxford, 1967
APOT . . . . . . *Apocrypha and Pseudepigrapha of the Old Testament*. Ed. R. H. Charles. 2 vols. Oxford: Oxford University Press, 1913
ARAB . . . . . . *Ancient Records of Assyria and Babylonia*. Daniel David Luckenbill. 2 vols. Chicago, 1926–1927
Arch . . . . *Archaeology*
ARI . . . . *Assyrian Royal Inscriptions*. A. K. Grayson. 2 vols. RANE. Wiesbaden, 1972–1976
ARM . . . . . . Archives royales de Mari
ARMT . . . . . Archives royales de Mari, transcrite et traduite
ArtH . . . . *Art History*

ARW . . . . *Archiv für Religionswissenschaft*
AS . . . . Assyriological Studies
ASJ . . . . *Acta Sumerologica (Japan)*
ASOR . . . . . . American Schools of Oriental Research
ASORDS . . . American Schools of Oriental Research Dissertation Series
ASTI . . . . *Annual of the Swedish Theological Institute*
ATJ . . . . *Ashland Theological Journal*
AThR . . . . . . *Anglican Theological Review*
ATSDS . . . . . Andrews Theological Seminary Dissertation Series
AuOr . . . . . . *Aula orientalis*
AUSDS . . . . . Andrews University Seminary Dissertation Series
AUSS. . . . . . . *Andrews University Seminary Studies*
AUU . . . . Acta Universitatis Upsaliensis
BA . . . . *Biblical Archaeologist*
BAIAS . . . . . *Bulletin of the Anglo-Israel Archeological Society*
BAR . . . . *Biblical Archaeology Review*
BARead . . . . *Biblical Archaeologist Reader*
BASOR . . . . . *Bulletin of the American Schools of Oriental Research*
BASORSup . . Bulletin of the American Schools of Oriental Research: Supplement Series
BAW . . . . Bayerischen Akademie der Wissen
BBB . . . . Bonner biblische Beiträge
BBET. . . . . . . Beiträge zur biblischen Exegese und Theologie
BBR . . . . *Bulletin for Biblical Research*
BBVO . . . . . . Berliner Beiträge zum Vorderen Orient
BCOTWP . . . Baker Commentary on the Old Testament Wisdom and Psalms
BDB. . . . . Brown, F., S. R. Driver, and C. A. Briggs. *A Hebrew and English Lexicon of the Old Testament.* Oxford, 1907
BeO . . . . *Bibbia e oriente*
BES . . . . *Bes*
BETL. . . . . . . Bibliotheca epheremeridum theologicarum lovaniensium
BETS . . . . *Bulletin of the Evangelical Society*
BHH . . . . *Biblisch-historisches Handwörterbuch*. B. Reicke and L. Rost. Göttingen, 1962-1966
Bib . . . . *Biblica*
BibOr . . . . . . Biblica et orientalia
BibSem . . . . . Biblical Seminar
BibRes . . . . . . *Biblical Research*
BiOr. . . . . *Biblioteca Orientalis*
BJRL . . . . *Bulletin of the John Rylands University Library of Manchester*
BJS . . . . Brown Judaic Studies
BM. . . . . British Museum
BN . . . . *Biblische Notizen*
BO. . . . . *Bibliotheca orientalis*
BR . . . . *Biblical Research*
BRev . . . . *Bible Review*
BRM . . . . Babylonian Religion and Mythology
BSac . . . . *Bibliotheca sacra*
BSC. . . . . Bible Student's Commentary
BSOAS . . . . . *Bulletin of the School of Oriental and African Studies*
BT . . . . *Bible Translator*
BTB . . . . *Biblical Theology Bulletin*
BWL . . . . *Babylonian Wisdom Literature.* W. G. Lambert. Oxford, 1960; reprinted Eisenbrauns, 1996
BZ . . . . *Biblische Zeitschrift*
BZABR . . . . . Beihefte zur Zeitschrift für altorientalische und biblische Rechtsgeschichte
BZAW . . . . . Beihefte zur Zeitschrift für die alttestamentliche Wissenschaft
CAD . . . . *The Assyrian Dictionary of the Oriental Institute of the University of Chicago.* Chicago, 1956–
CAH . . . . *Cambridge Ancient History*
CahRB. . . . . . Cahiers de la Revue biblique
CANE. . . . . . *Civilizations of the Ancient Near East*. J. Sasson. 4 vols. New York, 1995
CAT. . . . . Commentaire de l'Ancien Testament

CAT. . . . . *Cuneiform Alphabetic Texts from Ugarit, Ras Ibn Hani and Other Places*. M. Dietrich, O. Loretz, and J. Sanmartin. Munster, 1997
CBC . . . . Cambridge Bible Commentary
CBET . . . . . . Contributions to Biblical Exegesis and Theology
CBQ . . . . *Catholic Biblical Quarterly*
CBQMS . . . . Catholic Biblical Quarterly Monograph Series
CH. . . . . Code of Hammurabi
CHANE . . . . Culture and History of the Ancient Near East
CHI . . . . Cambridge History of Iran. 7 vols. 1968-91
CIS . . . . Corpus inscriptionum semiticarum
CIS . . . . *Corpus inscriptionum semiticarum*
CJ . . . . *Classical Journal*
CL . . . . Code of Lipit-Ishtar
CML . . . . *Canaanite Myths and Legends*. G. R. Driver. Edinburgh, 1956. J. C. L. Gibson, 1978[2]
CNI . . . . Carsten Niebuhr Institute
ConBOT . . . . Coniectanea biblica: Old Testament Series
COS . . . . *The Context of Scripture*. W. W. Hallo. 3 vols. Leiden, 1997–2002
CT . . . . *Cuneiform Texts from Babylonian Tablets in the British Museum*
CTA . . . . *Corpus des tablettes en cunéiformes alphabétiques découvertes à Ras Shamra-Ugarit de 1929 à 1939*. A. Herdner. Mission de Ras Shamra 10. Paris, 1963
CTH . . . . Catalogue des textes hittites
CTU . . . . *The Cuneiform Alphabetic Texts from Ugarit, Ras Ibn Hani, and Other Places*. M. Dietrich, O. Loretz, and J. Sanmartín. Münster, 1995
CU. . . . . Code of Ur-Nammu
CurTM. . . . . *Currents in Theology and Mission*
DANE . . . . . . *Dictionary of the Ancient Near East*
DBAT . . . . . . *Dielheimer Blätter zum Alten Testament*
DBI . . . . *Dictionary of Biblical Imagery*. T. Longman and L. Ryken. Downers Grove, 1998
DCH . . . . *Dictionary of Classical Hebrew*. D. J. A. Clines. Sheffield, 1993–
DDD . . . . *Dictionary of Deities and Demons in the Bible*. K. van der Toorn, B. Becking, and P. W. van der Horst. Leiden, 1995. 2nd ed., Grand Rapids, 1998
DISO . . . . . . Dictionnaire des inscriptions sémitiques de l'ouest. Ch. F. Jean and J. Hoftijzer. Leiden, 1965
DNWSI. . . . . Dictionary of the North-West Semitic Inscriptions. J. Hoftijzer and K. Jongeling. 2 vols. Leiden, 1995
DOTHB . . . . *Dictionary of the Old Testament: Historical Books*
DOTP . . . . . . *Dictionary of the Old Testament: Pentateuch*. T. D. Alexander and D. W. Baker. Downers Grove, 2003
DOTT . . . . . . *Documents from Old Testament Times*. D. W. Thomas, London, 1958
DSB. . . . . Daily Study Bible
EA . . . . El-Amarna tablets. According to the edition of J. A. Knudtzon. *Die el-Amarna-Tafeln*. Leipzig, 1908–1915. Reprint, Aalen, 1964. Continued in A. F. Rainey, *El-Amarna Tablets, 359–379*. 2nd revised ed. Kevelaer, 1978
EA . . . . *Epigraphica anatolica*
EAEHL . . . . Encyclopedia of Archaeological Excavations in the Holy Land. M. Avi-Yonah. 4 vols. Jerusalem, 1975

EBC . . . . *Expositor's Bible Commentary*
ECC. . . . . Eerdmans Critical Commentary
EPRO . . . . . . Études préliminaires aux religions orientales
ErIsr . . . . *Eretz-Israel*
ET . . . . *Evangelische Theologie*
ETS . . . . Evangelical Theological Society
ETSS . . . . Evangelical Theological Society Studies
EvQ . . . . *Evangelical Quarterly*
EvTh. . . . . *Evangelische Theologie*
FAOS. . . . . . . Freiburger altorientalische Studien
FAT . . . . Forschungen zum Alten Testament
FB . . . . Forschungen zur Bibel
FCI . . . . Foundations in Contemporary Interpretation
FOTL . . . . . . Forms of the Old Testament Literature
GKC . . . . *Gesenius' Hebrew Grammar.* E. Kautzsch. Translated by A. E. Cowley. 2nd ed. Oxford, 1910
GM . . . . *Göttinger Miszellen*
GTTOT . . . . *The Geographical and Topographical Texts of the Old Testament.* J. J. Simons. Studia Francisci Scholten memoriae dicata 2. Leiden, 1959
HALOT . . . . *The Hebrew and Aramaic Lexicon of the Old Testament.* L. Koehler, W. Baumgartner, and J. J. Stamm. Translated and edited under the supervision of M. E. J. Richardson. 4 vols. Leiden, 1994–1999
HANEL. . . . . *History of Ancient Near Eastern Law.* R. Westbrook. 2 vols. Leiden, 2003
HAR . . . . *Hebrew Annual Review*
HAT . . . . Handbuch zum Alten Testament
HBD . . . . *HarperCollins Bible Dictionary*
HBS. . . . . Herders Biblische Studien
HCOT. . . . . . Historical Commentary on the Old Testament
HDR . . . . Harvard Dissertations in Religion
HKM. . . . . . . *Hethitische Keilschrifttafeln aus Masat.* Ed. Sedat Alp. Ankara: Turk Tarih Kurumu Basimevi, 1991
HL. . . . . Hittite Laws
HO . . . . Handbuch der Orientalistik
HS . . . . *Hebrew Studies*
HSM . . . . Harvard Semitic Monographs
HSS . . . . Harvard Semitic Studies
HTR . . . . *Harvard Theological Review*
HUCA . . . . . *Hebrew Union College Annual*
IB . . . . *Interpreter's Bible.* G. A. Buttrick et al. 12 vols. New York, 1951–1957
IBC . . . . Interpretation Bible Commentary
IBD . . . . *Illustrated Bible Dictionary.* J. Douglas. 3 vols. Leicester, 1980
IBHS . . . . *An Introduction to Biblical Hebrew Syntax.* B. K. Waltke and M. O'Connor. Winona Lake, 1990
ICC . . . . International Critical Commentary
IDB . . . . *The Interpreter's Dictionary of the Bible.* G. A. Buttrick. 4 vols. Nashville, 1962
IDBSup . . . . . *The Interpreter's Dictionary of the Bible: Supplementary Volume.* K. Crim. Nashville, 1976
IEJ . . . . *Israel Exploration Journal*
IOS . . . . *Israel Oriental Society*
IrAnt . . . . *Iranica Antiqua*
Iraq . . . . *Iraq*
IRT . . . . Issues in Religion and Theology
ISBE . . . . *International Standard Bible Encyclopedia.* G. W. Bromiley. 4 vols. Grand Rapids, 1979–1988
IVPBBC-OT . *IVP Bible Background Commentary on the OT.* J. H. Walton, V. H. Matthews, and M. W. Chavalas. Downers Grove, 2000

JAGNES . . . . *Journal of the Association of Graduate Near Eastern Studies* (University of Berkeley)
JANESCU . . *Journal of the Ancient Near Eastern Society of Columbia University*
JAOS . . . . . . Journal of the American Oriental Society
JB . . . . Jerusalem Bible
JBL . . . . *Journal of Biblical Literature*
JCS . . . . *Journal of Cuneiform Studies*
JDS . . . . Judean Desert Studies
JEA . . . . *Journal of Egyptian Archaeology*
JEOL . . . . . . *Jaarbericht van het Vooraziatisch-Egyptisch Gezelschap (Genootschap) Ex oriente lux*
JESHO . . . . . *Journal of the Economic and Social History of the Orient*
JETS . . . . *Journal of the Evangelical Theological Society*
JJS . . . . *Journal of Jewish Studies*
JNES . . . . *Journal of Near Eastern Studies*
JNSL . . . . *Journal of Northwest Semitic Languages*
JPS. . . . . Jewish Publication Society
JPSTC . . . . . . JPS Torah Commentary
JQR . . . . *Jewish Quarterly Review*
JR. . . . . *Journal of Religion*
JRAS . . . . *Journal of the Royal Asiatic Society*
JSem . . . . *Journal of Semitics*
JSJ . . . . *Journal for the Study of Judaism (in the Persian, Hellenistic, and Roman Periods)*
JSOT . . . . *Journal for the Study of the Old Testament*
JSOTSup . . . Journal for the Study of the Old Testament: Supplement Series
JSS . . . . *Journal of Semitic Studies*
JSSEA . . . . . . *Journal of the Society for the Study of Egyptian Antiquities*
JTS . . . . *Journal of Theological Studies*
KAH . . . . *Keilshrifttexte aus Assur historischen Inhalts*
KAI . . . . *Kanaanäische und aramäische Inschriften*. H. Donner and W. Röllig. 2nd ed. Wiesbaden, 1966–1969
KAR . . . . *Keilschrifttexte aus Assur religiösen Inhalts*. E. Ebeling. Leipzig, 1919–1923
KAT . . . . Kommentar zum Alten Testament
KBo . . . . *Keilschrifttexte aus Boghazköi*
KHC . . . . Kurzer Hand-Kommentar zum Alten Testament
KTU . . . . *Die keilalphabetischen Texte aus Ugarit*. M. Dietrich, O. Loretz, and J. Sanmartín. AOAT 24/1. Neukirchen-Vluyn, 1976. 2nd enlarged ed. of *KTU: The Cuneiform Alphabetic Texts from Ugarit, Ras Ibn Hani, and Other Places*. M. Dietrich, O. Loretz, and J. Sanmartín. Münster, 1995 (= *CTU*)
KUB . . . . *Keilschrifturkunden aus Boghazköi*
LAE. . . . . *Literature of Ancient Egypt*. W. K. Simpson. 3rd ed. New Haven, 2003
LAPO . . . . . . Litteratures anciennes du Proche-Orient
LBI. . . . . Library of Biblical Interpretation
LCL. . . . . Loeb Classical Library
LE . . . . Laws of Eshunna
Levant . . . . . . *Levant*
LH. . . . . Laws of Hammurabi
LIMC . . . . . . *Lexicon iconographicum mythologiae classicae*. Edited by H. C. Ackerman and J.-R. Gisler. 8 vols. Zurich, 1981–1997
LL . . . . Laws of Lipit-Ishtar
LU . . . . Laws of Ur-Nammu
LXX . . . . Septuagint
Maarav . . . . . *Maarav*
MAL . . . . Middle Assyrian Laws
MANE . . . . . Monographs of the Ancient Near East
MAOG . . . . . Mitteilungen der Altorientalischen Gesellschaft
MARI . . . . . . *Mari: Annales de recherches interdisciplinaires*

MCAAS . . . . Memoires of the Connecticut Academy of Arts & Sciences
MDOG . . . . Mitteilungen der Deutschen Orient-Gesellschaft
MGWJ . . . . . *Monatschrift für Geschichte und Wissenschaft des Judentums*
MOS . . . . Midden-Oosten Studies
MSJ . . . . *The Master's Seminary Journal*
Muses. . . . . . . *Before the Muses: An Anthology of Akkadian Literature.* Benjamin R. Foster. 2 vols. Bethesda, 1993
MVAG. . . . . . Mitteilungen der Vordersasiatisch-ägyptischen Gesellschaft. Vols. 1-44. 1896-1939
NAC . . . . New American Commentary
NBD . . . . *New Bible Dictionary.* J. D. Douglas and N. Hillyer. 2nd ed. Downers Grove, 1982
NBL. . . . . Neo-Babylonian Laws
NCB . . . . New Century Bible
NCBC . . . . . . New Century Bible Commentary
NEA . . . . *Near Eastern Archaeology*
NEAEHL . . . The New Encyclopedia of Archaeological Excavations in the Holy Land. E. Stern. 4 vols. Jerusalem, 1993
NEB. . . . . New English Bible
NERT . . . . . . *Near Eastern Religious Texts Relating to the Old Testament.* W. Beyerlin. OTL. London, 1978
NGTT . . . . . . *Nederduitse gereformeerde teologiese tydskrif*
NIBC. . . . . . . New International Bible Commentary
NIBCOT . . . New International Biblical Commentary on the Old Testament
NICOT . . . . . New International Commentary on the Old Testament
NIDBA . . . . . *New International Dictionary of Biblical Archaeology.* E. M. Blaiklock and R. K. Harrison. Grand Rapids, 1983
NIDOTTE . . *New International Dictionary of Old Testament Theology and Exegesis.* W. A. VanGemeren. 5 vols. Grand Rapids, 1997
NIV. . . . . New International Version
NIVAC . . . . . NIV Application Commentary
NJPS . . . . Tanakh: The Holy Scriptures: The New JPS Translation according to the Traditional Hebrew Text
NRSV . . . . New Revised Standard Version
NSBT. . . . . . . New Studies in Biblical Theology
NTOA. . . . . . Novum Testamentum et orbis antiquus
OBC . . . . Orientalia biblica et christiana
OBO . . . . Orbis biblicus et orientalis
OCD. . . . . . . *Oxford Classical Dictionary.* S. Hornblower and A. Spawforth. 3rd ed. Oxford, 1996
OEAE . . . . . . *The Oxford Encyclopedia of Ancient Egypt.* D. Redford. 3 vols. New York, 2001
OEANE . . . . *The Oxford Encyclopedia of Archaeology in the Near East.* E. M. Meyers. 5 vols. New York, 1997
OIP . . . . Oriental Institute Publications
OLA . . . . Orientalia lovaniensia analecta
OLP . . . . Orientalia lovaniensia periodica
OLZ. . . . . *Orientalistische Literaturzeitung*
Or . . . . *Orientalia* (NS)
OrAnt . . . . . . *Oriens antiquus*
OS. . . . . Oudtestamentische studiën
OTE. . . . . *Old Testament Essays*
OTG . . . . Old Testament Guides
OTL . . . . Old Testament Library
OTP. . . . . *Old Testament Pseudepigrapha.* J. H. Charlesworth. 2 vols. Garden City, 1983, 1985
OTS. . . . . Old Testament Studies

OTWSA . . . . Ou-Testamentiese Werkgemeenskap van Suid-Afrika
OtSt . . . . *Oudtestamentische Studiën*
PAPS . . . . Proceedings of the American Philosophical Society
PBS . . . . Publications of the Babylonian Section
PEQ . . . . *Palestine Exploration Quarterly*
POTT . . . . . . *Peoples of Old Testament Times*. D. J. Wiseman. Oxford, 1973
POTW. . . . . . *Peoples of the Old Testament World*. A. Hoerth, G. Mattingly and E. Yamauchi. Grand Rapids, 1994
PRU . . . . *Le palais royal d'Ugarit*
PT . . . . Pyramid Texts
RA . . . . *Revue d'assyriologie et d'archéologie orientale*
RAI . . . . Recontre assyriologique internationale
RANE . . . . . . Records of the Ancient Near East
RANE . . . . . . *Readings from the Ancient Near East*. B. Arnold and B. Beyer. Grand Rapids, 2002
RB . . . . *Revue biblique*
RevB . . . . *Revue de Qumran*
RevistB . . . . . *Revista bíblica*
RGG . . . . *Religion in Geschichte und Gegenwart*. K. Galling. 7 vols. 3rd ed. Tübingen, 1957-65
RHA . . . . *Revue hittite et asianique*
RHPR . . . . . . Revue d'Histoire et de Philosophie Religieuse
RHR . . . . *Revue de l'histoire des religions*
RIDA. . . . . . . *Revue internationale des droits de l'antiquité*
RIM . . . . The Royal Inscriptions of Mesopotamia Project. Toronto
RIMA . . . . . . The Royal Inscriptions of Mesopotamia, Assyrian Periods
RIMB . . . . . . The Royal Inscriptions of Mesopotamia, Babylonian Periods
RIME . . . . . . The Royal Inscriptions of Mesopotamia, Early Periods
RISA . . . . Royal Inscriptions of Sumer and Akkad. G. A. Barton. New Haven, 1929
RivB. . . . . *Rivista biblica italiana*
RlA . . . . *Reallexikon der Assyriologie*. Erich Ebeling et al. Berlin, 1928–
RQ. . . . . *Römische Quartalschrift für christliche Altertumskunde und Kirchengeschichte*
RS . . . . Ras Shamra
RSP . . . . *Ras Shamra Parallels*
SAA . . . . State Archives of Assyria
SAALT . . . . . State Archives of Assyria Literary Texts
SAAS . . . . . . State Archives of Assyria Studies
SAOC . . . . . . Studies in Ancient Oriental Civilizations
SBAB . . . . . . Stuttgarter biblische Aufsatzbände
SBAW . . . . . . Sitzungsberichte der bayerischen Akademie der Wissenschaften
SBB . . . . Stuttgarter biblische Beiträge
SBC . . . . Student Bible Commentary
SBFLA. . . . . . *Studii biblici Franciscani liber annus*
SBH. . . . . *Sumerische-babylonische Hymnen nach Thonafeln griechischer Zeit*. G. A. Reisner. Berlin, 1896
SBLABS . . . . Society of Biblical Literature Archaeology and Biblical Studies
SBLDS . . . . . Society of Biblical Literature Dissertation Series
SBLMS . . . . . Society of Biblical Literature Monograph Series
SBLRBS. . . . . Society of Biblical Literature Resources for Biblical Study
SBLSP . . . . . . *Society of Biblical Literature Seminar Papers*
SBLSymS . . . Society of Biblical Literature Symposium Series
SBLWAW . . . Society of Biblical Literature Writings from the Ancient World
SBONT . . . . . Sacred Books of the Old and New Testament

SBS . . . . Suttgarter Bibelstudien
SBT . . . . Studes in Biblical Theology
SBTS . . . . Sources for Biblical and Theological Study
SC . . . . Sources chrétiennes. Paris, 1943–
ScrHier . . . . . Scripta hierosolymitana
SDOAP . . . . . Studia et Documenta ad Iura Orientis Antiqui Pertinentia
SE . . . . Studies in Egyptology
SemeiaSt . . . . Semeia Studies
SHANE . . . . Studies in the History of the Ancient Near East
SHCANE . . . Studies in the History and Culture of the Ancient Near East
SHJPLI . . . . . Studies in the History of the Jewish People and the Land of Israel
SHR. . . . . Studies in the History of Religion
SJLA . . . . Studies in Judaism in Late Antiquity
SJOT . . . . *Scandinavian Journal of the Old Testament*
SNN . . . . Studia Semitica Neerlandica
SO . . . . Symbolae osloenses
SOTSMS. . . . Society for Old Testament Studies Monograph Series
SSI . . . . *Textbook of Syrian Semitic Inscriptions*. 3 vols. Oxford, 1971–82
SSN . . . . Studia semitica neerlandica
SSS . . . . Semitic Study Series
ST . . . . *Studia theologica*
StBoT. . . . . . . Studien zu den Boghazkoi Texten
StudOr . . . . . Studia orientalia
Sumer . . . . . . *Sumer: A Journal of Archaeology and History in Iraq*
SWBA . . . . . . Social World of Biblical Antiquity
Syr . . . . *Syria*
TA . . . . *Tel Avi*
TAD. . . . . *Textbook of Aramaic Documents*. B. Porten and A. Yardeni. 4 vols. Jerusalem, 1986-99
TAPS. . . . . . . Transactions of the American Philosophical Society
TB . . . . Theologische Bücherei
TBC. . . . . Texts from the Babylonian Collection (Yale)
TCL. . . . . Textes cunéiforms. Musée du Louvre
TCS. . . . . Texts from Cuneiform Sources
TDOT . . . . . . *Theological Dictionary of the Old Testament*. G. J. Botterweck and H. Ringgren. Translated by J. T. Willis, G. W. Bromiley, and D. E. Green. 15 vols. Grand Rapids, 1974–
TGUOS. . . . . Transactions of the Glascow University Oriental Society
Them . . . . *Themelios*
TJ. . . . . *Trinity Journal*
TLOT . . . . . . *Theological Lexicon of the Old Testament*. E. Jenni, with assistance from C. Westermann. Translated by M. E. Biddle. 3 vols. Peabody, Mass., 1997
TOB. . . . . *Traduction Oecuménique de la Bible*
TOTC . . . . . Tyndale Old Testament Commentaries
Transeu . . . . . *Transeuphratène*
TS . . . . *Theological Studies*
TSF Bulletin . *Theological Student's Fellowship Bulletin*
TSTT. . . . . . . Toronto Semitic Texts and Studies
TWOT . . . . . *Theological Wordbook of the Old Testament*. R. L. Harris, G. L. Archer Jr. 2 vols. Chicago, 1980
TynBul . . . . . *Tyndale Bulletin*
TZ . . . . *Theologische Zeitschrift*
UBL . . . . Ugaritisch-biblische Literatur
UCOP . . . . . . University of Cambridge Oriental Publications
UF . . . . *Ugarit-Forschungen*
UNP . . . . Ugaritic Narrative Poetry. Simon B. Parker. SBLWAW 9. Atlanta, 1997

UT . . . . *Ugaritic Textbook.* C. H. Gordon. AnOr 38. Rome, 1965
VAB. . . . . Vorderasiatische Bibliothek
VAT . . . . Vorderasiatische Abteilung Tontafel. Vorderasiatisches Museum, Berlin
VB . . . . Vorderasiatische Bibliothek
VT . . . . *Vetus Testamentum*
VTE. . . . . Vassal Treaties of Esarhaddon
VTSup . . . . . Vetus Testamentum Supplements
WBC . . . . . . Word Biblical Commentary
WHJP . . . . . . World History of the Jewish People
WO . . . . *Die Welt des Orients*
WOO . . . . . . Wiener Offene Oreintalistik
WTJ . . . . *Westminster Theological Journal*
WVDOG . . . Wissenschaftliche Veröffentlichungen der deutschen Orientgesellschaft
WZKM . . . . . *Wiener Zeitschrift für die Kunde des Morgenlandes*
YNER . . . . . . Yale New Eastern, Researches
YOS . . . . Yale Oriental Series, Texts
ZA . . . . *Zeitschrift für Assyriologie*
ZABR . . . . . . *Zeitschrift für altorientalische und biblische Rechtgeschichte*
ZÄS . . . . *Zeitschrift für ägyptische Sprache und Altertumskunde*
ZAW . . . . *Zeitschrift für die alttestamentliche Wissenschaft*
ZDMG . . . . . Zeitschrift der deutschen morgenländischen Gesellschaft
ZDPV . . . . . . *Zeitschrift des deutschen Palästina-Vereins*
ZKT . . . . *Zeitschrift für katholische Theologie*
ZNW. . . . . . . Zeitschrift für die neutestamentliche Wissenschaft
ZPEB . . . . *Zondervan Pictorial Encyclopedia of the Bible.* M. C. Tenney. 5 vols. Grand Rapids, 1975
ZTK . . . . *Zeitschrift für Theologie und Kirche*

ISAIAH

by David W. Baker

Introduction

Isaiah's magnificent prophecy spans not only history, going from creation (e.g., 42:5) to eternity (e.g., 9:7), but also geography, with an interest ranging between God's own people through all of humanity (e.g., 2:2). Containing both words of hope and horror, its key theme is God himself, who is referred to hundreds of times.

Isaiah prophesies during the latter half of the eighth century B.C. during the reign

Sargon
Kim Walton, courtesy of the Oriental Institue Museum

Manuscript of Isaiah from the Dead Sea Scrolls
Erich Lessing/Art Resource, NY, courtesy of the Israel Museum (IDAM)

Judean Kings	
Amaziah	796–767 B.C.
Uzziah (Azariah)	(791)[1]–740/39
Jotham	(750)–732/731
Ahaz	(744/743)–716/715
Hezekiah	716/715–687/686
Manasseh	(696/695)–642/641
Amon	642/641–640/639
Josiah	640/639–609
Jehoahaz	609
Jehoiakim	609–597
Jehoiachin	597
Zedekiah	597–586

of four named kings (1:1). His prophecies do not simply concern his own era, however, but anticipate both horrifying and hopeful events in Judah's future. They describe a period of destruction and exile, with many of the people being deported far away from their own land, which will be ravaged and destroyed (586 B.C.). Some of Isaiah addresses the situation of exile (chs. 40–55). This is not the end, however, since the exiles will return and the land will be rebuilt (c. 535 B.C.); other sections of the book seem directed toward that situation (chs. 56–66).

The compositional history of Isaiah is debated, with numerous competing views as to the number of authors and the times of composition.[2] This discussion is beyond the scope of the present study, but whichever view is espoused, the historical scope of the prophecy covers a period of over two centuries. Here we summarize the sweep of history between the eighth and fifth centuries B.C.

In the beginning of this period, Israel was controlled by Assyria, a major world power whose capital, Nineveh (Mosul in contemporary Iraq), is on the Tigris River, but whose empire in this period stretched from what is now Iran as far west as Egypt. Lying in the midst of major land routes between Assyria and Egypt, Israel felt repeatedly the horrors of war and destruction.

Just prior to the time of Isaiah, a succession of three Assyrian kings arose who were weaker and less aggressive than their predecessors, so Israel and Judah enjoyed relative peace and prosperity. This came to an abrupt end in 745 B.C. when a new and powerful king gained the Assyrian throne. Tiglath-pileser III (744–727 B.C.; 2 Kings 15:29; cf. 15:19, where he is called Pul) reinvigorated Assyrian expansion and aggression

Tiglath-pileser III
© The Trustees of the British Museum

Family of Judah being taken into exile from Lachish
Caryn Reeder, courtesy of the British Museum

until the end of the Assyrian empire late in the following century. The northern kingdom of Israel faced more imminent external pressure. Her king, Jeroboam II, had just died and his dynasty was brought to an end by the assassination of his son Zechariah (2 Kings 15:8–12), followed by a rapid turnover of rulers, likely influenced by the Assyrian pressure (v. 19).

Uzziah, the king of Judah, also died (740 B.C.; Isa. 6:1), but his passing, though traumatic, was expected since he was suffering from an incapacitating skin disease and his son Jotham was effectively ruling in his place (2 Kings 15:5). Jotham's reign was not seriously affected by Assyria directly, but, ironically, by an alliance between Judah's sister nation, Israel under Pekah, with their northern neighbor Aram, under Rezin (15:37). These two allies wanted Judah to join their coalition against Assyria, though their actual motives are unstated; they were too small to oppose Assyria on their own.[3]

Judah refused to do join the coalition, leading to the confrontation known as the Syro-Ephraimite War (Isa. 6–7; 2 Kings 16:5–9; 2 Chr. 28:5–21), which affected especially Ahaz, Jotham's son. He dithered back and forth on whether to side with Assyria, who was strong and brutal, or Israel and Aram, who were stronger than Judah and also close by. He finally opted for a pro-Assyrian policy, against the urgings of Isaiah (Isa. 7:7–9), and bribed Tiglath-pileser to leave him alone and instead deal with the opposing alliance, which the Assyrian king did in 734–732 (2 Kings 16:7–9).[4]

When Tiglath-pileser died in 727 B.C., his subjects, including Hoshea, king of Israel, asserted their independence. His son and heir, Shalmaneser V (726–722 B.C.), besieged Samaria, the Israelite capital (2 Kings 17:4), and exiled its leaders under Sargon II (721–705 B.C.; vv. 5–6). In one of his annals he records: "I besieged and conquered Samaria, led away booty 27,290 inhabitants of it ... and imposed on them the tribute of the former king."[5] In the period immediately after Sargon's death, while his son Sennacherib (704–681 B.C.) was occupied securing the throne, several of his vassals rebelled, requesting help from Ahaz's son and successor, Hezekiah (2 Kings 18:14–16; 715–687 B.C.).

Assyria proved too strong for any such alliance, moving against it in 701 B.C., conquering many and extracting tribute from

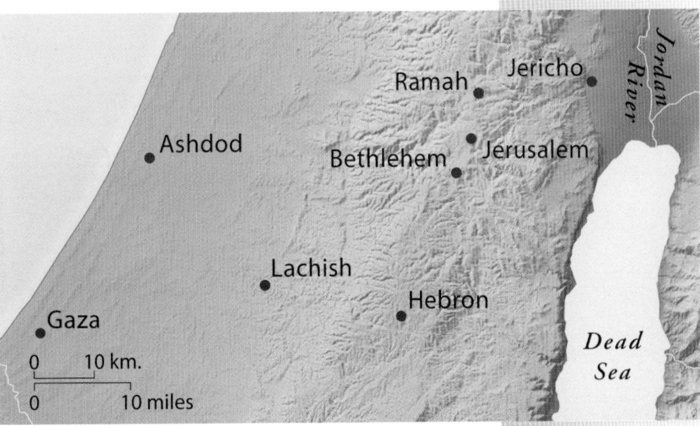

Judah and Jerusalem

them. Even so, Hezekiah did not join a coalition against them spearheaded by Philistia in 715–713, which was short-lived, with the Philistine capital, Ashdod, destroyed (Isa. 14:28–31; 20:1–6).[6] Sennacherib proved able and reestablished control over Babylon and then turned in his third campaign against Hezekiah and the west in 701.[7] He captured much of Judah, but was unable to take either Hezekiah or Jerusalem, possibly holding off because of payment of tribute. Sennacherib does boast: "He himself, I locked up within Jerusalem, his royal city, like a bird in a cage."[8] While the Bible records the siege (2 Kings 18:17–19:9), it records no defeat, saying rather that the Assyrian forces unexpectedly withdrew (vv. 35–36).

Judah still remained under Assyrian control, who continued to demand service from Manasseh, Hezekiah's son and successor (687–642 B.C.; cf. 2 Chr. 33:11)[9] as they were also battling in Egypt. Assyria started to weaken under the onslaught of their erstwhile vassals, the Scythians and the Medes, as well as the Babylonians, who expelled Assyria from their holdings in southern Mesopotamia in 625 B.C. under the leadership of Nabopolassar (626–605 B.C.).[10] Allying with the Medes, he captured Assyria in 614 B.C., and the Assyrian capital, Nineveh, in 612 B.C. (Nahum; Zeph. 2:13–15). The seemingly overwhelming enemy was thus laid low, but not before great loss for Judah and the end of the nation of Israel.

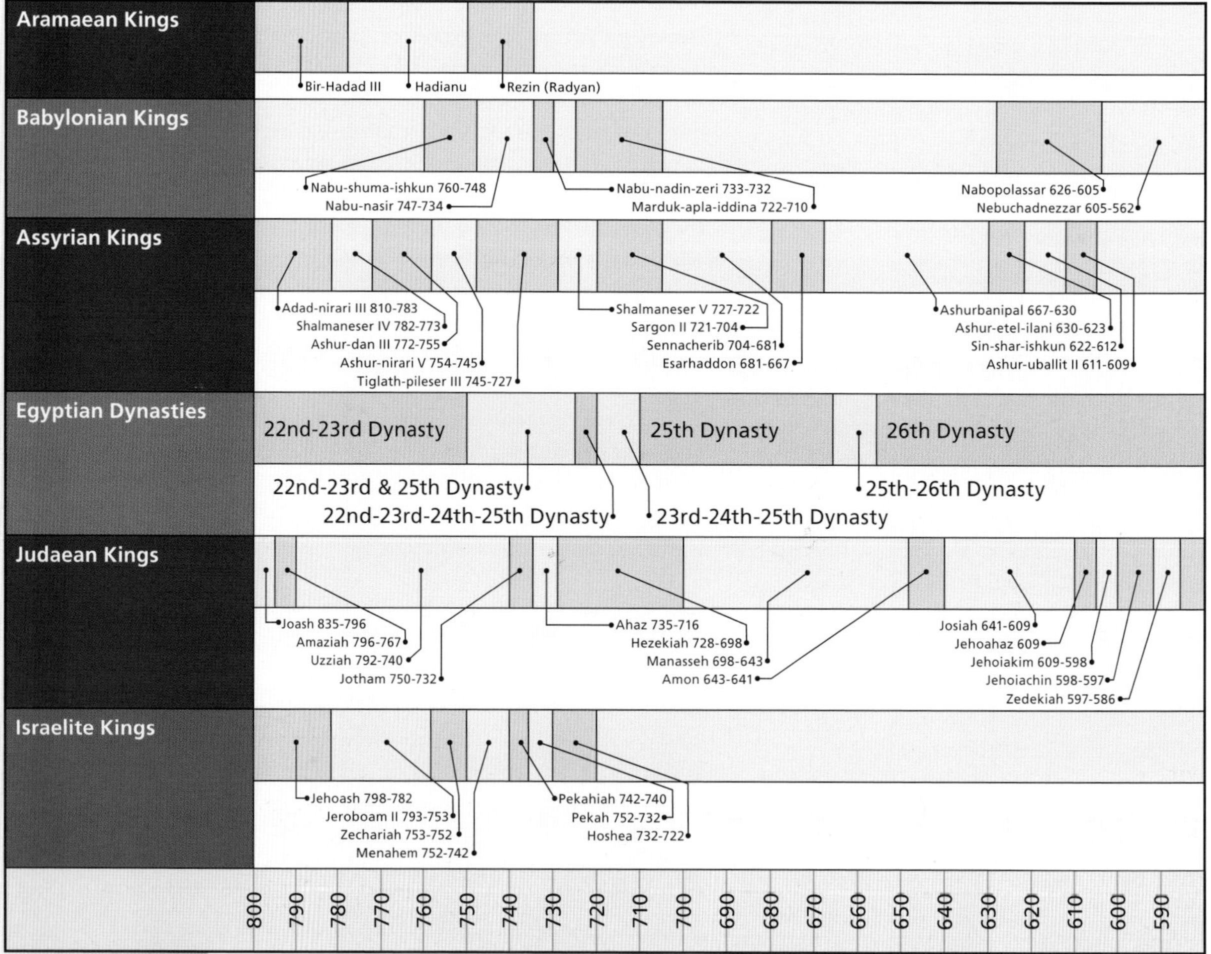

Manasseh remained under Assyrian subservience under Sennacherib's able son, Esarhaddon (680–669). Since Egypt had been instrumental in fomenting repeated rebellions, Assyria turned her military attention toward her, going as far as destroying Thebes in 663 under the leadership of Ashurbanipal (668–627), Esarhaddon's son.

Pressures continued to rise against Assyria, not only from Egypt and Babylon, but also from the Indo-Aryans from the north, including the Medes. Upon Ashurbanipal's death, his successors were unable to maintain control, with Babylonia gaining self-rule in 626 under Nabopolassar. Joining with the Medes, Babylonia brought Assyria to its knees, destroying its capital, Nineveh, in 612 B.C. and destroying the Assyrian empire in 609.

During this period of weakness, Josiah (640–609 B.C.) won Judah's independence and reestablished worship of Israel's God. Josiah's son, Jehoiakim, was an Egyptian vassal, but in 605 the Babylonian ruler Nebuchadnezzar defeated the Egyptians at Carchemish. Jehoiakim changed his allegiance, but he soon rebelled and died during a Babylonian siege, leaving a desperate situation for his son, Jehoiachin. At age eighteen, Jehoiachin was faced with an overwhelming force surrounding his city, which fell three months later, with the young king taken into exile.

Babylon then enthroned her own puppet king, Mattaniah (Jehoiachin's uncle), renaming him Zedekiah, thus showing complete control over him. The prophet Jeremiah warned Zedekiah that any defiance of Babylon was futile, since God himself was turning against his own wayward people. The king did not listen, so after a two-year siege, Jerusalem fell in July, 586 B.C. The king was blinded and taken into exile along with many of the people; the temple and other important buildings were destroyed as were the very walls of the city, and Babylon placed Gedaliah, who was not even of royal birth, over Judah as governor. This looked like the end of God's own people.

This was not the case, however, since the Neo-Babylonian empire was itself short-lived. After its strongest and longest ruling king, Nebuchadnezzar (605–562), died, three inferior monarchs reigned, but in the meantime a coalition was forming in the east between the Medes and the Persians. Under the able leadership of Cyrus, their armies moved in and brought the Neo-Babylonian empire to an end in 539 B.C. This had a direct impact on the Judean exiles since the Persians exercised a different foreign policy from either the Assyrians or Babylonians. The latter had taken leading citizens of captured nations into exile far away from their homes in order to lower the chances of their trying to liberate their country. Persia, by contrast, left conquered people in their homeland, or, in the case of Judah, allowed those who desired to return to their native land.

Not every Israelite in Babylonian exile took advantage of the opportunity to return to Judah (Ezra 2:64–65 numbers the returnees at 49,897). Life in Babylon and Persia was economically good for many, allowing some to reach high office (e.g., Esther) and live in relative comfort. The returnees to Judah found life difficult, facing hostile neighbors and a daunting rebuilding task. The latter chapters in Isaiah apparently offer encouragement to such returnees.

Heading (1:1)

The vision (1:1). Most prophecies begin with a self-identification that can contain elements such as the type of literature, the identity of the prophet, and the time period. These indicate that they contain actual messages to a real audience addressing real-life issues they were facing. "Vision" is a form of divine revelation that did not necessarily involve the physical eyes, since here it involves primarily words rather than images (cf. 2:1). Prophets of Yahweh and pagan prophets experienced them.[11] In Mesopotamia, even laypeople, both men and women, received visions or dreams from their gods.[12]

Horses feeding at a manger
Werner Forman Archive/The British Museum

Judah and Jerusalem (1:1). After the split of the nation of Israel into two parts following the reign of Solomon, the northern nation was known as "Israel" or "Ephraim" after its main tribe, with its capital in Samaria. The southern nation was "Judah" after the main tribe occupying the area. Its capital was Jerusalem, which was also the site of the national religious shrine, the temple of Yahweh.

Isaiah son of Amoz (1:1). In the ancient Near East a father's name commonly distinguished people with the same first name (cf. "Johnson"—son of John). This at times extended several generations, especially if an earlier ancestor had some claim to fame. Sometimes an earlier ancestor rather than the biological parent was used as an identifier.

Kings of Judah (1:1). Many Old Testament prophecies give their date either in relation to an important event or to the kings who ruled during a particular period. Similarly in Mesopotamia, documents are dated by using names of important officials, one of whose name was associated with each year.[13] The Old Testament is often more general, simply providing the reigns, though at times a specific year identification is given. Dating was important because the events discussed are not some theoretical abstraction, but rather relate to real people at a specific time and place (see the chart of Judean kings in the introduction).

Courtroom Summons (1:2–31)

Hear, O heavens! Listen, O earth! (1:2). Ancient Near Eastern covenants include witnesses to testify regarding covenant breach or obedience and to bring about the required punishment or blessing.[14] They also heard the indictment in a lawsuit brought against a covenant breaker. These witnesses among Israel's neighbors included deities[15] and elements of nature, such as heaven and earth here (see Deut. 4:26; 30:19; 31:28) and things like mountains, rivers, sea, and clouds.[16]

The ox knows his master, the donkey his owner's manger (1:3). Knowledgeable animals are proverbial. In their natural, untutored state, they know how to live and flourish in their environment. Egyptian wisdom acknowledges a dog as one recognizing its food source.[17] This contrasts with humanity, according to Isaiah, which seemingly lacks this basic survival instinct, turning against the very Creator and the order of his created universe. A Hurro-Hittite wisdom text has a deer irrationally turning against the source of its provisions, but the writer explicitly acknowledges that he is writing metaphorically of humanity: "It is not a deer, but a human."[18]

Israel (1:3). Deriving from the new name God conferred on Jacob (Gen. 32:28), "Israel" came to designate the people of all twelve tribes descended from him. When the nation divided after the reign of Solomon, the

▸ Covenant Lawsuit

Isaiah starts out his prophecy strong, issuing a summons to participate in a lawsuit against his people. This literary form, called a *rîb*, is more specifically a suit against covenant breakers, with Israel and Judah often named as defendants (e.g., 3:13).[A-1] The various personae in the suit show that it is heavily weighted against the defendant: Israel. The plaintiff is Yahweh, since it is his covenant that the defendant broke. The prosecuting attorney is the prophet, who *de jure* represents Yahweh. There is no defense attorney, and witnesses ("heaven" and "earth") are called either to testify to the wrongdoing or to observe the outcome of the trial. The judge, jury, and the one who carries out the punishment is Yahweh.

northern kingdom used that name, while the southern kingdom was known as Judah. But the term could still refer to Judah as it does here. It is therefore necessary to be careful in determining who "Israel" refers to.

Sinful nation (1:4). National sin is not only known of Israel but also her neighbors. The eighth-century Babylonian Myth of Erra and Ishum speaks of national destruction following humanity's abandoning the natural order ("A son will not ask for the health of his father, nor the father of his son. A mother will happily plot harm for her daughter"[19]) and departing from justice and righteousness.[20] Divine abandonment of God's people follows their abandoning his established order.

Turned their backs (1:4). Turning one's back is an insulting sign of lack of interest and abandonment, in marked contrast to turning one's face toward someone in attention or obedience. Queen Hatshepsut showed dedication to her god by stating: "I did not turn my back to the city of the All-Lord, rather did I turn my face to it."[21] Merneptah in the Merneptah Stele claimed that he was able to conquer Libya because the protective god "Seth turned his back upon their chief."[22]

Whole heart afflicted (1:5). Heart pain can derive either from physical bruising, as is the case here, or psychological battering, as it is for a letter writer in Lachish who stated, "For your servant has been *sick at heart* ever since you sent [that letter]."[23]

Not cleansed or bandaged or soothed with oil (1:6). These procedures aided healing for injuries. Oil was an important element for wound treatment.[24] While treatment of maladies is less frequently mentioned than their diagnosis,[25] an Old Babylonian letter requests: "Send me two measures of oil in a pot. A dog bit a man and I will bandage (him). Send the oil."[26] An Akkadian text prescribes a treatment: "You wash him with water ... and afterward he bathes with soap and anoints himself with oil."[27]

Your country is desolate, your cities burned with fire, your fields ... stripped (1:7). Conquerors often despoiled their captives either to provide for their own provisions while their army was on the move or to punish the conquered by making their land uninhabitable. This is shown physically by the number of burn levels found in archaeological excavations.[28] The Babylonian Myth of Erra and Ishum describes similar punishments to those found here:

> (II:52'–54') I shall finish off the land and count it as ruins. I shall devastate cities and make them a wilderness. I shall destroy mountains and fell their cattle.
>
> (II:66'–68') I shall let wild beasts of the mountains go down (into cities), I shall devastate public places, wherever people tread. I shall let wild beasts of the countryside which are not ... come into the public square.

(II:71') I shall devastate the royal palace and make it into a ruin.[29]

Trees were also denuded, as when Tiglath-pileser I stated, "Their orchards I cut down."[30] This was to deprive the enemy of food necessary to maintain a defense. Shalmaneser III stated of a captured ruler, "I uprooted his harvest, cut down his gardens."[31] The anguish caused by such devastation to one's home and land is powerfully portrayed not only in such places as Psalm 137 and Lamentations, but also in the Sumerian Lamentation over the Destruction of Sumer and Ur.[32]

Daughter of Zion (1:8). Zion was the original fortified mountain city that David conquered and claimed for his own.[33] Jerusalem grew around this fortress. Common ancient Near Eastern practice was that smaller, unfortified cities or "suburbs" grew in proximity to a fortified location. If the surrounding areas, commonly called "daughters" of the fortress in the Bible, were attacked, inhabitants took refuge behind its walls. Here Jerusalem is described as a daughter of Zion.

Like a shelter ... like a hut (1:8). Field workers at times found protection from the elements in temporary shelters (10:29) in their fields, using them in order to remain close by during times of intense agricultural activity, but also to provide protection for the ripening crops (4:6). When their need was over because the harvest season was finished, they were abandoned to fall apart. Jerusalem and Zion, the center of Israel's civil and religious life and a symbol of its national existence will, in its punishment, become like a temporary lean-to, crumbling because it filled no further function, nonguardians of a nonexistent crop.

Like a city under siege (1:8). Cities were generally fortified to protect against foreign incursion. Attackers had to find a way either to get in or to get the people out. The latter was accomplished by laying siege, surrounding the city (29:3), and not allowing any to either enter or leave. Ashurbanipal describes his siege of Tyre: "I strangled his food supply and forced them to submit to my yoke."[34] During the Amarna period, the Canaanite ruler of Megiddo complained to the pharaoh about attacks by the king of Shechem, "We are unable to do the plucking (harvesting),"[35] since they were unable to leave the city. This ultimately led either to capitulation or to disease, starvation, and death by thirst. The Hittites and Egyptians used the same tactics.[36]

Like Sodom ... like Gomorrah (1:9). Sodom and Gomorrah were prototypical bad cities in the Old Testament because of their wickedness and subsequent destruction by an angry God. Jerusalem, God's covenant city, because of her equivalent evil (v. 10),

Assyrians cutting down the trees outside a besieged city
Caryn Reeder, courtesy of the British Museum

▸ Cultic Activity

God himself established numerous ways for people to approach him in worship and petition. Regulations for such occasions occupy much of the Pentateuch (e.g., Lev. 1–7; Num. 28–29), and their practice was frequent and prolific. These acts were too easily perverted, however, with people thinking that the rituals themselves were important, not the obedience of heart (cf. Isa. 1:10–14). God strongly condemns worship of pagan deities and unethical and sinful actions that render true worship impossible.

Similar cultic activities played an important role in the life of Israel's neighbors.[A-2] Worship included sacrifices and feeding the gods,[A-3] hymns and prayers,[A-4] and periodic festivals.[A-5] These all necessitated numerous cultic personnel, some of which, such as diviners (see 2:6) and sorcerers, were unacceptable in Israel itself.[A-6]

will be wiped out like them, exemplifying a covenant-breaker's destruction (Deut. 29:23).

Sacrifices ... offerings (1:11). Creation traditions in Egypt and Mesopotamia portrayed humanity as servants or cattle of the gods.[37] Specifically, they were to provide food for the gods, relieving them of having to look after themselves. The means for doing so was sacrifice, at times identified as "food for the gods."[38] Official Yahwism denied this function to Israel's sacrificial system, rarely describing the altar as God's "table," since he did not eat. A "table" was common in Mesopotamian ritual practice, as when King Rimush "established as regular offerings per day for the table of Shamash."[39] Popular Israelite religion frequently forgot that God was not actually fed through sacrifice and sought to manipulate him through such offerings. It is this misuse of ritual that Isaiah and Amos condemn.

Trampling of my courts (1:12). The court was an open space enclosed by walls, surrounding or within a building; thus it had limited access. It was part of the palace and of the temple. In the case of the religious sites, entry was restricted to those bringing offerings since this was a holy place. At times, the courts could be populated with worshipers. Illicit entry even into the outer court of the sanctuary defiled it, resulting in a severe punishment.

Incense (1:13). See 17:8. Part of Israel's sacrificial ritual was burning incense, made from various aromatic herbs, spices, and resins. Among other ritual uses, it was burned on a special altar just in front of the entrance to the Most Holy Place in the tabernacle and temple. Apart from its symbolic significance,

Offerings made to the god Osiris on the funerary papyrus of Nebqed
Fredduf/Wikimedia Commons, courtesy of the Louvre

Incense
Kim Walton, courtesy of the Oriental Institute Museum

it muted the stench caused by slaughtering the sacrificial animals.[40]

New Moons, Sabbaths and convocations (1:13). Israel and other nations used a lunar calendar of about twenty-eight days rather than our solar calendar. The turn of the new moon, marking a new month, was thus ritually important not only for Israel,[41] but also for her neighbors. The Akkadian Atraḫasis Epic speaks of special activities revolving around the seven-day cycle: "On the first, seventh, and fifteenth days of the month, He [Enki] established a purification, a bath."[42] Ugarit records note special rituals on that day, and Emar in north Syria had an annual New Moon festival lasting several days.[43] In Israel, work was to cease and there were special offerings on these occasions.

Hands raised in worship before Re-Horakhty
Guillaume Blanchard/Wikimedia Commons, courtesy of the Louvre

Spread out your hands in prayer (1:15). Prayer and worship for Israel were not quiet, internal exercises with the eyes closed, but total body experiences. They could involve loud outbursts and weeping or quiet tears, lying prostrate, as well as lifting hands. The same action accompanies some prayers and incantations in Akkadian literature,[44] and one kind of prayer is called a "raising of the hands" (*nish qate*).[45] King Keret does this in the Ugaritic Keret Epic. He brings sacrificial material to a high place and raises "his hands heavenward, sacrificed to the Bull, his father."[46] The action symbolizes supplication to a deity viewed as being "on high."

Symbolic actions are used in many areas of life—religious (like here), relational (such as shaking hands today), and legal.[47] The fact that these symbolize an inner or interpersonal reality is significant. In Israel, all of these outward demonstrations without that inner reality are useless and not even noticed by God, who seeks inner motivation.

I will not listen (1:15). A disconcerting realization is that the one to whom one fervently prays is not listening. This is claimed by the speaker who says, "They do not hear my prayers and requests."[48] There are no known examples where the gods say they are not listening. The psalmist shows need for audience in a common plea to hear (e.g., Ps. 17:6; 27:7). A more poignant plea comes from the seventh century Prayer to Every God, a cry of dereliction by a petitioner who does not know if anyone is listening:

> May the god who is not known be quieted toward me;
> May the goddess who is not known be quieted toward me.
> May the god whom I know or do not know be quieted toward me;
> May the goddess whom I know or do not know be quieted toward me....
> Although I am constantly looking for help, no one takes me by the hand;
> when I weep they do not come to my side.
> I utter laments, but no one hears me.[49]

Wash and make yourself clean (1:16). In addition to physical cleanliness, washing has symbolic meaning on the ritual level, since it is part of many sacrificial ceremonies. A Ugaritic purification rite states of the officiant:

He washed himself and made himself up,
Washed his hands up to the elbow, his
arms up to the shoulder,
Entered the shade of his tent;
Took a ram in his hand,
A newborn (lamb) with both hands . . .
sacrificed to the Bull Ilu, his father.[50]

The Babylonian king Merodach-Baladan (39:1) describes himself in a brick stamp as "king with clean hands," apparently indicating that he was suitable to rule.[51] This is appropriate since Shamash, the god who enthrones and guides kings,[52] "approves of clean hands."[53] In an Akkadian cultic conflict text, after a fierce battle "when [Marduk] assumed kingship, he bathed himself in water,"[54] possibly with the dual purpose of physical and ritual cleansing.

Do right! Seek justice . . . oppressed . . . fatherless . . . widow (1:17). A desirable life not only looked after one's own well-being, but also that of those unable to look out for themselves. Virtue was thus not only vertical (how one related with God) but also horizontal (how one related with one's fellow Israelites). Similar admonitions to protect these social classes are common (1:23; 16:5), demonstrating the foundational importance of social ethics for Israel's covenant.[55] The covenant protects the rights of those unable to demand their own, and one of the functions of the king was to ensure that these rights were protected.

This is pictured in Mesopotamia when Shamash, the sun god (who is also judge), hands perfectly straight rods to King Hammurabi (eighteenth century B.C.) for him to use as a straight edge to evaluate his legal decisions. In his own self-justification, Hammurabi claims: "I established truth and justice as the declaration of the land; I enhance the well-being of the people."[56] The legendary Ugaritic king Keret apparently has not followed through on these obligations: "You did not judge the widow's case, you did not make a decision regarding the oppressed . . . you did not feed the orphan."[57] Widows were especially vulnerable since they not only were not married, but they had no social or financial support from a male family member.[58]

Scarlet . . . white . . . red as crimson (1:18). Even the cheapest dyes were likely not used regularly by the common folk for everyday wear, since they were associated with luxury. White material, in contrast to that which is dyed, was in its pure, "clean" state, and the adjective also describes wool in Akkadian texts.[59] In the Neo-Assyrian Marduk's Ordeal, the dead wear multicolored wool dyed that way by his red blood.[60]

In the Bible, the whiteness of snow is sometimes compared with a dreaded skin disease, so the color does not always indicate the positive notion, as it does here. There is a stark contrast between red and white in Mesopotamia as well. A ritual meant to avert evil refers to a red goat: "As a deflowered female will never be a virgin again and as red will never become white or white red, so may I and the evil be parted forever."[61] Both cases concern separation from evil.

Faithful city . . . harlot . . . murderers . . . rebels . . . thieves (1:21–23). If a king is supposed to maintain social order (1:17), social disintegration is a frightening prospect (59:3–8). In this case the turmoil has

Shamash, the god of justice, at the top of the Stele of Hammurabi
Kim Walton, courtesy of the Oriental Institute Museum

▸ Dyes

The ancients colored their fabrics with dyes derived from various materials from animals, plants, and minerals. Purple, from mussel shells found in Phoenicia, were hardest to get and thus more expensive. The cheaper, red dyes mentioned in 1:18 derived from worms and insects.[A-7]

A murex snail, one ancient source of purple dye, engraved with the name of Rimush, one of the kings of the Empire of Akkad.
Marie-Lan Nguyen/Wikimedia Commons, courtesy of the Louvre

completely reversed the desired order. The Egyptian Prophecies of Neferti (early twentieth century B.C.) describe similar horrors:

> A man sits with his back turned,
> While one man kills another.
> I show you a son as an enemy,
> A brother as a foe, a man slaying his father. . . .
> I show you the land in turmoil,
> The weak-armed is strong-armed,
> One salutes him who saluted.
> I show you the undermost uppermost. . . .
> The beggar will gain riches,
> The great [will rob] to live.
> The poor will eat bread,
> The slaves will be exalted.[62]

Choice wine is diluted with water (1:22). The exact nature of this intoxicating drink is unclear, though the Hebrew term *sb*ʾ usually relates to an Akkadian word for a kind of beer. Beer was made from grain, mainly barley and wheat, or even dates—a staple in Mesopotamia and Egypt,[63] where grapes for wine were harder to come by. It was also made in Israel, as evidenced by a brewery at Tel Goren, near Ein Gedi.[64] Its intoxicating power was proverbial, with an Egyptian lover expressing his "high" from his lover's kisses rather than from beer.[65]

The eighteenth-century Hymn to Ninkasi, the Sumerian beer goddess, claims that beer drinking "makes the liver happy, fills the heart with joy."[66] Numerous varieties of beer are mentioned, with one text speaking of dark beer, light beer, emmer beer, and barley beer.[67]

Wine was also available in great variety and ranged from poor to fine in quality.[68] One of the finest seems to be from Izalla (Izlo), mentioned not only in Mesopotamian but also biblical texts (Ezek. 27:19 ["Uzal"]). Another is said to be "the drink of the king."[69] Beer and wine are also part of the tax paid by villagers to the Ugaritic king.[70] The alcohol content and the flavor of these drinks would be adversely affected if water was added.

Bribes . . . gifts (1:23). Israelite leaders are to dispense justice impartially. It is all too easy, however, for the straight to be made crooked when financial incentives are involved. This specific term of "gifts" (*šalmōnîm*) can be an innocuous greeting gift, somewhat like our hostess gifts ("Now as a gift of greeting for my father 100 [shekels of] blue wool and 10 [shekels of] wool").[71] It easily becomes misused, however, since it can be used to secure a favorable response from an official ("the

▸ Silver and Dross

Fine metals such as silver must be separated from base metals such as lead sulphide in which they are usually suspended when found in their natural state (cf. 1:22). The process, called cupellation, heats the lead to 900–1000 Fahrenheit degrees in a small crucible (a cupel) made from bone ash. Most of the lead and other base metals oxidize because of the heat and are absorbed into the cupel, leaving purer silver or gold.

Often this did not result in the purity necessary to work the metal, so that further refinement was necessary. The metal was reheated, with impurities rising to the surface, where they could be skimmed off and discarded. The useless discard of the smelting process is the "dross" (cf. 1:22). Another possible interpretation is that there was a mishap in the smelting process, and the pure and base metals did not separate sufficiently, so one was left with a useless slag, which is the dross. Only the purified metal (1:25) could be worked to produce such things as fine jewelry. Several hordes of silver pieces have been excavated in Israel.[A-8]

Pieces of silver from a jeweler's workshop at Tell el-Ajjul
Z. Radovan/www.BibleLand Pictures.com

shepherds gave *bribes* to the governor and the temple administrator").[72]

"Bribe" may be overplaying the term, which could rather be a gratuity proffered in order that a case might be moved up in priority so it could be heard in an overcrowded court docket, not that the verdict might be swayed through payment.[73]

Be broken (1:28). Breaking people as a punishment or in defeat is a common literary metaphor (8:15; 28:13).[74] In Egypt, the physical practice of breaking people was done as part of a curse on one's enemies. Their names were written on pieces of clay pottery or on clay figurines and then smashed. Like the names that were broken, people prayed that the gods would work through sympathetic magic to break those named.[75]

Sacred oaks ... garden (1:29–30). Green trees and watered gardens were rare and special places among those living in (semi-)arid conditions like those found in the ancient Near East. Ashurnasirpal II boasted of collecting and planting

Execration figurine
Elke Noppes/Wikimedia Commons courtesy of the Musées Royaux d'Art et d'Histoire, Brussels

Sacred tree in a relief of Assyrian king Ashurnasirpal
Rob Rogers, courtesy of the British Museum

many exotic trees and plants in his garden in Calah/Nimrud,[76] while Nebuchadnezzar II of Babylon was proud of his terraced ("hanging") palace gardens,[77] which were among the seven wonders of the ancient world.

These were not only places of relaxation but also of worship, since gardens, sacred trees, and groves were important in Canaanite and Mesopotamian popular religion. Part of the royal funerary rites seems to take place in the royal garden,[78] and trees in particular seem to be imbued with life, not only for pagan neighbors of Israel, but even at creation. Israel herself is seduced by this cult of life and fertility and condemned for succumbing (57:5).

Trees even become objects of worship either in their own right or as symbols of a deity.[79] Seals and scarabs found in Israel show people kneeling and also raising their hands in worship before trees. One Egyptian scene depicts a life-giving divine tree with a female breast suckling a human;[80] in another it offers a kneeling worshiper a tray of foodstuffs.[81]

Trees were also associated with the goddess Asherah,[82] whose cultic tree symbol is associated with Yahweh in an enigmatic inscription from Kuntillet Ajrud, an Iron Age II site in Sinai: "Yahweh of Samaria and his asherah" (see comment on 44:24); there is an accompanying picture of two ibexes nibbling from a tree. This clearly illuminates syncretism among the Israelites, whose worship in gardens (65:3; 66:17) and groves God will turn to nothing by withholding water from them both (1:30).

The Last Days for the Lord's Mountain (2:1–22)

Mountain of the LORD's temple ... chief among the mountains ... raised (2:2). Jerusalem is situated high in the hill country of eastern Israel and physically looks down on the surrounding terrain. Visitors had to go up to visit it and within it had to climb even more to get to the temple, which overlooked the rest of the city. This city, the habitation of God, is associated with Mount Zion (8:18), God's holy hill. Another mountain, Horeb in the Sinai Peninsula, is also known as "the mountain of God."

Israel's neighbors also associated sanctuaries and divine worship with mountains. In Ugaritic texts, Mount Zaphon is the place of Baal's mountain palace,[83] and El, the chief Canaanite god, also resided on a mountain.[84] In Mesopotamia's plains artificial mountains, known as ziggurats, were built to provide sacred space for worshipers to come to a place that visually intersected with the heavenly realm.

Mesopotamian texts also equate building temples high like mountains. The Sumerian king Gudea recorded his temple building activities in the late third millennium B.C.: "They are making the temple grow (high) like a mountain range; making it float in mid-heavens like a cloud; making it raise its horns like an ox; making it raise (its) head high in the mountains ... making the temple raise (its) head high in heaven and earth like a mountain range."[85] The city of Babylon is also to be raised to the sky.[86]

All nations will stream to it (2:2). In this verse the mountain of Israel's God is elevated theologically. It is the central point of worship to which everyone will come up to worship. Gudea also envisions visitors from afar: "The great fearfulness of my temple is cast over all the foreign lands. At (the mention of) its name all the foreign lands assemble from the horizon, Magan and Meluhha descend from their mountains."[87] If a god displays wisdom and power, all who hear will receive benefit.

Let us go up (2:3). In a prophecy concerning Ashurbanipal when he was yet crown prince, it was "predicted" that "[the … king]s of the lands shall say to one another: ['Come let us] go to Ashurbanipal! The king has witnesses! [Whatever the god]s decreed for our fathers and forefathers, [let him now] arbitrate between us.' [Mulis] su said: '[You shall rul]e over [the king]s of the lands; you shall show them their frontiers and set the courses they take.'"[88] In terms similar to those in Isaiah, guidance for life and decision-making come from the great king, who is modeled after the Ashur, the ideal king.[89]

Beat their swords into plowshares and their spears into pruning hooks (2:4). Beating here has the connotation of breaking into pieces. When swords are broken, the resultant pieces of metal can be used to strengthen and sharpen the wooden tips of plow blades, called shares. This loosens the soil, scratching out a furrow in which to plant.

Spears could have straight or curved blades. When broken they could yield smaller, hand-held tools resembling a sickle. These could be sharpened and used as small, curved knives to trim grape vines (18:5). Since God will resolve international disputes, weapons can be put to more peaceful and productive use.

Full of superstitions (2:6). People desire to hear from the divine, especially as regards the future, and so seek revelation in a number of different ways. See sidebar on "Superstitions and Divination."

Horses … chariots (2:7). Horses and chariots were weapons of war. Military chariots required iron technology to provide strapping for the wheels, since wooden ones easily shattered. Lack of iron technology early in her history put Israel at a disadvantage against the Canaanites (Judg. 4).

Farm tools from the Old Babylonian period, including a plowshare
Mark Borisuk/www.BiblePlaces.com

Late Bronze Age spear heads
Todd Bolen/www.BiblePlaces.com, courtesy of Rockefeller Museum

Chariot with three occupants from the Balawat gate
Michael Greenhalgh/ArtServe, courtesy of the British Museum

Divine image from Qatna
Marie-Lan Nguyen/Wikimedia Commons, courtesy of the Louvre

Assyrian chariots, pulled by one or two horses, carried two or more passengers: the driver, an archer or spearman, and often a shield bearer.[90] Horses were emblematic not only of power but also wealth, since they were expensive. They needed special care to protect the huge economic and military investment, shown by Ugaritic texts describing treatment for disease.[91]

Full of idols (2:8). Idols are physical representations of deities. They were denied to Israel since she worshiped an invisible God who was not to be depicted in any concrete way. Idols were made of wood, stone, clay, or metal. They could be carefully shaped in human or animal form and covered with gold or silver leaf (e.g., 2:20; 30:22). Gold and silver were used for images of the divine in Ugarit,[92] Israel,[93] Egypt,[94] Mesopotamia,[95]and Syria.[96] At times idols were even given fine clothing.[97] The Canaanite worshipers at Ugarit had lists of garments for the gods.[98]

Some idols were small amulets that could be carried, while others were of human size. Still others were of superhuman size, such as the winged bulls standing over fifteen feet tall in the palace of Sargon II, a contemporary of Isaiah. These represented the protective *lamassu*-spirits bringing fortune to the city.[99]

Special rituals (called "washing/opening the mouth") were performed to imbue the images with divinity.[100] As representative or embodiment of the deity, idols were treated with respect, since the deity itself was believed to be represented in the idol.[101] Part of their worship was through offerings, which provided the gods with food and drink.[102] Israel itself found it too easy to slip from a worship of their God to worshiping a physical representation of him (see the temple as an idol of sorts in Jer. 7).

Dread of the LORD . . . splendor (2:10). Israel's God, Yahweh, is without physical body and form and so is not visible. He has, however, a divine aura or radiance, his "glory," which is apparent to the human eye. Medieval paintings used a halo to depict

▸ Superstitions and Divination

In Israel, God revealed himself through his prophets in the form of visions, dreams, and the like. He also responded to queries through other, less common means, such as casting lots. The latter, using physical, mechanical means to question a god, was common among Israel's neighbors and is called "divination." It comes in numerous forms and is strongly condemned as unsuitable for Israel, whose God is not to be so manipulated (e.g., Deut. 18:9–14).

Three forms of divination are mentioned in Ezekiel 21:21, where, when a Babylonian king needs to decide which direction to take, "he will cast lots with arrows, he will consult his idols, he will examine the liver." Rhabdomancy used arrows or sticks that were thrown to the ground, and an interpretation was made depending on how they fell. Idol consultation used a type of household god (*teraphim*) that was somehow expected to speak. Common in Mesopotamia was hepatoscopy or extispicy, the examination of animal entrails, especially the liver.[A-9] They were carefully inspected by trained priests who checked for abnormalities, which would communicate a message from the god regarding the future. In keeping Israel from misusing animal livers in this way, part of the liver taken from sacrifices was to be completely burnt.

Other types of divination were also used.[A-10] In necromancy one consulted with the dead,[A-11] such as when Saul consulted Samuel through a medium at Endor (1 Sam. 28:8–19).[A-12] Mesopotamia was also the source for astrology, consultation of the heavenly bodies (see Isa. 47:3).[A-13] In hydromancy, people interpreted the patterns of oil placed on water in a cup or bowl, much like reading tea leaves today.[A-14] In a practice not referred to in the Bible, Mesopotamian and Canaanite priests also inferred meaning from abnormal animal and human births.[A-15]

Though Scripture condemns these practices, this is not because they do not work. There is supernatural power in the occult, but it is not open to followers of the true God. Israel is to depend on God's self-revelation rather than manipulating nature to find out secrets (see comments on 7:11–14).

On an individual level, a reason to know the future was to be able to take action against any evil that might be coming. Incantations and magic charms were used for protection against these. A sixteenth-century B.C. Egyptian example of a charm to protect a child reads: "Hast thou come to kiss this child? I will not let thee kiss him!... Hast thou come to injure him? I will not let thee injure him! Hast thou come to take him away? I will not let thee take him away from me! I have made his magical protection against thee out of clover ... out of honey."[A-16] For Israel, the power to protect and heal did not lie in magic or in human strength, but in the Lord God, who welcomed prayer and was ready to protect and save (cf. 35:3–6).

Liver model used for divination
Caryn Reeder, courtesy of the British Museum

Cylinder seal impression with deity surrounded by glow of *melammu*
Kim Walton, courtesy of the Oriental Institute Museum

this. Egyptian art used the sun disk over the head of several of their deities to indicate their divine status. Akkadian texts refer to the (*pulhu*) *melammu*, the (fear-causing) radiance that characterized not only deities but also other awe-inspiring beings such as demons and kings.[103] The goddess Ishtar is often depicted as an armed war goddess.[104]

Several accounts of royal battles refer to this terror transferred to the king (and his army), overwhelming the enemy and leading to their defeat. For example, Adad-Nirari III describes his campaign against the Hittites in the early eighth century B.C.: "The kings of the extensive [land of Hatti] ... had become strong and withheld their [tribute] ... (my) *fearful splendor* overwhelmed them and they submitted to me."[105]

Cedars of Lebanon ... oaks of Bashan (2:13). Cedars from Lebanon were renowned for their height (37:24), and its wood was imported for building. The Canaanite god Baal also lived in a house/palace of cedar.[106] Shalmaneser III frequently mentions cedar beams among the tribute he received.[107] One of the earliest mentions of getting cedar wood comes from the texts of Gudea of Lagash.[108] The association of the cedar with Lebanon was strong enough to lead to its inclusion in the country's flag today.

Bashan is on the western edge of the Golan Heights, where mighty oaks once grew.[109] The height of both cedar and oak was noted even in Egypt, where a thirteenth-century B.C. letter speaks of part of Syria: "It is overgrown with junipers and oaks and cedars that have reached the sky."[110] Oak is associated with a Canaanite temple in Egypt,[111] and the term *ʾln* (GK473) is used in both Ugaritic and Akkadian texts.[112]

Iron Age walls at Dan
Kim Walton

Lofty tower ... fortified wall (2:15). City fortifications were necessary in the ancient Near East in order to protect inhabitants against marauders. An eighth-century Phoenician text states that the writer "built fortifications in those places so that they ... might dwell in the ease of their hearts."[113] It was a matter of pride for a city to be fortified. Built of stamped earth, brick, or stone, the walls of this period are solid[114] and could be massive, with towers placed periodically along them.

In some cases, there were both inner and outer protective walls (26:1). At Lachish, the outer wall was 3 meters (9 feet) thick and the inner wall 6 meters (19 feet).[115] At Khorsabad, the fortress of Sargon II, the city wall was 14 meters (45 feet) thick and 12 meters (38 feet) high;[116] at Nineveh among Sennacherib's building projects was a wall that could have been as much as 23 meters (nearly 75 feet) tall,[117] though the exact height is difficult to determine, since no walls are found completely intact and height was usually measured by brick-courses.[118]

Fortifications were also located outside of urban areas. For example, Egypt maintained border posts to the east to stop Bedouins and marauders from infiltrating their territory.[119] Three successive fortresses were built at Kadesh Barnea in periods later than Israel's passing through on the way to the Promised Land.[120]

Trading ships ... vessel (2:16). See also 23:1; 60:9. Shipping was not among Israel's major trades, since she had few good ports, though it had some role even early in her history (cf. Judg. 5:17). Solomon established a Red Sea port at Ezion Geber in cooperation with Hiram of Tyre. Shipping played a more major role in Ugarit, further up the Mediterranean coast in the area of Tyre, where there is a contract for ships rented to another king.[121] It was also an acceptable trade in Egypt, where a son of Ramesses II married the daughter of a sea captain.[122] The hazards of the trade are shown in a Middle Kingdom (early second millennium) Egyptian text about a shipwrecked sailor,[123] and archaeologists have found numerous shipwrecks.[124]

"Trading ships" are literally "ships of Tarshish" (60:9), merchant ships that carried heavy cargo.[125] They were probably single-masted vessels with a single row of oars. Warships were larger and could have several decks and oar banks. Both add to the prestige and wealth of their owner nations, but their pride will be brought down by God.

Idols will totally disappear (2:18). A disappearing personal god strikes its worshiper with despair, since help is no longer available. Antagonistic gods need to be repulsed, however, which is done by means of incantations and amulets. A seventh-century amulet from Syria reads: "As for Sasm [the warrior-god] let (the house) not be opened to him, and let him not come down to the doorposts.... Pass away, and forever fly away."[126]

Shake the earth (2:19, 21). The awe-inspiring coming of God (see 2:10) causes not only people but also nature to quake in terror. His coming, called a theophany, is often accompanied by earth-shaking phenomena. Assyrian kings associate the same convulsion with their coming, who describes himself as one "at whose warlike ferocity the lands are convulsed down to their foundations."[127]

Trading ship from Punt from Hatshepsut's temple in Deir el-Bahri
Erich Lessing/Art Resource, NY

Caves ... holes ... rodents and bats (2:19–20). The powerful strongholds will be ineffective, and people will take up living in unnatural conditions. Their ineffective idols will be discarded to be with unclean rodents. The Sumerian poetess Enheduanna, in a third-millennium B.C. text, exalts the goddess Inanna, before whom none of the other gods are able to stand. Of them she writes: "Oh my lady, the Anunna, the great gods, fluttering like bats fly off before you in the clefts, they who dare not walk in your terrible glance, who dare not proceed before your terrible countenance."[128] Lifeless idols will flee to crannies before the all-powerful God just as the other gods do before Inanna.

Judgment on Jerusalem, Judah, and Their Women (3:1–4:1)

Take ... all supplies of food and ... water (3:1). Sitting behind massive fortifications (2:15), enemies were difficult to root out through direct attack. Often the siege was a more effective means of subduing them. They were completely cut off, surrounded in their stronghold by what essentially now served as a prison. Food, which had to come from surrounding fields, and water, which sometimes came from sources outside city walls, was no longer accessible; thus, the inhabitants either capitulated or died of hunger or thirst (see 1:8). This tactic is clear from the later site of Masada, where Roman camps surrounding an Israelite stronghold are still visible.

The hero and the warrior, the judge and prophet, the soothsayer and elder, the captain of fifty and man of rank, the counselor, skilled craftsman and clever enchanter (3:2–3). During a siege, the besieged needed not only supplies of food and drink but also the support of skilled leadership. This is a fairly comprehensive list of those who provided civic, military, and religious leadership. If they were removed, the city was hard-pressed to stand. Such officials also played important roles in Mesopotamia and Egypt.[129]

Military operations were an everyday part of life and had their own personnel.[130] Judges in Israel were tribal leaders, especially during periods of war. They were subsequently replaced by kings (surprisingly absent from this list) when the monarchy was established in Israel. Neo-Assyrian judges were actively involved in judicial cases.[131] The prophet was the regular intermediary between the divine and the people.[132] Since the list consists mainly of recognized officials, the prophets referred to here could be the court prophets, who often did not present God's viewpoint but rather the message the king wanted to hear (9:15).

The diviner was an illegitimate source of divine revelation used by Israel's pagan neighbors and forbidden for her (see sidebar on "Superstitions and Divination" at 2:6). Enchanters, or "whisperers," were also unacceptable in Israel, but were still found among the people, charming snakes (Eccl. 10:11). A work written in a Canaanite dialect from Syria reads: "Incantation ('whispering') against the Flyers, the goddesses...."[133] All of these, considered to supply leadership support for the people, whether officially or in a clandestine manner, will be removed and replaced by unexpected leaders (3:4).

You have a cloak (3:6). The cloak or robe is the outer garment used to cover oneself. This could indicate that people were so destitute that the last one having all of his clothes left would be chosen leader. This is also a soldier's garment (9:4); it could have been fringed and embroidered as were robes of various social classes and nationalities as shown on the Black Obelisk of Shalmaneser III. This, then, could be a call for leadership from anyone who had some evidence of being able to offer it, even if only through their official-looking garments.

The LORD takes his place ... rises to judge (3:13). Numerous pictures of ancient Near Eastern deities show them seated while receiving worship. When standing, the deities are more aggressive, often with weapons as instruments of judgment.

Crushing my people and grinding the faces (3:15). Ashurnasirpal II describes Tukulti-Ninurta II as someone "who crushes those who are not compliant to him, who severs the back of the warriors."[134] A Middle Babylonian boundary stone includes a curse: "May they curse him with an irrevocable curse, may they crush his descendants forever."[135] The metaphor of military defeat is also depicted literally, with the king actually walking on his defeated enemies.

Anklet from the mummy of Psusennes I
Werner Forman Archive/The Egyptian Museum, Cairo

Haughty ... outstretched necks ... ornaments jingling on their ankles (3:16). Pictorial representation of common folk is rare in the period of the Bible, since the upper classes receive more attention. Commoners probably wore little personal adornment. Others used greater finery, including solid bronze rings placed on the ankle. The outstretched neck could be simply a prideful posture, or it could have been caused by wearing numerous necklaces, physically forcing the outstretched posture.

Bald ... baldness (3:17, 24). Baldness, especially among women, was not customary, and most wore well-coifed hair. Shaving all or part of the head of someone was a sign of disrespect (7:20) or mourning (15:2). A special haircut also seemed to be the mark of a slave, since one of the Hammurabi's laws reads: "If a barber shaves off the hairlock of a slave not belonging to him without the consent of the slave's owner, they shall cut off the barber's hand."[136] The formally prim and proper upper-class women will be either humiliated or enslaved.

Finery (3:18–23). These verses give the most extensive list of personal adornment in the Bible. Some terms are rare and not at all clearly understood. "Finery" is the general term, encompassing the list that follows, referring first to jewelry and then to clothing. "Bangles" are the ankle bracelets mentioned in v. 16; "headbands" are ornaments resembling or representing the sun, which are common in Israelite seals, showing Egyptian influence.[137] "Crescent necklaces" are like the moon, possibly showing influence from the moon god of Haran or from the Canaanites at Ugarit.[138]

"Earrings" (lit. "drops," indicating their pendant shape) were worn by men and women, and "bracelets" were also common. Headbands or turbans were worn by Israel and her neighbors, though it is hard to imagine "perfume bottles," which have been found in excavations serving as an item of

Finery of Queen Pu-Abi found in the royal burial pits at Ur at the end of the third millennium
Michael Greenhalgh/ArtServe, courtesy of British Museum

clothing, so they are possibly a type of amulet, paralleling the "charms" mentioned next (cf. the same root "whispering" in 3:3).

Signet or seal rings were used by some officials as a symbol of authority and worn on the finger. They left an impression when pressed into a clay writing tablet. Other rings were worn in the nose.[139]

Well-dressed hair (3:24). Hair not only distinguished individuals, as it does to today, but ethnic groups could be discerned by their differing hairstyles.[140] Elaborate hairstyles were worn by gods and leaders in Mesopotamia and Egypt.[141] Nice hair was prized, as shown by an Old Babylonian text describing someone as "provided with beautiful hair."[142] Included among other gifts in a letter from el-Amarna were "29 silver ladles, with boxwood and ebony handles, which are for curling hair."[143]

Sit on the ground (3:26). Extreme emotion is debilitating, affecting the ability to stand. Utnapishtim experienced this when he saw the destruction of his fellow human beings after the flood in the Babylonian Gilgamesh Epic. He said: "Consequently I crouched, I sat down, I wept."[144] This pose of abject despair and defeat is shown in first-century A.D. Roman coins showing the female figure known as *Judaea capta*.

Seven women will take hold of one man ... take away our disgrace (4:1). One of the unfortunate results of war is the depletion of men, resulting in a higher ratio of women. In the ancient world, women were under the care of various men during their lives—first their fathers, then their husbands, then their sons. If these were lost, through death or divorce, the woman and her children were placed in a precarious position, not the least reason being that land, the major resource of an agricultural people, was traditionally held by the man. Without a man and the sustenance supplied by the association with him, life was in jeopardy. This economic need is not the case here, however, since the women will provide their own provisions, apparently willing to bypass the traditional bride price.

"Disgrace" points toward a societal rather than an economic lack. This word occurs in the context of rape, an unfortunate concomitant of war. The women are either seeking protection from such violation, or else a return of status to one who has already been raped and so humiliated—a state shared by a woman who was widowed (54:4).

"Seven" is a significant number in the Bible, indicating completeness. One indication of this is that the symbol for seven in Akkadian also means "totality."[145] This number also seems to represent an unspecified high number, as we might say, "I told you a hundred times" (e.g., 11:15; 30:26). Akkadian incantations parallel this use, for example, when speaking of "seven young men and seven young women,"[146] and Inanna is given "seven divine attributes."[147]

The Branch of Yahweh (4:2–6)

Recorded among the living (4:3). The righteous followers of God are inscribed in a book of life. It is also known in Mesopotamian thought, where instead of a book we read of Tablets of Destiny (cf. 46:10).[148] These contained the destiny of everything and were given by Tiamat to her general Kingu.[149] In a prayer to Nabu (who subsequently controlled the tablets), Nebuchadnezzar II prays: "On your reliable writing board which establishes the border of heaven and the netherworld, decree the lengthening of my days, inscribe for me extreme old age."[150] In the Babylonian wisdom Poem of the Righteous Sufferer, the sufferer in the end receives several blessings, including "I was reckoned among the living."[151]

Cloud of smoke by day and a glow of flaming fire by night (4:5). God's protection and guidance was marked by these two elements when Israel departed from Egypt (Ex. 13:21–22), and they will be restored to Israel's survivors in the eschatological Day of the Lord. The powerful radiance of

Mesopotamian gods (2:10) is also associated with fire, smoke, and cloud.[152] In Ugaritic literature, several times the term translated in Hebrew as "cloud" is used of a divine messenger or herald, a representative of a god.[153]

Allegory of the Vineyard (5:1–7)

My loved one (5:1). One expects to hear of the writer's human beloved, but instead sees an agricultural reference. A lover compared to a garden is familiar (see Song 4:12–5:1), and the same comparison is found in Sumerian and Akkadian texts. A collection of the first lines of Akkadian poems identifies three: "She seeks the beautiful garden of your (to a male) charms"; "The lover-king goes down to the garden"; "The chief gardener of the pleasure garden."[154]

The Egyptian Ptah-Hotep (mid-third millennium B.C.) instructed his son to love his wife appropriately because "she is a profitable field for her lord."[155] Akkadian letters from the king of Byblos, Rib-Hadda, found at Amarna in Egypt, contain a proverb that compares a woman to a field four times: "For lack of a cultivator, my field is like a woman without a husband."[156]

A song about my vineyard (5:1). Vineyards were common in the agricultural life of Israel, with evidence of them from the ancient Near East as early as the third millennium B.C. While grapes were necessary for wine production, many steps were needed to produce the final product. Isaiah 5 describes several of these. The rocky hill country of Israel had to be cleared of rocks and were also often terraced; the collected rocks reduced erosion caused by water runoff and retained moisture for the vines. Some of the rocks could also be used for walls surrounding the vineyards, for watchtowers where guards could protect against marauders, and also for huts where workers could sleep.

Planting was done from cuttings rather than from seeds, and the growing plants

Winemaking from a tomb painting in Thebes
The Yorck Project/ Wikimedia Commons

Allegories

Symbolic stories are not rare in the Bible, occurring as fables or parables. They can hide a meaning that might be dangerous to state literally, such as preaching against Rome in the guise of Babylon (Rev. 17:5), or they can evoke emotions more readily through metaphor than through literality (e.g., the two lustful sisters in Ezek. 23). Such stories can draw clear word pictures from the daily life of the hearers.

A fable similar to that between the trees in Judges 9 is an Akkadian dispute between the date palm and the tamarisk as to which is most beneficial.[A-17] Though not in an allegorical text, in the Akkadian Myth of Erra Marduk utters a woe to Babylon in similar words. This metaphor is explicit, while that of the vineyard in Isaiah remains hidden until the end:

> Woe to Babylon, which I made as lofty as a date-palm's crown, but the wind shriveled it.
> Woe to Babylon, which I filled with seeds like a pine-cone, but whose abundance I did not bring to fruition.
> Woe to Babylon, which I planted like a luxuriant orchard, but never tasted its fruit....
> Woe to Babylon, which I have taken in my hands like the Tablet of Destinies [see comment on 4:3] and will not deliver to anyone else.[A-18]

needed to be carefully tended and pruned. Even with this careful tending, it took several seasons before usable grapes could be harvested.

After harvest, the grapes were placed in baskets and carried to the winepress. These were either built or hewn out of the rock, sometimes in the vineyard itself or else some distance away. The grapes were trodden underfoot in order to release their juice, which flowed to a lower section of the press, where it was collected. It was then placed in jars for fermenting.[157]

Vintners experienced this labor firsthand. They were thus attentive to Isaiah's message and would have reacted with disgust at the news of the "bad," useless grapes after all of the effort expended. Their astonishment would have been magnified when they realized that the presentation was allegorical and that they themselves were the useless vineyard.

Watchtower in a field
Z. Radovan/www.BibleLandPictures.com

Built a watchtower (5:2). In order to guard from marauders or scavengers, watchtowers were built. The concept of guarding has a sexual nuance in Akkadian, where it refers to protecting one's chastity. "If a woman 'hates' her husband, saying 'You shall not take me' ... if she is chaste ('guarded'), it is

▸ Wordplay

Plays on meaning and sounds, called paronomasia, appear to be linguistic universals, engaging the human sense of play. Sound play is generally language specific, not immediately clear in another, unrelated language. An example in 5:7 is words using similar sounding consonants (alliteration) and vowels (assonance) placed near each other but in contrast to each other. In 5:7 God looks for "justice" (*mišpāṭ*), but finds "bloodshed" (*miśpāḥ*). He seeks "righteousness" (*ṣᵉdāqâ*), but gets "cries of distress" (*ṣᵉʿāqâ*) instead.

Someone has suggested an English equivalent: "He sought *equity*, but found *iniquity*, a righteous *nation*, but instead, lament*ation*."[A-19]

Plays like this capture the attention and imagination of the audience. Israel's neighbors used these as well. The Akkadian *Enuma Elish* describes Marduk: *nakhlapta aplukhti pulkhati khalipma*, "an armor garment, he was clothed with terror."[A-20] Similar plays have been discovered in Egyptian,[A-21] Sumerian,[A-22] and Ugaritic.[A-23]

not a sin," but "if she is not chaste ('guarded'), she is a wayward woman ... they shall throw that woman into the water."[158] This nuance fits well in this lover's metaphor.

Woes and Judgments against Oppressors (5:8–30)

Till no space is left (5:8). Landowners regularly seek to expand their holdings, but this has dire consequences in an agricultural society where family land is not only the place where you live but also the source of your food supply. To protect people from losing this vital resource, laws such as the Year of Jubilee were enacted, by which land was to be returned to its original owners every fifty years. This served as a reminder of the identity of the ultimate landowner, God himself.

While using different legal mechanisms, Akkadian law also protected the unfettered disaffection of land outside the family or tribal unit.[159] One means for this was public disclosure of a pending sale. One of the Middle Assyrian laws states that one who purchased field or house in Ashur "shall have the herald make proclamation 3 times during 1 full month ... concerning the field and house which he is about to acquire, saying: 'I am about to take possession by purchase (of) the field and house of such a one ... let those who have any right or claim to possession bring forth their deeds.'" Lacking a response, the purchase could be finalized.[160]

Others restrict use of another's land without permission: "If a man has either laid out an orchard or dug a well or grown vegetables or trees on waste land which is not his ... when the owner of the field comes forward, he (the owner) shall take the orchard together with (the produce of) his labors."[161]

In Egypt, the arability of land was ensured by Hapy, the divine Nile in its inundation of the land,[162] without whose beneficence land ownership was problematic.[163] The importance of landholding over a long period of time is exemplified there by the Inscription of Mes from the time of Ramesses. It shows the transmission of land over several generations and litigation brought before the royal court when there were problems concerning that transmission.[164]

Laws are not necessary to regulate something that no one ever does or thinks about doing; this suggests that there were people seeking to take advantage of unfortunate neighbors, as reflected in 5:8. In times of drought or other crop loss, people sometimes had to sell their property or even their

Egyptian musicians from a tomb painting from the time of Thutmose IV
Z. Radovan/www.BibleLandPictures.com

family and themselves into slavery in order to live. This woe condemns those with financial means enough to exploit this situation, amassing not only all of the land into their own hands, but also all of the civic power that resides with landowners.

A ten-acre vineyard will produce only a bath of wine, a homer of seed only an ephah of grain (5:10). Several terms here refer to Hebrew measurements. The area of the vineyard is literally described as "ten-yoke," where a "yoke" is the amount of land a single pair of oxen can plow in a day, though the exact size is unknown. This would be a fairly large vineyard; most English translations (arbitrarily) take it as ten acres. A "bath" is a liquid measure that equals the "ephah," a dry measure for grain. They are estimated to be between 4.5 and 9.5 gallons. A "homer" (lit., a "donkey load"), the amount of grain a donkey can carry, is one-tenth of an ephah.[165] These results are so pitiful, resulting in a net loss for grain and only about 1 percent of regular production, that planting is useless.

Drinks ... wine (5:11). Carousing and inebriation, following too much consumption of the results of the good fruit from the vine, are not good. The Bible elsewhere condemns it (Prov. 20:1). The Egyptian Instruction of Ani (c. 1100 B.C.) also warns: "Don't indulge in drinking beer, lest you utter evil speech."[166] Banquets with drinking were well known, ranging from the Persian period (Esth. 1:8), clear back to creation, according to the Akkadian *Enuma Elish*. It reads concerning a divine gathering:

> They conversed, sat down at a feast, on produce of the field they fed, imbibed of the vine, with sweet liquor they made their gullets run, they felt good from drinking beer.[167]

Harps and lyres ... tambourines and flutes (5:12). The translations for these terms are approximations, though they are found in other ancient texts as well as in visual representations. The harp (16:11; 23:16) and lyre (14:11) are wooden stringed instruments—one with ten strings (Josephus, *Ant.* 7.12.3) and one probably with less, which are held in the hand. Tambourines (24:8; 30:32) are also hand instruments often played by women, though men also played them. Flutes (30:29, probably better "pipes") are hollow tubes made from metal, reed, or bone. Numerous figures show them being double-pipes.[168] A Sumerian proverb seems to hold pipers and flutists in low regard: "A disgraced singer becomes a piper; a disgraced *kalûm*-priest becomes a flutist."[169]

My people will go into exile (5:13). The customary foreign policy of both Assyria and Babylonia was to deport the rulers and leading citizens of conquered states, exiling them far away from their home.[170] One study places the number of such exiles during the Neo-Assyrian period at over 1.2 million,[171] dispersed throughout the Assyrian empire.[172] A result of this policy was the depletion of power at home as well as separating leaders from bases for resistance in their native land so they would be less likely to rebel against their overlords.[173] Deporting entire families also aided resettlement in the new land, lessening the draw home.[174]

Assyria did this to the northern nation of Israel in 721 B.C.,[175] as Babylonia did to Judah in 597 and 586 B.C. To avoid Babylonian wrath for killing her figurehead governor, Gedaliah, people from Judah voluntarily exiled themselves to Egypt in 581. Such deportation is evident not only textually,[176] including names mentioned indicating people of different ethnic origin, but also on reliefs on the walls of some palaces.[177]

Grave ... opens its mouth without limit (5:14). The grave is the entryway to *šeʾôl,* the term used in this verse. It is the netherworld, the place of the dead, of which the grave is the gateway (38:10). Since it is the ultimate destination of everyone, it is insatiable. This is also a characteristic of the Canaanite god Mot, the god of the dead. He says of himself in the Baal Cycle:

> Is my appetite the appetite of the lion in the wild, or the desire of the dolphin in the sea? Or does it go to a pool like a buffalo? Or travel to a spring like a hind, or, truly, does my appetite consume like an ass? So will I truly eat with both my hands, or my portions amount to seven bowls' worth, or my cup contain a whole river?[178]

The Egyptian Book of the Dead pictures a goddess monster named "Devourer" or "Eater of the Dead" (Amam) standing beside scales on which a human's heart is weighed opposite Maʾat ("order"). She waits to devour those who do not weigh up to this norm.

Draw sin along with cords of deceit (5:18). One draws along behind those things over which one has control. This is shown in numerous reliefs of bound and joined prisoners being led away. Ironically, at this point in their history, all that Isaiah's audience can parade after themselves as their greatest achievement is their sin.

Heroes at drinking wine and champions at mixing drinks (5:22). Two military terms are used satirically, since the only opponent conquered is alcohol. Wine is a common beverage in the area, made from grapes, honey, or dates.[179] Drinks could be flavored by adding herbs and spices. Intoxicants were often consumed through a long, straw-like tube, which also served as a strainer.[180]

Cylinder seal impression shows a banquet scene, including seated figures drinking beer from long tubes.
Kim Walton, courtesy of the Oriental Institute Museum

Bribe (5:23). A major role for a national leader was to establish justice for those unable to secure it for themselves—the weak and the disenfranchised (see comment on 1:23). For this reason, law codes were common. The whole enterprise is brought to nothing, however, when those charged with administering the law are corrupt, basing their decision on their own economic advantage rather than on justice, which they pervert. Making the entire enterprise of governance problematic, bribery is dealt with harshly. One of Hammurabi's laws states: "If a judge decides a case ... and then changes his decision, if they prove he changed his decision, he shall pay twelve times the penalty. He shall be disbarred, never to go back and sit with the judges in court."[181]

Dead bodies are like refuse in the streets (5:25). The lack of a proper burial was scandalous in Israel and among her neighbors—a

Devourer from the Book of the Dead
Allan Hise, courtesy of the Agyptisches Museum, Berlin

sign of disrespect for the departed. The Sumerian Marriage of Martu describes an uncivilized man: "A tent-dweller ... he dwells in the mountains ... he eats uncooked meat, in his lifetime he has no house, when he dies, he will not be buried."[182] An Amarna letter views it as a necessity: "Since there is no water, no straw, no supplies, no burial of the dead, may the king my lord take cognizance ... that life be given."[183]

Mesopotamians understood that after death a spirit or ghost left the departed. It sought to join its fellows in the netherworld. This was accomplished through burial, when the soul was at peace. After death, the departed was remembered through various rites such as offerings of food, drink, and prayer. Peace and memory would not be possible if there was no burial.[184]

Lack of burial is especially poignant in a description of war in Myth of Erra and Ishum, in which a man must bury his slain son, "but he will have none to bury him."[185] The abhorrence is also expressed in curses against those who break the law or a covenant. A Middle Assyrian law says of a woman who is proven to have self-induced an abortion: "They will impale her; she shall not be buried."[186] Esarhaddon says: "May Ninurta ... fill the plain with your corpses, give your flesh to eagles and vultures to feed upon ... may the earth not receive your body for burial, may the bellies of dogs and pigs be your burial place."[187]

Not a belt is loosed at the waist, not a sandal thong is broken (5:27). Preparation for battle or for work is exemplified by one's clothing being in good repair and functioning properly. A Twentieth Dynasty schoolbook praising the scribal art contrasts that profession to the soldier, who faces difficulties similar to those in Isaiah: "He may not rest. There are no clothes, no sandals."[188] In the Egyptian Tale of the Two Brothers, when Anubis finishes engaging in battle and other work, he takes off "his staff and his sandals, as well as his clothes and his weapons."[189] This suggests a possible military connotation for the Isaiah passage.

Arrows ... bows ... horses' hoofs ... chariot wheels (5:28). Composite bows, so called because they were formed of several materials, possibly originated in Assyria and were curved, which made for greater distance. Arrows were made from reeds, tipped with stone, bone, or metal. Shoeing of horses was not practiced, so some terrain was difficult for them; however, they developed hard hoofs. On chariots and horses, see comments on 2:7.

Lions ... young lions (5:29). The ferocity and roar of lions proverbially inspires fear. They are shown roaring in numerous Israelite seal impressions[190] and in other representations.[191] They are pictured as mauling unfortunate prey and are themselves prey of mighty hunters. A hero is shown in his power holding a lion. Nebuchadnezzar I (1124–1104 B.C.) writes of himself: "He rages like a lion ... his senior officers like a lion he roars,"[192] and Ashurnasirpal II describes himself: "I am a warrior, I am a lion."[193]

Lion attacking bull in a relief from Persepolis
Brian J. McMorrow

Isaiah's Commission and Message (6:1–13)

Aramaic plaque of Uzziah's reburial
Z. Radovan/www.BibleLand Pictures.com

King Uzziah died (6:1). Uzziah became the tenth king of Judah after the assassination of his father, Amaziah, though they probably shared the throne while Amaziah was a prisoner of war. Uzziah in turn shared the throne with his son Jotham after being infected with leprosy, which perhaps led to his death. It made him ritually unclean and therefore unable to fulfill any public duties. Grief in Judah must have been great since Uzziah was the only king whom many, including Isaiah, knew, since his reign was so long. Isaiah's vision is a reminder that, in spite of his passing, the true King still reigns: "The king (Uzziah) is dead; long live the King (Yahweh)!"

The anguish could well have been exacerbated by fear, since just prior to Uzziah's death in 742 B.C., the great Assyrian king Tiglath-pileser III had ascended his throne (745), reviving the waning Neo-Assyrian empire. He turned his attention to Israel and the west, starting with military campaigns in 743. One such campaign encountered "[Azr]iau (Azariah) of Judah,"[194] an alternate name for Uzziah (2 Kings 14:21), leading some to suggest that he was the opponent mentioned.[195] Fear at this juncture in Israel's history provided opportunity for a prophet to be heard, as it did in the reign of Ahaz in Isaiah 7.

I saw the Lord (6:1). Israel's neighbors could physically see manifestations of their gods, who were understood as being present in natural phenomena such as sun or storm, or in their cult images.[196] Mention of people seeing them is rare in the texts, however. Even when the goddess Ishtar proposes that the King Gilgamesh become her lover, she sees him, but there is no mention of his seeing her.[197] Most commonly the existing mentions are in the form of names, such as "I shall see the face of god X."[198] The Babylonian Theodicy states that "the one looking at the face of a god gains good fortune,"[199] and Tiglath-pileser I (1115–1077 B.C.) wrote: "I reckoned them with those who see the face of the god Aššur," understood as indicating the subject of the god, an appropriate meaning for this Isaiah passage.[200]

Yahwistic orthodoxy understood Israel's God as not being physically visible since he was associated with neither natural phenomena nor images. The possibility of perceiving him with the eyes was generally denied. Thus, the meaning of the verb "see" expands in the physical realm to include perception through other senses besides the eyes. It also

Cylinder seal impression showing Ishtar in a shrine flanked by guardian creatures
The Metropolitan Museum of Art/Art Resource, NY

Dating Methods

Old Testament writers did not have the luxury of one fixed point in time from which to date events. Rather, they dated occurrences in their texts as they related to other important events in the memory or tradition of their audience. This could have been a noteworthy natural phenomenon (e.g., the earthquake in Amos 1:1) or a memorable historical occasion, such as this death of a king (see Isa. 14:28) or a military attack (20:1). This convention is called "relative dating" since it relates one event to another in sequence. A contemporary example might be saying that something happened "three years ago."

Judaean Kings	
Amaziah	796–767
Uzziah (Azariah)	(791)–740/39
Jotham	(750)–732/731
Ahaz	(744/743)–716/715
Hezekiah	716/715–687/686
Manasseh	(696/695)–642/641
Amon	642/641–640/639
Josiah	640/639–609
Jehoahaz	609
Jehoiakim	609–597
Jehoiachin	597
Zedekiah	597–587

Relative dating leaves it difficult to correlate one such system with another. For our example, to what year in our B.C./A.D. system does the year of Uzziah's death correspond? One of the ways to accomplish this correlation is by finding "synchronisms," events involving two groups that are known from within each group. Such a correlation (which does not provide an exact date) was Israel's paying tribute to Assyria. This event is mentioned in records of both of the kings involved, Menahem of Israel (2 Kings 15:19) and Tiglath-pileser III (called "Pul" in the biblical text) of Assyria.[A-24] These synchronisms, of which there are several between Israel/Judah and Mesopotamia, as well as between Israel/Judah and Egypt and between Egypt and Mesopotamia, serve as anchors, binding together separate relative dating systems.

The next step to accurate dating is helped by the detailed records kept by the Egyptians. For them, the exact moment that the star Sirius appeared in a certain position marked the beginning of the agricultural year. Their records noted these dates, and modern astronomers have determined that the star follows a cycle of 1,460 years. Putting the Egyptian records together with the astronomical data allows us to relate events in those records to our dating system.

Assyrian records also help in this way. They collected the names for each year in what are called "Eponym Lists," which provided a relative chronology (see comments on 1:1).[A-25] An anchor point to other chronological systems, resulting in a more absolute chronology, is provided in the Eponym List by reference to a solar eclipse, which has been identified astronomically as occurring in 763 B.C.[A-26]

widens metaphorically to include inner perception such as in a vision and even understanding or comprehension.

Isaiah must here be having a vision rather than seeing the Lord with physical eyes. Israel's God has no physical body that can be seated; note that he wears no robes. Isaiah may well be standing in the earthly temple; the wording indicates that he sees something huge, though not necessarily a physical statue of God.[201] A large Egyptian god was associated with the temple at ʿAin Dara, a contemporary of the Solomonic temple, as shown by giant footprints on its steps.[202]

Lord/LORD (6:1, 3). The personal name of the God of Israel is "Yahweh" (*yhwh*), occurring over 460 times in Isaiah. Its exact pronunciation is uncertain, since Jews who worried about breaking the command against misusing God's name ceased using it orally by the time of the Second Temple. Instead, they substituted the Hebrew term for "Lord" (*ʾᵃdōnāy*, used in 6:1). Most English Bibles have maintained this legalistic avoidance of the divine name, but show its presence in the original through writing it in small capital letters (i.e., "LORD," as in 6:3). This helps English readers get back to the Hebrew.

"Lord" (*ʾᵃdōnāy*) can be a polite form of address to a stranger, equivalent to English "sir." It also can refer to one higher in social status than oneself, such as a slave addressing his master (24:2) or a person speaking to a king (e.g., 19:4; 26:13) or to God (e.g., Gen. 15:2).[203] Here the term shows a combination of the last two uses, referring to a God who is royally enthroned. Numerous ancient Near Eastern representations of deities show them enthroned in a manner similar to royalty.

High and exalted (6:1). In a hierarchy of power and authority, God is followed by the king, with the people falling below them. We use this extended spatial meaning of the term when we speak of someone "moving up the ladder." It is also used of God in relation to the rest of creation. It can also have a literal meaning, where something is physically raised. This physical representation of God's metaphorical superiority is meant here, reflecting the practice of standing the divine image on a dais or pedestal in its temple. The description of the temple in Jerusalem suggests that the floor of the Most Holy Place was raised since its internal height is ten cubits less than that of the temple proper. An important Babylonian temple to the national god Marduk was named Esagila, "House whose head is high."[204]

Train of his robe (6:1). The common mode of male dress was an outer robe, which generally fell between the knee and the ankle but did not have a train per se. The term is better translated as "his hems," the very edges of his garments, which were sufficient in themselves to fill the temple. This graphically illustrates the power, majesty, and size of God. The anthropomorphic picture of his garments, and in that, their farthest extremity dwarfs the physical reality of Israel's grandest architectural production. Whether Isaiah's vision refers to the physical structure he knows in Jerusalem or to a heavenly temple, the greatness of God is overpowering.

The hem was not only part of the magnificent garment; it also could play a legal role, symbolically and legally representing a person in Mesopotamian legal documents. Most of the writing needed to be done by scribes, since this skill was beyond most people, including royalty. The person legally bound by the documented agreement needed to sign it, even though that person could not read. Whereas today one might use an "X,"

Goddess borne by winged griffin is sitting on throne
Erich Lessing/Art Resource, NY, courtesy of the Louvre

Hem of the royal robe of Shalmaneser III
Heather Wassing, courtesy of the British Museum

at that period one could "sign" by leaving either an impression of one's thumbnail or of the fringe at the hem of one's robe. It is a means of personal identification.[205] Using this symbolism, God was closely associating himself with his temple in Jerusalem.

The hem also had legal implications in West Semitic texts from Isaiah's period.[206] There "seizing the hem" of a god acknowledged one's submission, so this relationship was still possible to Israel since at least the hem was accessible to them.

Filled the temple (6:1). The word for "temple" (*hêkāl*) used here is not the common Hebrew phrase "house of Yahweh," but rather a rare word of Mesopotamian origin. Originating among the non-Semitic Sumerians, the term was borrowed by the Semitic speakers of Akkadian in Mesopotamia and by Hebrew speakers. The term indicates two "great houses," that of the king (our "palace"; e.g., 13:22; 39:7) and of God (our "temple"; e.g., 44:28; 66:6). The ambiguity of the word does well here where Yahweh is portrayed as both God and King.

Clay bulla is decorated with two winged serpents (uraeus). The inscription reads "belonging to Amos, servant of Hezekiah."
Z. Radovan/www.BibleLandPictures.com

Seraphs, each with six wings (6:2). Seraphim (the

Six-winged figure from Tel Halaf
Matthew Wilson, courtesy of the Walters Museum, Baltimore, MD

Hebrew plural of *śārap*, "seraph") are one of two types of heavenly being mentioned by Isaiah, the other being "cherubim" (37:16). The latter, having a single pair of wings, are associated closely with the throne, while the seraphs are flying above it. The Hebrew term itself means "burning," which has led some to associate them with lightning,[207] but seraphs are not associated elsewhere with fire but with serpents (14:29; 30:6), possibly alluding to the metaphorical burn of venom. The serpents biting the Israelites in the wilderness are called "seraphs" (Num. 21:6–9).

The ancient Near East does know of serpents associated with divinity as well as with royalty.[208] A ninth-century tablet from Sippar shows a two headed serpent man, Mush-igimin ("two-faced serpent"), who was the chief constable of Shamash, the sun god.[209] In Egyptian art, part of the crown of the pharaoh is a *uraeus*, a black-necked cobra. The seraph is also found in numerous seals, often winged, though those having three pairs are rare; most have four wings.[210] A number of these have been found in Israel, so these figures were familiar to Isaiah and his readers.[211]

Even though Israel was banned from having images of God, his attendants or symbols were available at least in popular religion. Most such creatures are portrayed as standing

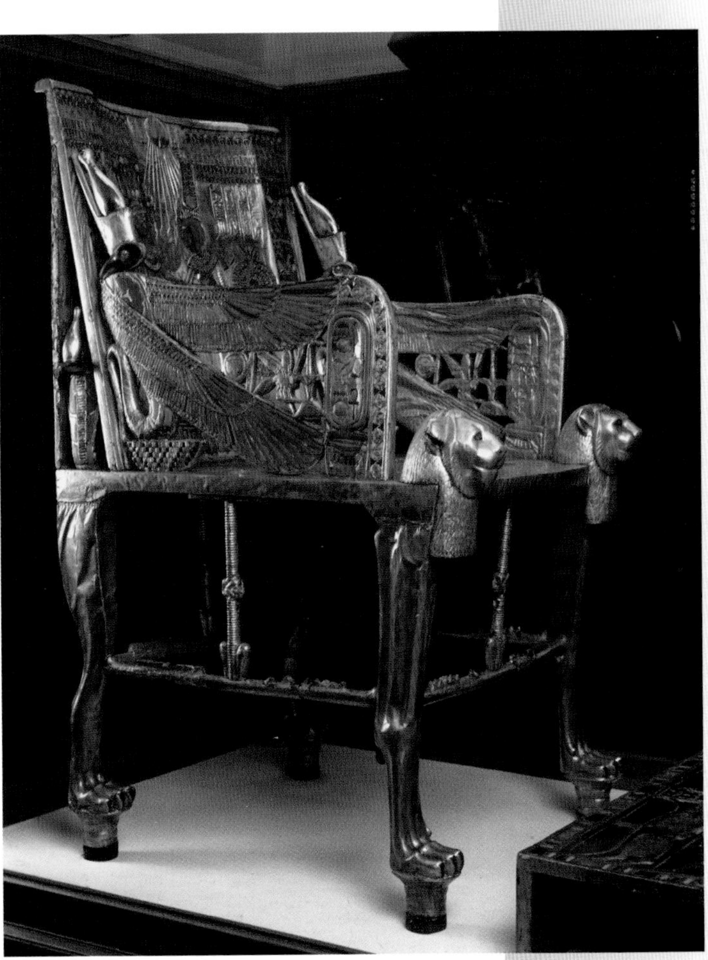

The throne of pharaoh Tutankhamun features armrests picturing winged serpents who would therefore flank the king, reminiscent of the seraphim around the throne of Yahweh.
Scala/Art Resource, NY, courtesy of the Egyptian Museum, Cairo, Egypt

or walking rather than flying like the seraphim. Besides the two wings used for locomotion, two cover their face in the presence of the holy God, and two cover their "feet." This is most probably a euphemism for the genital area (e.g., 7:20, where NIV uses "legs"), which was also covered in God's presence.

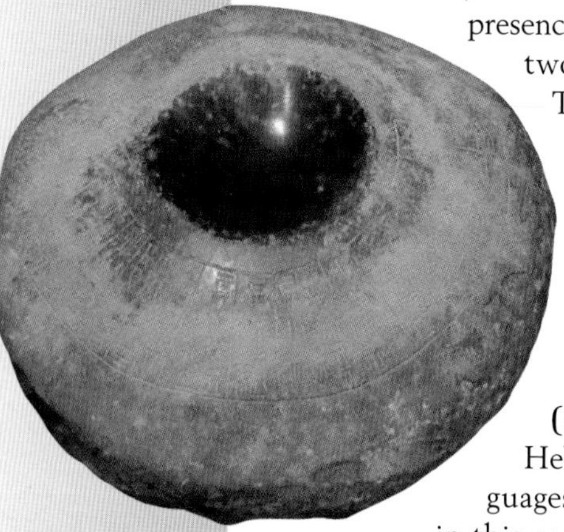

Holy, holy, holy (6:3). Repetition in Hebrew, as in other languages, provides emphasis, in this case, of the superlative holiness of God.[212] Akkadian priests also used threefold repetition in some incantations, with magical words calling for divine action.[213] Some of these repetitions were in the context of the "mouth washing" ritual (cf. 6:7).[214]

Descriptions of the gods emphasize their key characteristics. These frequently involve their prowess[215] or lofty status.[216] Neither of these attributes of power is important to Israel's God on this occasion; rather, attention is drawn to his holiness.

Doorposts and thresholds shook (6:4). Door technology in the ancient world differed from our doors. Rather than using hinges, most doors pivoted on a vertical supporting post set into an indentation to one side of the lower, stone threshold.

It is unclear why these architectural features are singled out here. While Isaiah himself may have been in the temple doorway, that is not indicated in the text. In Assyria, fantastic supernatural beings flanked gateways, and this could have been the original role of the seraphim, who now take up new positions worshiping God. While the entire temple probably shook, these parts are perhaps chosen as representative because of this association with the seraphim.

Woe to me! (6:5). Woe oracles are common expressions of affliction and trouble in Isaiah (3:9, 11; 24:16) and elsewhere in the Old Testament. In this verse it is brought forth by the realization of the distance between the holy God and the unclean prophet. Israel's neighbors also used similar woe formulae—for example, when woe is called on those responsible for the death of Aqhat in the Ugaritic myth,[217] or when Sargon inflicts wartime violence.[218]

Touched my mouth (6:7). Upon his encounter with the holy God, Isaiah realizes that he himself is ritually unclean. As such, he cannot join in voicing God's praise with unclean lips. He is also disqualified from proclaiming God's message to his people if the very instrument of his ministry as a prophet, his speech, is polluted by impurity. Ritual purification comes through cauterization by a coal from the temple's incense altar.

Ritual purification of the mouth as practiced in Mesopotamia is known through a number of *mīs pî* ("mouth-washing") texts.[219] This was most frequently performed on cult statues in preparation for their installation in a temple, where they became objects of worship and revelation, their mouths having been prepared. Part of the ritual called for threefold repetitions of spoken incantations (cf. 6:6)[220] and multiple washing rituals, in contrast to the single purification of Isaiah. The purification resulting from the rituals are similar, though the instruments bringing it about (a live coal vs. water) are different. One parallel is suggestive for the Isaiah context, since the special *bārû* or incantation priest had his mouth cleansed in order to make his presentation of the divine will more clear.[221] In both cases, the instrument of revelation must be pure.

Egypt also provides a parallel when contact by a fiery serpent rod (*wrt.hk'w*; cf. the seraphs of 6:2) opens or purifies the mouth.[222] Whichever society provides background for Isaiah's purification, a procedure is necessary before he can enter into the presence of a holy God. The unclean cannot be in the divine presence.

Socket from a temple gate
Kim Walton, courtesy of the Oriental Institute Museum

Your sin [is] atoned for (6:7). Atonement, or the ritual removal of impurity caused by sin or other means, is a main theme in Leviticus (cf. Lev. 22:14; 27:9; 47:11). The cognate verb in Akkadian (*kpr*) also indicates purification and cleansing, both literally, such as brushing one's teeth, and in the cult, such as purifying a temple through rituals or magic.[223]

One Akkadian ritual series is named "burning" (*šurpu*), since fire plays a central role in it. Various spoken incantations and burning numerous objects resulting in smoke (cf. v. 4) comprise the key rituals.[224] The second tablet of this ritual provides for purification from numerous transgressions involving the mouth (e.g., eating taboo things, evil speech, contempt, lying, etc.), but no specific mention is made of purifying the lips.

Whom shall I send? And who will go for us? (6:8). Incantation texts seek divine intervention against some type of malady. Numerous Akkadian incantations ask which deity should be the one called to present the case for assistance. They concern the interaction between the divine and human realms through the use of a messenger, much as the discussion does in Isaiah. They read: "Whom shall I send and whom shall I order?"[225]

Us (6:8). Several instances in the Old Testament where plural forms refer to Israel's sole God have raised questions: Is God one or several? The same plural form is also used by rulers (e.g., Gen. 26:10, 16; 2 Sam. 24:14), either referring to themselves through the "royal we" (*pluralis majestatis*) or else including their royal retinue. Israel's neighbors envisioned a heavenly council of deities surrounding the heavenly throne. These are known from Ugarit,[226] Byblos,[227] and Mesopotamia.[228] Israelite orthodoxy acknowledged only one God, but lesser, semidivine beings are found in his presence, not as advisors or exercising authority over him, but as his servants. Based on this information, God's speaking with his retinue is a possibility here.

Go and tell (6:9). In the ancient Near East, messengers were important as a means of contact between a ruler and others, including his subjects and other rulers. They served administrative, business, and diplomatic functions.[229] They were at times carefully selected and acted with the authority of the one who sent them (e.g., Num. 22:15, where the messengers were themselves royalty). They were to be trustworthy in passing on the charge entrusted to them[230] and usually were commissioned to deliver their messages orally,[231] which were often accompanied by written texts, such as letters. In Mari, one Itur-Asdu commissions someone saying: "Now go, I send you. Thus you shall speak to Zimri-Lim saying. . . ."[232] In the Egyptian tale of

Ritual series *Shurpu*
Bildarchiv Preussischer Kulturbesitz/Art Resource, NY, courtesy of the Vorderasiatisches Museum, Staatliche Museen zu Berlin, Berlin, Germany

A dignitary stands before King Sargon perhaps being sent on behalf of Sargon or coming before him with a message.
Marie-Lan Nguyen/Wikimedia Commons, courtesy of the Louvre

Wen-Amun's journey to Phoenicia, he is sent as Amon's messenger.[233]

Some suggest that the prophets were messengers coming not solely from God, but rather delivering the message of a divine council.[234] In the ancient Near Eastern world, this was a collection of the gods who met together to decide matters, such as in the Babylonian creation account, commissioning Marduk to battle Tiamat and then elevating him to chief among the gods.[235] There are hints of such a council in the Old Testament as well; while there is only one God, there are other supernatural beings.

Among Israel's neighbors, gods also used messengers to pass along their instructions. At times they sent other deities,[236] but they also used humans. This is common in epic texts,[237] but also in other genres. In an Akkadian incantation a deity asks a familiar question: "Whom may I send?" (Isa. 6:8).[238] The reason for messengers was that the message would be heard and responded to, not the opposite, as was expected of Isaiah's message (vv. 9–11).

Make their ears dull and close their eyes (6:10). Isaiah's prophetic role was to call the people back to repentance and a relationship with God. This is impossible if the people cannot receive the message. Nonfunctioning organs have several interpretations. In the Akkadian Poem of the Righteous Sufferer, physical debility seems to come from a supernatural attack of some kind. Among the physical symptoms, the sufferer says: "My eyes stare, they cannot see, my ears prick up, they cannot hear."[239] In a Sumerian prayer, similar symptoms arise when a penitent realizes that he has sinned (cf. 6:5–7). For him, a scribe, it is his hand and mouth, the tools of his trade, that are useless.[240] Also, when faced with shock or fear, the body reacts with numbness, as when Nabal heard the news that he had almost been destroyed by David's band, "and his heart failed him and he became like a stone" (1 Sam. 25:37; see Hab. 3:16).

Another suggestion is that the symptoms are to parallel those of the dumb idols Israel too often worships. Instead of maintaining allegiance with a living and responsive God, they turn to sightless, deaf idols for aid.[241] God warns that Israel will become like what they worship.

Sent everyone far away (6:12). See comment on 5:13.

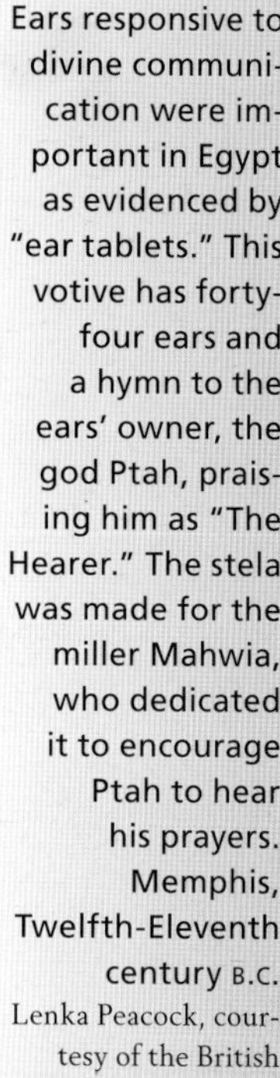

Ears responsive to divine communication were important in Egypt as evidenced by "ear tablets." This votive has forty-four ears and a hymn to the ears' owner, the god Ptah, praising him as "The Hearer." The stela was made for the miller Mahwia, who dedicated it to encourage Ptah to hear his prayers. Memphis, Twelfth-Eleventh century B.C.
Lenka Peacock, courtesy of the British Museum

Isaiah and Ahaz (7:1–9)

Aqueduct of the Upper Pool (7:3). The existence of an "upper" pool, apparently outside the city walls to the north, suggests a lower one, which is also mentioned by Isaiah (22:9), perhaps within the walls and thus more secure during siege conditions. The aqueduct apparently carried water to the upper pool. Water was a major problem for Jerusalem throughout her history, and identification of the various elements of her water system is a matter of some debate.[242] It appears that the king is here inspecting the water supply of the city, which would soon be under siege.

Washerman's Field (7:3). Washing and working new cloth is called "fulling," which leads to many translations identifying this as the "Fuller's Field." It rid the material of natural oils before it could be used and was an important part of cloth preparation.[243] The place where it was done seems well known, since it is the site of two important meetings (36:2; also 2 Kings 18:17).

Be careful (7:4). Lachish in Judah has produced several letters from the first quarter of the sixth century B.C. One says: "I am also sending to my lord the letter of Tobyahu, servant of the king, which came to Shallum son of Yada from the prophet and which says, 'Beware.'"[244] Exactly who is warning whom is unclear,[245] but it appears to involve a confrontation between prophet and king, though in Isaiah the message is encouraging, which might not be the case in Lachish.

Son of Tabeel (7:6). Two people are shown little respect, since only their father's name is given. They are Pekah, simply called "son of Remaliah," and another who is "son of Tabeel." The name is Aramaic, so it may indicate someone who had pro-Aram/Syria sympathies, that is, who would oppose Judah and side with her enemies in this Syro-Ephraimite conflict.[246] Another possibility is that it refers to Tubail/Etbaal, the king of Tyre who paid tribute to Assyria, along with Rezin, in about 738 B.C.[247] One of the two enemies will take over Judah for himself.

Sovereign LORD (7:7). "Lord" (*bēl*) is a common descriptor of Mesopotamian gods,[248] and a special name assumed by Marduk when he gained ascendancy over the other gods in the *Enuma Elish* creation epic.[249] A common Semitic noun for "lord, ruler," *baʿal* is the name of an important god at Ugarit,[250] who is also well known in the Old Testament. The Phoenician god Melqart

Parties in the Syro-Ephraimite War

Rezin and Pekah

Rezin (known as Rah/qyanu from Akkadian texts, *rdyn* in Aramaic) was an Aramean (Syrian) king who was dethroned when his nation was incorporated into the Assyrian empire in 732 B.C. He had been paying tribute to them for some time, as a list of vassals dated from the reign of Tiglath-pileser III (Pul, 2 Kings 15:19; 745–727 B.C.) shows.[A-27] In order to forestall incorporation, Rezin joined Pekah, son of Remaliah (Isa. 7:4, 5; 8:6) and king of Israel from c. 737–732, to oppose Assyria. They, and Pekah's son and successor, Hoshea (732–724 B.C.; Pekah was killed by the Assyrians[A-28]), pressured Jotham, king of Judah (c. 750–732 B.C.), to join their anti-Assyrian coalition, but he refused. To present a united front against their common enemy, Syria and Israel (designated by the name of its major tribe, Ephraim) united against Judah now led by Ahaz (735–715 B.C.) to force cooperation, in what is called the Syro-Ephraimite war.[A-29]

Having been earlier concerned with rebellions in other parts of his empire, in 734 B.C. Tiglath-pileser turned his attention to his holdings along the Mediterranean, where he campaigned for several years. A list of year names of his reign designate 734 B.C. through 732 B.C. respectively as "against Philistia ... against Damascus [Syria's capital."[A-30] Judah rightly perceived the overwhelming superiority of Assyria over any western alliance, so took the part of discretion (or cowardice) and did not join the coalition. In fact, she allied herself with Assyria, paying tribute.

This is acknowledged in an inscription of Tiglath-pileser dated 727 B.C., which reads: "[I received tribute] of ... Jehoahaz [Ahaz's full name] the Judahite."[A-31] The Assyrian army soon crushed the alliance, surrounding Israel on three sides by its army and allies, cutting Syria and Damascus off from its support.[A-32] The entire episode proved theologically vexing to Israel and Judah; does one follow logic or God?[A-33]

is also called "lord."[251] What should distinguish Yahweh from these other "lords" is that he is indeed sovereign.

Sixty-five years (7:8). This specific period of time is given as that in which Ephraim will become no more. Since the events of this story take place about 735 B.C., the period ends in 670 B.C., which is a puzzling figure since the Assyrians captured Israel's capital, Samaria, and ended its monarchy fifteen years later in 722 B.C., with its people exiled and foreigners transplanted into its territory. The end of the reign of Esarhaddon and the start of that of Ashurbanipal took place about 669 B.C.

Both of these kings engaged in exile and resettlement during their reigns. Esarhaddon says concerning a campaign against Sidon in Syria: "I drove to Assyria his teeming people which could not be counted,"[252] while Ashurbanipal says much the same concerning his campaigns against Egypt and Tyre.[253] He mentions receiving tribute, "ten minas of gold from the land of the Judeans,"[254] but neither of them mentions taking exiles from Israel, though their records are far from complete.

Immanuel's Sign (7:10–25)

Sign (7:11–14). Seeking revelation or confirmation from the divine is common in the ancient Near East. In the Old Testament signs could look back, reminders of what was (55:13) or proof of what was said (Ex. 3:12), or they could point forward, a portent of what was to be (Isa. 8:18). Omens were

Captives from Syria in an Assyrian relief from Nineveh
Todd Bolen/www.BiblePlaces.com

signs commonly used in the area, though unacceptable for Israel. Through them a skilled interpreter sought to analyze some natural phenomenon to determine the message from the gods (see sidebar on "Superstitions and Divination" at 2:6).

Nabonidus speaks of "the goddess Annunitu who, at sunrise, makes my signs good ones."[255]An Akkadian prophecy was offered by Ishtar of Arbela: "To the king's [Esarhaddon] mother because you implored me,"[256] and Ashurbanipal claims: "I asked Shamash and Adad and they gave me a firm positive answer."[257] This indicates that prophecies were both requested and provided.

Prophecies were sought because of a worldview that saw a tie between past and present, though not in the cause-effect relationship. Life could be described as a number of discrete but interconnected episodes in which B followed A, not through causality but rather through some sort of natural progression. If one knew that the last time A happened, B followed behind, one kept on the lookout for A so as to be able to anticipate B, since the two were inexorably connected. Written collections of omens were common in order to be able to "foretell," or better, to simply know, the future.[258]

Ahaz declines a sign, which God provides anyway. Perhaps his hesitancy is due to a pagan understanding, that a sign once given inevitably leads to the next event, which Ahaz does not want to encounter, whatever it might be.

House of David (7:13). While earlier kings were referred to dismissively simply by their father's name (7:6), here Ahaz is identified only by his line: he is a Davidic descendant, as were all the kings of Judah. It was a great and perpetual line, but Ahaz was not representing it well in this instance.

The phrase also occurs in extrabiblical texts. An eighth-century Aramaic inscription found at Tel Dan apparently mentions "the house of David."[259] There has been heated debate about both the text's authenticity and its meaning,[260] as well as about the proposed identification of the "house of David" in the ninth-century Mesha inscription, also called the Moabite Stone.[261] There is no a priori reason why the name should not be authentic, since David was the founder of a long-lasting dynasty with extensive contact with its neighbors. The dynasty of a lesser king, Omri, is found outside the Bible, also in the Moabite Stone,[262] so David would not be surprising.

The virgin ... will give birth to a son (7:14). Annunciations of birth, heralding such an important event through supernatural means, are not rare.[263] Hagar heard of Ishmael's birth (Gen.16:11), as did Manoah's wife of the birth of Samson (Judg. 13:3, 5). A bilingual Akkadian-Sumerian psalm dedicated to Assur is broken, but it may refer to a supernatural "virgin" birth of Tukulti-Ninurta I. It speaks of one "who was begotten by Enlil, [pure seed?] set in a maiden, a male she bore you."[264]A Canaanite text has the exact Ugaritic equivalent of this text, saying of the moon goddess Nikkal, "Behold, the young woman will bear a son."[265] The baby remains unnamed in the text, whose main focus is the marriage of two lovers more than the identity of their offspring.

David's success and influence was such that he was recognized as the founder of the long-lasting dynastic line both in the Bible and in ancient Near Eastern records such as this Aramaic inscription from a century and a half after his time. This inscription contains the only reference to David yet found in extra-biblical documents from the Iron Age.
Z. Radovan/www.BibleLandPictures.com

Immanuel (7:14). In ancient Israel, naming had more significance than it does today, when names are usually chosen for reasons of sound, fad, or association with a family member. Hebrew names have meaning transparent to one who understands the language, and attention is often drawn to the significance of this meaning to the birth event or some other aspect of life. For example, Benjamin, "son of the right [hand]" (a position of honor) was so renamed by his father Jacob from the original name Ben-Oni, "son of my pain," given by his mother Rachel, who was dying in childbirth (Gen. 35:19). The former is much more propitious for the life of the child than was the latter.

In Egypt, the pharaohs were given portentous names, usually five, when they ascended the throne (see 9:6). This particular name ("God is with us") is similar to one found on several Israelite seal impressions, "Yahweh is with us."[266]

Curds and honey (7:15). Milk in Israel was mainly from goats and could be con-

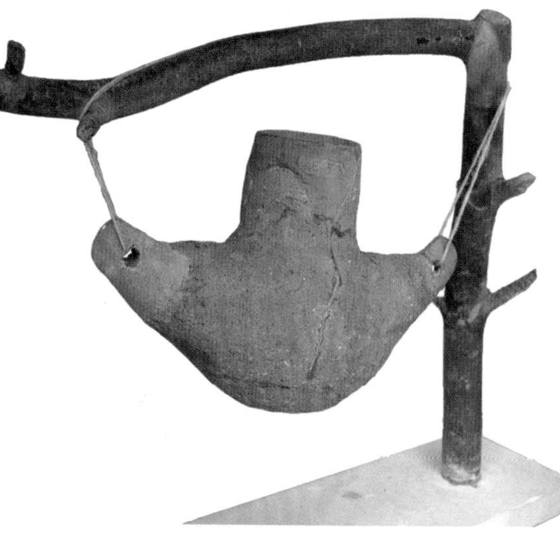

Churn from the Chalcolithic period. Pottery containers were suspended and rocked to produce cheese and ghee.
Todd Bolen/www.BiblePlaces.com

▸ Virgin—Semantics

Words contain different components of meaning that distinguish them from other related terms. For example, gender is the main distinguishing element between "man" and "woman," while age distinguishes "woman" from "girl." The two terms relevant to this passage are "girl" and "virgin." Both share the elements "female" and "youth," but the latter has the additional element of sexual inexperience. It is more specific in this area than is "girl," which may be used of those with or without sexual experience.

The Hebrew term used in 7:14 (*ʿalmâ*) seems to have the elements of female, young, fertile, and marriageable, since Proverbs 30:19 indicates sexual experience, while other texts speak of unmarried daughters (Gen. 24:43; Ex. 2:8). It would then be equivalent to "girl" in the example above.[A-34] The related Ugaritic (Canaanite) term (*ǵlmt*), among other things, describes a king's wife[A-35] and even a mother. The Isaiah passage seems to be speaking of a young, fertile female who may or may not be married at the time, but will bear a son within a certain period.

Interpretational controversy arises with the LXX's translation of the term as *parthenos* ("virgin"), which adds the element of sexual inexperience as an explicit part of the meaning. The application of this verse to Jesus's birth, using *parthenos* (Matt. 1:23) has skewed the interpretation of the Isaiah passage. In the New Testament, Mary's sexual inexperience is a key issue (Luke 1:27), while that is not an issue in Isaiah; rather, timing is the focal point of the message to Ahaz.

sumed straight or processed. One of the processing means was pressing or churning, which produced what is translated here as curds, though it more likely refers to something like yogurt or butter, since curds are formed from coagulation. "Ghee" is a possible translation, as for like the related word in Akkadian, it refers to refining and clarifying butter for longer "shelf life."[267] Mesopotamians used ghee for food and medicine as well as in religious rituals.[268]

A number of texts associate this milk product with honey. This was usually made from pressing dates or grapes,[269] although wild honey from bees was also used. There is no evidence of domestication of the honeybee until later in Israel.[270] An Egyptian relief from the mid-third millennium shows containers of bee honey.[271] Shamash-resha-utsur, an eighth-century ruler of the area of Suhu in the Middle Euphrates, claims that he "brought down from the mountain ... the bees which gather honey—which none from among my forefathers had seen or brought down to the land of Suhu."[272] Honey is also used for food and for medicine (as a poultice or ingested) and rituals in conjunction with ghee.[273] Both could keep well, so they were important for people on the move, as well as being enjoyable condiments for everyone who could find them.

Razor ... shave ... legs (7:20). From wall reliefs from the period of the Old Testament one can see that men from Israel and Syria had pointed, goatee-type beards, while the Assyrians had full, bushy beards. This is in contrast to the Egyptians, whose men were generally clean shaven, except for an artificial bound beard on the end of the chin. Involuntary shaving was an insult for those

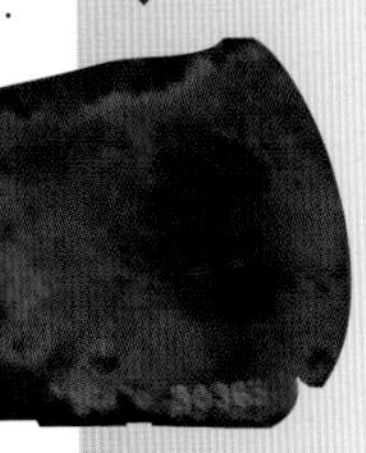

Razor
Kim Walton, courtesy of the Field Museum, Chicago

Land to Be Laid Waste

Tiglath-pileser III moved west with his armies on several occasions. In his ninth year (737 B.C.) he states: "I received tribute from ... Rezon of Damascus [cf. 7:1], Menahem of Samaria."[A-36] When Pekah faced this army, which took several of his cities (2 Kings 15:29), he apparently did not capitulate to them, because pro-Assyrian Hoshea assassinated him and took the throne (v. 30). In a later, fragmentary text speaking of these events of 732 B.C. Tiglath-pileser III states: "The house of Rezin of Aram [i.e., Damascus] I besieged, I captured. I destroyed sixteen districts of Aram."[A-37] Also, "The land of Bit-Humria [Israel] ... I carried off [to] Assyria. Peqah, their king [I/they killed] and I installed Hoshea [as king] over them. 10 talents of gold, x talents of silver, [with] their [property] I received from them and to Assyrian I carried them."[A-38] Hoshea therefore had a pro-Assyrian stance, ruling as their vassal for a while. But then he turned for help to Egypt, which proved his undoing. Shalmaneser V attacked him, and Samaria fell in 722 B.C.

In this way, the two kings whom Ahaz fears, Pekah and Rezin, disappear from the scene through the agency of Assyria, the tool God uses to answer Ahaz's prayer. This is not in Judah's best interest, however, since they will soon observe that the Assyrian cure is worse than the Syro-Ephraimite threat.

Assyria under Tiglath-pileser III flourished and expanded in what is known as the Neo-Assyrian empire. He campaigned to the south, subduing Babylonia, and then to the west, against Syria and her allies. For a time, the empire stretched even into Egypt. In its height, the Assyrians were able to besiege and capture Samaria, ending the Israelite monarchy and exiling its leading citizens (722 B.C.; 1 Kings 17:24–41). While Judah became a vassal nation, she did not suffer the same fate under the Assyrians.

Several of Assyria's kings are known from the biblical texts as well as from their own inscriptions. They include: Tiglath-pileser III,[A-39] Shalmaneser V (2 Kings 17:3–4; 18:9), Sargon II (Isa. 20:1),[A-40] Sennacherib (Isa. 36:1; 37:9, 17, 21, 37),[A-41] Esarhaddon (2 Kings 19:37;

	Israelite Kings	Judaean Kings	Assyrian Kings
750	Menahem 752-742	Uzziah 792-740	Ashur-nirari V 754-745
			Tiglath-pileser III 745-727
740	Pekahiah 742-740	Jotham 750-732	
	Pekah 752-732	Ahaz 735-716	
730	Hoshea 732-722	Hezekiah 728-698	Shalmaneser V 727-722
720			Sargon II 721-704
710			Sennacherib 704-681
700		Manasseh 698-643	

Ezra 4:2; Isa. 37:38),[A-42] and Ashurbanipal (Ezra 4:10).[A-43] They were known throughout the area for their ferocity and cruelty, with a mighty army that would trample over its weaker neighbors, often torturing and killing their defeated leaders and leading citizens. For example, during his campaigns Shalmaneser III claims: "I erected a tower of heads in front of the city (and) burned their adolescent boys (and) girls."[A-44]

Tiglath-pileser III's capture of Astartu, 730 BC.
Todd Bolen/www.BiblePlaces.com

Bearded Syrian on Kilamuwa inscription
N. S. Curthoys, courtesy of the Pergamon Museum, Berlin

whose society favored beards and was at times done to prisoners of war. Sennacherib wrote of defeated enemy warriors: "I cut off their beards."[274] Mourners also shaved themselves (15:2). In Isaiah, all the hair was shaven, including that of the "legs," usually understood as a euphemism for the genitals (Isa. 6:2; 36:12). Here it is used metaphorically and ironically, since the razor used against Israel is one she had "hired" to protect her in the first place.

Assyria Is Coming (8:1–10)

Reliable witnesses (8:2). Important, official documents in the ancient world were not only sealed but also witnessed by reliable folk whose names were inscribed toward the end of the tablet. They are indicated in Akkadian texts by the designation "in the presence of X," their signature assuring that the one claimed to have produced the document did indeed do so.[275] Contracts are serious undertakings, such as one for a delivery of straw having seven witnesses.[276] The presence of two such witnesses here in 8:2 indicates some sort of official document, whether a marriage contract (v. 3) or some other record of a significant naming.

Uriah (8:2). Uriah was chief priest at the time and in charge of anything to be placed in the sanctuary. A Hebrew ostracon,

Writing in the Ancient Near East

Scribal kit from Egypt
Kim Walton, courtesy of the Oriental Institute Museum

Among the earliest Middle Eastern writing implements was a stylus, a piece of reed or wood used to make marks on clay tablets. Clay was a common writing material, especially in Mesopotamia. In Canaan, clay was also used, either in the form of a tablet such as those found at Megiddo, or as pieces of broken pottery called ostraca, on which people wrote with ink.

In Egypt, other writing material included a type of paper made from the papyrus plant and parchment made from animal skins scraped and preserved. Both of these were inscribed with ink. These techniques were also used in Israel itself, with a prize example of a large parchment scroll being that of Isaiah itself found among the Dead Sea documents.[A-45] The document is large, close to twenty-five feet long. A combination of the two methods, writing on clay in Akkadian and on a pliable material in Aramaic, was used simultaneously at times by Mesopotamian scribes.

The "pen" elsewhere only describes an implement, some kind of carver or incisor, used in making the golden calves (Ex. 32:4). This use could indicate that what is written in Isaiah 8 is some kind of inscribed tablet or even a cylinder seal.

Since most Mesopotamians, including the upper classes, were illiterate, they often had seals carved and inscribed with their names to serve as official endorsements embossed on a text. They were often worn on a cord around the neck, not only as ornamentation, but also to be at hand when a document needed endorsement. The use of these for identification and the importance of names on them suggest that this may refer to a large seal.

probably dating from the late seventh or early sixth century B.C. and found in the area immediately south of the temple mount in Jerusalem, lists a number of names. Though broken, the last legible one is of an Uriyahu/Uriah.[277]

Prophetess (8:3). Although all of the writing prophets in Israel were male, females also fulfilled a prophetic role. Prophetesses are mentioned in letters concerning prophecies from nineteenth-century Mari in north Syria,[278] and numerous women are named as oracle givers, though not always designated as "prophet," in seventh-century prophecies concerning the Assyrian kings Esarhaddon and Ashurbanipal.[279] On the history of this time period, see the introduction.

The gently flowing waters of Shiloah (8:6). Lying in the hills, Jerusalem had a limited water supply in the form of springs, mainly the Gihon. Water needed to be directed from them to neighboring parts of the city by aqueducts or tunnels.[280] Heze-

Siloam channel used to distribute water from the Gihon spring to the valley below
Todd Bolen/www.BiblePlaces.com

kiah, Ahaz's son and successor, cut a tunnel from the Gihon Spring, but this verse cannot refer to that channel, since that was later; moreover, it was of such a pitch that the water would not be called "gently flowing." An earlier Siloam, or Shiloah, channel carried water from Gihon down the eastern side of David's city and irrigated the Kidron Valley.[281] Its lower pitch allowed the water it carried to flow more gently.

Floodwaters ... overflow all of its channels (8:7–8). Flooding can metaphorically describe overwhelming military force that cannot be held in check. The same metaphor was used in Mesopotamia, where flooding was damaging, rather than providing necessary irrigation as it did in Egypt. It is personified as an overwhelming force in the Sumerian Curse of Agade from the early second millennium: "The rampant Flood who knows no rival."[282]

The Old Babylonian king Naram-Sin describes his foe in floodlike terms: "It leveled cities, tells, and temples. It transformed everywhere equally. Like the deluge of water that had been unleashed among the first peoples, it transformed the land of Akkade."[283] Ashurnasirpal II (883–859 B.C.) describes himself as "an impetuous flood,"[284] and Shalmaneser III (858–824 B.C.) describes his onslaught on his opponents in similar terms: "I slew their warriors with the sword, descending upon them like Adad [the storm god][285] when he makes a rainstorm pour down."[286]

The River (8:7). While the Jordan River was important for Israel because of its geographical location in the land, the river par excellence, the "great river," was the Euphrates. On several occasions it is called "the River" (e.g., 31:21). The army of the Assyrians, whose homeland was along the more eastern Tigris River, needed to cross the more westerly Euphrates to approach Israel.

Outspread wings (8:8). While a bird's wings could protect her young, they also were the means of locomotion (e.g., 6:2), including propelling a raptor in swift attack, which is the picture painted here. An eighth-century Phoenician amulet from Arslan Tash depicts a winged sphinx and speaks of it as a "flyer" and "night demon," which is to be driven away from its attacks by the text's incantations.[287]

Wings are part of the representation of numerous ancient Near Eastern deities. Many are on symbolic representations of gods shown as a winged disk.[288] Other deities are portrayed in either human or animal form with wings. A winged disk in Assyria shows a superimposed anthropomorphic Shamash, the sun god, in his "flight" through the sky.[289] An Egyptian scene shows a ram-headed representation of the sun god whose widespread wings shelter several other figures parallels the widespread wings in Isaiah.[290] The goddess Maʾat, personifying the cosmic order, is depicted with outspread wings, perhaps indicating the universality of her influence,[291] as do those of Nut, the heavenly vault.[292]

Some winged beings represent malevolent forces, such as the bull of Heaven sent by Ishtar to destroy Uruk,[293] while others,

Winged disk in Assyria symbolized Shamash, the sun god, in his "flight" through the sky
Caryn Reeder, courtesy of the British Museum

Defeated soldiers captured in net
Jill Walton, courtesy of the Louvre

such as the composite human-headed, winged guardian bulls placed athwart Assyrian palace gates[294] served benevolent functions. For Isaiah, the wings stress the widespread, malevolent influence of the approaching army.

Immanuel (8:8). "God is with us" was a propitious name in 7:14 and is here applied to the nation of Judah as a whole. Some see verses 9–10 as applying the term again to Judah, but the context may rather suggest that these verses are taunting words of the arrogant Assyrian army. Sennacherib's officers used similar words to dispirit Jerusalem when it was under siege, claiming that the gods of other nations had been unable to save them, implying that they were now with Assyria (2 Chr. 32:17). Mesopotamian rulers regularly claimed the favor of the gods.[295]

Cyrus (557–529 B.C.), the Persian king who brought the Babylonians to their knees (see 44:28), claimed that his ability to do so was because the Babylonians had neglected the true worship of Marduk, their god. "He surveyed and looked throughout all the lands, searching for a righteous king whom he would support. He called out his name: Cyrus."[296] In other words, Cyrus also is claiming "the gods are with us."

Wait for God (8:11–22)

Stone that causes men to stumble (8:14). An Aramaic inscription from this period speaks of Panamuwa bringing a gift to Tiglath-pileser III, who "made him king over the house of his father. And he killed the stone of destruction from the house of his father."[297] This apparently refers to Panamuwa's predecessor on the throne, using terms that impugn his legitimacy. Travelers on a journey were impeded by uncleared roads (62:10), metaphorically referring to rebel leadership impeding legitimate rule.[298]

Snare (8:14). See also 51:20 on "nets." Nets and snares were used for hunting animals and birds. In the Akkadian Etana story, a snake cries to Shamash: "Truly, O Shamash, your net is as wide as earth, your snare as broad as the sky,"[299] intimating that no one could hope to escape him. Nets also were used metaphorically for capturing people in an inescapable trap. At times, nets were also used for protection, as in the Neo-Sumerian hymn describing the birth of Shulgi (2094–2047 B.C.). In praise of the god Enlil, he is said to be "the life-giving light, who guides the multitudes ... the huge net, spread over heaven and earth, a rope, stretched over all the lands."[300] Israel's God, rather than being the protective sanctuary

Cuneiform tablet with envelope
Kim Walton, courtesy of the Oriental Institute Museum

that Israel expects, will instead serve as the means of their capture and destruction.

Bind up ... seal (8:16). (See 3:18–23; see also the sidebar on "Writing in the Ancient Near East" at 8:1.) Important documents needed to be preserved for posterity. In the case of Mesopotamian texts, which were written on clay, they were sealed and/or enclosed in a clay envelope, which would have been removed if the official document needed to be consulted for some reason. Documents written on pliable material such as papyrus could be folded and secured by twine, which itself was fixed by a seal (29:11).

I, and the children ... are signs (8:18). A Mesopotamian practice views people, particularly newborns, as signs or omens. The person or some abnormality they have are indicative, as seen in at least two omen collections, *Shumma Izbu*, "If a fetal anomaly" and *Shumma Ālu*, "If a city."[301] Isaiah chides his fellows for ignoring the signs from God standing before them and instead consulting pagan sources.

Consult the dead (8:19). Necromancy, consulting the dead, has already been condemned by Isaiah (2:6; cf. also 29:4). Here some of its participants are identified. The "medium" (*ʾōb*, one who consults the ghost) or perhaps the spirit of the dead could infest living people and be consulted for esoteric knowledge (19:3).[302] A similar Sumerian term in the Gilgamesh epic indicates a hole into the netherworld from which a divine spirit could issue.[303] Mesopotamian texts refer to those who "bring up" the shades of the dead.[304] A Sumerian proverb speaks of offering to the dead,[305] and archaeological evidence of such offerings for the dead indicates awareness of them even in Israel.

The "spiritist" (*yiddᵉʿōnîm*, GK3362, the one consulting the spirit) most frequently parallels the ghost.[306] Resorting to these was an abomination, prohibited in Israel. Rather than asking of God, who knows the past and determines the future, people consult the dead, who are beyond knowing anything. Rather than listening to God through his lucid prophets, they resort to entities that only chirp and mutter.

Distress and darkness and fearful gloom (8:22). An omen from Ugarit also associates the appearance of trouble (here, "distress") with famine (v. 21).[307] It is found in a list of birth omens. These are based on events in human experience that in the past have happened subsequent to an irregular birth and so are likely to follow a similar birth anomaly in the future. Famine was often the result of inadequate rainfall, resulting in greatly diminished crop yields. Inability to find adequate food could result in widespread death or population dispersion to areas better supplied (see comment on 9:20).

A Child Is Born (9:1–7)

Land of Zebulun and the land of Naphtali ... Galilee of the Gentiles, by the way of the sea (9:1). Zebulun and Naphtali lay in the area of Galilee astride a major highway through Israel from the north.[308] They therefore were among the first people to be attacked from the north, such as that upon Pekah under Tiglath-pileser III in 733 B.C. (2 Kings 15:29).[309] When he had conquered the region, he left only the hill country of Ephraim to Israel, making the rest into three of the provinces of his empire.

The Mediterranean coastal area was the province of Duru, named after the city Dor on the coast, where Assyrian archaeological remains have been found.[310] This "way of the sea" may refer to a route further north toward Tyre, running from Abel Beth Maacah westward (seaward) toward Janoah.[311] Magiddu, named for one of its major cities, Megiddo,[312] included "Galilee of the Gentiles," and Galʾazi (Gilead, 2 Kings 15:29)[313] was in Transjordan ("along the Jordan").[314]

Northern Kingdom of Israel under Assyrian Rule

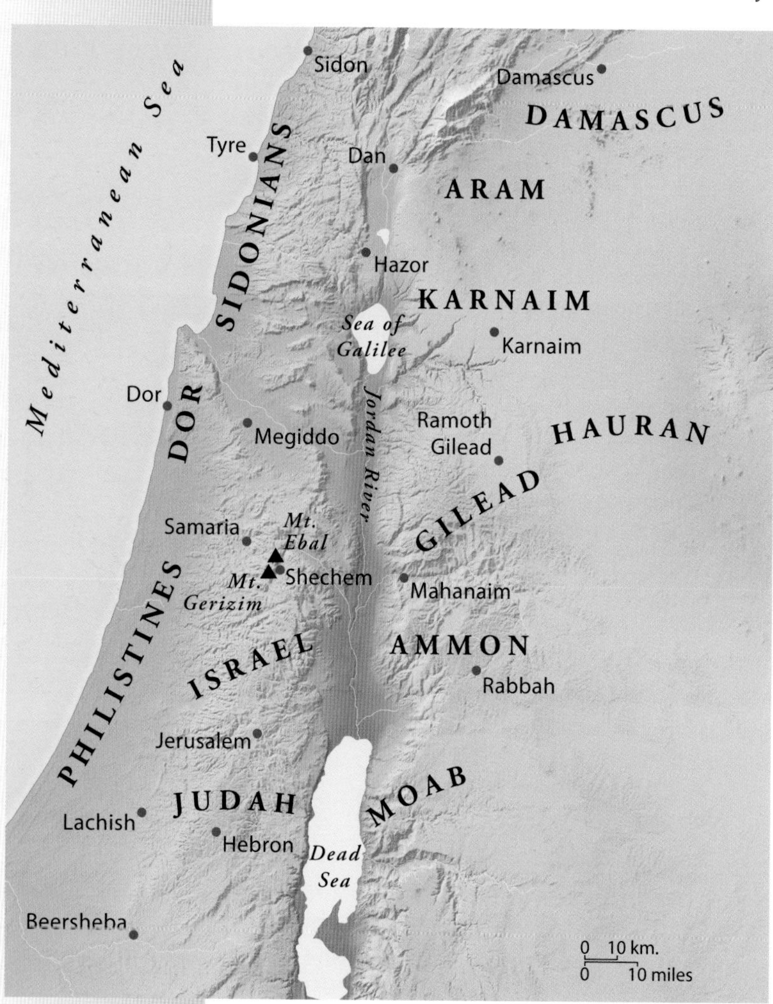

Great light ... a light has dawned (9:2). A major Assyrian deity was Shamash, the sun god, the source of light. Hammurabi (c. 1792–1750 B.C.) says, "When the god Shamash, great lord of heaven and earth, king of the gods, with his shining face, joyfully looked at me, Hammu-rapi ... he granted me everlasting kingship."[315] Hammurabi also describes himself as "solar disk of the city of Babylon, who spreads light over the lands of Sumer and Akkad,"[316] thus assuming the illuminating role of his patron. The Egyptians and Canaanites also had important solar deities.[317] For Israel, light symbolizes the presence of God.

Midian's defeat (9:4). Midian, related to Israel through one of Abraham's concubines, was a nomadic people without a fixed geographical location. The episode of their defeat at the hand of the Israelites is most likely when Gideon was able to defeat the Midianite army with only three hundred men (Judg. 7). Then, as here, it is ultimately Yahweh who is the victor (Isa. 7:14–15).

Yoke (9:4). A yoke joins a pair of draft animals at the shoulders in order for them to be able to pull in unison.[318] It could also join together people used as draft animals.[319] It is a common biblical metaphor for heavy service, especially to foreign powers. Liberation from such oppression is expressed by breaking the yoke.

The same metaphor is common in the ancient Near East. In a text from the middle second-millennium Amarna, a leader vows that he has the yoke of his lord on his neck,[320] and eighth-century Assyrian rulers used the same image, such as Esarhaddon (680–669 B.C.): "I imposed the heavy yoke of my rule upon them."[321]

Freedom from domination was achieved in a similar manner: "Let us break the yoke."[322] When one is under the yoke of a beneficent being, it can be to one's advantage, for "he who bears his god's yoke never lacks food, though it be sparse."[323] The non-Semitic Hittites in Asia Minor used the metaphor as well, so it was well at home in Israel's literary and sociological environment.[324]

Narmer palette shows pharaoh beating enemy with rod.
Erich Lessing/Art Resource, NY, courtesy of the Egyptian Museum, Cairo

The rod of their oppressor (9:4). The rod is that borne by an oppressing ruler, which can also be translated as a "scepter." It could be used for aggressive purposes or simply held as a symbol of the leader's potential power. Breaking it symbolizes the loss of that power.

Warrior's boot ... garment (9:5). "Boots" only occur here in the Old Testament, but the term in Akkadian indicates sandals or shoes.[325] Many soldiers are shown barefoot or with sandals, though some wear higher boots.[326] These and their outer garments, bloodied in battle, were banned from Israelite reuse, but were to be destroyed by fire. The bloody aftermath of battle is accentuated by an Ugaritic reference to the goddess Anat, who kills so many opponents that "up to her knees she wades in the blood of soldiers, to her neck in the gore of fighters."[327]

Child is born ... son is given (9:6). The birth of a son was viewed as a matter of rejoicing in ordinary circumstances. Having a royal son to assume the throne was even more important. Panamuwa I, a Syrian king in the mid-eighth century, wrote an Aramaic document stating a blessing on "whoever of my sons seizes the scepter, and sits upon my throne, and maintains power."[328] The Assyrian Esarhaddon enacted a treaty with vassals to ensure that they recognized his desire that his son, Ashurbanipal, succeed him to the throne.[329]

Everlasting Father (9:6). An undated seal impression in Phoenician, Ammonite, or Hebrew belongs to a man named Abiʿad, "eternal father."[330]

Neo-Assyrian boots
Z. Radovan/www.BibleLand Pictures.com

Increase of his government and peace (9:7). It is the last of the royal titles of v. 6 that is highlighted through this phrase. "Peace" denotes more than just a lack of war; it encompasses well-being, safety, and plenty, along with good relationships with one's brother, neighbor, and God (e.g., 27:5). It is a longed-for end of one's life as well as an anticipated goal of Israel's settlement of the land after years of wandering (Lev. 26:6).

Royal Birth

While the birth of any child is important, that of a future ruler is even more momentous. In the Ugaritic Aqhat text, when Danʾel hears he will have a son:

> Danʾel's face lit up with joy,
> His countenance glowed....
> He cried out loud:
> I can sit and be at rest, my innermost being can rest,
> For a son will be born to me,[A-46] as to my brothers,
> a scion, as to my kinsmen.[A-47]

There then follows a list of the benefits that he expects, including performing religious rituals and protecting and helping his father when he is incapacitated.

An Egyptian myth tells the story of the conception and birth of Hatshepsut. Amun-Ra tells Ahmose that she is to bear a daughter: "Hatshepsut-Henemt-Amon is the name of this son [sic!].... She will carry out the beneficial actions of this kingdom throughout the whole land.... I have united the two lands for her, with all her names upon the throne of Horus the living one.... He [sic!] gives all life, all continuation and all welfare, all health and all largeness of heart upon the throne."[A-48] In other words, royal birth announcements, indicating the name along with personal and national benefits, find a home in the literary and historical context of Isaiah. Here the prophet celebrates the birth of one who will continue the royal line of David.

The Mesopotamian god Marduk is purported to prophesy of a coming ruler, one who sounds much like Nebuchadnezzar I (1124–1103 B.C.), who probably had the piece written for propaganda purposes. Marduk prophesies:

> A king of Babylon will arise, he will renew the marvelous temple.... He will create the plans of heaven and earth.... He will lead me in procession to my city Babylon [reestablishing him as the city's main god]. He will restore my (processional) boat, he will overlay its rudder with precious metal ... with gold leaf. [... this prince] will see the benevolence of the god. [The years of] his reign will be long.... He will provide for the city and gather in the scattered ones.... This prince will cause his land to browse on the splendors of his pastures, and his days will be long.... This prince will [ru]le [all] lands.[331]

This lengthy rule of peace and plenty echoes well with that of Isaiah's messianic vision. In another of his texts, Marduk describes the gods as "bailiffs of peace,"[332] showing that peace has royal and divine sources. It is also important in the realm of the here and now. Numerous Amarna letters mention a desire for it, and in one a Hittite ruler writes to his Egyptian counterpart: "Now, my brother, [yo]u have ascended the throne of your father, and just as your father and I were desirous of peace between us, so now too should you and I be friendly with one another."[333]

He will reign on David's throne ... from that time on and forever (9:7). When political stability is not a given, a long-standing throne is a *desideratum*. Esarhaddon received a message from Ishtar of Arbela that "for lengthy days and eternal years I established your throne."[334] This is not a statement of absolute eternity, never-ending time in an ontological sense. Rather, it is a wish for a long life. This was a common blessing wished on others as well, as noted in several Amarna letters.[335] Absolute eternity was not a concern in the ancient world, since even most deities had a finite existence. What is in view is perpetuity either through a single lifetime or into the foreseeable future.[336]

▶ Names and Naming

Four of five Sesostris I names appear here on the side of the White Chapel.
Manfred Näder, Gabana Studios, Germany

The significance of names in the ancient Near East has already been noted (7:14).[A-49] In the Old Testament names not only looked to the circumstances of birth (e.g., Jonathan, "Yahweh has given [a son]"; Reuben, "Look! A son"), but could also wish a blessing (e.g., Isaiah, "Yahweh's salvation"; Immanuel, "God be/is with us").

Royal names could change when a person attained the throne. Several Israelite kings found their names changed by their overlords, showing that they were under authority of an outside power (e.g., Eliakim changed to Jehoiakim by the Egyptians, 2 Kings 23:34). Others seem to have adopted their own throne name, as some have suggested for Azzariya ("Yahweh aided") adopting the name Uzziah ("Yahweh is my strength").[A-50] King David was identified at his death by four titles: son of Jesse, man[A-51] exalted by the High One, anointed by Jacob's God, Israel's favorite singer (2 Sam. 23:1).

Whether chosen by this ruler for himself in 9:6b (supported by the Hebrew form of the verb[A-52]) or by another on his behalf,[A-53] the names are auspicious for his reign. Some suggest parallels with the Egyptian practice of a five-part royal title,[A-54] though only four are listed here. The Ugaritic king Niqmepa had four titles: "master of justice, he who builds a (royal) house/dynasty, royal guardian, royal builder,"[A-55] while Mesopotamian kings employed numerous titles or epithets. Although not all are used of one ruler, they include, "counselor,"[A-56] "(very) strong/mighty,"[A-57] "mighty, heroic,"[A-58] "eternal/everlasting,"[A-59] "father,"[A-60] "prince,"[A-61] and "one who quiets, brings peace";[A-62] so the concepts applied to Isaiah's ruler are well represented in their literary environment.

Condemnation of Israel's Sinful Pride (9:8–10:4)

Bricks ... dressed stone ... fig trees ... cedars (9:10). A broad range of quality in products available to builders is presented here, from common and ordinary to fine and rare. Cheaply available were mud bricks, which could be easily handmade from readily available material and sun-dried. Isaiah brags that this common house-building stuff will be replaced by finished, hewn ashlar

The upper blocks of Ashlar masonry contrast to the fieldstone base near the gate of Tel Dan.
Kim Walton

stone, which has been dressed on all sides by a chisel.[337] Requiring more work and being much more durable, these stones were also more expensive than common brick.

Roof beams were generally made from the commonly available wood of the sycamore fig, which was used in spite of its softness and lack of durability. In contrast, the speakers, in their braggadocio, purport to replace it with the harder and therefore stronger, taller, and more precious cedar (cf. 2:13). This is reminiscent of the days of Solomon, who "made silver as common in Jerusalem as stones, and he made cedars as numerous as the sycamore-fig trees" (1 Kings 10:27; 2 Chr. 9:27).

Rezin's foes (9:11). Rezin, the Aramean king of 7:1, was conquered by Assyria in the campaign of 734–732 B.C.[338] Undoubtedly Assyria is the enemy noted here.

Arameans from the east and Philistines from the west (9:12). When Assyria campaigned in the area, it moved against all the inhabitants, including Israel, the Arameans, and the Philistines. Tiglath-pileser III says, "I received tribute from ... Mitinti of Ashkelon [a Philistine city], Jehoahaz of Judah";[339] "I received tribute from ... Rezon of Damascus";[340] and "as for Hanno of Gaza [a Philistine city] who had fled from my army ... I imposed tribute upon them."[341] Since this verse sees Israel suffering attack from these two neighbors, this could indicate that some of their soldiers were either conscripted into the Assyrian army or were hired as mercenaries.

His hand is still upraised (9:12, 17, 21). The anthropomorphism of God's outstretched hand most often indicates anger and judgment (5:25; 23:11), though it can also bestow blessing (Deut. 4:34). In the Akkadian folktale Poor Man of

Pharaoh with outstretched arm in relief at Karnak
Manfred Näder, Gabana Studios, Germany

Unjust Laws

A major role of Israel's ruler was to establish justice and righteousness, the very foundation of Yahweh's kingship. They were to make sure that everyone received protection under the law (e.g., 9:7; 33:5). Hammurabi, in the prologue to his law code, lists some of his accomplishments: "I established law and justice in the language of the land, thereby promoting the welfare of the people."[A-63] The epilogue begins: "The laws of justice, which Hammurabi, the efficient king, set up, and by which he caused the land to take the right way and have good government."[A-64] Those who did not rule in such a manner were judged harshly.

In Isaiah legal moves against individuals unable to defend themselves are condemned; the rulers are unacceptably misusing power. Hammurabi also states that he wrote his laws "in order that the strong might not oppress the weak, that justice might be dealt to the orphan (and) the widow . . . to give justice to the oppressed."

Some legal collections provide insight as to what oppression and injustice looked like. The Laws of Ur-Nammu (c. 2112–2005 B.C.) declare that their ruler stopped oppression by heavy-handed rulers, setting out to "establish equity in the land (and) he banished malediction, violence and strife."[A-65] The Lipit-Ishtar Lawcode (nineteenth century B.C.) mentions slavery, and children and parents standing in opposition to each other,[A-66] while the Edict of Ammisaduqa mentions several elements that were made right, having been carried over from his predecessor. They include forgiveness of debt arrears for unpaid taxes and deceptive business practices.[A-67] This kind of economic wrong would have been known and detrimental to Isaiah's audience as well, as would royal use of conscript labor for royal gain, and onerous taxes and conscript labor.

Stele of Hammurabi with legal sayings to demonstrate he is a just and wise king

Scott MacLeod Liddle, courtesy of the Louvre

Nippur, the poor man "with his right hand he greeted the mayor, 'May Enlil and Nippur bless the mayor.'"[342]

In iconography, the hand seems most often stretched out in blessing or supplication, though it at times indicates aggression. A text of Sargon states, "I raised both of my hands in fervent prayer."[343] In the Gilgamesh Epic, the cow-goddess, Ninsun, "climbed the staircase and went up on the roof.... Scattering incense she lifted her arms in appeal to the Sun God."[344] A more sinister connotation is in a Sumerian/Akkadian bilingual text where "when you lift your arms, a long shadow is spread."[345]

On the right they will devour, but still be hungry; on the left they will eat, but not be satisfied (9:20). A similar description is given of two baby sons of the chief Ugaritic god, Ilu. Upon their birth, Shahru-wa-shalimu, personified dawn and dusk, "prepare (food for themselves) on right and left, into their mouth (it goes) but never are they satisfied."[346]

Feed on the flesh of his own offspring (9:20). In times of siege, when all outside supplies were cut off by the surrounding enemy, people were driven to eating the unthinkable, even their own children. This could be metaphorical, indicative of the barbaric way people treated each other. An Egyptian pyramid text from the time of the Pharaoh Unas (c. 2375–2345 B.C.) seems to use the idea metaphorically:

> [Unas is] a god who lives on his fathers, who feeds on his mothers!... who lives on the being of every god, who eats their entrails ... their bodies full of magic.... Unas is he who eats men, feeds on gods.... Unas eats their magic, swallows their spirits; their big ones are for his morning meal, their little ones for his evening meal, their little ones for his night meal, and the oldest males and females for his fuel.[347]

However, there is no reason to argue it is not literal in Isaiah. Cannibalism was one of the curses for breaking the covenant between Israel and her God (Deut. 28:53–57).

In the Assyrian story of the flood, *Atraḫasis*, mankind is punished by deprivation of food. This happened for so long that "[when the sixth year arrived, they served up] the daughter for dinner, they served up [the son for food]."[348] Among the curses that Esarhaddon placed on his vassals if they should break their treaty with him was cannibalism:

> Let the barley rations to be ground disappear for you, so that they grind your bones, (the bones of) your sons and daughters instead of barley rations ... may you eat in your hunger the flesh of your children, may, through want and famine, one man eat the other's flesh ... may he make you eat in your hunger the flesh of your brothers, your sons and your daughters.[349]

Deprive the poor ... widows ... fatherless (10:2). As noted in the sidebar on "Unjust Laws," Hammurabi singled out "the orphan (and) the widow," while Ur-Nammu states that "the orphan was not delivered up to the rich man; the widow was not delivered up to the mighty man."[350] King Keret from Ugarit is condemned: "You let your hands fall slack; you do not judge the widow's case, you do not make a decision regarding the oppressed.... Before you, you do not feed the orphan, behind your back the widow."[351] The Egyptian wisdom text The Eloquent Peasant commends someone by saying: "For you are the father of the orphan, the husband of the widow, the brother of the desolate, the garment of the motherless."[352] These are commonly mentioned in the Old Testament.

Condemnation of Assyria's Sinful Pride (10:5–19)

Seize loot and snatch plunder (10:6). Military action was, and still is, largely a matter of acquisition. The Amarna letters contain numerous mentions of raids, commonly in letters from Rib-hadda, mayor of Byblos. He complains of the ʿApiru and other marauders taking grain,[353] ships,[354] surrounding vil-

▸ Calno, Carchemish, Hamath, Arpad, Samaria, Damascus, Jerusalem

These seven cities mentioned in 10:9–11 are presented in pairs, with Samaria occupying space in two pairs. The first in each case lies geographically south of the second, which had previously been conquered. The writer is positing that the same fate will befall each southern city.

In north Syria, Carchemish lies on the Euphrates, while Calno/Calneh is not surely identified, but is probably known in Akkadian texts as Kullani. Assyrian years were identified by eponyms, which associate each year with the name of a dignitary and an event that happened that year. For example, 734 B.C. is known as the year "Kullani (is) captured."[A-68] Carchemish was plundered by Egypt under Thutmoses III in the mid-fifteenth century B.C.,[A-69] as well as by Ramesses III some three centuries later.[A-70] Capture by Assyria is more relevant to Isaiah, and it was taken by Ashurnasirpal II[A-71] and his son Shalmaneser III in 857 B.C.[A-72] It was still paying tribute to Assyria in the person of Tiglath-pileser III a century later,[A-73] but it rebelled and had to be subdued in 717 B.C. by Sargon II.[A-74] It is probably the latter event to which Isaiah refers, so a subsequent conquest of Calneh must be intended.

Hamath and Arpad lie further south in Syria. Hamath was also mentioned in earlier Egyptian texts[A-75] and in ninth-century Akkadian texts.[A-76] It became a vassal of Tiglath-pileser III in 734 B.C.[A-77] and was completely destroyed with its inhabitants exiled in 720 B.C. under Sargon II.[A-78] Arpad is mentioned in several places in the eponym lists, including 805, 754,[A-79] 743, 742, 741 B.C.,[A-80] so it was apparently not a willing vassal (see 36:19; 37:13). Though not mentioned by name, it could have been a member of the anti-Assyrian alliance with Hamath that was defeated so soundly in 720 B.C.[A-81]

In southern Syria, Damascus was the Aramean capital that had earlier attracted Egyptian[A-82] and ninth-century Assyrian attention.[A-83] In 732 B.C., Assyria, at the instigation of Ahaz, came against Damascus (7:1), conquering it and making it one of its provincial capitals.[A-84] Samaria, the Israelite capital, repeatedly rebelled against Assyria and finally fell in 722 B.C.

The last geographical pair, Jerusalem and Samaria, is listed south-north in verse 10, but is reversed in verse 11. The example of Samaria and its defeat is offered to Jerusalem, trying to convince her to turn back to God, but she does not, and so is also captured by Babylonia in 586 B.C.

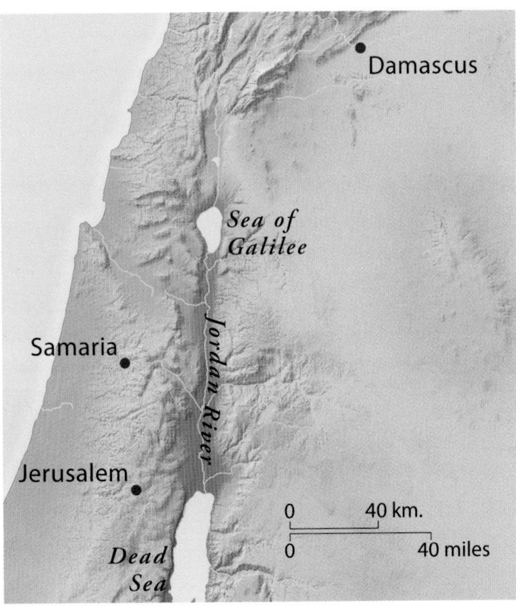

Capital Cities Subject to Assyria

Bulla from seal of Hezekiah identified as son of Ahaz, king of Judah
Z. Radovan/www.BibleLandPictures.com

lages,[355] and the very bronze from his city gates.[356] A Ugaritic letter describes an incident in which "your messenger came, he clobbered the militia, and he plundered the town. He has burnt up our food, and even destroyed the vineyards."[357]

Images (10:10–11). Jerusalem is indistinguishable from her neighbors, including Samaria, in their use of images, even though they were banned in her foundational covenant document, the Decalogue. The only difference mentioned is that the idols of Assyria are superior, not that Israel has disavowed them as they ought. This may indicate their relative power, since Assyria with her idols were able to subdue both Israel and Judah. Part of any ancient conquest was to take away the god images of the conquered.

Ahaz used idols, and Isaiah and his contemporaries condemn their worship (e.g., 30:22; 31:7). Archaeology has not found many idol figurines from the first millennium, but there are a number of seals and seal impressions from this period. Some show deities, especially from Egypt. For example, one is inscribed, "Of Abiyau, servant of Uzziah," possibly referring to the Judean king (Isa. 6:1), showing an infant Horus kneeling on lotus or papyrus plants.[358] Another belonged to a servant of King Ahaz of Judah (733–727 B.C.)[359] and has a winged sun disk, three Egyptian crowns, and two uraeia or Egyptian cobras on it.[360] Another reads, "Of Hezekiah, [son of] Ahaz, king of Judah."[361] More rarely, Mesopotamian iconography is shown on a seal.[362]

By the strength of my hand I have done this (10:13–14). The Assyrian king is condemned for his pride (v. 12). His statements are like those found in contemporary Assyrian royal inscriptions. For example, Ashurnasirpal II introduces himself:

> Ashurnasirpal, strong king, king of the universe, unrivalled king, king of all the four quarters, sun(god) of all people, chosen of the gods ... beloved of the gods ... destructive weapon of the great gods, the pious, beloved of your (Ninurta's) heart, prince, favorite of the god Enlil ... attentive prince, worshipper of the great gods, ferocious dragon, conqueror of cities and the entire highlands, encircler of the obstinate, crowned with splendor, fearless in battle, lofty merciless hero ... king of all princes, lord of lords ... king of kings ... the king who has always acted justly ... has always contested with every last enemy ... and imposed on them tribute and tax.... I am king, I am lord, I am praiseworthy, I am exalted, I am important, I am magnificent, I am foremost, I am a hero, I am a warrior, I am a lion, I am virile.[363]

In another inscription the Assyrian king picks up another theme found in Isaiah: "I, Ashurnasirpal, sage, expert, intelligent one, open to counsel, wisdom which the god ... destined for me."[364]

Egyptian pharaohs are not immune from such self-aggrandizement either. Ramesses II described a battle at Qadesh in 1275 B.C. in poetic form:

> His majesty was a youthful lord, a hero
> without peer ...
> Mighty in victories over all foreign
> countries....

Man felling a tree with axe, from wall painting in the tomb of Nakht
Werner Forman Archive

Going straight ahead, entering the throng, his heart confident in his strength . . .
Effective in counsel, good at planning.[365]

I removed the boundaries (10:13). Boundaries between holdings, whether at the national or the local level, were important to maintain, as established by law (Deut. 19:14; 27:17). Some boundaries were marked by stones, similar to survey markers of today, which should not be moved. This practice was used in Mesopotamia during the Kassite period (mid-second millennium B.C.). More than simply delineating land holdings, they also describe their granting, along with other entitlements that provided an income for the holder.[366] Encroachment on such entitlements was a serious business, so strong curses are placed on any who move, deface, or challenge the stone and its contents.[367] These could comprise a third of the entire text.[368]

Neo-Assyrian royal inscriptions frequently mention the perspective Isaiah presents here, effectively removing any boundary stones by taking over the territory of others. Tiglath-pileser III speaks of taking a territory: "These lands I restored to the border/territory of Assyria,"[369] a de facto removal of another's boundary stone and replacing it with his own.

Wasting disease upon his sturdy warriors (10:16). Those affected are not warriors, since the term used here never refers to them in the Old Testament, but rather to fat people (17:4) or luxuriant places (Gen. 27:28, 29). "Wasting" applies to both humans and to a dry measure for such things as grain, so God here threatens the depletion of either the Assyrian people or their produce.

The curses at the end of Hammurabi's law collection include the name of Ninkarrak: "Summon up a terrible illness in his body, with demonic pain, and fever, and weeping sores, one which cannot be relieved, one which no physician understands, one which cannot be soothed by bandaging, one which, like the sting of death, cannot be removed."[370] Rib-Addi of Byblos wrote the pharaoh of his weakness: "I am old and there is a serious illness in my body. The king, my lord, knows that ... the pains (illness) are severe, for I committed sins against the gods."[371] Such symptoms were not simply physical but could have a divine origin.

Light of Israel (10:17). Several Mesopotamian kings included among their epithets one claiming to be "the Sun of all people."[372] They now face destruction at the hand of Israel's God, the Creator of light and light itself (2:5).

Forests ... trees (10:18–19). Most of the ancient Near East was not heavily forested, so trees were valuable for building as well as for their fruit. One of Hammurabi's laws penalizes someone for tree-cutting without permission.[373] Israel was not to destroy them in battle (Deut. 20:19), but they will be destroyed if she turns against God (Jer. 6:6). Loss of trees was one of the curses for breach of covenant (Deut. 28:42). Some Assyrian conquerors prided themselves in cutting and burning their enemy's trees: "I gathered the tall trees, the pride of his palace, as many as I could fell, and burned them."[374]

A Returning Remnant (10:20–34)

Destruction has been decreed (10:22). As humanity was created by God, so their destruction is decreed by him. Newly created humanity is threatened with death in the Atraḫasis Epic: "The god got disturbed with [the humans'] uproar. Enlil heard their noise and addressed the great gods, ' ... With their uproar I am deprived of sleep ... let there be plague, ... let there be a scarcity of plant-life to satisfy their hunger' ";[375] finally humanity faced a flood. A mid-second millennium lament over Ur sings of the gods: "After they had pronounced the utter destruction of my city, after they had pronounced the utter destruction of Ur, after they had directed that its people be killed...."[376]

The Weidner Chronicle records that Bel/Marduk was upset because "Naram-Sin ravaged the people of Babylon. Twice he (Bel) summoned the Gutian armies against him and [put to flight] his people.... He (Marduk) has given his royal dominion to the Gutian army."[377] In the eighth-century Erra Epic, "Ishtar was enraged and became angry with Uruk (her city). She summoned an enemy and despoiled the land like corn before (flood)-water."[378] It does not pay to get on the wrong side of one's god, whether in Israel or in Mesopotamia.

This is what the Lord, the LORD Almighty, says (10:24). Since the prophet is relaying a message from his God, he often uses what is called a messenger formula (see 6:9). It is also frequent outside the Bible, with many Akkadian letters including "thus says X."[379]

Egypt (10:24). Egypt held Israel's ancestors as slaves for four centuries, until they released them at the exodus. During the reign of Tiglath-pileser III, Egypt played little part in the international arena, apart from an attack in 734 B.C. on Assyrian holdings by two rulers: "Hanno, king of Gaza and also Sibe, the *turtan*-official of Egypt set out ... against me.... I defeated them ... Hanno I captured personally."[380]

Rock of Oreb (10:26). In Judges 7:35, two Midianite leaders, Oreb and Zeeb, were captured by men helping Gideon. Oreb was killed at the "Rock of Oreb," an unidentified site along the Jordan River.

Itinerary for Assyrian Invasion ▸

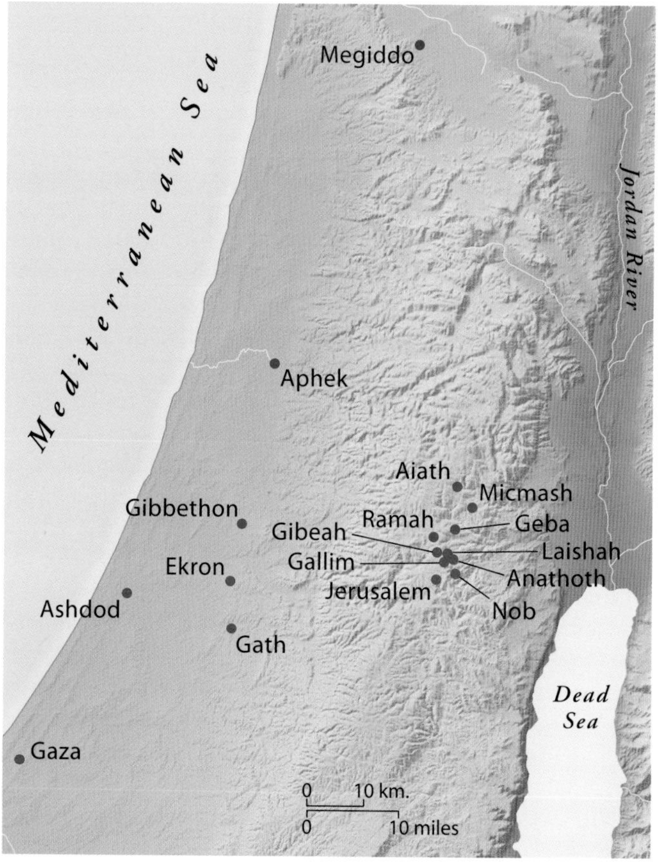

▸ The Ideal King

The concept of an idealized future ruler continues from 9:6–7. Tranquility and lack of conflict again characterize the future reign—both important elements even from early in the history of tribal Israel (cf. Josh. 11:23).

A beneficent and tranquil rule is also an Akkadian ideal, in spite of their bloody and brutal reality. For example, "[A prince will arise] and rule for eighteen years. The land will rest secure, fare well, people will [enjoy] prosperity. The gods will ordain good things for the land, favorable winds [will blow].... Shakkan (the god of the beasts) and Nisaba (the god of grain) will [...] in the land."[A-85] Not only people, but animals and plants will benefit in this prophecy, most likely written after the event of an actual king's reign.[A-86] A letter to Ashurbanipal describes a time of justice and equity where every age and all people will enjoy fullness of health and joy (9:7; 11:4; see discussion at 61:1).[A-87]

Yoke (10:27). See comments on 9:4.

They enter ... pass (10:28–32). The twelve cities mentioned here lie to the north of Jerusalem and show the Assyrian path along established routes aimed directly toward the Judean capital.[381] This could refer to a campaign by Sargon II, who moved against an uprising among the Philistines of Ashdod and their allies, which could have included Israel.[382] He wrote: "Azuri, king of Ashdod, had schemed not to deliver tribute any more and sent messages of hostilities against Assyria to the kings in his neighborhood.... I besieged, conquered the cities Ashdod, Gath."[383] There is also the possibility of an Assyrian palace in Ashdod built by Sargon.[384] While not including all the cities mentioned in Sennacherib's campaign in 701 B.C. (2 Kings 18:13),[385] since that incursion came from a different direction, there is some overlap between the two itineraries.

Anathoth (10:30). This city in Benjamin reflects the name of Anath, a Canaanite goddess mentioned as early as the Mari texts as well as those from Ugarit.[386]

Oracle of the Coming Ideal King (11:1–16)

Shoot ... stump ... roots (11:1). Arboreal imagery is used to show the rebirth of a people from what looks to all outward appearances like dead growth (cf. Job 14:8).

New tree growing out of stump
Kim Walton

Ishtar of Arbela standing on lion, with symbol of sun above her head from Til-Barsib
Z. Radovan/www.BibleLand Pictures.com

The Ugaritic Aqhat Legend speaks of Dan'el in these terms: "He who had no son like his brothers (did), or shoot/scion like his kin. May he have a son like his brothers, and a shoot like his kin."[387] In a Phoenician text from the late eighth to early seventh century, Azitawada claims that, among other things he did for his ruler, "I did good to the root of my lord, and I enthroned him on his father's throne."[388]

The Spirit of the Lord will rest upon him (11:2). Israelite kings received not only divine election but also divine empowerment through God's Spirit. They, like the judges, did not rise to the position on their own merits, but through God's selection and enabling. In Akkadian texts, the impersonal equivalent of the empowering Spirit of God is the awesome radiance (*melammu*) possessed by gods and at times granted to kings. It is in many ways equivalent to the "glory" (*kābōd*) attributed to Israel's God (e.g., 6:3).

Sennacherib credits to it his ability to subdue Hezekiah: "As for Hezekiah, the fear of the awe-inspiring radiance of my lordship overwhelmed him."[389] Some reliefs from Syria and Mesopotamia show various symbols above both gods[390] and kings,[391] indicating some continuum between the two, not in identity but in power and enablement.

Judge (11:3–4). See comment on 1:17. Discerning judgment is important for God's ruler, and similar attributes were valued elsewhere as well. An old Babylonian ruler of Der is described as "just judge, not harming any man, one who secures justice for male and female victims of wrong."[392] A Ugaritic king fulsomely addresses the pharaoh as "great king, king of Egypt, gracious king, just king, king of kings,"[393] highlighting the importance of justice and equity in their dealings. Such discernment is a divine gift, and in Mesopotamia it was exercised in particular by Shamash and Adad,[394] and in Egypt by Thoth, god of wisdom.[395] A Sixth Dynasty Egyptian dignitary describes himself in terms similar to those of Isaiah:

> I spoke truly, I did right, I spoke fairly, I repeated fairly, I seized the right moment, so as to stand well with people. I judged between two so as to content them, I rescued the weak from one stronger than he as much as was in my power.[396]

A little child will lead them (11:6). The upside down nature of the coming period is exemplified by who is in control. Usually it is gods or kings who lead, as in a Sumerian text from Ebla when speaking of "Nisaba, the first born of Enlil ... in (her?) hand is the lead-rope of the land."[397] The Instructions of Ptah-Hotep also reflect the expected: "If you are a man who leads, who controls the affairs of others. . . ."[398] The god Amen-Re, speaking to Thutmose III on that Pharaoh's stele, concludes a hymn by saying: "I have

Utopian Animal Behavior

Ferocious animals were a constant threat, so the elimination of this threat would be part of an ideal kingdom. In the Sumerian Myth of Enki and Ninhursag, the paradise of Dilmun is described as a pure and clean land where "the lion kills not, the wolf snatches not the lamb, unknown is the kid-devouring wild dog."[A-88] Another Sumerian text, Enmerkar and the Lord of Aratta, contains an incantation: "On that day when there is no snake, when there is no scorpion, when there is no hyena, when there is no lion, when there is neither dog nor wolf, when there is thus neither fear nor trembling."[A-89] In each of these cases, the beasts will disappear.

There is debate whether the Sumerian texts describe an idyllic place or just "an inchoate primeval period before things received their ultimate definition."[A-90] There is little evidence in Mesopotamia for a return to paradise,[A-91] and evidence for such is not clear here. The context in Isaiah, however, is clearly future oriented, and none of the animal imagery relates specifically to the Genesis creation account. The clearer Genesis tie is the presence of the "Spirit" (v. 2), whose presence is clear in the precreation story (Gen.1:2).

The Instructions of Ani, a New Kingdom Egyptian text, take a different approach to such beasts, one closer to that in Isaiah. It spells out some of the benefits of education, which can tame even the nature of the beasts: "The fighting bull who kills in the stable, he forgets and abandons the arena; he conquers his nature ... and becomes the like of a fatted ox. The savage lion abandons his wrath."[A-92] The animals are not removed, just their ferocity.

Four Corners of the World

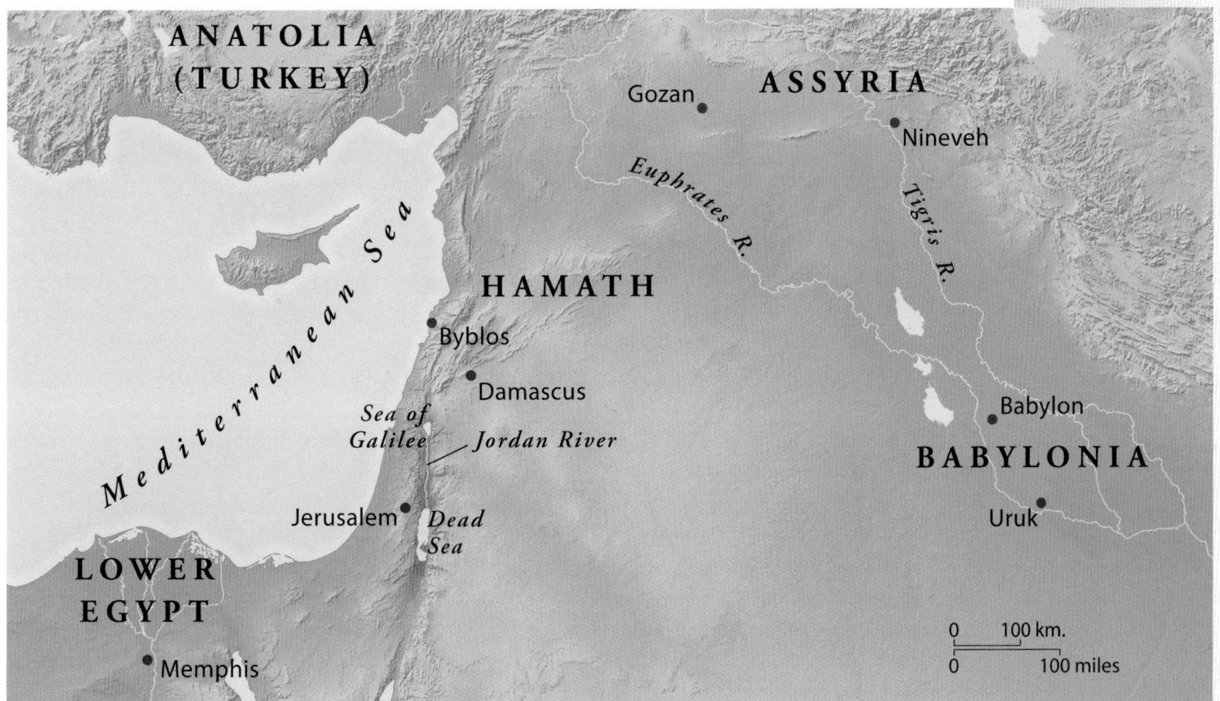

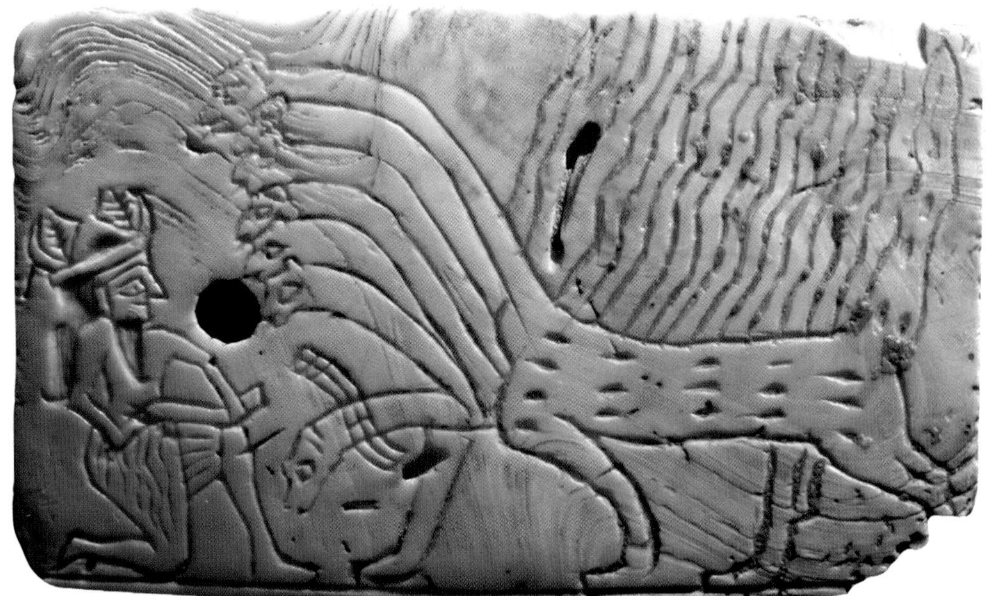

Engraving on shell shows god kneeling before fiery seven-headed monster.
Z. Radovan/www.BibleLandPictures.com

placed you on the Horus-throne for millions of years, that you may lead the living forever."[399]

Gather the exiles ... assemble the scattered (11:12). The map shows that the locations mentioned in 11:11 surround Israel, illustrating the "four quarters of the earth." Israel was actually exiled to Assyria, representing the northeast (2 Kings 17:23), and Babylonia (2 Kings 25:8–30), which, along with Elam, represents the southeast. The name used for Babylonia (Shinar) is an old designation for the area (Gen.11:2; 14:1). Amenhotep II (1427–1400 B.C.) mentions receiving gifts since "the chieftain of Hatti [the Hittites in central Turkey] and the chieftain of Sangar [Shinar] heard of the great victories which [I] had done."[400]

Some refugees ended up in Egypt to the southwest, designated by three areas, each further upstream on the Nile than the last (Jer. 41:16–44). Farther northwest lie the "islands of the sea," that is, the Mediterranean, the prototypical "land far away" (Isa. 24:15–16), though no specific mention is made to an actual exile to such places.

Restoration of a divided and dispersed land is an ideal also in Egypt. The prophecies of Neferti (early second millennium) speak of an ideal king. After a time of turmoil and dissolution, "a king will come from the south.... He will unite the Two Mighty Ones (Upper and Lower Egypt and their representative deities)."[401]

Four quarters of the earth (11:12). Assyrian kings, including those in the Neo-Assyrian period, regularly designated themselves as "king of the four quarters (of the earth)," that is, of the entire inhabited world.[402] These relate to the four directions of the wind.[403] Distant lands are emphasized on a Late Babylonian world map.[404]

Dry up the gulf of the Egyptian sea (11:15). Nowhere else in the Old Testament is there mention of such a water feature as this. Most probably the event referred to is Israel's exodus from Egypt when the power of the Red Sea was "destroyed," dried up for Israel to cross through.

Break it [the Euphrates] up into seven streams (11:15). The River, referring to the Euphrates (9:7), will also be handled in such a way as to allow exiles to return from there. Seven channels instead of the one major body will make each smaller and shallower, and thus easier to cross. Also, "seven" in the ancient world denotes an indeterminate but large number (see comment on 4:1).

From Ugarit, Baal describes himself in similar terms: "Indeed I killed Il's beloved, Yam (Sea); indeed I finished off Nahar (River), the great god; indeed I muzzled Dragon, I closed his mouth. I killed the twisting serpent, the seven-headed tyrant."[405] An Early Dynastic plaque shows a man battling a seven-headed dragon,[406] and an Akkadian text, speaking of evil demons, says "in heaven there are seven, in the earth (or 'underworld'), seven."[407] Yahweh here seems to depersonify the often malevolent seven.

A Praise Hymn (12:1–6)

I will praise you, O Lord (12:1). When God's anger is over and danger is past, praise is given to God (Ps. 40). The psalms speak of such praise after punishment (e.g., Ps. 51). Praise after pain inflicted by his god is also found in the words of Mesha: "Omri was king of Israel, and he oppressed Moab many days because Chemosh [the Moabite god] was angry against his land. And his son [Ahab] succeeded him and he said, 'I will oppress Moab.... Now Omri occupied the land of Medaba ... but Chemosh restored (it) to me in my days.'"[408]

Numerous others praise their gods for victory, even though they do not mention prior defeat. Tiglath-pileser I (1114–1076 B.C.) designates himself as "the courageous hero who lives by the trust-inspiring oracles given by Ashur and Ninurta, the great gods and his lords, (and who thus) overthrew his enemies."[409] Shalmaneser III says of a coalition that included Ahab of Israel, "I fought with them with (the support) the mighty forces which Ashur, my lord, has given to me, and the strong weapons which Nergal, my leader, has presented to me."[410] Sargon II says of the ruler of Carchemish, "I lifted up my hands (in prayer) to my god Ashur ... I made him and his family surrender."[411]

Sing to the Lord (12:5). Song was an expression of thanks in Mesopotamia as well. Old Babylonian texts say, "I will sing a song of the goddess Belet-ili/Ishtar,"[412] and "the song of the goddess Mama is better than honey."[413] Sumerian proverbs show the value of good singing: "When a singer knows the hymns and performs well the wailing, he is indeed a singer!"[414] Also, "A scribe without a hand is like a singer without a throat."[415]

An Oracle against Babylon (13:1–22)

Gates of the nobles (13:2). Gates were prominent places in the city, since everyone had to pass through them. Often they were given ceremonial names and epithetic descriptions, similar to the description used here, apparently for its main users.[416] Nebuchadnezzar II (614–562 B.C.) built several huge gates in Babylon, including the well-known Ishtar gate, to whom it was dedicated.[417]

▸ Oracles against Foreign Nations

International relations were often as strained in the ancient world as they are today. In the Old Testament, this is seen by the number of collections of prophecies against foreign nations (e.g., Isa. 13–24; 34; Jer. 46–51; Ezek. 25–32; Amos 1–2). They wronged God's people, so God brought woe down on them.

Egypt had an equivalent to these in her Execration Texts. These were magical curses in which those people and nations cursed were listed on pottery bowls or clay figurines, which were then to be smashed, breaking the power of those inscribed. One of these speaks of "the Ruler of Jerusalem, Yaqar-ʿAmmu, and all the retainers who are with him; the Ruler of Jerusalem Setj-ʿAnu, and all the retainers who are with him."[A-93]

▶ Eighth-Century Babylon

During Isaiah's lifetime in the eighth century, Assyria was the dominant power;[A-94] Babylon would play a more major role in the following centuries. Assyria was the nation that exiled Samaria and its people, and the king of Babylon, Merodach-Baladan (Marduk-Apal-Iddin II, 722–711 B.C.), sent envoys to Hezekiah, supporting his political aspirations against Assyria (39:1–8). So why does Isaiah begin with an oracle against Babylon? While some credit this section to a much later period (e.g., the time of the fall of the Neo-Assyrian empire during the sixth century), there is no compelling reason to do so, since it equally well represents the eighth-century situation.[A-95]

A group of West Semites of unclear origin, though apparently associated with the northern Arabian peninsula,[A-96] the Chaldeans/Babylonians (see 13:19–20) settled in the swamps of lower Mesopotamia and quickly acculturated to the Assyro-Babylonian culture. More urbanized than their better-known neighbors, the Arameans who settled a bit further north along the Tigris,[A-97] they paid tribute to the Assyrian overlords, but quickly gained power over them.

In the early eighth century, a temporarily weakened Assyria enabled Babylonia to gain political power in the area. To thwart the threat to their southern flank, a strengthened Assyria under Tiglath-pileser III moved in, fought against, and assumed the Babylonian throne, uniting Assyria and Babylonia for the first time in over four centuries. They maintained a dual monarchy through the next century.[A-98] It could have been this move south against Babylonia that prompted this oracle.[A-99]

Melishipak II brings his son before Nannaya as main deities portrayed as astral symbols look on. Kassite boundary marker.
Jill Walton, courtesy of the Louvre ▶

Day of the LORD ... will come like destruction (13:6–10). "The day of the LORD" is a common theme in the Old Testament prophets. It commonly refers to a time of judgment on Israel, but it also is used of other nations facing judgment from Israel's God (e.g., 34:8). A judgment day receives mention in a late first millennium Egyptian text of Petosiris. He lists his good deeds, "I did this remembering I would reach god after death, knowing the day of the lords of justice, when they separate in judgment!"[418]

Almighty [Shaddai] (13:6). One among numerous titles for God is "El Shaddai," here translated "Almighty" (*šadday*). Isaiah chose this designation here to produce a sound play with the word "destruction" (*šōd*). The meaning of Shaddai is debated,[419] but an attractive interpretation is that it

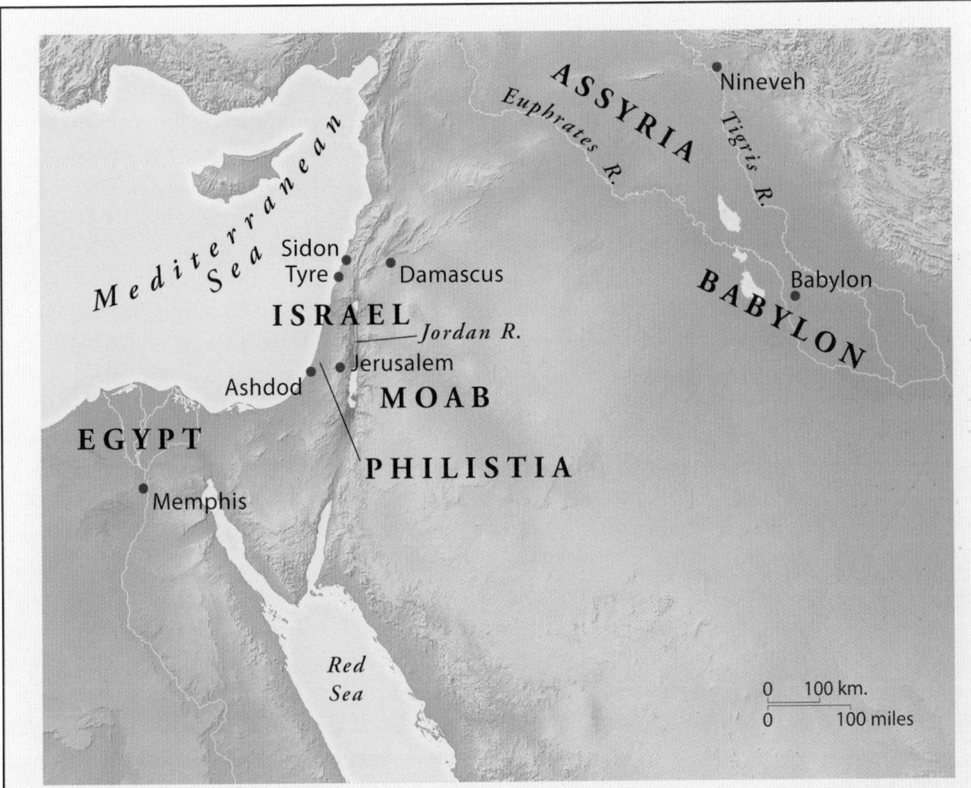

Nations Targeted in Isaiah's Prophecies

relates to the Akkadian *šadû* ("mountain"). Assyrian gods are often associated with mountains, and some are even called "great mountain."[420] The Aramaic Balaam inscription also attests to gods with this name, when the heavenly assembly calls Balaam to hear of the plans of the Shaddai gods in council.[421] The mountain deities will suffer defeat at the hands of the real Shaddai.

Stars ... constellations ... sun ... moon (13:10). The day of the Lord will bring darkness to the cosmic light-givers of Israel's neighbors. This could be an implicit threat against their deities, since Egypt, the Assyrians, and the Canaanites worshiped sun (Amun-Re, Utu/Shamash, and Shemesh respectively),[422] moon (Nikkal/Ningal/Nanna and Sin in Mesopotamia, Yerah in Canaan),[423] and stars as gods.[424] It is through the worship and consultation of the astral deities, with several astronomical diaries in which celestial observations were recorded, that the Babylonians developed the predecessor of the today's horoscope.[425] The "constellations" are specifically those associated with Orion (e.g., Sirius, the Dog Star, Amos 5:8).[426]

Israelite captives being flayed during the Assyrian conquest of Lachish
Caryn Reeder, courtesy of the British Museum

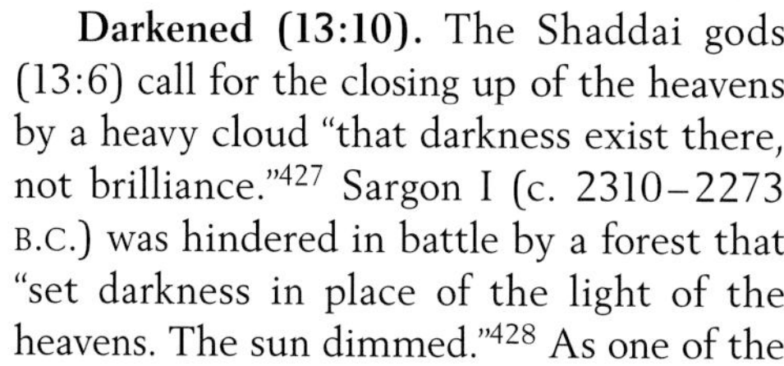

Darkened (13:10). The Shaddai gods (13:6) call for the closing up of the heavens by a heavy cloud "that darkness exist there, not brilliance."[427] Sargon I (c. 2310–2273 B.C.) was hindered in battle by a forest that "set darkness in place of the light of the heavens. The sun dimmed."[428] As one of the curses for breaking a covenant with him, Esarhaddon says: "In your eyes may darkness be, and so you may walk in darkness."[429] This is a blow against the Assyrian gods, who are often described as "one characterized by enlightening the darkness."[430]

Mede from the staircase at Persepolis
Brian J. McMorrow

The gods themselves were unnerved by darkness in the Gilgamesh Epic: "Adad's awesome power passed over the heavens, whatever was light he turned into darkness.... No one could see his neighbor, nor could people see each other in the downpour. The gods became frightened at the deluge."[431]

Ruthless (13:11). Babylonian policy toward those who rebelled against them was physically harsh, employing various atrocities such as flaying people by removing their skin. This policy was adopted from the Assyrians, whose empire preceded their own. This was not sadistic but rather an aspect of foreign policy, an aspect of psychological warfare that served to debilitate enemies who heard of the atrocities.[432] This was a means of keeping vassal peoples under control through terror. It could also be an example of hyperbolic language, stretching the truth enough to intimidate those who might oppose her.[433] Reliefs on the palace walls of Assyrian kings fulfilled the same function, filling visitors and foreign emissaries with awe and terror at the might and brutality of their overlord.[434]

Gold of Ophir (13:12). According to the metaphor used here, gold from Ophir is particularly fine. The location of Ophir is disputed, though areas along the Red Sea (Saudi Arabia or East Africa) are favored. An inscription from Tell Qasile, a Philistine site in what is now Tel Aviv, records, "Gold of Ophir, for Beth-Horon, 30 shekels."[435]

Heavens tremble ... earth will shake (13:13). Convulsion of heaven and earth is commonly associated with the appearance of God. It is also associated with Baal, the Canaanite storm god: "Baal gives his holy voice, he repeats the thundering product of his lips. His holy voice makes the earth shake; the thundering of his lips makes the hills tremble."[436]

Hunted gazelle (13:14). The Assyrian king Ashurnasirpal II held a banquet as part of the inauguration of his new palace. For it he served, among other things, "1,000 spring lambs, 500 stags, 500 gazelles."[437] Gazelle meat served a more prominent role before the domestication of meat sources, but it continued to be hunted not only for food but also for sport.[438] The gazelle or ibex is depicted on only a few Hebrew seal impressions.[439]

The Medes (13:17). The Medes, living in northern Iran, south of the Caspian Sea, were an Aryan people (Gen.10:2).[440] In the ninth century, Shalmaneser III and subsequent Assyrian kings mention them in inscriptions, especially as a source of horses. Isaiah's contemporaries Tiglath-pileser III and Sargon II led numerous military campaigns into Median territory.[441] The Medes came more to the fore in the seventh century when their king Cyaxares (c. 625–585 B.C.), in alliance with the Chaldeans/Babylonians under Nabopolassar (626–605 B.C.), captured the Assyrian capital Nineveh in 612 B.C., ending the Assyrian empire.

Babylon's Defeat

The Chaldeans from the southern Babylonian marshlands, especially the Bit-Yakin tribe, exercised control over the entire Babylonian region several times in the mid to late eighth century. Mukin-Zeri took power in 731 B.C.,[A-100] but he was deposed by the Assyrian Tiglath-pileser III. Within a decade, Merodach-Baladan II of Babylonia regained the throne, ousting the Assyrians until 710 B.C. Sargon II then reestablished Assyrian dominance for five years, illustrating the constant shift of power in the region.[A-101] Isaiah 13 could refer to one of the periods of the loss of Babylonian power.

The Neo-Babylonian (Chaldean) empire was established in 625 B.C. under Nabopolassar, uniting with the Medes to bring the Assyrian hegemony to an end in 612 B.C. It in turn fell to the Persians under Cyrus II in 539 B.C.[A-102] The fate of Babylon thus parallels some aspects of destruction associated with the Day of the Lord. The ultimate, final Day is preceded by numerous other "days" in which God brings punishment on his people, seeking repentance from them before the final judgment falls on them.

Ruins of Babylon
Bible Scene Multimedia/Maurice Thompson

Who do not care for silver ... gold (13:17). Sometimes attacking armies could be bought off so that they would leave without destroying those under attack (2 Kings 18:13–16). This was, in fact, the function of tribute, which functioned on a national level like extortion payments do on a personal level. Such tribute by subject kings to their overlord is common in Akkadian texts; Esarhaddon increases the expected payment "above the previous annually given tribute."[442] Another king says, "Indeed I received a tribute gift of a chariot of gold."[443] The actual metals in weighed portions served as currency before coinage spread in use to Babylonia in the sixth century.[444] The Medes are pictured as so ferocious that they cannot be satisfied with anything less than conquest.

Like Sodom and Gomorrah ... will never be inhabited (13:19–20). Sodom and

▸ Sheol and the Afterlife

Sheol (*šᵉʾôl*) denotes the underworld (Greek "Hades"), the place of the dead. It is a place to which one goes down. It is associated with dust and also separation from God. The Old Testament does not have a clearly articulated understanding of its nature, showing more concern for one's relationship to God and his covenant in the present life than for a theological articulation of death and what follows.[A-103]

The afterlife was a central concept in Egyptian culture.[A-104] Early in their history, blessing was reserved for the king, but as time went by, it became available to others who had sufficient economic means. A large portion of the wealth of the upper classes came to be applied toward preparation for a good afterlife. This included building a suitable tomb well-stocked with objects needed in the afterlife, and arranging for mummification and regular offerings at the tomb. Knowledge of the route through the underworld and of protection from dangers accompanying the journey were provided through spells and litanies in the Coffin Texts and the Book of the Dead.[A-105]

The soul would reunite with the body in the afterlife, necessitating the preservation of the latter through mummification.[A-106] On the point of introducing the mummified remains into the tomb, numerous funerary rites were performed, including the "Opening of the Mouth" ritual, which is preserved in pictures as well as text.[A-107] This revivified the dead to be able to function in the netherworld.[A-108] The king, having descended from divinity, returned to that state after death, a state also open to others later in Egyptian history. Many of the same activities were undertaken by the dead as they were among the living, just in a different location. In contrast to royalty and the wealthy, commoners did not have a positive view of death, since they were relegated to earth.[A-109]

The netherworld was not so desirable in Mesopotamian understanding.[A-110] When Enkidu is allowed out of the

Gomorrah, lying beside the Dead (Salt) Sea, were destroyed by God and thereafter symbolized utter destruction. Thorns and salty soil, rendering most plant growth impossible, were characteristics of the destroyed area. A similar destruction is wished on those who break the eighth-century Aramaic Sefire treaty: "May Hadad sow salt and weeds/cress on [Arpad and its surrounding area]."[445] In the next century, Ashurbanipal says of one of his conquests, "I turned his cities into ruin-hills."[446]

Desert creatures will lie there (13:21). When a place is totally desolate and empty of people, the native animals can take up residence there. Among the desert creatures mentioned here are "jackals" (a unique term; NRSV, "howling creatures"), "owls" (NRSV, "ostriches," though owls are more apt to live in ruins, 34:13), "wild goats" (though the term can also refer to domesticated goats, Lev. 4:23), "hyenas" (Isa. 34:13), and another unidentified breed of canine ("jackal," a different word from v. 21; cf. 35:7; 43:20). The eighth-century B.C. Aramaic Sefire treaty has a similar curse on a covenant breaker: "And may Arpad become a mound to [house the desert animal], the gazelle and the fox and the hare and the wild-cat and the owl."[447]

Babylon Taunted (14:1–23)

Taunt (14:4). The genre of the taunt song in verses 4b–21 is based on a lament or dirge.

netherworld in a Sumerian forerunner of the Gilgamesh Epic, he says: "If I am to tell you the way things are ordered in the Netherworld, O sit you down and weep. The one you touched with joy in your heart (i.e., Enkidu), he says, 'I am going to ruin.' Like an [old garment] he is infested with lice, like a crack [in the floor] he is filled with dust."[A-111] A Vision of the Netherworld from the seventh century describes what is seen by one Kumma. After describing fifteen terrifying gods found there, he says, "The netherworld was filled with terror." He approaches the enthroned underworld god, Nergal: "With a fierce cry he shrieked at me wrathfully like a furious storm; the scepter ... one which is full of terror, like a viper. He drew towards me in order to kill me."[A-112]

Various aspects of Egyptian beliefs about the afterlife illustrated in the Book of the Dead, Nebqed
Werner Forman Archive/The Louvre

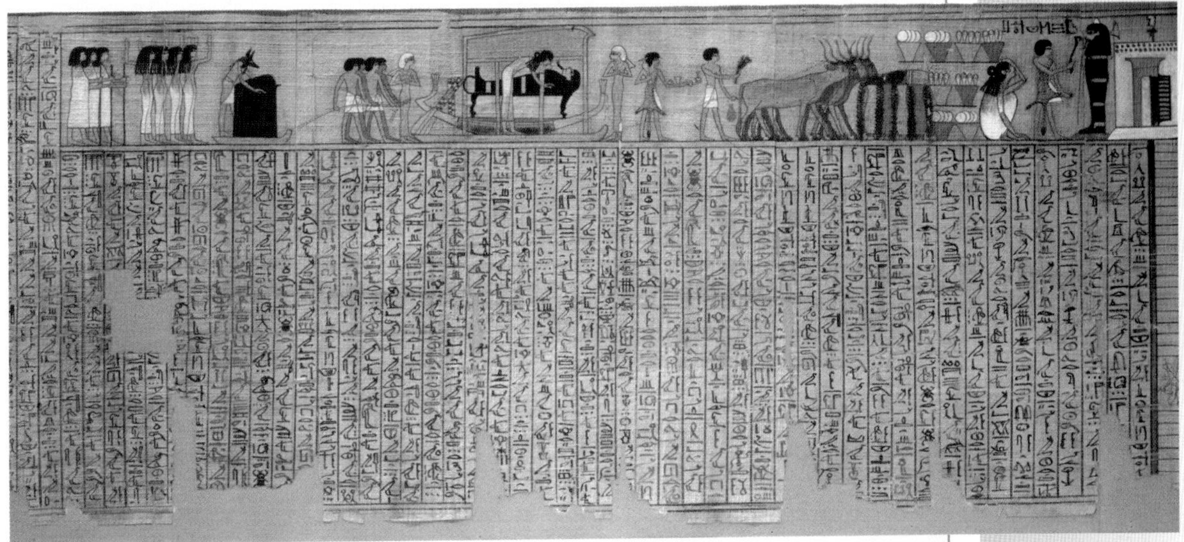

In Hebrew this is marked by a 3–2 beat pattern (cf. Amos 5:2),[448] and contains the typical word "How" (v. 12). The "taunt" is a mocking speech that does not reflect actual sorrow, but rather joy at the demise of the hated ruler who is as good as dead.

Broken the rod ... the scepter (14:5). See comment on 9:4. Shalmaneser I wrote, "Ashur ... gave me the sceptre, weapon, and staff (to rule),"[449] while Tiglath-pileser I attributed them to Shamash. This shows an understanding that royal power was divinely given. Isaiah's taunt is thus not only against Babylon's king, but against his gods who placed him on the throne.

All the lands are at rest and at peace (14:7). See comment on 9:7.

Cedars of Lebanon (14:8). See comment on 2:13.

Woodsman (14:8). The woodsman is literally the "(tree)-cutter" (37:24), the one who harvests this valuable timber. Cedar wood is particularly suited for building palaces and temples. In the Instructions of Merikare, among benefits of the Egyptian subduing land to the west was that "it pays taxes, it gives cedar wood."[450]

The cedar forests of Lebanon were an important territory even from the time of Naram-Sin toward the end of the third millennium.[451] Gilgamesh and his friend Enkidu traveled to the cedar forest and took it from the hands of Humbaba, cutting its trees,[452] even though it was "the seat of gods and goddesses' throne."[453] Nebuchadnezzar much later refers to it as "the luxurious forest of Marduk," and, "What no former king had done (I achieved): I cut through the steep mountains ... and constructed a straight road for the (transport of the) cedars."[454]

In the Old Testament, Yahweh himself has power over the cedars. While arrogant Babylon had exploited the forests of its conquests, it is Yahweh who is the woodsman par excellence, who will cut off Babylon (14:22).

Spirits of the departed ... leaders ... who were kings (14:9). The dead were not viewed as completely separated from the living. Their spirit could be summoned back (e.g., 1 Sam. 29:11–20). The emphasis here is the powerlessness of the shades on the living, in contrast to the royal power they used to wield.

"Spirits" or "shades" are the same as the Ugaritic *rapium*, who represent the departed Canaanite ancestors. They parallel "the dead" (Isa. 26:14) and are at times beneficent spirits, like Samuel, invoked to visit and aid.[455] Some suggest an etymological link with the Ugaritic verb *rpʾ*, "to heal," but this is debated.[456] A Ugaritic enthronement liturgy summons the *rapium* and names previous kings who had died to honor the new king: "You have summoned the Rephaim of the netherworld."[457] Joining them in death is one's expected and desired end, as evidenced by the Phoenician sarcophagus inscription of Eshmunazor, king of Tyre. He calls a curse on anyone disturbing his final rest: "Let him have no resting-place with the Rephaim, let him not be buried in a grave."[458]

Neo-Assyrian copy of a tablet of observations of the planet Venus from the time of Ammisaduqa in the Old Babylonian period
Erich Lessing/Art Resource, NY, courtesy of the British Museum

Fallen ... morning star, son of the dawn (14:12). An Assyrian omen concerning birth anomalies states that "a large star will fall," perhaps referring to a meteor.[459] A broken Ugaritic omen text states: "If a star falls on the thirtieth day."[460] The Hebrew behind "morning star" (*hêlēl*) occurs only here in the Old Testament, though the root means "shine" (13:10; 31:26). This "shining one" probably refers to Venus and is found also in Ugaritic mythology, with mention of "daughters of the morning star."[461] The Vulgate translators rendered this as "*luciferos*," also the morning star, Venus. This led English interpreters to associate this passage with Satan, though it is not he who is the subject under discussion, but rather the Babylonian king.

The morning star descends from "dawn" (*šāḥar*), another denizen of Canaanite mythology. It is part of a divine astral pair, "Dawn and Dusk" (or morning and evening star), and is descended from the head of the pantheon, Ilu, and a human female.[462] Isaiah is probably referring to some well-known mythological event in which a lofty figure was relegated to the lowest depths, the netherworld itself, though is unclear which myth he means. "Dawn" is personified in the Old Testament (Ps. 57:8), but it is never deified.

You who once laid low the nations (14:12). At the height of its power, the Babylonian empire controlled the region stretching from Iran to Egypt, and from Turkey to Saudi Arabia. Its power gained control over neighbors great and small, but it will meet the same fate at the hand of others.

I will ascend to heaven (14:13). As humans chafed against overbearing rulers on earth, seeking freedom from their oppression, so did the gods rebel. In the *Enuma Elish* creation story, Tiamat and her minions rebelled against the high gods for what seemed to her were their overbearing demands,[463] while in the Myth of Anzu, a created being seeks to steal the Tablets of Destiny, which are to be under divine control (see sidebar on "Divine Purpose" at 46:10).

Mount Zaphon
John Monson

Brought down ... to the depths of the pit (14:15). Initially indicating a literal pit or cistern, the Hebrew term used here (*bôr*) metaphorically refers to the grave. The cognate Akkadian term (*buru*) most regularly shares the same literal meaning, though some also suggest an underworld link for it.[471]

You are cast out of your tomb ... you will not join them in burial (14:19–20). While burial is the desired end of life, allowing a final peace, disinterment was done to move a body to a more appropriate place, as evidenced by Jacob and Joseph. Also a body could be moved within a family tomb to make room for later arrivals.[472] Lack of a proper burial or actual removal from a grave was abhorrent (see 5:25).

On an Akkadian boundary stone a curse is uttered against anyone who defaces the stone: "May his life come to an end through oppression and hunger, may his corpse be cast aside and may there be no one to bury (him)."[473] This lack of final honor shows that one has reached the end of life without anyone who cares.

Stars of God (14:13). See comment on 13:10.

Mount of assembly ... sacred mountain (14:13). This is literally "heights of the north [*ṣāpôn*]." In Ugaritic texts, Saphon/Zaphon is identified with a mountain, Jebel al-ʿAqra, or Casius in classical sources (deriving from the Hittite Chazzi),[464] which lies north of Ugarit. It is considered holy because it is capped by Baal's palace in the Baal Epic and is also the site of his burial.[465] Possibly the Baal text considers the mountain divine,[466] though the text could equally speak of "the gods of Zaphon," a divine assembly such as that mentioned by Isaiah.[467] The Babylonian king arrogates himself to divinity by establishing himself to the location of the gods.

Most High (14:14). Elyon ("Most High") as a title usually describes Israel's God, sometimes in association with his name and other times on its own. Since deities are considered lofty, it is not surprising that similar titles apply to gods of Israel's neighbors. Their supremacy is indicated spatially by several being cosmic, that is, solar, lunar, or astral deities.[468] An Akkadian hymn title is "Exalted Ea."[469] A Canaanite divine epithet like that used by Isaiah is "the Most High" (*ʿly*), and Baal is known as "Most High Baal." An eighth-century Aramaic treaty text speaks of the deities before whom the treaty is concluded, including "El" and "Elyon."[470]

Oracle against Assyria (14:24–27)

Trample him down (14:25). This harsh treatment of the Assyrians is appropriate since Assyria was doing the same to its Israelite vassals. An Akkadian theodicy speaks of the wicked who "ruin the weakling, they trample on the powerless."[474]

Yoke (14:25). See comment on 9:4.

Assyria (14:24–27). See sidebar on "Land to be Laid Waste" at 7:16.

Plan determined for the whole world ... hand stretched out over all nations (14:26–27). See 40:8. In a monotheistic religion such as that of Israel, one could speak of

Naram-Sin victory stele with enemy trampled underfoot
Rama/Wikimedia Commons, courtesy of the Louvre

a universal divine plan since there is but a single divine planner. In polytheistic religions, however, the multiplicity of deities works against a unitary divine plan. For example, Tiamat's plan for domination was thwarted by the plan of other deities under the leadership of Marduk in the *Enuma Elish* epic.[475]

Each instance of divine conflict reflects opposing divine plans. Plans could be claimed for specific cities by their gods, as when Cyrus claimed of the chief god of Babylon: "And Marduk, the great lord, leader of his people, looked happily at the good deeds and steadfast mind of Cyrus and ordered him to march on his own city Babylon ... and went alongside him like a friend and companion ... [Marduk] allowed him to enter Babylon without battle or fight."[476] In contrast, Yahweh, as universal Creator and Lord, can make and bring to fruition universal plans.

Oracle against Philistia (14:28–32)

Philistines (14:29). The Philistines were among the Sea People who moved from the Aegean to the western Mediterranean coast in the twelfth century B.C.[477] By the tenth century, the Philistines were flourishing in their five city states: Ashdod, Ashkelon, Ekron, Gath, and Gaza.[478] Though they contended over territory with the Israelites during their settlement in the land and later,[479] it was the Assyrians, mainly under Tiglath-pileser III and his successors, who threatened their autonomy.[480]

Tiglath-pileser campaigned against a coalition of nations including Philistia during the Syro-Ephraimite War in 734–732 B.C. (see sidebar on "Rezin and Pekah" in Isa. 7). The Assyrian eponym for 734 B.C. is of "Bel-Dan of Kalah, to Philistia," referring to this campaign.[481] It is also mentioned is his Calah Annals, which, though poorly preserved, state: "Mitinti of Ashkelon [broke] the loyalty oath and re[volted] against me";[482] more is mentioned in another inscription concerning Hanum of Gaza, who was dethroned and then reinstated by him, making Gaza an Assyrian tributary.[483]

After Tiglath-pileser's death in 727 B.C., some of the Philistines assumed self-rule until Sargon II crushed them in a battle near Qarqar.[484] The same thing happened when Ashdod rebelled in 712 (see 20:1) and when Sargon himself died in 705 B.C., with this rebellion quashed by Sennacherib in 701.[485] Any of these Assyrian kings could be the ruler referred to here.

Oracle against Moab (15:1–16:14)

Destroyed (15:1–4). Several northern Moabite cities are destroyed, with others left to mourn their destruction. Such destruction, especially of royal cities such as Kir, was common among Assyria and others. For example, Shamshi-Adad V (824–811 B.C.) claimed to destroy several royal cities and 250 surrounding towns.[486] The precariousness of national existence could be what is meant by a Sumerian proverb: "The palace—one day it is a mother who gives birth; the next day, it is a mother in mourning."[487]

Moab

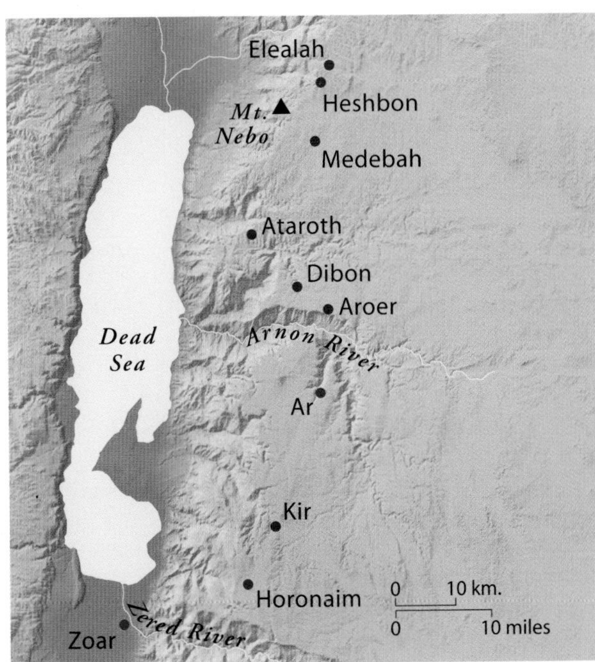

Moab lies in Transjordan, east of the Dead Sea.[A-113] Genesis portrays its inhabitants as descending from Lot's incestuous relationship with his oldest daughter (Gen. 19:30–38). Under their king Balak, they opposed Israel's passage toward the Promised Land after the exodus (Num. 22–24), though they ultimately caused Israel more problems through sex than through the sword (Num. 25). King David defeated Moab (2 Sam. 8:2), though in the ninth century, under their king Mesha, they regained independence for a time (2 Kings 3:4–27).[A-114]

During the eighth century, Moab and its neighbors fell under Assyrian control, with its kings paying tribute to Tiglath-pileser III (747–727 B.C.),[A-115] Sargon II (721–705 B.C.), and Sennacherib (704–681 B.C.). It was not happy with its subjugation and so joined a revolt instigated by Ashdod in 713 B.C., but later fawned before Sennacherib when he campaigned through the area: "Kammusunadbi from Moab (and) Aiarammu from Edom, they brought sumptuous gifts ... and kissed my feet."[A-116] Moab's opposition to Israel and possibly its lack of resistance to the encroaching Assyrians resulted in its inclusion in oracles against nations found in several prophets (Amos 2:1–36; Jer. 48).[A-117]

Dibon (15:2). Dibon lay in the Transjordanian territory of Moab, but it was captured by the Amorites just prior to the Israelite journey through the area in their move from Egypt to Israel (Num. 21:26–30), when they took it for their own (21:21–25, 31).[488] King Mesha of Moab (2 Kings 3:4) was from Dibon,[489] the Moabite capital. He rebelled against the foreign, Israelite hegemony over his land and wrested control of it, including Dibon, from them (2 Kings 3:4–27).

High places (15:2). Canaanites (as well as Israelites) worshiped at high places (1 Kings 3:1–4), here parallel to "temple" (lit., "house"). Their exact nature is debated, most likely being platforms associated with sacred standing stones.[490] The Moabite king Mesha states, "I made this high-place for Kemosh [Moab's national deity],"[491] which might be the destination here. Worship has turned to mourning, as in the Lamentation over the Destruction of Ur from a millennium earlier: "The Ekishnugal [Sin's temple], my royal house, the righteous house, my house which has been given over to tears."[492]

Mourning Rites

Grief, while an inner emotional state, is often demonstrated by outward signs. Weeping is a common response to loss, not only in the Bible but elsewhere as well. The Ugaritic king Keret, after losing his family and "entering into his room, he wept ... he shed tears."[A-118] A vocal response like wailing or keening, coming from a Hebrew term (*yll*), gives rise to the English term "ululation."[A-119]

Emotions of grief are also indicated by clothing oneself in sackcloth (15:3) or placing dust or ashes on one's head (58:5), as Il does when he hears of Baal's death: "He pours dirt/ashes of mourning on his head."[A-120] The physical body is also at times mutilated, as both Il and Anat perform the same acts: "With a stone he scratches incisions on (his) skin, with a razor he cuts cheeks and chin. He harrows his upper arms, plows the chest like a garden, harrows the back."[A-121]

Gilgamesh, upon the death of his friend Enkidu, is sure that all creation, humans, rivers, forests, and wild animals will join in weeping.[A-122] Gilgamesh himself says, "I will neglect my appearance after your death. Clad only in a lionskin, I will roam the open country,"[A-123] making himself unsightly and unkempt, like those mourning in Isaiah's time. Sumerian and Akkadian literature is rich in oral expressions of grief, often inspired by the destruction of city or temple.[A-124]

In the Egyptian Admonitions of Ipuwer, mourning and lament are specifically contrasted with joy: "Lo, merriment has ceased, is made no more, groaning is throughout the land, mingled with laments."[A-125] For Egypt, however, laments were less common, since a thriving life, and a good transition to an even better afterlife, were of more central significance to them.[A-126]

Mourners from tomb of Ramose in Luxor
Manfred Näder, Gabana Studios, Germany

High place and standing stone outside of the Iron Age Gate at Bethsaida
Kim Walton

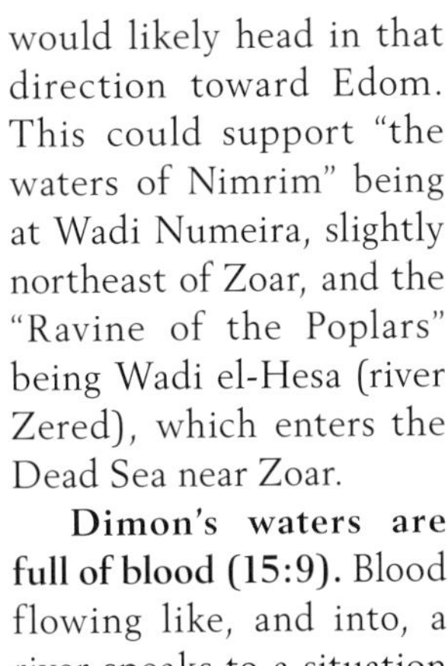

Her fugitives flee (15:5–9). People are fleeing from the Assyrian destruction in northern Moab. Their waypoints are uncertain, apart from Zoar (most likely located at the southern end of the Dead Sea) and Dimon (probably a word- and sound-play on Dibon, deriving from the Hebrew word *dm*, "blood"). The "border of Moab" (v. 8) could be that to its south, since those fleeing would likely head in that direction toward Edom. This could support "the waters of Nimrim" being at Wadi Numeira, slightly northeast of Zoar, and the "Ravine of the Poplars" being Wadi el-Hesa (river Zered), which enters the Dead Sea near Zoar.

Dimon's waters are full of blood (15:9). Blood flowing like, and into, a river speaks to a situation of utter destruction. A Neo-Assyrian prophecy uses the same imagery, "I 'sacrificed' your enemies, filling up the river with their blood."[493]

Lambs as tribute (16:1). Often tribute given from a vassal to an overlord consisted of luxury goods or money.[494] Livestock was also levied as tribute from areas in which it was raised, such as the Persian province "Beyond the River" (Ezra 6:8–9). This refers to the area west of the Euphrates,

Sela
Todd Bolen/www.BiblePlaces.com

Fruit and Harvests

Israel relied to a large extent on their agricultural produce for subsistence. Even after a number of her inhabitants had moved to urban areas, crop production was vital. Its importance is highlighted in one of the earliest Hebrew inscriptions ever discovered, the Gezer Calendar, which traces the agricultural year. It uses two of the words used by Isaiah describing the "harvest" (*qṣr*) and "fruit" (*qṣ*) (see comment on 8:4; Jer. 40:10).[A-127]

which includes the Moabite plateau, known for herds of cattle and sheep. The Moabite king had previously supplied great quantities of livestock as tribute to Israel (2 Kings 3:4).

Sela (16:1). Sela (lit., "rock") is best known as the capital city of the Edomites (2 Kings 14:7), who lived just south of Moab. This may have been the refugees' final destination, from which they contact Judah and Jerusalem. There is no known place in Moab with this name, though somewhere in its south fits best into the context in Isaiah.[495] Rocky sites would be appropriately so named in both territories.

Fords of the Arnon (16:2). The Arnon gorge enters the Dead Sea about in the center of its eastern side. Mesha, the Moabite king, claimed, "I made the military road in the Arnon,"[496] and the fords may well be where the main north-south King's Highway crossed it.[497]

A detail of a painting in the tomb of Sennedjem showing the reaping wheat in the mythical fields of Iaru
Z. Radovan/www.BibleLandPictures.com

Fields ... wither ... vines (16:8). Grief is equated to languishing crops in Ugaritic literature as well. In the context of a rod of bereavement and widowhood, "the vine-pruners prune it/him ... they fell it ... like a vine."[498]

Oracle against Damascus (17:1–14)

Aroer (17:2). Aroer lay on the Arnon River southeast of Dibon and just east of the King's Highway.[499] Its fortress (which at one period measured fifty yards on each side) marked the southernmost boundary of Moab. Mesha, in his inscription, credits himself with refortifying it when he says: "I built Aroer."[500]

Glory ... will fade (17:4). Using the same verb as in this Isaiah passage, a Ugaritic birth omen states that of a certain anomaly is seen, "the king's spear will lay low [*dll*; see NRSV] the land."[501]

Body will waste away (17:4). See comment on 14:9.

Reaper (17:5). Grain is harvested by a reaper who, while gathering the stalks in the left hand, cuts them just below the grain itself with a sickle held in the right hand. This is shown in several Egyptian reliefs.

Valley of Rephaim (17:5). This valley divided the territories of Benjamin and Judah, extending from Jerusalem to the southwest. From this passage it is evident that the valley was fertile and apparently a source of much of the provision for Jerusalem. A recent research project has been

▸ Damascus

Damascus was the capital of Syria (Aram) during the tenth to eighth centuries B.C. Under its king Rezin, it joined Israel to pressure Judah to join an anti-Assyrian coalition (7:1–9). When Judah refused, the two allied against her in the Syro-Ephraimite War, but soon fell to Tiglath-pileser III (734–732 B.C.), a defeat Yahweh had promised to Ahaz (7:16). Tiglath-pileser declared: "I received tribute from ... *Ra-hi-a-nu* (Rezin) of Damascus, Menahem the Samarian," and also captured Rezon's very birthplace.[A-128] It rebelled against Assyria under Sargon II, but was quickly brought back under their hegemony,[A-129] remaining under foreign domination through the Babylonian and Persian empires.

examining the agricultural technology of the vicinity.[502]

Olive tree is beaten (17:6). Since some of the olive crop grew higher on the tree than one was able to reach, harvesters beat the branches with sticks. Some of the crop that did not readily fall must be left for those unable to produce their own food (Isa. 24:13).

Valley of Rephaim
Bible Scene Multimedia/Maurice Thompson
▲

Asherah poles (17:8). Trees were associated with the Canaanite goddess Asherah, who is the Canaanite mother goddess and apparently consort of the chief god, El (see 1:29–30; *m. Sukkah* 3:1–3).[503] On several occasions the verbs indicate that an Asherah, apparently a cultic representation of the goddess, was made by human hands. Consensus is that they were some form of wooden pole, perhaps a stylized tree, which was variously "made," "shaped," "cut down," or "burned." Deities associated with wood or trees are also known among Israel's neighbors (see 57:5). Since wood is perishable, no sure physical examples have been identified.

Incense altars (17:8). Large altars were used for animal sacrifices, but smaller ones were used for other sacrifices, including burning incense.[504] The incense was burned for its smell, on a mundane level, counteracting some of the noxious odors associated with slaughter and sacrifice, instead producing a pleasing aroma ascending to the deity, partly masking other smells. An Old Babylonian prayer shows its appealing function: "Let the incense burn high, let it summon the great gods."[505]

This also points out another characteristic of incense smoke, that it permeates the area, acting as a fumigant. It is used with the sick, as when in the Akkadian Maqlu ritual text an incantation is stated over some salt, "put it in the censer for fumigants that is at the head of the bed."[506] The term used here (*ḥmn*) is restricted to pagan, Canaanite altars in the Old Testament.

Lot (17:14). A decision-making tool used among Israel and her neighbors was the lot. Distribution of quantifiable items could be made by casting a lot,[507] probably some sort of marked or colored stone (called psephomancy), producing a binary response, either "yes" or "no," to a question asked. Apparently the deity was viewed as determining the outcome of the process. A text of Tiglath-pileser I speaks of "Ashur who bestowed upon me for my lot authority and power."[508] It was used in Israel for allocating land and war booty, including prisoners of war. Land distribution was a major use of the lot in Mesopotamia so that the term extended in meaning from the means of determination to the share determined by the process.[509] Mesopotamian texts also show the lot was used to assign people to some offices such as a priesthood, determined as part of an inheritance.[510] The practice is also known from a late seventh-century Phoenician text.[511]

Offering stand from Megiddo
Kim Walton, courtesy of the Oriental Institute Museum

A relief depicting hunters in papyrus reed boats
Werner Forman Archive/The Egyptian Museum, Cairo

Oracle against Cush (18:1–7)

Cush (18:1–7). In the Old Testament, Cush refers to two different areas. The Kassites lived in Mesopotamia (2:13), while Cush also refers to the territory immediately south of Egypt, the territory in view here. Translated in the LXX as "Ethiopia," Cush probably lies north and west of what we know today as Ethiopia—that is, in what is now northern Sudan, ancient Nubia, populated by black African people.[512]

Early in the history of Cush, its northern boundary was between the first and second Nile cataracts, though later it was pushed a bit further south.[513] Egypt and its neighbor to the south were constantly jockeying for power in the region. In the late eighth and early seventh centuries B.C., during the Third Intermediate Period, the Twenty-Fifth (Ethiopian) Dynasty controlled Egypt and had contact with Israelite rulers (e.g., 2 Kings 17:4).[514]

Akkadian texts refer both to Kus and to Meluhha (Nubia). Sargon made several campaigns to the west against a group of anti-Assyrian allies, probably including Judah and Cush.[515] One of his inscriptions speaks of a person named Yamanni who fled Sargon's approaching army: "He fled to the border area of Egypt which is on the border with Meluhha."[516] References to either "Egypt" or "Cush" in Isaiah most likely refer to this dynasty. They challenged Assyria's territorial expansion to the west, including Israel.

Land of whirring wings (18:1). Locusts or other flying insects plague the Middle East (see Joel), and another occurrence of the same Hebrew term refers to such creatures (Deut. 28:42). These could be used to describe Cush, which undoubtedly suffered locust infestations, but it is curious that such a ubiquitous feature should define a distant nation. The LXX and the Targums interpret the term as a kind of boat, possibly another referent to the swiftly darting crafts of 18:2. The Egyptians, and by implication, the Cushites, used boats with sails,[517] whose flapping would sound like the whirring of many insect wings.

Envoys (18:2). International relations were influenced by both military encounters and diplomatic contact (see comments on 6:9; 39:7). While the former receive the greatest mention in the texts, the latter was also important in trying to maintain the peace or at least to subvert the powers of war. This type of messenger or envoy (*ṣîr*) made international contact, though here in Isaiah it is unclear who the messengers represent or to whom they are being sent. It appears that they are to take a general, unspecified call to the world (18:3).

Papyrus boats (18:2). Reeds are common both in the Nile region and in the Mesopotamian marshes. In ancient times reeds were bundled together to make light rafts, which could move with speed and stealth, if necessary.[518] Third millennium Mesopotamian seals show a divine figure, probably the sun god, seated in a crescent-shaped boat (of unknown material), showing his journey through the sky.[519] One is depicted on an Israelite seal.[520]

Swift messengers (18:2). Urgency required speed, which is frequently noted in letters from Mari. One reads: "This tablet is urgent. Let your swift messengers deliver it."[521] Nabonidus speaks of being a "swift envoy of the great gods."[522]

Tall and smooth-skinned (18:2). Pictorial representations of people of this period portray different groups distinctively (cf. comment on 7:20). Men from Syria-Palestine had short, thin beards that ran along the jaw line.[523] Assyrian and Babylonian men generally sported fuller and longer beards.[524] Egyptians were largely clean-shaven ("smooth") or had a goatee.[525] Nubians, from Cush, are also "smooth" and shaven—a noticeable characteristic for an Israelite prophet. These people are also said to be "tall," fitting a description by Herodotus: "And the Ethiopians ... are said to be the tallest and finest people of all."[526] Association of these peoples with "rivers" (18:3) has led to their identification with inhabitants of Mesopotamia with its two rivers,[527] but those living along the Nile and its tributaries are not ruled out.

Strange speech (18:2). This unique term is a reduplicated adjective (*qaw-qāw*), literally meaning "very strong." It may be an onomatopoetic term resembling the babbling sound of a foreign tongue, much like "barbarian" (one whose language sounds like "bar-bar").[528]

A ripening grape (18:5). This metaphor of God's pruning of peoples on the earth provides insights into Israel's viticultural practices (cf. 5:1–7). This is not the time of grape harvest, since none is mentioned, only that of grain (*qāṣîr*, v. 4), which happens in April-May. During this time of the year, grape blossoms are followed by the formation of ripening grape clusters. The Gezer Calendar designates the month following grain harvest as that of "pruning," when unproductive shoots and extraneous leaves and branches were removed so that the nutrients could flow to the remaining grapes, providing optimum nourishment. Here attention is not directed toward the burgeoning vines, but rather to the discarded detritus of the pruning.[529]

Birds of prey (18:6). Carrion birds (cf. 46:11) feed on flesh. Falcons, for example, are depicted on several Hebrew seals, though they are not necessarily depicted as threatening.[530] One of the curses against anyone breaking the 672 B.C. treaty with Esarhaddon reads: "May he fill the steppe with your corpses; may he cause the eagle to eat your flesh."[531] The repugnance at this state of

Relief from palace of Nimrud depicting birds picking at the exposed carcasses of the slaughtered enemy, ninth century.
Z. Radovan/www.BibleLandPictures.com

affairs derives from the respect one should show to the dead by burying them (see 5:25).

Gifts will be brought to the LORD (18:7). Bringing gifts was a means of paying homage to a respected person (see 18:7). Naaman showed respect in this way to Elijah, although he refused the gifts (2 Kings 5:1–19). An Aramaic inscription from a date close to Isaiah's writing (733–727 B.C.) reads: "My father, Pana[muwa, son of Ba]rsur, brought a gift (*šay*)[532] to the king of Assyria."[533] Sometimes there is no clear demarcation between a gift and tribute, the latter deriving from

Background of Egypt

Egypt's long history is characterized by strong rulers who established a dynasty able to unite various parts of the country, interspersed with weak rulers and dynasties where unification dissolved. During the latter periods, competing power centers operated simultaneously, and ruler turnover was rapid. Particularly chaotic periods in Egyptian history are designated as the First, Second, and Third Intermediate Periods (twenty-second to twenty-first, eighteenth to sixteenth, and eleventh to eighth centuries B.C., respectively).

The period of Isaiah thus falls toward the end of the last period of internal Egyptian turmoil. The weakening of the Ramessides led to the Twenty-First Dynasty (eleventh to tenth centuries B.C.), in which Upper and Lower Egypt went their separate ways. The Twenty-Second and Twenty-Third Dynasties were founded by a foreigner, a Libyan, Soshenq (945 B.C.). Cushite princes Kashta and Piankhy claimed Upper Egypt, while Shabaka took the entire country about 712 B.C., consolidating the Twenty-Fifth (Ethiopian) Dynasty (716–663 B.C.).[A-130]

This unification was needed to counter the increasing pressure from Assyria to the east under Tiglath-pileser III, Shalmaneser V, and Sargon II. The confrontations between these two major powers led to turmoil in their neighbors, as the Israelites, the Philistines, and others in the vicinity found their allegiances pulled first in one direction and then in the other, depending on the waxing and waning of the relative power of the two major nations.

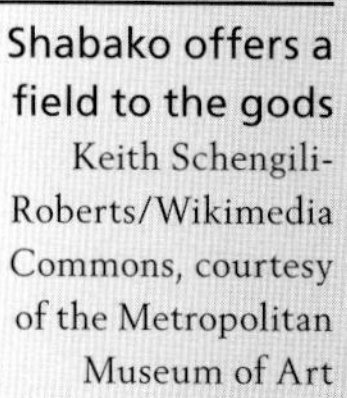

Shabako offers a field to the gods
Keith Schengili-Roberts/Wikimedia Commons, courtesy of the Metropolitan Museum of Art

some coercion such as taxation. Thutmose III (early fifteenth century B.C.) writes of receiving tribute from Cush (Nubia).[534] Whichever the case for Isaiah, Israel's God is being acknowledged as sovereign.

Oracle against Egypt (19:1–25)

Rides on a swift cloud (19:1). Yahweh is depicted as riding on the clouds (see 18:4, where he is compared to a cloud), as one who is their powerful master (5:6). The Canaanite god Baal/Hadad is also frequently described as "rider on the clouds,"[535] though a different word for "cloud" is used (see Ps. 68:4). This is understandable since Baal/Hadad is the god of the storm, with some of his functions described as: "Baal will appoint the season of his rain, a season for moisture to appear and snow. He will set his voice in the clouds, his lightning bolts to the earth."[536] The Mesopotamian storm god, Adad (cognate of Baal's designation Hadad, also designated Ishkur), controls the clouds as he "herds together the rain-clouds."[537]

Though not identifying Baal explicitly, God's control over elements such as clouds, rain (vv. 5–7), thunder, and lightning (see 1 Kings 18)[538] is a veiled polemic against Baal. The polemic is more explicit in Hosea 2. In each case, Yahweh, who is not worshiped as a storm god, is shown to have actual control over the storm.[539]

The idols of Egypt tremble (19:1). An encounter with the all-powerful God causes fear and trembling in the presence of someone greater and mightier than the lifeless and powerless idols. Weakness of the body and its organs regularly accompanies fear (7:2). The gods, when faced with the violent deluge in the Gilgamesh Epic, "feared because of the flood. They recoiled, ascending to Anu's heavens. The gods cringed like dogs, crouching outside."[540]

Egyptian against Egyptian (19:2). Family squabbles, even fratricide, are an ancient phenomenon (e.g., Cain and Abel; Joseph and his brothers). Civil strife also occurred within a nation split apart for some reason (e.g., Israel and Judah, Isa. 7). This internal squabbling was expected in Egypt, with its various power centers and vying royal households. One of the Prophecies of Neferti (early second millennium B.C.) states: "I show you the land in turmoil. . . . One will seize the weapons of warfare,

Admonitions of Ipuwer
Erich Lessing/Art Resource, NY, courtesy of the Louvre

the land lives in confusion."[541] The earlier Admonitions of Ipuwer state: "You would set confusion throughout the land, together with the noise of contention. Behold, one thrusts against another."[542] A Sumerian proverb describes fraternal conflict: "The brothers in anger have destroyed the estate of their father."[543]

	Egyptian Dynasties Third Intermediatre Period	Egyptian (Low Chronology)
1080		Ramesses XI 1099-1069
1070	21st Dynasty	Smendes 1069-1043
1060		
1050		Amenemnisu 1043-1039
1040		Psusennes I 1039-991
1030		
1020		
1010		
1000		
990		Amenemhet 993-984
980		Osochor 984-978
970		Siamun 978-959
960		Psusennes II 959-945
950	22nd Dynasty	Sheshonq 945-924
940		
930		Osorkon I 924-889
920		
910		
900		
890		Takelot I 889-874
880		Osorkon II 874-850
870		
860		
850		Takelot II 850-825
840		
830	22nd-23rd Dynasty	Sheshonq III 825-773
820		
810		
800		
790		
780		
770		

They will consult the idols and the spirits of the dead, the mediums and the spiritists (19:3). Egypt, like other nations, wished to know and influence the future and used various means for this, including dreams and divination (see sidebar on "Superstitions and Divination" at 2:6). The Admonitions of Ipu-Wer bemoan the uncertainty of powerless magic and silent divine guidance, when the normal gets turned on its head: "Lo, the private chamber, its books are stolen, the secrets in it are laid bare. Lo, magic spells are divulged, spells are made worthless through being repeated by people. Lo, offices are opened, their records stolen; the serf becomes an owner of serfs."[544]

Letters to the dead were written by Egyptians to ask the departed to take up their cause in the netherworld against those who were persecuting them from beyond the grave.[545] A First Intermediate Period letter from a husband to his deceased wife is touching: "How are you? Is the West (the place of the dead) taking care of you [according to] your desire? Now since I am your beloved on earth, fight on my behalf and intercede on behalf of my name.... Please become a spirit for me [before] my eyes so that I may see you in a dream fighting on my behalf."[546] This is not properly necromancy, an arcane, magical art that was not practiced per se in Egypt.[547] Such consultations and supplications, says Isaiah, will be ineffective.

Cruel master ... fierce king (19:4). From an internal Egyptian perspective, this could refer to either the foreign Ethiopian ruler Piankhy (740–716 B.C.) or his brother Shabaka (716–695 B.C.). The former describes his campaign to the north toward Lower Egypt to stop encroachment on his territory. In formulaic language, which could also reflect reality, he states concerning his troops: "They went forth against them; they made a great slaughter against them, exceedingly great.... They slew many of their men and many horses."[548]

A hand that Israel would also find harsh is that of the Assyrians, who could also be meant here. The Egyptian Osorkon IV (probably king "So" in 2 Kings 17:4) had been sought for support by Hoshea in 725 B.C., an action probably not viewed favorably by Assyria. Under Ashurbanipal in 663 Assyria conquered Egypt as far south as Thebes.[549] He describes some of his actions in the campaign: "They did not spare anybody among (them). They hung their corpses from stakes, flayed their skins and covered (with them) the wall of the town."[550]

Fishermen will groan and lament (19:8). Fish was an important element of the diet of Israel and her neighbors. The Egyptian Instructions of Merikare describe the benefits given to humanity by the creator god, such as: "He made for them plants and cattle, fowl and fish to feed them."[551] According to the Admonitions of Ipuwer, the bounteous storage barns of the king should make available for everyone "emmer, barley, fowl and fish; it should have white cloth, fine linen, copper and oil."[552]

Mesopotamian fishermen provided regular supplies to numerous gods at their temples,[553] and Egyptian fishermen are among the skilled workers deported by Esarhaddon from Egypt.[554] Archaeological excavations in Jerusalem have found indications of a trade in fish there, with several species evident.[555] Fish are also represented on a number of Hebrew seal impressions.[556] It is therefore a serious matter when, as recorded in an Akkadian hemerological text, "a huntsman must not catch fish, birds, or animals."[557] Egypt feels this loss as well in the Prophecies of Neferti where, among other natural disasters, "the River of Egypt is empty.... Perished indeed are those good things, those fish ponds ... overflowing with fish and fowl."[558] This lack of a catch is bemoaned in Isaiah.

Zoan (19:11). Zoan is usually identified with Tanis, a city on the eastern Egyptian delta about thirty miles south of the Mediterranean.[559] It served as the capital of the

Fishing shown in Egyptian relief on the Mastaba of Mereruka
Manfred Näder, Gabana Studios, Germany

Egypt and the Nile

The majority of the land of Egypt is arid, with less than 100 mm. (four inches) of precipitation per year.[A-131] The only productive land was in the narrow strip along the Nile, relying on irrigation from the river.[A-132] When the river flow was hindered, the country found itself in dire circumstances. An Eighteenth Dynasty Egyptian prophetic text of Neferti, set in the earlier Fourth Dynasty, exclaims: "The river of Egypt is empty, one can cross the water on foot.... Perished indeed are those good things.... All good things have passed away."[A-133] A Ptolemaic work, purporting to come from the Old Kingdom, is the Famine Stela: "I was in mourning on my throne. Those of the palace were in grief, my heart was in great affliction, because Hapy [the divine Nile River] had failed to come in time, in a period of seven years. Grain was scant, kernels were dried up, scarce was every kind of food."[A-134] The fate described in such detail in 19:5–10 was a constant dread of the people of Egypt.

Foreigners, including Israelites and their ancestors, had been seeking residence in Egypt for centuries. As far back as Genesis, the patriarchs spent time there, usually for famine relief (Gen. 12:10–20; 37–50). Contact continued during the monarchy, with Solomon strengthening ties with Egypt, though refugees running from him also found haven there. Other times relationships were strained, with Egyptian armies moving north against Solomon's successor, Rehoboam. Later, Jeremiah ended up in Egypt, much to his chagrin, when Judeans rebelled against their Babylonian overlords and fled there for their lives.

Nile River
Todd Bolen/www.BiblePlaces.com

Flax Industry

Wooden model depicting a weavers workshop
Werner Forman Archive/The Egyptian Museum, Cairo

Flax is used, among other things, to make linen, one of the oldest of the world's fabrics.[A-135] The Hebrew Gezer Calendar reads: "the month [March to April] of flax cutting."[A-136] Its fibrous leaves were softened by soaking so that the long fibers could be removed, dried, bleached, combed/carded, and spun to produce thread. This was then woven on a loom to produce linen fabric. Shorter fibers could be made into wicks for lamps (42:3). Linseed oil from the flax seeds was potable and had medicinal purposes.[A-137]

Flax was grown in Egypt and Mesopotamia as well as Canaan. Requiring plentiful water, irrigation was often necessary.[A-138] The Egyptian Hymn to Hapy, the personified Nile River, lists among its other bounties: "People are clothed with the flax of his fields,"[A-139] and it is listed in a papyrus schoolbook from the Twentieth Dynasty among many other edible and useful things with which a grateful student wished to bless his teacher.[A-140]

Flax and linen are mentioned in Mesopotamian texts from as early as the Pre-Sargonic through the Neo-Babylonian periods for use in clothing, bed coverings, curtains, and rope.[A-141] Linen weavers are also mentioned in several Neo-Babylonian texts.[A-142] While linen was a sturdy cloth, the frailty of the plant itself is used metaphorically in the First Intermediate Period Admonitions of Ipuwer: "The land is left to its weakness like a cutting of flax."[A-143] Linen fabric and garments made from it are also included in several lists from Canaanite Ugarit.[A-144]

Man and wife harvesting flax in the afterlife shown in the tomb of Sennedjem
Werner Forman Archive

pharaohs of the Twenty-First to Twenty-Third Dynasties and was an important religious site also for the Twenty-Fifth dynasty.[560] When Zoan was elevated to capital status, material from other sites connected with earlier rulers, including Ramesses II, was brought in. Major building was undertaken by Siamun, Osorkon III, and Shoshenq III in the ninth to eighth centuries.[561]

Disciple (19:11). The term "disciple" is literally "son" (*ben*), a term commonly expanded from biological descent to include tutelage, passing on one's accumulated wisdom. Akkadian kings claimed sonship from predecessors or even from the gods as a mark of their legitimate claim to the throne.[562] Egyptian rulers commonly combined both functions, passing on royal wisdom to their sons, the crown prince, so they might be able to rule wisely.[563] This ancient wisdom is shown here to be worthless in the face of Israel's God.

Memphis (19:13). Memphis (Heb. *nōp*) is on the Nile's west bank about fifteen miles south of Cairo.[564] It periodically served as the northern capital of Egypt. An important religious site, it had a temple identified with the creator god Ptah, who, according to eighth-century Memphite theology, was universal creator.[565] The Ethiopian pharaoh Piankhy held it briefly in 728 B.C., but his brother Shabaka controlled it from 715 B.C. on. This period was chaotic in Egypt, with no less than four claimants to the throne, with Shabaka finally gaining the upper hand.[566] Concerning his campaign in 672 B.C., Esarhaddon writes: "As far as Memphis, his royal residence ... I fought daily, without interruption, very bloody battles against Tirhakah, king of Egypt and Ethiopia.... I entered Memphis, his royal residence."[567]

Blessings for Egypt, Assyria, and Israel (19:16–25)

Egyptians will be like women (19:16). A stele of Piankhy/Piye describes him as the personification of the god Horus, defeating opposing kings, designated as "bulls": "Hail to you, Horus, mighty King, Bull attacking bulls." The stele closes with praise to the pharaoh: "O mighty ruler, O mighty ruler, Piye, mighty ruler! You return having taken Lower Egypt, you made bulls into women!"[568] The mighty and fearless will lose their strength. A treaty between Ashurnirari V of Assyria and Matiʾilu of Arpad places a curse on the latter if he breaks it: "May Matiʾilu become a prostitute, his soldiers women."[569]

Five cities (19:18). The identity of these five is unclear, though four cities in Egypt are mentioned by Jeremiah as being inhabited by Jews over a century later (Jer. 44:1). They include Migdol, apparently a fortified site in the northeastern Nile delta[570] and listed among the cities conquered by Thutmoses III and later Egyptian kings;[571] Tahpanhes, possibly in the same area;[572] Memphis (see 19:13), longtime Egyptian capital settled during the First Dynasty and residence of the Twenty-Fifth Dynasty pharaohs just south of Cairo,[573] taken by the Assyrian king Esarhaddon and occupied by his son Ashurbanipal in the seventh century;[574] and Pathros/Upper Egypt, an unidentified area taken by Esarhaddon, who calls it Paturisi, lying between Egypt and Nubia further south.[574] Aramaic archives from Elephantine show the existence of Jewish communities in the area at this period.[576]

Language of Canaan (19:18). "Canaanite" is the general designation of one branch of Northwest Semitic that includes Old Canaanite, Hebrew, Phoenician, Ammonite, Moabite, and Edomite.[577] This language was probably Hebrew, though other Semitic groups were also settled in Egypt as slaves and captives, so this could refer to their dialect.[578] This would reflect a major change of heart among the Egyptians, who at some points in their history did not generally take kindly to foreigners. The Egyptian Tale of Sinuhe pictures him living among the barbarian "sandfarers" and being encouraged by one person he met who said, "You will be

Tale of Sinuhe
Lenka Peacock, courtesy of the British Museum

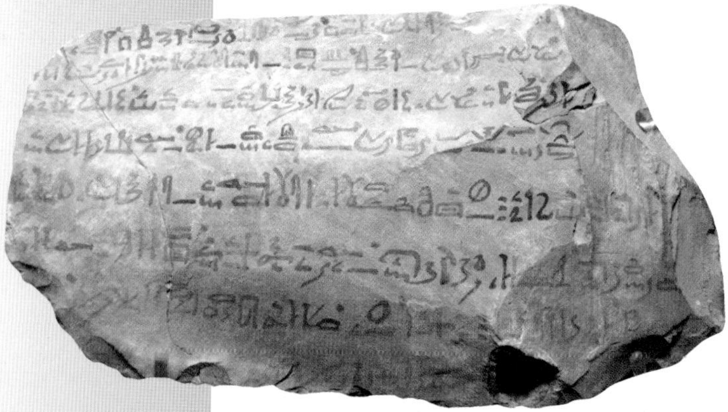

happy with me; you will hear the language of Egypt."[579]

Altar to the LORD in the heart of Egypt (19:19). The numerous Jewish residents in Egypt continued to worship their God, and so they needed shrines in which to do so. They are joined by Egyptians who, in times of crisis, will also call on Israel's God for help (v. 21).[580] A fifth-century Aramaic letter from Elephantine speaks of a temple of Yaho (Yahweh): "Now, our forefathers built this temple in the fortress of Elephantine back in the days of the kingdom of Egypt, and when Cambyses came to Egypt he found it built"[581] (Cambyses undertook this campaign in 525 B.C.).[582] This shrine, which was requested to be rebuilt in this same letter, served the Jews living in Egypt. There is no evidence of a Yahwistic temple serving as a place of worship for the Egyptians, the situation envisioned by Isaiah.

Monument to the LORD at its border (19:19). This term (*maṣṣēbâ*) designates a sacred standing stone and is viewed, either positively or negatively, as part of pagan practice.[583] Their exact function is unclear.[584] In Israel examples have been found from Tel Dan in the north to Arad in the south.[585] Those in Israel are without inscription, though some found in the Sinai desert at Serabit el-Khadem are inscribed with Egyptian hieroglyphics.[586] An Old Aramaic stela bears the inscription, "Monument of Bir-Hadad ... erected for his lord Melqart."[587]

Here the *maṣṣēbâ* is dedicated to Yahweh, the God of Israel, rather than to a pagan deity. Its location at the border could show that it is a boundary stone, set up to guard a border or even to claim it as Yahweh's territory (see 10:13).

Vows to the LORD (19:21). Solemn promises to one's god are not only part of Israel's experience with her covenant with God, but also among her neighbors. Mesopotamian legal practice helped ascertain the truth of a claim by taking a vow before a deity.[588] Esarhaddon remembers his father's actions with his older brothers: "He made them swear a powerful oath before Assur, Sin, Shamash, Nabu, and Marduk, the gods of Assyria, the divine inhabitants of heaven and earth."[589] The purpose of doing such a thing in the god's presence is spelled out in an Akkadian text from Turkey, where, after a list of gods, we read: "May they be witnesses to this oath."[590] While these can be designated "oaths of the gods," they differ from the vow made here, which is made "to," not "by," Israel's God.

Israel my inheritance (19:25). Ugaritic texts also see territory as the "inheritance" of a god. Of Mot, the god of death, "a low

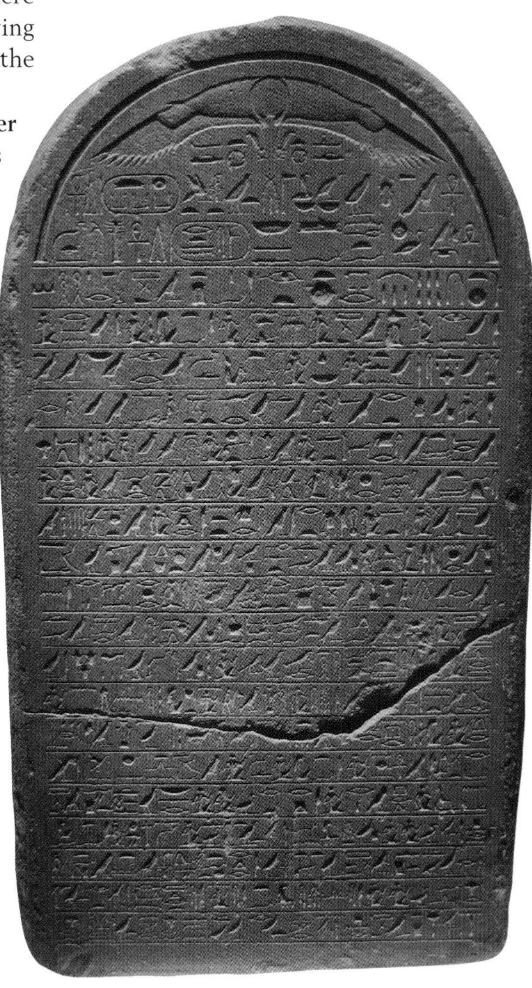

Boundary stele of Senusret III
Magnus Manske/ Wikimedia Commons, CC-BY-SA

bog (?) is the seat of his dwelling; a mire his inheritance land."[591]

Prophetic Signs for Egypt and Cush (20:1–5)

Supreme commander (20:1). This term (*tartān*) is transliterated from Akkadian (*tu/artānu*;[592] 2 Kings 18:17). A certain Shamshu-ilu, a *turtānu*, is described as "great herald, [the administrator of] temples, chief of the extensive army, governor of the land of Hatti ... conqueror of the mountains in the West,"[593] so this person coming against Ashdod was of some stature.[594] Several important officials listed in the Assyrian Eponym list have the designation *turtānu*.[595]

Stripped and barefoot (20:2–4). While nakedness was originally innocent, it often came to denote defeat and punishment. Removal of foot coverings also indicated humiliation. A Hittite text explains the punishment brought upon a guard found guilty of the "sin" of dereliction of duty: "[The gateman] shall remove [the guard's] shoe."[596] The Megiddo Ivory shows two bound prisoners, naked and barefoot, being brought before a dignitary, and naked, captive leaders are being tortured in the depiction of the siege of Lachish.[597] A Hebrew ostracon from seventh-century Horvat Uza includes a threat: "You shall be stripped naked in judgment."[598]

Egyptian captives and Cushite exiles (20:4). In battle, prisoners of war were common, not only in order to deplete the enemy forces but also to serve as potential hostages. They are portrayed in art[599] and mentioned in texts. Tukulti-Ninurta I (1294–1197 B.C.) describes a campaign in which he captured 180 cities, and "I took their hostages."[600]

Babylon's Doom (21:1–10)

Desert by the Sea (21:1). This is another descriptor of Babylon (v. 9).

Elam ... Media (21:2). As Israel was constantly pressed by the Mesopotamians from the east, so Mesopotamia itself experienced incursions of people like the Elamites and Medes from the east (present-day Iran). From their capital in Susa, Elamites supported Merodach-Baladan's successful takeover of the Babylonian throne in 720 B.C. Their help ebbed and flowed, however. By 710 it had withdrawn such aid, allowing Sargon to take Babylon, but it sent more support in 703 (probably referred to here; cf. 22:6), and in 700, though unsuccessfully. It was finally defeated by Assyria in 646.[601]

The Medes joined the Babylonians to defeat Assyria in the late seventh century and soon thereafter expanded control into Asia Minor. They themselves were soon incorporated into the Persian empire.[602]

Pangs seize me, like those of a woman in labor (21:3). Labor pains are a common symbol of physical and mental distress and anguish (13:8; 26:17–18).[603] In the Gilgamesh Epic, when the goddess Ishtar realized the ramifications of destroying humanity, she "screamed like a woman giv-

Megiddo ivory shows two bound prisoners, naked and barefoot, being brought before a dignitary.
Z. Radovan/www.BibleLand Pictures.com

▸ Sargon's Campaign against Ashdod

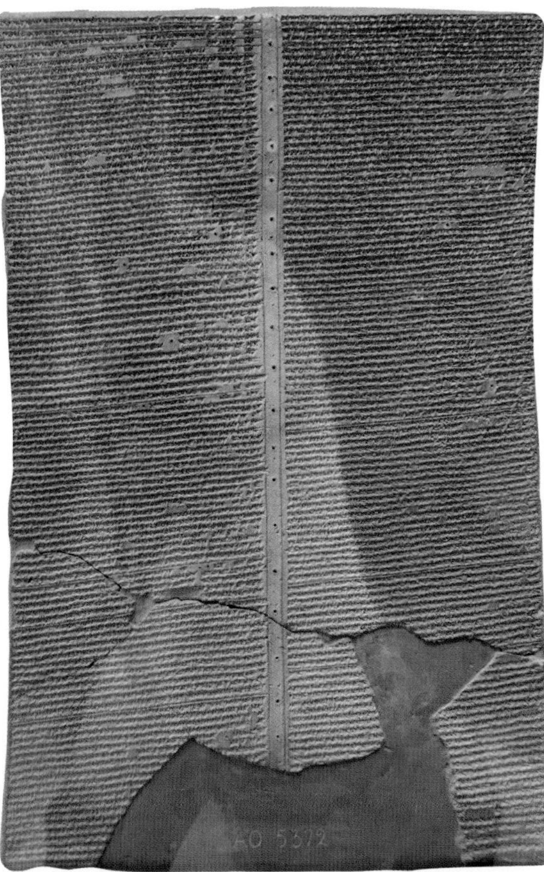

The army of Sargon II of Assyria moved against Ashdod and its king, Azuri, in 712 B.C. (20:1; cf. Amos 1:8), prompted by a revolt.[A-145] Ashdod was one of the five Philistine cities (along with Gaza, Gath, Ashkelon, Ekron) that had opposed Israel in the past (e.g., 1 Sam. 5). Azuri "schemed not to deliver tribute ... and sent messages of hostilities against Assyria to the kings in his neighborhood," hoping they would join his rebellion.[A-146] These kings may have included Hezekiah.

Sargon claims to have dethroned Azuri, replacing him with his brother Ahimittu, as well as exacting tribute.[A-147] Archaeological evidence of the attack can be found in level VIII at Ashdod, which was destroyed at about this time, with burials of over 3,000 individuals. There are also fragments of an Assyrian victory stela attributed to Sargon II. Though it does not contain the name of Ashdod, Assyrian practice of recording conquests on such stele suggests its presence would have been on the complete stele.[A-148]

Account of Sargon's campaign to Urartu in 714, two years before Ashdod
Marie-Lan Nguyen/Wikimedia Commons, courtesy of the Louvre
◂ 

ing birth, the Mistress of the gods wailed" because, she said, "I bore my people."[604]

My heart falters (21:4). Fear and suffering often present themselves metaphorically through physical manifestations such as this (see 19:1). A Middle Kingdom Egyptian complaint says, "My limbs are weighed down; I grieve in my heart."[605]

They set the tables, they spread the rugs, they eat, they drink! (21:5). Preparations for banquets could be elaborate, showing off the wealth and power of the host.[606] When the Ugaritic god Kothar-wa-Hasis arrived, he was similarly feted: "They arrange a chair and he sits to the right of Mighty Baal, while [the gods] ate and drank."[607] A Hittite banquet scene shows a guest seated before a set table,[608] and a Punic banquet scene from Spain shows a sumptuous meal.[609]

Riders on donkeys or riders on camels (21:7). Assyrian wall reliefs show soldiers riding horses in battle, including one scene where they pursue a camel rider.[610] Camels were more regularly used as beasts of burden,[611] as were donkeys,[612] though at times camels were also ridden.

Babylon has fallen (21:9). This prophecy anticipates the fall of Babylon to a Medio-Persian alliance when Nabonidus, the last Babylonian king, lost his own power base. He was defeated by Gubaru, a former Babylonian general who had defected to the Persians in October, 539.[613]

All the images of its gods lie shattered (21:9). A nation's gods were supposed to protect them, leading them in military conquest. Their weakness and defeat are symbolized by their destruction. An Aramaic text from Elephantine in Egypt from 407 B.C. describes an attack by the Egyptians on the temple there: "They went up against the Temple, destroyed it to the ground, and the stone pillars there, they smashed them."[614]

Threshing floor (21:10). See comment on 27:12.

Prophecies against Edom and Arabia (21:11–17)

Dumah ... Seir (21:11). Dumah is a sound play on the land of Edom in Transjordan, also called Seir. Edom and Israel shared a long and not always congenial history. The two nations especially contested control of the Arabah, south of the Dead Sea, along with the copper mines there.[615] Several Israelite kings gained control of Edom,[616] but she was apparently complicit in the fall of Jerusalem in 586 B.C. and the exile of its chief inhabitants (see Obadiah). She herself was dispossessed by the Arabs and Nabateans during the Persian and Hellenistic periods.[617]

Arabia (21:13–17). The Arabian tribes were mainly nomads inhabiting the desert regions of the Arabian peninsula and southern Negev.[618] The Bible refers to them mainly in relation to their direction "east" of Israel (*qedem*), as in the twentieth-century B.C. Egyptian Tale of Sinuhe, which refers to the "Sandfarers" associated with the east

Raiders riding camels on stone relief from the palace of Ashurbanipal
Werner Forman Archive/The British Museum

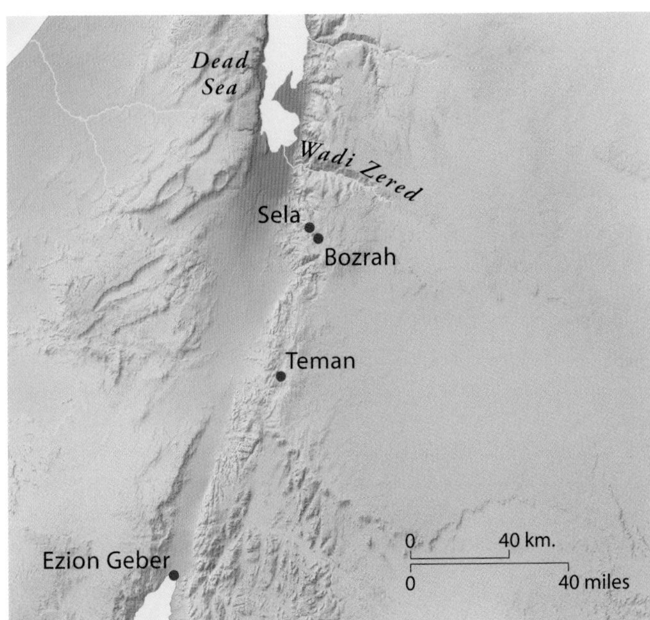

(*qedem*).[619] As well as encroaching on the neighboring settled areas, they also acted as traders and merchants.

Shalmaneser III records that in one of his campaigns to the west he destroyed "1,000 camels of Gindibu of Arabia,"[620] and a stele of Tiglath-pileser III speaks of "the kings of the land of ... Qedar (and) the land of Arabia" as among those who paid tribute to him.[621] The former could be an alternative name for the latter (i.e., "Qedar, that is, Arabia"),[622] though it probably denotes two separate places.[623] Modern maps of the Assyrian empire indicate that it probably never included the Arabian peninsula under its direct control, in spite of its claims.[624]

Qaynu from the royal line of Qedar lived in fifth-century Egypt,[625] and another Aramaic text from the same period describes the establishment of a new cult in the oasis city of Tema in northern Arabia. Lying athwart trade routes between Yemen, Mesopotamia, Egypt, and Syria, it was an important cosmopolitan site.[626]

The Arabs gained importance during the Greco-Roman period, some of them establishing the Nabatean empire with a stronghold in Petra.[627] With the advent of Islam in the seventh century A.D., Arab influence took an exponential leap forward and continues today.

Oracle against Jerusalem (22:1–25)

Gone up on the roofs (22:1). House roofs were accessible to the inhabitants, at times serving as an area for sleeping and living. They were also used as places of worship, especially of pagan deities. Sacrifices on roofs were also known in Ugarit. King Keret, having lost his family, prayed for more children and was told to sacrifice: "Climb to the summit of the tower.... The Keret must descend from the rooftops."[628] Special Akkadian rituals also took place on the roof, as "with the preparation you daub the roof, the loft rooms (on the roof), the windows."[629] This present passage may indicate that Israel is turning to other gods in thanks for their perceived deliverance, which in fact is not going to happen.

O town full of commotion (22:2). When Sargon died in 705 B.C., many of the Assyrian vassals in the west revolted, Israel's king Hezekiah among them. He moved also against other of his opponents such as the Philistines and sought to strengthen his own defenses. But when Sargon's successor, Sennacherib, attacked him in 701, those defenses were not the determinative factor (see 2 Kings 19:34–36).

Sennacherib's armies were able to take much of Judah according to Isaiah 36:31–37:38 and Sennacherib's own records: "Hezekiah the Judean, who did not submit to my yoke, 46 of his strong, fortified cities and the innumerable towns surrounding them ... I besieged and I conquered."[630] He claims to have besieged Jerusalem, but he does not say it fell to him. This reflects the biblical picture that shows Hezekiah being spared the humiliation of his capital falling to the enemy.

Palace of the Forest (22:8). Solomon built this armory/storehouse in 1 Kings 7, so named because of its extensive use of cedar from Lebanon. King Mesha of Moab also claims to have built "the walls of the forests,"[631] which probably refers to the material of the wall, or more likely a small copse of trees associated with it.[632]

Put on sackcloth (22:12). Sackcloth is a coarse, black goat's hair fabric (50:3) worn against the skin as a sign of mourning. The constant chafing accentuated the pain of loss. A text from the period of Nabonidus speaks of humiliating oneself before the gods by removing fine clothes. "I wear a torn garment, my cloth is sackcloth."[633]

Let us eat and drink ... for tomorrow we die (22:13). Profligacy before perishing is reflected in an Akkadian proverb, which also contains the opposite. "Very soon he will be dead; (so he says) 'Let me eat up (all I have)!' Soon he will be well; (so he says), 'Let me economize!' "[634]

This steward, to Shebna, who is in charge of the palace (22:15). Shebna's title, "steward" (*sōkēn*), is known also from an Old Aramaic graffito from Hamath, referring to ʾAdon-lu-ram,[635] as well as in the Phoenician Ahiram inscription from the late second millennium where it is used of a governor.[636] His job description is applied to several people in the Old Testament, two of whom, Shebna and Eliakim (see 36:3), have it during the reign of Hezekiah. A *sōkēn* came to designate an important government official.[637]

A stone lintel over a tomb was found in an eight- to seventh-century cemetery in the Silwan area on the eastern slope of the Kidron Valley in Jerusalem.[638] It reads: "This is [the tomb of *Shbn*]*yhu*,[639] who is over the house. No silver or gold is here, but rather [his bones] and the bones of his servant-woman with him. May the one who opens this be accursed."[640] This fits the time and circumstances of tomb building mentioned in the Isaiah passage. The name Shebna is also inscribed on an eighth- to seventh-century scarab found in Israel,[641] with the fuller Shebnayahu on other inscriptions.[642]

Hewing your grave (22:16). In Jerusalem, tombs were often hewn from the limestone rock, especially by people with means (e.g., Gen. 50:5; 2 Chr. 16:14; Matt. 27:60).

Like a ball (22:18). An exact translation of this comparison is tentative at best, since the term only occurs here in the Bible. The only other known case of this word is in the Canaanite Baal epic. There Anat slaughters people: "Under her like balls are heads; above her like locusts are hands."[643]

Robe (22:21). This long tunic was worn by both genders and was also part of the priestly regalia. In the latter case, such

Shebna inscription from Silwan tomb
Caryn Reeder, courtesy of the British Museum

▸ Hezekiah's Tunnel and Water Projects

Jerusalem's water supply was vulnerable to enemy attack, since it lay outside the city wall, and was limited in scope for an area of its size (see also comment on 7:3). Hezekiah sought to secure it from attack and siege. The intermittently running spring at Gihon lay in the valley just east of David's city.[A-149] It was joined by aqueducts and a tunnel of some 1,800 feet in length to other locations, including the Pool of Shiloh, this "Lower Pool."[A-150]

The tunnel has an inscription above one end that details the arduous digging task. It describes two digging teams working toward each other following a circuitous route. "When there were still 3 cubits to be excavated, there were the sounds of a man calling to his companion. On the day of the (completed) excavation, the stone-hewers struck out, each toward his opposite number, pick toward pick."[A-151]

Hezekiah's tunnel
Todd Bolen/www.BiblePlaces.com
◂

Pool of Shiloh at southern end of city of David
Kim Walton
▴

tunics were items of value, important gifts. Correspondence regarding trade and transport of such garments is well documented in fifth-century Aramaic texts from the Jewish colony at Elephantine in Egypt.[644]

Father (22:21). A leader is not regularly designated as "father" in the Old Testament, but is so in texts of her neighbors.[645] The Phoenician king Kilamuwa wrote in the late ninth century: "To some I am father and to some mother and to some brother."[646]

Key to the house of David (22:22). Keys in the biblical period were not small pieces of metal fitting into one's pocket, but large wooden objects, at times needing to be carried on the shoulder.[647] Eliakim, as keeper of the key, will be custodian of the affairs of the Davidic dynasty.

Assyrian relief from Lachish shows tents in Assyrian camp held up by tent pegs.
Todd Bolen/www.BiblePlaces.com

Peg (22:23–25). Eliakim's installation into office is metaphorically compared to a peg, either in the ground as a tent peg (e.g., 33:20) or on a wall, to which things may be safely attached. The metaphor highlights fixity and security, which will prove illusory.

Oracle against Tyre (23:1–18)

Tyre ... Sidon (23:1–2). Tyre and Sidon were two of the main Phoenician cities in what is now southern Lebanon. The former was built on an island some six hundred yards offshore. It lay approximately twenty-five miles south of Sidon. Both cities served as seaports and trading centers, brokering products from inland as well as from across the waters.

The Phoenicians had associations with Israel throughout most of the monarchy period, with Hiram I of Tyre (980–950 B.C.) providing aid to both David and Solomon.[648] Assyrian interest in the region was long-standing, with Tiglath-pileser I (1114–1076 B.C.) receiving tribute from this wealthy locale following a campaign in their area.[649] Tiglath-pileser III records receiving tribute from "Hirummu [Hiram II] of Tyre."[650] Sennacherib speaks of overwhelming the Sidonian king and the city of Tyre.[651] Phoenicians apparently tried to remain at least trading allies of Egypt against Assyria in this period, but they found no successful military alliance with them.

Ships of Tarshish (23:1). The description is ambiguous, since it could indicate either the vessel type or the place of origin. Etymologically related to smelting, these could be large ore ships, carrying crude ore to smelting sites or finished metal from them (e.g., 60:9). Some indications are geographical (e.g., v. 6), though the site of Tarshish is disputed, with suggestions ranging from Spain to Carthage.[652]

Cyprus (23:1, 12). Cyprus (Heb. *kittîm*) became a Phoenician colony just prior to this time period.[653] Some Cypriotes lived in early sixth-century Arad as shown by their inclusion in Hebrew ration lists from that site, one of which says, "Give 4 baths of wine to the Kittim."[654] It fell to Sargon II in 709,[655] at about the same time as did Midas, king of Phrygia,[656] leaving Tyre and Sidon without important anti-Assyrian allies in the area.

Be silent (23:2). Silence (*dmm*) is appropriate in the presence of serious events or

Relief on bronze bands of Balawat gate showing trading ships leaving Tyre
Werner Forman Archive/The British Museum

important people. It is contrasted to rejoicing or open grief. The Hebrew root apparently has a second, almost antonymous meaning of "weep, wail," which equally well fits this context (v. 1). Facing death, a Ugaritic text urges, "Don't you cry, don't you wail/be silent (*dmm*) over me, don't drain, O son, your eye's spring ... tears."[657]

Fortress of the sea (23:4). Tyre's location on an island is said in Egyptian and Assyrian sources to be "in the sea."[658] It lay about 2,000 feet offshore and so was relatively secure until a causeway was built out to it by Alexander the Great in about 332 B.C.[659] While mentioned in the Amarna texts from the mid-second millennium, Tyre reached it peak under the Phoenicians during the time of David and Solomon, when it became a support trading partner of Israel. From there, Phoenician influence spread throughout the Mediterranean.

In addition to its protection by the sea, it also boasted large fortifying walls.[660] The Tyrians in their island stronghold withstood capture by the Neo-Assyrian kings, though its mainland holdings were much more vulnerable. They did pay Assyria tribute, as Tiglath-pileser III records: "I sent an officer of mine, the *rabšaq* (see 36:2) to Tyre [and received] 150 talents of gold."[661]

City of revelry (23:7). Arbela, a city in northeastern Mesopotamia, is described in a hymn: "Arbela, city of celebration. Arbela, city of festivals. Arbela, city of the palace of celebrations ... city of celebrations. Arbela, dwelling place of jubilation."[662] While being the city where Ishtar dwelt, or perhaps because she, the goddess of sexuality and fertility, resided there, it is also a city of riotous life.

Bestower of crowns (23:8). Phoenicia's power and wealth are such that even her merchants, the main source of her revenues, are like royalty. Their abundance of goods is shown by the tribute levied against them by Assyria under Shalmaneser III, pictured on the Balawat gates.[663] A crown was worn by rulers and deities. The distinguishing feature between the two was the horns, or their symbolic representation, which often decorated the divine crown.[664]

Seventy years (23:15). A seventy-year period of Tyre's destruction takes Israel's history to the time of Josiah.[665] The number is symbolic ("a king's life"). An Esarhaddon inscription also refers to a seventy-year period of divine displeasure caused by people's evil behavior, precipitating Marduk's acting against them by sending them into slavery: "70 years, the calculated time of its abandonment."[666] Yahweh is claiming for himself the authority over foreign nations claimed elsewhere by Assyria's gods.[667]

Hire as a prostitute (23:17). Prostitutes practiced their trade for payment. An Old

Assyrian Siege Tactics

Assyrian siege tactics are known from inscriptions and reliefs (cf. 23:13). Supplies were first cut off from an enemy stronghold so that it would capitulate when facing starvation or death from thirst. Fortified cities were also attacked directly. For this, the attackers at times used scaling ladders.[A-152] As the Lachish reliefs show, soldiers on the walls repelled such attackers by raining down on them arrows, stones, or boiling liquids. An offensive priority was thus to drive the defenders off the walls. For this the Assyrians employed siege towers with battering rams in order to break through the wall. A frontal assault on thick walls took a long time, so the tower was run up with a siege ramp,[A-153] in order to knock off the top of the wall, which was more vulnerable.

Siege ramps were made of stone covered with tamped earth angling up the city wall. Since the towers were heavy, they would have sunk into the soft earth and become immobilized, so the ramps were topped by wooded planks to support the weight. The defenders, in the meantime, had countermeasures. Since the towers were made of wood and covered with leather for protection from archers, they were flammable. Defenders threw burning torches down on them, but the attackers doused the resultant fires with large water ladles.

When the defenders had been driven from their positions, the attackers could concentrate on the walls themselves. Rather than using a direct assault, they often used an oblique attack. Sappers or miners would tunnel under the walls, shoring up their excavations with wooden timbers. After the hole was considered large enough, it was filled with dry brush, which was then set on fire. This burned through the supporting timbers, which collapsed, bringing down the wall. The attacking forces could then easily enter the city, taking it captive.[A-154]

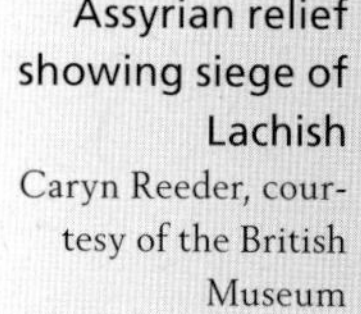

Assyrian relief showing siege of Lachish
Caryn Reeder, courtesy of the British Museum

Babylonian text refers to "the one who stands at the cross-roads and roams the streets,"[668] though trade was also found in taverns.[669] In a Ugaritic snake charm, the term used here (ʾtnn) is less specifically defined as a "gift": "give a snake as [my dowry] and sons of snakes as my 'gift.'"[670]

Judging the Earth (24:1–23)

Drink wine ... beer ... drinkers (24:9). See comment on 1:22. Beer drinking was common in Egypt and Mesopotamia, but it was also known in Israel.[671] Its use accompanied parties, which included sexual activity, as shown in several graphic seal impressions.[672] Beer could have a sexual nuance in itself, since it is paralleled in a Sumerian text with the external female sex organ: "Her vulva is sweet like her beer—and her beer is sweet!"[673] Pleasures of drinking are exemplified in a Sumerian proverb: "Pleasure—it is beer; discomfort—it is an expedition."[674]

Caught in a snare (24:18). See comment on 8:14.

The floodgates of the heavens are opened (24:18). A profligate deluge from heaven (cf. Gen. 7:11) after removing protective barriers also occurs in the Gilgamesh Epic: "The god Erragal pulled out the irrigation regulating poles.... For a day the storm [...]; quickly it stormed, passing over the people like a battle so that people couldn't even see each other.... Even the gods feared because of the deluge."[675] This envisions a cosmic geography in which waters are kept above the earth, held back by a barrier. When this barrier is breached by opening gateways or windows in it, water pours forth, flooding the earth beneath (see 34:4).[676]

Shut up in a prison (24:22). The context may refer to imprisoned foreign kings, though they were usually executed or exiled. Thus, this phrase likely refers to pagan powers opposed to God ("powers ... above"). Cyrus speaks of allowing the gods of Sumer and Akkad to return to their homes from their captivity under Nabonidus in Babylon (see 30:22 regarding imprisoned gods).[677]

Be punished (24:22). This Hebrew military term (*pqd*) indicates a mustering of the troops for an official visit, inspecting them, finding them wanting, and meting out the appropriate response. Here God is the inspector, determining the destiny of people based on their actions in relation to him.[678]

Detail from coffin of Nespawershepi, chief scribe of the Temple of Amun. Rain falls from the sky goddess Nut, bringing forth seedlings from the mummified body of Osiris, illustrating his role as a sign of resurrection and new life.
Werner Forman Archive/Fitzwilliam Museum, Cambridge

Lament

When faced with either anticipated or actualized calamity, the human response is to wail and to ask "Why?" This is generally done through the literary genre of lament. As a human characteristic, it is found across many cultures and periods. When the Ur III dynasty fell at the close of the third millennium, two known laments were written. The Lamentation over Sumer and Ur bemoans the city's destruction: "My city has verily been destroyed before me.... In the fields ... there is no grain."[A-155] The Egyptian Prophecy of Neferti (later second millennium) bewails the fact that "the land has completely perished ... the rivers of Egypt are empty."[A-156]

Moon ... sun (24:23). See comments on 3:18–23; 13:10.

LORD Almighty will reign on Mount Zion (24:23). People in the ancient Near East understood deities having special interest in different towns and cities. Yahweh rules in Zion just as Marduk does in Babylon.[679] Divine ties to specific locations are physically demonstrated by the dedication of temples to them, which serve the gods in a way similar to the function of a palace for a king.

God's Blessing on Zion (25:1–12)

Made the city a heap of rubble (25:2). Some objects, including cities, were "put to the ban" (*ḥerem*), dedicated to the exclusive use of God, and so destroyed so as to be unusable to others (43:28).[680] An Old Babylonian inscription of Idi-Sin describes a prince who "destroyed the city and dedicated (*qadāšu*, 'sanctified') it to those gods."[681] The Moabite king Mesha describes campaigns against Ataroth and Nebo: "I captured it [Ataroth], and I killed all the people of the city as a sacrifice for Kemosh [the Moabite god] and for Moab.... I killed [Nebo's] whole population ... for I had put it to the ban (*ḥerem*) for Ashtar Kemosh"[682] A Hittite text also states that the ruler took numerous cities and "I devoted (them) to the Storm god of Nesha."[683]

Such destruction also fulfilled a sociopolitical function. If a society was unable to use captives as slave labor, it might not be wise to leave them to form a resistance movement, so destruction was for protection.[684] On a theological level, destruction, often by fire, transfered the objects burned from the physical to the divine realm. An example of this, though not seen as *ḥerem*, concerns some

When cities were destroyed, the walls were often entirely dismantled with the cast down stones making a pile of rubble. These stones are from the Roman dismantling of Jerusalem.
Kim Walton

offerings, part of which was for the offerer or the priest to eat, but part was completely burned, transferring it to God.

Banquet (25:6). Royalty and people of means sponsored banquets to honor victories and special occasions.[685] The gods also did this, especially when one of them was enthroned. For example, when Marduk was honored for subduing Tiamat, all the great gods "had a palaver, held an invited banquet" that consisted of food and drink, including wine, strong liquor, and beer.[686] Ashurnasirpal II recorded a feast on his Banquet Stele celebrating the dedication of a palace at Calah. The menu included "100 fat oxen, 1,000 calves and sheep of the stable ... 500 ducks, 500 geese ... 10,000 eggs, 10,000 loaves of bread, 10,000 jugs of beer, 10,000 skins of wine" as well as grapes, pistachios, onions, garlic, turnips, honey, ghee, mustard, milk, cheese, dates, cumin, and olives in great quantity.[687]

Destroy the shroud ... the sheet ... he will swallow up death (25:7–8). Among some of Israel's neighbors "Death" (*mwt*) was a god, and there is evidence of its personification in the Old Testament as well (Ps. 49:14). In Akkadian literature, death (*mūtu*) eats people, since one person says, "He took me out of the mouth of death."[688]

The Canaanite god Mot devours others voraciously, including his fellow god Baal, the god of fertility.[689] Of him it says, "Baal will enter his innards (lit., 'liver'); he will enter his mouth like a shriveled olive."[690] This devouring is a cyclical event, happening in the fall, which leads to the "death" of winter. In the spring Baal is released from the netherworld. For Isaiah the tables will be turned; death, rather than devouring, will be devoured by Israel's God. The sphere here is not agriculture but international relations, where Israel's God has total sway, even over seemingly overwhelming odds.

Judah's Salvation Song (26:1–21)

Walls and ramparts (26:1). City walls were important for protection against marauders. There was often an inner wall above an inclined earthen rampart, with a second, outer wall below.[691]

Dead will live (26:19). See comment on 14:9. Resurrection as the actual revivification of the dead is within God's power and has here just been denied to God's enemies. Resuscitation of the newly dead occurs three times (1 Kings 17:17–23; 2 Kings 4:20–37; 13:20–21; cf. John 11:1–44). While resurrection can be applied metaphorically to the Israelite nation, it can also apply literally to individual people here.[692]

A detail of the painting of the sixth section of the Book of Caverns on the wall of the sarcophagus hall of the tomb of Ramses VI. Above the dado of decapited enemies, the journey of the sun disc through the underworld is depicted.
Werner Forman Archive

The fullest understanding of life after death was among the Egyptians. This is reflected through their elaborate burial practices, preparing the departed to make a suitable transition into the next life. The Egyptian Book of the Dead was a guide for those entering the afterlife.[693] This should not be seen as a resurrection, returning to life in this world, but rather, from the Egyptian worldview, a step beyond this life to the next.[694]

Mesopotamians did not entertain the possibility of resurrection from the underworld inhabited by shades.[695] Gilgamesh is told, after facing the death of his companion Enkidu, "the life you pursue you will not find. When the gods created humanity, they set aside death for humanity, keeping eternal life in their own hands."[696]

Libation vase of Gudea dedicated to Ninghishzidda
Jill Walton, courtesy of the Louvre

Enkidu himself, a semihuman beast man, is allowed, with the help of the sun god, to return from the netherworld in a Sumerian predecessor of the Gilgamesh story: "He [the sun god, Utu] made an opening in the Netherworld, by means of his phantom he brought his servant up to him from the Netherworld."[697]

The goddess Ishtar decides to visit the netherworld of her own volition, but then is brought back to earthly existence in the Descent of Ishtar to the Netherworld.[698] The Canaanite fertility god also dies and rises again.[699]

But none of these examples indicates a possibility of human resurrection.[700] It is precisely ordinary humans, residents of Judah, who are promised restoration of life by Isaiah, whether personally or nationally. This is in contrast to their foreign oppressors, who will not enjoy the same future (v. 14).

Dew (26:19). Dew was the only source of moisture in the drier parts of the year for areas of Israel. The Canaanite inhabitants of Ugarit understood it as coming from Baal: "Seven years Baal goes missing, eight the cloud rider. No dew, no drizzle, no flow of the deep, no sweetness of Baal's voice."[701]

Israel's Restoration (27:1–13)

Leviathan the gliding serpent, Leviathan the coiling serpent (27:1). Serpents/dragons accompanied several ancient Near Eastern deities. Tiamat designed serpents and dragons to join her in battle against Marduk,[702] and snakes also accompanied Marduk.[703] A seven-headed serpent/dragon is shown on a carved shell from Mesopotamia in battle with a god.[704] In Ugaritic literature, Baal battles Lotan, a cognate of Leviathan, who is described as "Lotan the gliding (fleeing) serpent ... the coiling serpent ... with seven heads"[705] (using the same words as Isaiah; cf. 11:15).[706]

The situation in regards to Lotan/Leviathan is usually one of conflict.[707] A Neo-Assyrian seal shows a male in combat with a dragon,[708] as does a West Semitic stamp seal.[709] A similar motif occurs in Egypt, where Seth kills the snake deity Apophis.[710]

In Egypt, different creation myths sought to elevate the cities in which they were held by giving a key role to the deities of each in creation, kingship, and the netherworld: in Hermopolis, the Ogdoad ("group of eight"), in Heliopolis, the Ennead ("group of nine"), and in Memphis, Ptah the craftsman.[711] Isaiah here takes a mythological creature and historicizes it, associating it with Tyre much as Jeremiah associates Rahab with Egypt (30:7).

Monster of the sea (27:1). Battle between sea and dry land is not only literally visible, but is also found in mythological texts. Many references in the previous comment place the ser-

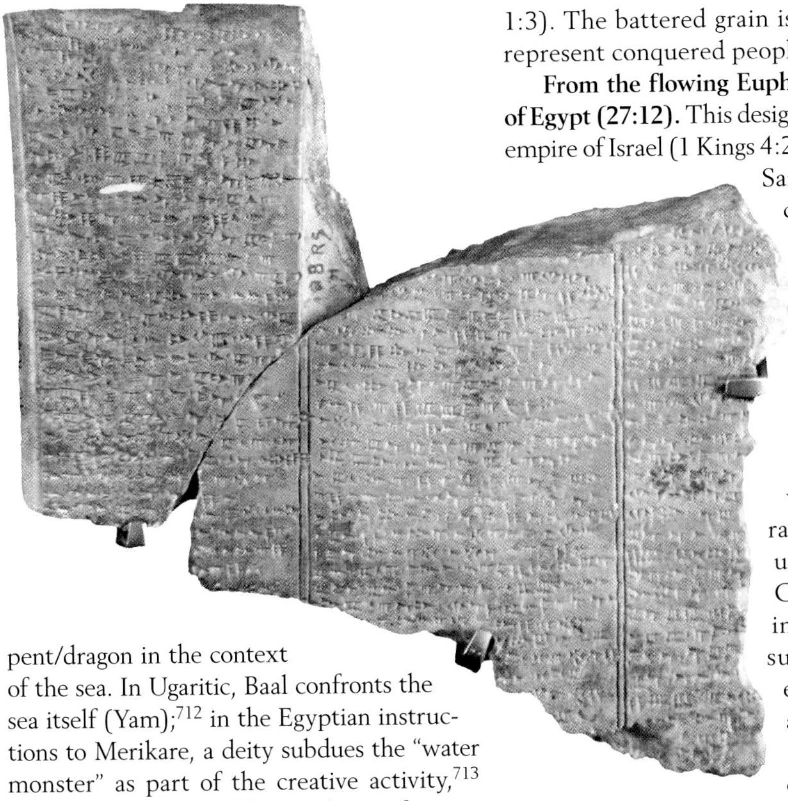

Tablet of the Baal Epic that speaks of Baal's defeat of Lotan
Rama/Wikimedia Commons, courtesy of the Louvre

pent/dragon in the context of the sea. In Ugaritic, Baal confronts the sea itself (Yam);[712] in the Egyptian instructions to Merikare, a deity subdues the "water monster" as part of the creative activity,[713] and Tiamat, a sea goddess in dragon form, is defeated by Marduk in the Akkadian creation epic *Enuma Elish*.[714] Here Yahweh will be triumphant. While he is said to use a ferocious sword, the text highlights God's triumph over any ferocious enemy.

I guard it (27:3). As Yahweh guards the vineyard, so in the Ugaritic tale of Dawn and Dusk one god is called "guard of the sown,"[715] and another is "guard of the vineyard."[716]

Chalk stones (27:9). Stone altars were made of limestone, a building material common in Israel.[717] When crushed into powder, the resultant lime could be used for sealing plaster for cisterns[718] or as a covering for a defensive wall as at Lachish.[719]

Incense altars (27:9). See comment on 17:8.

Thresh (27:12). Threshing separated the grain from its encasing husk. This was usually done on a special threshing floor either by driving animals over the stalks or by using a wooden sledge with teeth (cf. Amos 1:3). The battered grain is used at times to represent conquered people (e.g., 21:10).

From the flowing Euphrates to the Wadi of Egypt (27:12). This designates the idealized empire of Israel (1 Kings 4:21; cf. Gen. 15:18). Sargon II, during his campaign against Egypt, is said to conquer "all the desert up to the Wadi of Egypt."[720]

Trumpet (27:13). The trumpet (*šôpār*) was made out of ram's horn and was used to announce God's appearance in a theophany, to summon worshipers for holy days and ceremonies, and also to warn of an approaching enemy (e.g., 18:3). This particular trumpet summons exiles back to worship God in their native land. In Akkadian, the same word root (*š/spr*) refers to a horned animal or part of the horn itself.[721] Neither it, nor the more common Akkadian word for "horn" (*qarnu*), is used of a trumpet in texts, though horns were used as vessels.[722]

Drunken Ephraim (28:1–13)

Wreath (28:1). While this term (*ᶜᵃṭārâ*) can refer to a garland or crown of gold or silver, as it does in Akkadian documents,[723] here it refers to one made of a more transitory substance: flowers formed into a garland. They, like the city of Samaria for which it stands at the head of Ephraim (7:9), will soon fade away (40:6–8). Instead of being a symbol of splendor and blessing (e.g., 62:3), it will vanish before the Assyrian onslaught against Israel (Ephraim) in 722 B.C. Akkadian documents also refer to such a headdress

▸ Theophany

God's self-disclosure, called a "theophany," is always an event of great import.[A-157] Here (28:2–4) his power is shown, not through the customary noisy thunder and trumpet blast,[A-158] but through the destructive power of the storm and rain. There is ambiguity of these phenomena in a marginal climate where water is desperately needed, but its excess can destroy.

The Assyrian king Sennacherib follows the behest of his god: "At the command of Assur, the great lord, my lord ... I blew over the enemy like the onrush of a raging storm."[A-159] The Ugaritic epics of Keret and Aqhat describe the high god Il appearing to Keret in a dream theophany[A-160] and Baal appearing to Aqhat,[A-161] but none of these phenomena accompanies them.

More often, Mesopotamian theophanies picture deities accompanied by their more unspecific awe-inspiring splendor (*melammu*; cf. 2:10; 11:2). Tiglath-pileser I declares: "The awe-inspiring fear of Assur my lord overwhelmed them."[A-162] The deity, like the king himself, was personally involved in military activity. Baal also receives a warlike description: "He takes possession of sixty-six cities, of seventy-seven towns; eighty does Baal [...], ninety does he [...]."[A-163]

of purple wool adorning the Aramean goddess Ishtar.[724] A special festival building is described: "I had it surrounded like a wreath with a garden with all sorts of fruit-(trees) and fragrant plants,"[725] their leaves flourishing while Samaria's fade.

Funerary model of a brewery and bakery from the Eleventh Dynasty found at Thebes
Keith Schengili-Roberts/Wikimedia Commons, courtesy of the Metropolitan Museum of Art
▸

Battle at the gate (28:6). The city gate was usually the most vulnerable area of a city's defense and so it needed special attention. As God supports those in Isaiah's battle, so does Baal in an Ugaritic prayer: "When someone strong attacks your gates, a warrior your walls, raise your eyes to Baal," and "he will repulse the strong from your gate."[726]

Stagger from wine (28:7). See comments on 1:22; 5:11. Alcohol use was common in the ancient Near East, so inebriation was ambiguous. The Egyptian Admonitions of Ipuwer state that in times of joy, "it is however good when people get drunk."[727] The Instruction of Ani takes the opposite view, one closer to that of Isaiah: "Don't indulge in drinking beer, lest you utter evil speech and don't know what you're saying."[728] Those whose minds need clarity find befuddlement (cf. Lev. 10:9–10).

Jerusalem's Covenant with Death (28:14–29)

Covenant with death, with the grave (28:15). See comment on 5:14. This is probably ironically metaphorical. Israel is trying to escape Assyria's control through military alliances with the Canaanites, with their deity Mot ("death"[729]) or Molech (see 57:5), or with Egypt (30:1–7) and her god of death, Osiris.[730] Politically, Israel is turning its back on Yahweh, the life-giving God, to submit to someone who not only worships death deities, but whose submission to them renders Israel's own national existence dead. While these death deities are at the head of the pantheon of neither Canaan nor Egypt, their existence in their respective pantheons makes a useful hook on which Isaiah can hang his expressions of shock at the actions of residents of Jerusalem.

Cornerstone for a sure foundation (28:16). A building stands or falls based on the solidness of its foundation (see 44:28), and the cornerstone is what aligns and founds it. As the first stone laid, everything else needs to square to it. Laying the foundation also has important symbolism, and kings took part in a special ceremony. Esarhaddon wrote, for example: "In a favorable month, on a propitious day, on gold, silver ... and wine I laid its foundation with limestone, hard stone of the mountains.... I made monuments and inscriptions with my name and laid them in it."[731]

Assyrian king with basket on head carrying ceremonial first brick for temple building
Z. Radovan/www.BibleLandPictures.com

In Mesopotamia, often foundation inscriptions were either inscribed on bricks or tablets buried in the foundation, dedicating the building to a deity or lauding the building king.[732] Here it is Zion, residence of God and depository of his expectations for Israel, that is to align their national life and upon whose solidity they can depend.

Mount Perazim ... Valley of Gibeon (28:21). David defeated the Philistines at Mount Perazim (2 Sam. 5:20) near Jerusalem. Its elevation provided a tactical advantage over the enemy moving in the valley below. Joshua successfully fought the Amorites at Gibeon, situated on a smaller hill above surrounding fields near Jerusalem, a site identified with el-Jib.[733]

Planting ... plow ... harrowing (28:24). Since agriculture was central to the existence of most people in this period, it is well represented in texts and pictures. Plowing late in the year loosened the soil to accept seed.[734] Some crops were seeded by throwing ("broadcasting"; e.g., dill and cumin),[735] while others were planted more carefully by seed drills, to keep each crop type separated. An Akkadian seal shows a wooden plow being pulled by two oxen.[736]

His God instructs him (28:26). Farming is here not something easily come by; rather it needs divine guidance. The Sumerians also had a "farmer's almanac," which, according to its colophon, was given by the farmer goddess Ninurta to help humans in this endeavor.[737]

Siege of Ariel (29:1–10)

Ariel (29:1, 2, 7). Designating all or part of Jerusalem, Ariel is related to God's "altar hearth" (see v. 2). This is the top of the altar on which the fire was laid. The same term appears in the Mesha Inscription, where

Festivals[738]			
Month Number/Day(s)	Month Name	Contemporary Month	Festival Name
All year long	All	Every 28 days	New moon
1/14	Nisan	March-April	Passover
1/15–21			Unleavened Bread
2/14	Iyyar	April-May	Second Passover
3/	Sivan	May–June	Weeks
7/1	Tishri	September-October	Trumpets
7/10			Day of Atonement
7/15–21			Feast of Tabernacles
12/14	Adar	February-March	Purim

Mesha claims to have captured and brought it back from Israel to Moab.[739] This could be an example of metonymy, when a part, the altar surface, stands for the whole, the city in which the altar is located. Ironically, the cultic implement that should purify the people so they could worship God will itself be destroyed for its cultic perfidy.

Siege (29:3, 7). See sidebar on "Assyrian Siege Tactics" at 23:13.

Your voice will come ghostlike from the earth (29:4). See comments on 2:6; 8:19.

Plowing scenes on Egyptian relief
Manfred Näder, Gabana Studios, Germany

Hittite storm god
Michael Greenhalgh/ArtServe, courtesy of the Istanbul Museum

The city of David, from which the word of the true God is to issue forth (2:3), is instead seeking occult messages from ghosts.

The LORD Almighty will come (29:6). See sidebar on "Theophany" at 28:2.

Thunder (29:6). The Mesopotamian storm god was Ishkur (Sumerian), Adad (Akkadian),[740] or Hadad/Baal (Canaanite).[741] As such, he controlled thunder and lightning through close association with them. This control is shown graphically for Baal, who holds a club that can

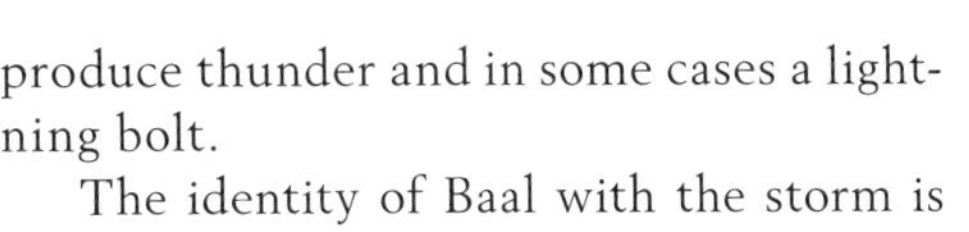

produce thunder and in some cases a lightning bolt.

The identity of Baal with the storm is shown in the Elijah story, where the storm god is denied power and productivity by Israel's more powerful Yahweh (1 Kings 18). In that episode and here, thunder, lightning, and rain are shown as tools of Israel's God, not as integral parts of his very being. He controls them and all of his creation, but he is not identified with or limited to any of these parts.

Blind yourselves (29:9). Jerusalem under attack will be helpless, blinding itself. Shalmaneser I described what he did to conquered enemies: "Most of them I slaughtered; 14,400 of their survivors I blinded, I carried off as spoil."[742] In an Akkadian text describing a cultic battle between the gods, Marduk gains the upper hand: "He tears out the eyes of the Enlil-gods."[743]

Vision of Restoration (29:11–24)

Sealed in a scroll (29:11). See sidebar on "Writing in the Ancient Near East" at 8:1. Seals were used much like a signature is today, certifying that a document was valid. Here it is placed on the outside of a rolled scroll, not only verifying the validity of its contents but also keeping it closed.

Shall what is formed say to him who formed it, "He did not make me"? (29:16). Isaiah expresses incredulity that something created might claim self-existence and thus self-sufficiency. An early eleventh-century Egyptian hymn dedicated to Ptah attributes to him self-existence, something Isaiah implies is reserved for Yahweh alone: "There is no father of yours who begat you … no mother of yours who gave you birth: your own [creator]."[744] Any human entertaining these thoughts is deluded.

Will not Lebanon be turned into a fertile field? (29:17). Lebanon, Israel's northern neighbor, is famed for its mighty cedar forests (see 2:13; 14:8). They are the habitation of the legendary Humbaba in the Gilgamesh

Egyptian Relationships under Hezekiah

Chafing from Assyrian domination, Hezekiah would have been tempted to turn to Egypt, the other major player of the period, for aid. The Twenty-Fifth (Ethiopian) Dynasty was on the Egyptian throne, though not with the unanimous support of the Egyptian population. There had been military and trade ties between Egypt and Nubia/Ethiopia for centuries, but the Ethiopians did not endear themselves to the Egyptians with their military superiority and taking control of the country.

When Thebes was threatened by an incursion from the west, however, the Egyptians were more welcoming of aid under the Ethiopian Piankhy/Pi (see comments on 19:1–20).[A-164] His brother and successor, Shabaka, encountered Assyrian expansion toward the south. Sargon II moved as far as Philistia, where he had previously encountered and defeated the army of Osorkon IV in 720.[A-165] Subsequently, Egypt under Shabaka developed a more conciliatory stance toward Assyria, since they probably did not have expansionistic tendencies toward their northeast. This temporary amity could be indicated by two seal impressions of Shabaka found at the Assyrian capital, Nineveh.[A-166]

Shabaka turned against Assyria at Sargon's death and the accession of his successor, Sennacherib. Shabaka's successor, Shebiktu, supported Hezekiah who faced Assyria at Eltekeh, helping to fend off Assyria's capture of Israel's capital. He had brought up from Ethiopia additional troops, including his brother Tirhakah, a future king (see 37:9). It is not clear from the present sources what the motivation was for this move. At the least, Ethiopia sought to slow Assyria's expansion and possibly looked toward increasing her own territory in Syria-Palestine.[A-167] While Judah was ultimately delivered from the immediate Assyrian threat by other means (37:36–37), Egypt's power was insufficient to expel Assyria completely and so Tirhakah and his forces returned home.

Taharqa presenting wine offerings to the god Hemen
Guillaume Blanchard/Wikimedia Commons, courtesy of the Louvre

Epic[745] and the destination of Wenamon to get timber in a report from late eleventh-century Egypt.[746] These national symbols will be felled, leaving only a field, while the fertile fields such as those on Mount Carmel (35:2) will become forested.

Woe to the Obstinate (30:1–5)

An alliance, but not by my Spirit (30:1). See comment on 28:15.

Egypt's shade (30:2). Smaller nations and city-states regularly requested aid and protection from their overlord or neighbor. The word used here for "shade" (*ṣēl*) is a cognate of the Akkadian *sillu* ("shadow"). Seeking protection from other countries

	Egyptian Pharaohs (low)	Assyrian Kings
750		Ashur-nirari V 754-745
740	Piankhy 747-716	Tiglath-pileser III 745-727
730		Shalmaneser V 727-722
720	Shabako 716-702	Sargon II 721-704
710		Sennacherib 704-681
700	Shebitku 702-690	
690	Taharqa 690-664	
680		Esarhaddon 681-667
670		Ashurbanipal 667-630
660	Psamtik I 664-610	

was common in the Amarna period.[747] This term is also used of divine protection, as when Gilgamesh requests of Shamash, "lay your protection [upon me]."[748]

Shame (30:3). Shame, a feeling of intrinsic worthlessness, is expressed in Mesopotamian letters in the sphere of diplomacy, coming when a relationship has been broken. In a letter to Sennacherib, Bel-Ibni asks that his previous status be restored "so that I will not be treated with contempt any more by my fellow Babylonians and will not have to (bow) my head in shame."[749] As Bel-Ibni is shamed by turning against his lord, so Israel will be by turning to another "lord," Egypt.

Zoan ... Hanes (30:4). Zoan (Tanis) lay thirty miles south of the Mediterranean and was an Egyptian capital city until just prior to this period.[750] Hanes is probably Heracleopolis, sixty miles south of Cairo and a regional capital during the Twenty-Fifth Dynasty. To seek aid, Hezekiah sent envoys to both places, but to no avail.

Oracle against Animals of the Negev (30:6–14)

Animals of the Negev (30:6). Travel through the Negev and Sinai was by donkey and camel. Dangers from lions and poisonous snakes awaited the unwary. The "adder" is literally a "burning" snake, this one having wings (6:2; 14:29), perhaps a metaphorical description of its swift, darting attack. This description might also be based on the gecko lizard, some of which can sail along on flaps of skin under their front legs (these are not poisonous, however).[751] Esarhaddon describes a campaign against Egypt during which he encountered serpents and flying creatures.[752]

Rahab (30:7). Rahab is a cosmic sea creature associated with chaos. It seems to have several names or at least is associated with other mythological creatures in the Old Testament: for example, Leviathan, Yam ("sea"; cf. Ps. 89:9–10), and "monster" (cf. Isa. 51:9).[753] It also has several manifestations: a creature defeated by God at creation (Job 9:13) and a metaphorical title for Egypt (Isa. 30:7). No creature with this name is known among Israel's contemporaries, though various monsters do oppose deities, such as the threatening Tiamat and her minions in the *Enuma Elish* epic (see 27:1) or the chaotic Tannin monsters who battle Anat in Canaanite lore.[754]

Write it on a tablet ... inscribe it on a scroll (30:8). See sidebar on "Writing in the Ancient Near East" at 8:1.

Seers ... prophets (30:10). "Seer" (*rōʾeh*) is an older term for what becomes known as a "prophet" (*nābîʾ*; see 1 Sam. 9:9). The term translated here as "prophet" is in fact "visionary" (*ḥōzeh*; Isa. 28:15; 29:10). This term is applied to Balaam both in the Bible (Num. 24:4, 16) as well as outside it.[755]

Akkadian also referred to the intermediaries between the divine and humanity by several terms.

Viper
Jack Hazut

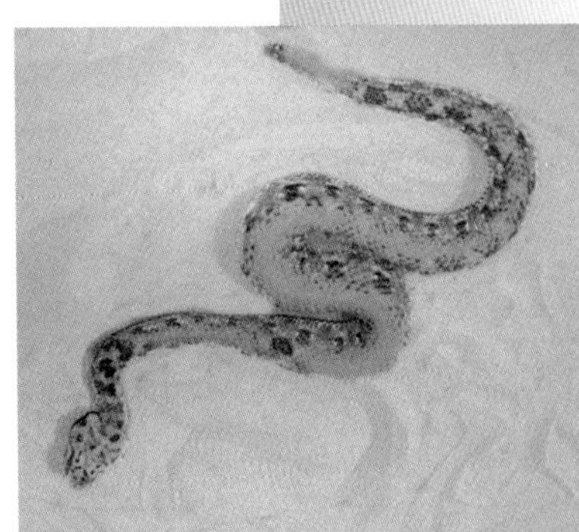

Silencing the Prophets

The prophetic message was frequently unwelcome, so prophets were often silenced by force or coercion (cf. Jeremiah). The view that a prophet predicted the future could easily morph to seeing the prophet as speaking the future into being, so silencing them could be seen as averting their dire predictions. This is perhaps why Esarhaddon made his vassals swear that they would not "listen to, or conceal, any word which is evil, improper, (or) unsuitable ... from the mouth of a prophet."[A-168] This reaction to prophetic messages in Assyria is surprising, since prophets are usually under royal control according to the extant texts, though the palace as a chief preserver of texts would be expected to censor material deemed to be to its detriment.

A seventh-century letter speaks of a prophecy supporting one Sasi, a claimant to the Assyrian throne: "A slave girl ... speaks a good word about him: 'This is the word of Nusku: The kingship is for Sasi! I will destroy the name and seed of Sennacherib.' " In addition to dealing with the prophet, other steps are called for to forestall the prophecy itself through a curse: "May the name and seed of Sasi ... perish, and may Bel and Nabu establish the name and seed of the king, my lord, until far off days."[A-169]

The ecstatic prophet (*makhkhu*) appeared in Old Babylonian texts from Mari, but the term had decreased in use by the Neo-Assyrian period.[756] Another term used only in Mari texts was the *ʾapilu* ("answerer"), though those with the title are said to come from Babylon and Syria as well.[757] A later term, *raggimu*, derives from the verb "to shout" and is used by Neo-Assyrian prophets of their divine message.[758]

Indirect messages from the gods came by visions and dreams to the *šabru* ("visionary")[759] and *šail(t)u* ("questioner").[760] While prophets who pass messages along directly from the gods also interpret dreams and visions, not all visionaries are considered prophets. For example, during one of Ashurbanipal's campaigns, "Ishtar who dwells in Arbela, let my troops have a dream in the night."[761]

Prophecy was more limited in Egypt, which more widely practiced divination (see sidebar on "Superstitions and Divination" at 2:6).[762]

Wall cracked and bulging ... break in pieces like pottery (30:13–14). Both brick and pottery are made from clay, which can be strong or friable. Water weakened brick walls, causing them to warp and collapse from their own weight, at times leading to disaster (9:10). Pottery was baked, making it less permeable but more brittle and prone to breaking. The broken pieces could be seen as worthless, but did serve some useful purposes, as noted here. Clay was used by the Egyptians to write their Execration Texts[763]—lists of neighboring enemies that were then cursed, to be broken like shattered pottery.

Grace Offered to Zion (30:15–26)

Bread of adversity (30:20). The value of bread and water, the two mainstays of life, are inverted. A Ugaritic incantation against sorcery uses a similar inversion, with the curse: "You will eat the bread of fasting."[764]

Defile your idols ... and your images ... throw them away (30:22). Destruction or removal of a cultic statue could make the attendant god depart or lose power. Esarhaddon claims in one of his campaigns that "gods and goddesses dwelling within it [the captured town] fled to heaven above like birds,"[765] while

Stele from Palace of Ashurbanipal depicting army musicians with cymbals and harps
Erich Lessing/Art Resource, NY, courtesy of the Louvre

Ashurbanipal, destroying temples and statues of Susa, wrote that "their gods, their goddesses I reckoned among the phantoms."[766] Many inscriptions record destruction or capture of the enemy's gods.[767]

Idols overlaid with silver and your images covered with gold (30:22). On the construction of idols, see comments on 2:8. Whatever value these idols purport to have will be no cause to keep them, since they are found to be lifeless and not life-giving.

Like a menstrual cloth (30:22). Literally "menstrual flow," such blood defiles and must be avoided (Lev. 15:33; 20:18), as are unholy pagan idols.

Judgment on Assyria (30:27–33)

Music of tambourines and harps (30:32). The tambourine, a percussion instrument related to a drum, was commonly played for celebrations. The Hebrew term *top*, like the English word "drum," is probably onomatopoetic.[768] The harp (*kinnôr*), or lyre, was a stringed instrument used widely in the ancient Near East.[769] A Sumerian proverb speaks of "a tearful lyre,"[770] which allies the instrument with pain, as here.

His arm (30:32). The arm, especially the right arm, symbolized power and strength. In numerous ancient Near Eastern depictions, the powerful right arm is raised.

Topheth (30:33). This was the place in the Hinnom Valley of Jerusalem where the Molech cult was practiced (see 57:5).[771]

Woe to Those Turning to Egypt (31:1–9)

Lion ... prey (31:4). The lion, among the largest carnivores in the ancient Near East, captured the imagination for its ferocity and voracity and appeared regularly in texts and

Black obelisk of Shalmaneser III depicting lion taking prey
Todd Bolen/www.BiblePlaces.com

iconography. An Israelite seal on a jar handle depicts a lion attacking a gazelle,[772] as does a late third millennium Akkadian cylinder seal.[773] Lions battle with bulls in ivories from Megiddo and Lachish[774] and attack humans in Late Bronze and Iron Age seals from Israel.[775]

Similar motifs are found in Mesopotamian, Egyptian, and Syro-Palestinian art.[776] Pharaoh Amenemhet I claims, "I subdued lions, I captured crocodiles,"[777] while Mesopotamian kings exhibit their fearless prowess by facing them in hunting scenes.[778] While being literal hunts, they also had metaphorical, symbolic value, identifying the king with the hunted creature over which he was master; the lion also embodied the warrior god Ninurta.[779]

Assyria will fall (31:8). Though Assyria appeared invincible in the eighth century, the ongoing rivalry between her and her southern neighbor, Babylonia, will soon escalate, to Assyria's detriment (see comments on Isa. 37). Though dominated by the Assyrians, Babylonia, especially its Chaldean elements, kept pushing its own sovereignty, with anti-Assyrian support at times coming directly from Elam to its east, and indirectly from Egypt to the west and Lydia to the north.

At the death of the mighty Assyrian king Ashurbanipal, family squabbles over succession allowed the Medes to attack them under Cyaxares (c. 625–585 B.C.), and the Babylonians under Nabopolassar (626–605 B.C.) to gain independence. Egypt, perhaps preferring the devil they knew rather than what they did not, sided with Assyria, but the Median and Babylonian armies proved too much even for this alliance, conquering Ashur in 614 B.C. and Nineveh in 612 B.C.[780]

Righteous Rule (32:1–8)

The eyes of those who see will no longer be closed, the ears of those who hear will listen (32:3). Wisdom and understanding are associated with the eyes and ears. Wisdom and skill characterize the mighty Marduk in the *Enuma Elish* epic, where his eyes and ears receive special attention. In creating Marduk, it is said of his father Ea: "He rendered him perfect and endowed him with double godhead. Greatly exalted was he above them, exceeding throughout. Perfect were his members beyond comprehension.... Four were his eyes, four were his ears.... Large were all four hearing organs, and the eyes, in like number, scanned all things."[781]

In Akkadian, two words for "ear" (*uznu, hasīsu*) expand in meaning to include awareness and even wisdom. Tiglath-pileser wrote of acting "with the skilled ear (*uzni*) and vast ear (*hasīsi*) which noble Nudimmud, the gods' sage, bestowed on me."[782] The process of the "civilization" and enlightenment of the wild man Enkidu in the Gilgamesh Epic begins with the ear as well.[783]

Sheep grazing on ruins of Arad with Early Bronze ruins in background
Kim Walton

Warning to Women (32:9–20)

Grape harvest … harvest of fruit (32:10). On the annual events in Israel's agricultural life as noted in the Gezer Calendar, see sidebar on "Fruit and Harvest" at 16:9. The two events noted here could be highlighted in a metonymy, where the part represents the whole, so that that entire agricultural process will be thwarted. The time period, early fall, may indicate a time just prior to the rainy season when marauding troops found it harder to carry out their campaigns (cf. 2 Sam. 11:1).

Sackcloth (32:11). See comment on 22:12.

Abandoned … deserted … a wasteland (32:14). In the Lament over the Destruction of Sumer and Ur from the late third millennium, part of the lamented destruction is shown by the gods abandoning their temples and towns.[784] One of the reasons for building, maintaining, and provisioning temples was to maintain the support of the gods who served there (see 44:28). Should such provisioning cease, so would divine sustenance. A lack of divine support would result in the physical destruction of the cities and abandonment by their inhabitants.

Citadel (32:14). This citadel (Heb. *ʿōpel*) refers to a section of the ridge crest southeast of the temple mount, which was part of the royal administrative area.[785] It most likely specifies the acropolis citadel placed on this strategic height overlooking the city. This term is known from other sites, such as Dibon in the Mesha Inscription, where the Moabite king describes his fortification efforts: "I built the Qarcho and the forest wall, and the wall of the citadel. And I built its gates, and I built its towers, and I built the king's house."[786] This area of a city needs special protection, particularly if it holds the king's residence. This hub of political life will be abandoned.

Watchtower (32:14). The only use of this term in the Bible, it is etymologically related to the "siege towers" of 23:13. Based on those discovered archaeologically, the towers usually had rectangular, heavy stone foundations not only to support their height, but also to withstand attack. Towers have been found at Giloh (near Jerusalem),[787] Ashdod,[788] Shechem,[789] and Edom.[790] These mighty, protective features will themselves be laid waste.

Promised Help in Distress (33:1–24)

Locusts (33:4). An agriculturally based economy like Israel's was in constant danger from any crop disruption. One particularly dreadful danger was that of locust swarms, which periodically move through the region of Israel even today. Covering the ground as thick as four to five thousand per square yard, they denude the land of any greenery. Their invasion, and the anguish and fear which followed, are clearly spelled out in the book of Joel, where the two locust types mentioned here are supplemented by two more (Joel 1:4).[791]

Locusts were one of the plagues brought on Egypt (Ex. 10:1–20). Their devastation is mentioned in a hymn for Sargon II, which speaks of "the malevolent locust, destroyer of grain, the evil grasshopper, dessicator of fruit orchards."[792] Their overwhelming number metaphorically can denote an overwhelming military force. The Ugaritic Legend of Keret states: "Like grasshoppers

Locust swarm in Eilat
Merav Maroody

▸ The Lord Dwells on High

Israel's God is associated with heights (e.g., 6:1; 57:15), including Zion and Sinai (see 1:8; 2:2). Among the later Israelite expatriates in Egypt, God dwelt in the heights.[A-170] Canaanite Baal also lived in mountain heights, on Mount Zaphon.[A-171] In Mesopotamia, mountains called forth several connotations. They were viewed as distant places, home of unsavory demons and wild beasts. It was the place of banishment of the *lamaštu*-demon in an Akkadian wisdom poem.[A-172] The inaccessibility of mountains could be a positive thing, when one used them for refuge. Ashurbanipal notes that an opponent of his "fled before my weapons and went up (for refuge) toward the mountains."[A-173] Some gods are identified as a mountain in an epithet, as when Enlil is called "Great Mountain Enlil."[A-174]

Temples were regularly built on heights, either natural or artificial (like the Mesopotamian ziggurat).[A-175] Ziggurats were built either to symbolize mountains in an otherwise flat terrain, or more likely to provide a closer approach to heaven for these shrines,[A-176] since they are often described as reaching or approaching heaven.[A-177] The Sumerian Gudea Cylinder exemplifies the tie between temple and mountain: "The house ... grown up 'twixt heaven and earth ... green foothill ... jutting out from the highland as the great mountain that it was."[A-178] Esarhaddon used similar words: "I raised to heaven the head of Esharra, my lord Assur's dwelling.... I piled it up like a mountain."[A-179]

Mount Sinai, the mountain of God
Wikimedia Commons
▸

Sharon plain
Todd Bolen/www.BiblePlaces.com

you will settle in the fields, like locusts the steppe-land's fringes," an event taking several days.[793] Some Mesopotamian texts refer to an infestation over the course of three years.[794] A Hebrew seal belonging to "'Azaryau, (son of) Locust" has a locust carved below the inscription.[795]

The fear of the LORD (33:6). Fear in this case is not a distressing emotion from facing pain or evil, but rather the reverence and awe before a superior. This is a desired response to one's ruler, whether divine or human. An Akkadian proverb makes this positive element clear: "Reverence gives birth to goodness."[796] Marduk, enthroned after defeating Tiamat, "is indeed Bel ['lord'] of the gods of heaven and earth, all of them. The king at whose instruction the gods are awed above and below."[797] A lack of awe and reverence is undesirable, leading to destruction. Ashurbanipal executed Ahsheri, whom he describes as "one not fearing my lordship."[798]

Treaty (33:8). Treaties are formal agreements between two or more parties with expectations for performance from both sides, each looking after the welfare of the other. Most biblical mentions of "covenant, treaty" refer to the one between Israel and her God (54:10), though a more universal covenant with God is also mentioned (24:5; 42:6), as are those between nations. Such a treaty—between the "destroyer" (v.1), probably Assyria, and Israel, which the former is breaking—is in view here.

An example of this type of treaty is one from the mid-eighth century between Bargayah and Mattel found in Sefire.[799] Treaty breach between these two could be in stipulated matters such as freedom of passage or turning over fugitives from one of the parties hiding in the country of the other. This treaty, which would have assured peaceful relations, is broken, resulting in uncertainty and fear.

Its witnesses are despised, no one is respected (33:8). The "witnesses" are those deities expected to bring about the punishments called for if the covenant was broken (see 1:2). In despising such gods, one is denying either their power or their interest in the treaty. An alternative reading for "no one" with the same Hebrew consonants (*ʾnš*) is the Akkadian term for some kind of landholder's obligation for state service (*unuššu*).[800] In that case, neglect of this duty was an element of the breach of contract.[801]

Lebanon ... Sharon ... Bashan ... Carmel (33:9). These four geographical areas, moving from north to south, are particularly fertile in an area surrounded by deserts, one of which is the Arabah.[802] Amenhotep II (1427–1400 B.C.) remarks on traveling from Ugarit and Qadesh, going "south within the valley of Sharon."[803] When these areas dry out, losing their fertility, agricultural disaster follows. The late third millennium Lament over the Destruction of Sumer and Ur bewails: "My plain, covered with vegetation, has become parched like an oven."[804]

Chief officer ... the one who took the revenue ... the officer in charge of the towers (33:18). The first of these is simply a general designation ("officer"), possibly for someone associated with taxation, as is the second, the "weigher"; both of these measured incoming precious metals, coins, and commodities. The last one appears to be in charge of fortifications; his relationship with the former two is unclear. These people of erstwhile power will disappear before God's actual power. These are examples of administrative bureaucracy that played an important role in the administration of both court and cult among Israel's neighbors, especially those who had sizable empires.[805]

Obscure speech ... strange, incomprehensible tongue (33:19). While the Israelites undoubtedly spoke Hebrew as their home language, these foreign officials, if Assyrian, would have spoken Akkadian, or if from other parts of the Assyrian empire, would have had other home languages. Any of these could have used Aramaic as the language of communication in their postings (36:11), since it was known in areas under Assyrian control from as early as the ninth century, as indicated by the ninth century bilingual Akkadian-Aramaic inscription found at Tell Fekheriye.[806]

The relative simplicity of the Aramaic writing system would have been recognized by the Assyrian overlords when they moved to their west, and it soon became the diplomatic, international language of the empire, with correspondence during the seventh century between Babylonia and Assyria taking place at least once in Aramaic.[807]

The discernable differences between dialects spoken among the Israelites (e.g., Judg. 12:5–6) would have been noticed by these imported officials and probably derided, if indeed Aramaic is understood here. Though not their native tongue, Aramaic and Hebrew were closely enough allied that the Israelites could have

Phoenician seagoing vessel from sarcophagus dating to the second half of the first millennium B.C.
Erich Lessing/Art Resource, NY, courtesy of the National Archaeological Museum, Beirut, Lebanon

understood either.[808] If Akkadian is meant here, the linguistic distance between that East Semitic language and the West Semitic Hebrew would have made them mutually incomprehensible—actually removed "from hearing," as the term here is literally translated.

Stakes (33:20). See comments on 22:23–25.

Galley with oars ... ship ... sail (33:21). Though the Israelites were not a seafaring people (see 1 Kings 9:26), they did use the sea to some extent. Her neighbors, both Egypt[809] and Mesopotamia,[810] relied more on seagoing and river vessels not only for trade but also for military activity. They used oared craft that could also have sails. An eighth-century Hebrew seal also shows a sailing ship,[811] most probably on the Mediterranean or the Galilean sea, but Zion/Jerusalem, situated in the highlands and far from any water body sufficient to allow such craft, could not depend on them for protection, but rather turned to her God.

The LORD is our judge, the LORD is our lawgiver, the LORD is our king (33:22). Various ancient Near Eastern deities fulfill these functions for different ethnic groups. Canaanite El is king for the Canaanites,[812] and numerous Mesopotamian deities are so identified.[813] Several Mesopotamian gods, including Adad (the storm god) and Shamash (the sun god; see comment on 1:17), are judges.[814] The Akkadian incantation text Maqlû requests: "Stand by, O great gods; hear my complaint; render my judgment; learn my behavior."[815] They are not accredited with themselves dispensing laws, but rather as acting justly and providing kings the wherewithal to promulgate just laws.

Hammurabi, in the prologue to his law code, states that the laws were not his impetus; rather, "when Marduk urged me to direct the people of the land to adopt correct behavior, I made the land speak with justice and truth."[816] Shamash is identified as "the solicitous judge who pronounces a judgment of righteousness,"[817] and a bilingual hymn reads: "O Shamash ... may Right stand at your right side, may Righteousness stand at your left side."[818] Israel is reminded that it is Yahweh, not any of his rivals, who fulfills these roles.

All Nations Judged (34:1–17)

Stars ... dissolved ... will fall (34:4). See comment on 13:10. As God created heaven and earth and all within them, so he can do away with them, reversing terrestrial creation in the flood and celestial creation here. Events here are a polemic against pagan deities, many of whom are astral, and worship of astral phenomena attracted even Israel. Astral deities are often pictured symbolically, including a star among Israel's neighbors.[819] These stars will disappear, along with the pagan deities they represent.

Sky rolled up like a scroll (34:4). One Mesopotamian view of the "heavens" was that it was solid, akin to the biblical concept of the "firmament, expanse" (Heb. *rāqiaᶜ* rather than *šāmayim*, as is used here; see Gen. 1:7).[820] In the *Enuma Elish* creation account, Marduk defeats and kills Tiamat: "He split her in two, like a fish for drying, half of her he set up and made as a cover, heaven. He stretched out the hide and assigned watchmen."[821] Something like this skin parchment scroll may be in mind here.

The Sumerian sign for "heaven, sky" also designates the sky god, An (Akkadian Anu), father of all gods.[822] He had control over the central part of the starry heaven on either side of the equator;[823] another god, Enlil, had control of the northern region,[824] and Ea, the southern region.[825] Yahweh, in rolling up the heavens, exercised power over the realm of all these powerful Mesopotamian gods.

Edom (34:5). See 21:11–12. Edom, lying to the southeast of the Dead Sea, descended from Esau. The first extrabiblical mention of Edom is a twelfth-century Egyptian text that notes some Bedouin tribes passing a Edomite border fortress.[826] Edom sought to thwart

Israel's passage after the Exodus, but Balaam prophesies her capture by Israel, which David accomplished with great bloodshed and ensuing hatred. Edom rebelled under Solomon as well as later under Joram.

Assyria under Tiglath-pileser III subdued Edom, among others, in 732 B.C., forcing tribute from her.[827] They were not annihilated, however, since cities such as Bozrah flourished at this time.[828] When Hezekiah was besieged for lack of tribute payment in 701 B.C., Edom was among those who paid up.[829] Under Assyria, Edom started to expand into the south of Judah (2 Kings 16:6; 1 Chr. 28:16–17), and she may have actively assisted the Babylonians in the sack of Jerusalem in 586 B.C.[830] The continuing animosity between Israel and Edom makes it a welcome candidate for destruction, possibly as representative of other hostile nations who face the same fate (see the book of Obadiah; see also Isa. 21:11–12 and comments there).

Bozrah (34:6).[831] Bozrah was the Edomite capital on the site of what is now Buseirah on the north-south Kings' Highway at its junction with a major east-west route some twenty miles south of the Dead Sea.[832] Proximity to copper mines also added to its wealth. It is a natural stronghold, surrounded by steep valleys. Excavations have uncovered a building with courtyard similar to those of the Neo-Assyrian period, indicating that it was occupied during this period of Isaiah. Remains also indicate continued occupation into the Babylonian/Persian periods.[833]

Wild oxen will fall with them, the bull calves and the great bulls (34:7). These beasts, known for their power (Num. 23:22), will become powerless. In Ur III and Old Babylonian Mesopotamia, the bull, especially the wild bull, represented royalty. Hammurabi is described as "aggressive bull, one who butts the enemies."[834] One of these terms (*pr*) is also used in Egyptian of a "ferocious bull."[835] This metaphor does not seem to occur in a time period close to Isaiah, who in the context more directly has his eye on the sacrificial function of the animals.

Blazing pitch (34:9–10). As one of several materials used to seal watercraft, the association of this word here with other, petroleum-based terms (bitumen, natural asphalt) suggests that "pitch," a tree resin, is an inappropriate translation. Smearing hot bitumen on the head of one who brought a false legal claim was a punishment in Old Babylonian texts.[836] Here an entire land is to be so punished. This was accompanied by the stench of "sulfur," also associated with the southern Dead Sea region.

Measuring line ... plumb line (34:11). To assure correct building alignment for a Sumerian temple, King Gudea pronounces a blessing on laying a temple foundation: "The plumbline aligns the bricks."[837] In The Eloquent Peasant, an Egyptian work from the Middle Kingdom, the peasant addresses the high steward as a "plumb-line which carries the weight!... Beam, do not tilt, plumb-line, do not swing awry!"[838] This refers to someone who makes sure that justice and honesty are carried out.

Bozrah
Todd Bolen/www.BiblePlaces.com

The measuring line and plumb-line, associated with certainty and truth (28:17), are given opposite functions here through the use of irony. The flip side of using these tools to make something straight is what happens when something is found out of plumb. Edom is found crooked so she cannot stand and will be destroyed.

Desert owl and screech owl ... desert creatures (34:11–15). See 13:21. The specific identity of each bird is unclear, but their symbolism is not. Such groupings of birds and other desert animals suggest that the inhabited area will become desolate after God's judgment. The Lament over the Destruction of Sumer and Ur bemoans the ruined city becoming a place, not of humans, but of foxholes.[839] The Egyptian Prophecy of Neferti pictures the land so decimated that "strange birds[840] will breed in the marshes.... The wild beasts of the desert will drink from the river of Egypt."[841]

Night creatures (34:14). This is the sole biblical occurrence of the Hebrew word *lîlît*. It derives from the feminine Akkadian word *lilītu*, which itself derives from Sumerian *líl* ("wind"), so it must refer to some wind or storm demon.[842] This demon, usually with the alternative designation "girl of Lili," is also important for her aberrant sexuality, which is not for procreation since she is sterile and produces poison instead of milk.[843] The sexual aspects were picked up in rabbinic Judaism, where she has the character of a seductive succubus.[844] She was feared also in Syria, as shown by the seventh-century Phoenician inscription from Arslan Tash: "From the dark chamber pass away ... O night demons."[845]

Bursting Joy (35:1–10)

The glory of the LORD, the splendor of our God (35:2). The attributed radiance of the Mesopotamian gods has been noted (see comments on 2:10; 11:2). It is a visible, awe-inspiring sheen indicating the god's otherness and might.[846] Marduk in his war power faces Tiamat: "On his head he was covered with terrifying sheen."[847] This could be transferred to others, whether terrifying creatures ("There were scorpion-men guarding the gate, whose terror was dread, whose glance was death, whose radiance was fearful"[848]) or a king ruling in power as representative of the gods.[849] It also is transferred to objects such as temples.[850] In 2:12–13 Isaiah pictures the powerful aura of God, in parallel with the glory of the pagan Lebanon, coming to a desolate desert.

Carmel (35:2). At the time of King Ahab, the area of Carmel, southeast of Haifa, was a lush area, with up to twenty-eight inches of annual rainfall.[851] It was the site of Canaanite worship and of the great showdown between Yahweh and Baal under Elijah. A headland jutting into the Mediterranean, it appears as "Holy Head" in Egyptian records and as Baal-Rosh in Akkadian texts.[852] Shalmaneser III records, "I went to the mountain of Mt. Baᶜli-râsi, a headland on the sea."[853]

Ahkenaten and family with the sun god Aten
Keith Schengili-Roberts/Wikimedia Commons, courtesy of the Altes Museum, Berlin

Carmel and the Mediterranean
Todd Bolen/www.BiblePlaces.com

One of King Sargon's high officials
Jill Walton, courtesy of the Louvre

Sharon (35:2). Sharon is a plain on the Mediterranean coast running about thirty miles north from the Yarkon River.[854] It was conquered by Thutmoses III and Amenhotep II,[855] and people from there are mentioned by Mesha in the Moabite Stone.[856] Two of its areas, Dor and Joppa, are mentioned on the fifth-century sarcophagus of Eshmunazer of Sidon.[857]

Strengthen the feeble hands ... knees (35:3–6). Healing from physical frailty is ever welcome and anticipated, here as a promised blessing from God. Numerous Akkadian prayers and blessings highlight the importance of long life and good health.[858] The incantation series Šurpu states: "Let Nusku stand by and grant health to the sick."[859] An Akkadian greeting formula reads: "May Shamash and Marduk grant you good health."[860]

When the Egyptian goddess Hathor finds Horus blinded by Seth, she tells him: "Open your eyes, that I may put this milk in." He opened his eyes and she put the milk in both eyes; then she said to him: "Open your eyes!" He opened his eyes. She looked at them and found them healed.[861] The ailments mentioned here are common in the period. A late Egyptian wisdom text, the Instructions of Papyrus Insinger, speaks of "the blind one whom the god blesses, his way is open. The lame one whose heart is on the way of the god, his way is smooth."[862]

Lion ... ferocious beast (35:9). See comment on 5:29; 31:4; also sidebar on "Utopian Animal Behavior" at 11:6.

Ransomed of the LORD (35:10). It is in Yahweh's hand to free those held in captivity or slavery. An Akkadian texts asserts,

"To free the captive, Shamash, is in your power,"[863] though more commonly this was done by a wealthy family or rulers. By doing this, the redeemer shows not only compassion for those suffering this fate, but also the power to be able to release them from it.

Assyria Besieges Jerusalem (36:1–22)

Field commander (36:2). This is one of the three high military officials whom Sennacherib sent against Hezekiah (2 Kings 8:17). He bears an Akkadian title *rab šāqê* (lit., "chief cup-bearer"),[864] which is transliterated into Hebrew here (cf. KJV, "Rabshakeh"). The position was a vital one, serving right beside the king and at times controlling access to him. This proximity led to trust between the king and the official, which may be why he is the official spokesman here. The Assyrian Eponym list records several officials with this title.[865]

Eliakim son of Hilkiah the palace administrator (36:3). Eliakim is literally "over the house" (22:15), the royal steward. Equivalent to an Egyptian vizier, he is in charge of daily palace operations. Several Hebrew seal inscriptions from the eighth and seventh centuries have the name "Eliakim,"[866] though not all refer to this son of Hilkiah. Ones that are likely to do so are found on jar handles from the period of Hezekiah. The royal larder would have been under his purview as steward, so wine and oil for royal consumption could well bear his official stamp. Several seals and other inscriptions also belong to people designated as "over the house."[867]

Shebna (36:3). See comment on 22:15.

Joah ... the recorder (36:3). Literally, a "recorder" (*mazkîr*) is "one who reminds," a secretary, who occupied an important place in palace administration.[868] The term is used on a Moabite seal from the mid-first millennium, "Belonging to Paltay, son of Maʾosh, the recorder."[869] In the Assyrian Eponym Canon, an identification of successive years by the name and office of important officials, 741 B.C. is associated with Bel-Harran-Belu-Utsur, "palace herald," the equivalent of this term.[870]

The great king, the king of Assyria (36:4). "Great king" is a common title of Assyrian royalty, used even by Sennacherib in his own inscriptions.[871] "King of Assyria" or "of Assyria and Babylonia" is also well attested.[872]

On what are you basing this confidence? (36:4). Israel is to put her trust in Yahweh, her God (8:16), but the Assyrians mock them for trusting on what they view as a powerless god. Tiglath-pileser I writes: "At the beginning of my kingship, 20,000 Mushkean men and five of their kings ... trusted in their own strength.... With trust in Ashur, my lord, I really inflicted a defeat on them."[873]

The Assyrian view of history was that events on earth reflected those in heaven. For example, Marduk's gaining supremacy over the other deities in the *Enuma Elish* epic[874] is reflected by Babylonian ascendancy over its neighbors. The Egyptians' powerlessness to aid Israel derives from weakness of their gods, and Yahweh himself has lost power if Judah's own king can remove his shrines. The Assyrian mockers fail to realize that these shrines are removed instead because of the powerful Yahweh (2 Kings 18:4). Orthodox Yahwism understands this theology, being convinced that Yahweh alone is in control of both heaven and earth.

You are depending on Egypt, that splintered reed of a staff (36:6). A rod or staff needed strength in order to provide weight-bearing support. A reed, which is pliable, cannot supply needed support, and even less if it is broken (see 42:3). Sargon made this same claim concerning the king of Ashdod who sought to lead the kings of Palestine, Judah, Edom, and Moab away from following Assyria. "To Piru, king of Egypt, a ruler unable to save them, they brought their greeting gifts [see 1:23], they repeatedly pestered him (to be their) ally."[875]

High places and altars Hezekiah removed (36:7). See 30:22. Destruction of a temple or deportation of a divine statue removed

Sennacherib and Hezekiah

Hezekiah constructed a tunnel through rock underneath the city to channel water from the Gihon spring to a location inside the city in preparation for the Assyrian siege (for picture of tunnel, see entry at Isa. 22). This inscription was found inside the tunnel commemorating the meeting of the crews digging from either end.
Deror Avi/Wikimedia Commons, courtesy of the Istanbul Archaeological Museum

Sennacherib as crown prince
Kim Walton, courtesy of the Oriental Institute Museum

The confrontation between Assyria and Judah is not only well documented in the Bible (2 Kings 18–19; 2 Chr. 32), but is known from Sennacherib's own records.[A-180] He writes:

> As for Hezekiah the Judean who did not submit to my yoke: 46 of his strong, fortified cities and innumerable of the smaller surrounding towns around them I besieged ... I conquered. 200,150 people, big and small, men and women, (as well as) innumerable horses, mules, donkeys, camels, oxen, and flocks I "liberated" from among them. I reckoned them as booty. (Hezekiah) himself I enclosed like a caged bird in Jerusalem, his royal city. I built fortifications around him, preventing any exit through his city gate.[A-181]

Relief of Lachish under siege by Sennacherib
Caryn Reeder, courtesy of the British Museum

Prism inscription of Sennacherib
Kim Walton, courtesy of the Oriental Institute Museum

Sennacherib does not mention actually capturing Jerusalem and its king, though he does mention that for the other cities in the area, including Lachish (36:2). Pictorial and archaeological evidence has been found for this attack.[A-182] Not mentioning the capture of more important Jerusalem leads to the assumption that he did not do so, or else he would have mentioned it. This reflects the biblical record: siege but no capture.[A-183]

the deity's influence. It meant that this god was so ineffective that he could not even look after his own interests. Sennacherib, describing the capture of Babylon, states: "My men took the gods who dwelt there and smashed them."[876] The Assyrian military leader claims that a king who neglects or opposes a god will suffer that god's displeasure, even as far as losing his position.

The Hittite Proclamation of Anitta of Kushshar claims: "Previously Uha, king of Zalpuwa, had carried off our goddess [Halmashuit].... [Regarding the city Hattusha], their goddess Halmashuit gave it over [to me], and I took it at night by storm."[877] Cyrus made the same claim: Neglecting worship led the gods to turn Babylon over to him.[878]

Aramaic ... Hebrew (36:11). See comment on 33:19. The Israelites distinguish here between two languages used in their area. Aramaic was the *lingua franca* of the Near East at this time (see 19:18), but most

Osorkon I hieroglyphic inscription with accompanying NW Semitic/Byblos
Rama/Wikimedia Commons, courtesy of the Louvre

Filth ... urine (36:12). Filth (lit., "feces, excrement") is naturally repulsive and is the last thing a starving people would eat (2 Kings 6:25). This shows the desperate and helpless state of the besieged Israelites. The helplessness and degradation of the Canaanite god Ilu is shown when he arrives at his palace completely drunk and carried by others: "HBY ... soils him in his feces and his urine."[882]

Drink water from his own cistern (36:16). Cisterns, artificial water reservoirs cut into bedrock, were important for a people without a steady and certain water supply. Public cisterns were supplemented by private ones for those of sufficient means to dig one. This propaganda promises this advantage to everyone.[883]

Prophecy of Deliverance (37:1–13)

Tore his clothes and put on sackcloth (37:1). See sidebar on "Mourning Rites" at 15:2 and comment on 22:12. These are two common signs of mourning among the Israelites and their immediate neighbors (Gen. 37:29, 34; Jer. 41:5; 49:3). A late Akkadian text speaks of a mourning ritual, probably influenced by West Semitic practice: "I was clad in a rent garment, my fabric is sackcloth."[884]

Tirhakah (37:9). Tirhakah (Taharqa) was the third king of the Twenty-Fifth (Ethiopian) Dynasty. A prodigious builder during his initial

native Israelites did not understand it—a situation that changed during the exile, when it became the home language of many exiled Israelites. The other language was Hebrew (lit., "Judean"), a southern dialect that the people understood,[879] which Shebna was trying to prevent from being spoken.

Simultaneous use of two languages for different purposes was not uncommon. Sumerian and Akkadian were used simultaneously in Mesopotamia. The Amarna tablets show Akkadian texts with Canaanite glosses,[880] and there is a hieroglyphic inscription with an accompanying version in Northwest Semitic.[881]

Taharqa in sphinx form
Guillaume Blanchard/Wikimedia Commons, courtesy of the Louvre

years of relative peace, he also campaigned to the north, encountering Sennacherib and Esarhaddon and their armies. The latter probably viewed Egypt as the instigator of unrest among their vassals in Syro-Palestine. He was forced to flea to Thebes, where he subsequently died.[885]

Rezeph (37:12). This was a city on the Euphrates north of Palmyra; a governor of Rasappa (Rezeph) is mentioned in the Assyrian Eponym List for 803 B.C.[886]

Protective creatures flanking doorway
Heather Liau, courtesy of the Louvre

Hezekiah's Prayer and God's Response (37:14–38)

Hezekiah ... read it (37:14). Hezekiah is said to have read, while Sennacherib is said to have heard. The relative difficulty of the writing systems of the two languages made Hebrew, with twenty-two letters, more accessible while Akkadian, with hundreds of different signs, was inaccessible to most officials. Ashurbanipal is among few who could boast of bilingual literacy: "I can read learned texts of which the Sumerian is obscure (and) the Akkadian is difficult to interpret."[887] For the most part, messengers carried communication that, while often written, was orally delivered to the recipient.[888]

Enthroned between the cherubim (37:16). Akkadian *kuribu* are protective deities represented by figures combining human, animal, and bird characteristics. Such figures appear frequently in ancient Near Eastern iconography of Assyria and Syro-Palestine.[889] They and other protective beings flanked doorways and were carved on each side of thrones, symbolizing their protection of the enthroned ruler. Warad-Sin (1834–1823 B.C.) wrote of building his throne: "A pair of protective genii I set up on either side of it."[890] Yahweh sitting between the cherubim occupied the true, universal throne, superior to that of any Assyrian opponent.

Open your eyes, O LORD (37:17). In a call for divine attention, an Aramaic treaty inscription from mid-eighth century Sefire, speaking to all the deities, calls: "Open your eyes to gaze upon the treaty."[891] This contrasts with an Israelite understanding that pagan deities, or their idol representations, neither see (44:18) nor speak, so must have their mouths opened (see comment on 2:8). In Akkadian idiom, opening the eyes signifies encouragement and happiness,[892] though here it will bring anger to the one who sees inappropriate actions.[893]

May know that you alone ... are God (37:20). Hezekiah argues for the uniqueness of God. Knowledge of the divine was important to Shalmaneser I, who describes himself: "I,

Stele from Sam'al (Zincirli) with the report of Assyrian king Esarhaddon's victory over Egypt and two prisoners with hooks in mouth attached to leashes
Bildarchiv Preussischer Kulturbesitz/ Art Resource, NY, courtesy of the Vorderasiatisches Museum, Staatliche Museen zu Berlin, Berlin, Germany

eternal offspring, one who knows the gods."[894] Knowledge of the gods in a polytheistic society was more problematic than in Israel. One had personal or city gods with whom one could have a more intimate relationship, but there were numerous deities, often powerful and potentially malevolent, whom one had not yet encountered. God's character is generally known through the outward manifestation of his awesome power and majesty (*melammu*; see 2:10). Isaiah, emphasizing the uniqueness of Israel's God, completely nullifies any claim others might make.

I have ascended the heights of the mountains, the utmost heights of Lebanon. I have cut down its tallest cedars, the choicest of its pines (37:24). The power of conquering a distant country with its mighty trees is a motif used by Assyrian kings to glorify themselves. Shalmaneser III wrote that he went up "to the Amanus Mountains (in western Syria[895]). I cut down cedar wood and juniper wood [cognate to the Hebrew 'pine,' *brš*]."[896] Since the cedar symbolized Lebanese power and pride, Assyrian destruction of it brought Lebanon shame (see 1:7; 10:18–19). This type of claim is noteworthy for an Assyrian king, since trees were sparse in Mesopotamia, and denuding another's valuable resources such as this resulted in a bare landscape much like Assyria's own (see 10:18–19).

I will put my hook in your nose and my bit in your mouth (37:29). God will treat Assyria like recalcitrant animals, turning the tables on those who treated others similarly. Tukulti-Ninurta I stated metaphorically: "with a bridle I controlled the land of...."[897] This treatment is also depicted on reliefs, showing that it was literally applied to captive people in addition to animals.[898]

Take root below and bear fruit above (37:31). The agricultural society of Israel was aware of the relationship between good root and good fruit, often associating the two (11:1). Curses written on a fifth-century Phoenician sarcophagus against any who might desecrate it include this one: "Let him have neither root below nor fruit above nor form among those living under the sun."[899]

Shield ... siege ramp (37:33). See sidebar on "Assyria's Siege Tactics" at 23:13.

One hundred and eighty-five thousand men (37:36). Although the number seems large, Sennacherib himself states, regarding the Judean villages he captured from Hezekiah, that he deported 200,150 people.[900] Soon thereafter Ashurbanipal wrote that during one of his campaigns, "Irra [the plague god], the Warrior struck down Uate, as well as his army, who had not kept the oaths sworn to me.... Famine broke out among them and they ate the flesh of their children."[901] Plague best explains this divine decimation of the Assyrian forces. The severity of plague is illustrated by the Plague Prayers of Mursislis, a fourteenth-century Hittite king whose realm had suffered for twenty years.[902] Several Hittite ritual texts to avert plague also exist.[903]

Adrammelech cut [Sennacherib] down with the sword.... And Esarhaddon his son succeeded him as king (37:38). Esarhaddon, Sennacherib's son and heir, writes of violent conniving to wrest away the throne by unnamed "brothers."[904] A Babylonian chronicle records that in 681 B.C.: "Month of Tebet, day 20: Sennacherib, king of Assur, his son killed him in a rebellion."[905] An Assyrian letter perhaps mentions the murderer, a son Arad-Mullissu, a possible variation of Adrammelech.[906] He was Sennacherib's second son who, after the capture and deportation of his older brother, the crown prince, would have expected to inherit the throne. Sennacherib's grooming of Esarhaddon as his successor may have enraged Arad-Mulissu enough to murder his father in hopes of gaining the throne.

Esarhaddon (37:38). Esarhaddon, though the youngest of Sennacherib's sons, was designated his heir just prior to his death.[907] Since this was an unpopular move among his brothers, he left the area for Cilicia until the murder of his father.[908] He then returned and took the throne after a civil war.[909] He led campaigns against Egypt under Tirhakah, which means he traversed Judah, but no biblical mention is made of him turning against Judah itself.[910] Judah under Manasseh was his vassal and provided him service. He died in 669 B.C., but not before securing the position of his heir designate, Ashurbanipal, so he would not have to contend with pretenders as he had done.

Ararat (37:38). Known as the resting place of Noah's ark, Ararat, or Urartu, is a mountainous region in northwest Assyria lying between lakes Van and Urmia in what is now Armenia.[911] Its mountains gave it some measure of protection against repeated Assyrian incursion. In the height of its power in the early eighth century, Urartu pushed west, but soon was forced back by Assyrian attacks under Tiglath-pileser III.[912] Its relative inaccessibility and geographic distance from the centers of Assyrian power made it a suitable place for fugitives such as Sennacherib's assassins to seek refuge.

Hezekiah's Illness and Extension of Life (38:1–22)

You are going to die; you will not recover (38:1). A lack of parallel to this kind of statement to a king elsewhere derives from the understanding of a prophet's role. Professional prophets received a livelihood from the palace and were loathe to jeopardize it. They and diviners could circumvent a negative pronouncement by pursuing omens until a satisfactory one appeared. There also were rituals and incantations available to subvert the projected calamity.[913] Isaiah does not depend on these magical means; rather, he turns to his God, who is not loathe confronting even kings with illness and death.

I will add fifteen years to your life (38:5). As patrons of individuals as well as nations, gods were to look after their well-being, as people reminded them in prayers and petitions. Shalmaneser III erected a statue in honor of Adad and prayed, "When the god Adad, my lord, looks upon this statue, may he be pleased (and) so command the lengthening of my days, proclaim the multiplication of my years, daily decree the removal of illness from my body."[914]

A writing of Hezekiah (38:9). This psalm-like heading identifies the genre and author of this poem. Akkadian texts often included similar

Stele of Esarhaddon
Francesco Dazzi, courtesy of the Pergamon Museum

▸ Psalm of Thanks for Healing

This genre of psalm is well known, being a natural response of gratitude for physical help. Sin-Iddinam, a king of Larsa, wrote a similar letter prayer to his patron goddess.[A-184] It begins with a salutation, identifying the god being petitioned, an element not found here, since there is only One to whom Hezekiah might pray. Then follows the writer's complaint (cf. 38:10–12), remembering illness and danger: "There is no escaping from my fears by myself; I am seized by an evil sickness."[A-185] The writer protests his innocence (cf. 38:13): "I did not neglect my duties."

The sufferer then prays for help (cf. 38:14): "As for me, let me enter your lap in the face of Death, save me from (its) hand.... Like a mother-cow, have mercy on me." A final praise for healing in Isaiah (38:20) is paralleled by the concluding request by a rival king: "Let him live!"[A-186] Individual prayers are rare in both the Bible and its environment, since written documentation mainly concerns those with power, such as the king in both of these examples.[A-187]

information such as genre and scribe in a colophon at the end of a document.[915]

Gates of death (38:10). See comment on 5:14. In a Sumerian text, Gilgamesh approached the netherworld: "At the Gate of Ganzir, the entrance to the Netherworld, he took a seat."[916] In the Akkadian Descent of Ishtar to the Netherworld, Ishtar says, "O gatekeeper, open thy gate, open thy gate that I might enter," and he leads her through seven gates into the "Land of No Return."[917] In the Aramaic Balaam text from Deir ʿAlla, a corpse "approaches [Sheol] ... to the edge of She[ol], and the shadow of the wall,"[918] which shows an understanding of a marked division between the places of the living and the dead common to the area and period.

The existence of gates guarding the Netherworld suggests that it is viewed architecturally as a city, though its walls are not specifically mentioned.[919] Instead of being a place of imprisonment, the ancient Near Eastern gates served to deter entry.[920]

A painting in the tomb of Sennedjem. The tomb owner stands at the gate of the Other World.
Werner Forman Archive/E. Strouhal

Like a shepherd's tent ... like a weaver (38:12). Using metaphors from Israel's life experience, Hezekiah highlights the transitory nature of life. Shepherds, frequently moving their flocks, had to uproot and move quickly, while weavers, when completing their product, rolled it up and snipped the threads connected to the loom. The hard life of the latter is caricatured in the Egyptian Satire on the Trades: "If he skips a day of weaving, he is beaten fifty strokes."[921] Hezekiah views his life as on the verge of uprooting and being cut off from among the living.

Like a lion (38:13). See comments on 5:29.

We will sing (38:20). The biblical association of leadership and the arts, in particular music, goes back most notably to King David, who not only wrote but played music (using the same verb, *ngn*).[922] Other musical forms are attributed to Moses and Miriam (Ex. 15:1, 21). The Sumerian king Shulgi (*c.* 2000 B.C.) wrote of himself: "I, the king, a warrior from the womb am I, I, Shulgi ... entered the Ekishnugal [temple], made resound there the drum and timbrel, took charge there of the *tigi*-music, the sweet."[923] Writing is also associated with royalty. Sargon of Akkad, several centuries earlier, had a daughter Enheduanna, who is the earliest known author.[924]

Poultice of figs (38:21). Figs were used medicinally in this period. Ugaritic texts describe treatments for horses, taking "rancid figs, and rancid raisins, and malt flour. He will pour it together into its nostrils."[925] They are also used to treat human maladies.[926]

Babylonian Envoys (39:1–8)

Merodoch-Baladan (39:1). Merodach-Baladan (Marduk-Apla-Iddina[927]) was king of Babylon twice: 722–710[928] and 705–703 B.C. (in between he lost his throne to Sargon II, who states, "My hands defeated Marduk-Apla-Iddina, king of the land of Chaldea").[929] Merodach-Baladan is called a king of Chaldea since he came from the group of Chaldean tribes taking power in Babylonia during this period.[930]

To thwart Assyrian expansion into his territory, Merodach-Baladan united Babylonian and Aramean tribes along with other neighbors such as the Arabs and the Elamites by taking advantage of Assyrian political instability and maintaining independent rule until 710 B.C.[931] The yoke was not thrown off for long, since Sargon and the Assyrians wanted to control their borders.[932] Sargon's son Sennacherib also had to contend with Merodach-Baladan, who regained his independence immediately after Sargon's death.[933]

Merodach-Baladan's military and political acumen is shown by these alliances, including the one sought here from Hezekiah. These emissaries were probably from this period, trying to persuade him to take up the Babylonian cause against Assyria.[934]

Sent Hezekiah letters and a gift (39:1). In international diplomacy, envoys from one nation delivered not only greetings ("letters") but gifts to the other. In a typical letter heading from the fourteenth-century B.C. archive at el-Amarna, Abdi-Heba of Jerusalem writes to the pharaoh: "Say to the king, my lord: Message of Abdi-Heba, your servant. I fall at the feet of my lord, the king, seven times and seven times." The letter concludes with instructions to the scribe to pass the message on to the pharaoh: "To the scribe ... Present eloquent words to the king."[935]

Kudurru (boundary stone) of King Marduk-apla-iddina II (Merodach Baladan)
Bildarchiv Preussischer Kulturbesitz/Art Resource, NY, courtesy of the Vorderasiatisches Museum, Staatliche Museen zu Berlin, Berlin, Germany

Exchange of gifts was a common practice among leaders, leading to a chain of counter-gifts and accusations if appropriate gifts were not forthcoming.[936] The practice continued, since Osorkon IV (Shilkanni) sent gifts to Sargon in 716 B.C.[937] To gain the favor of the king of Elam, Merodach-Baladan sent him gifts,[938] a similar motive for his contacts with Hezekiah.

Currying favor with Babylon is a mistake, according to Isaiah (39:6–7). Esarhaddon, in a building inscription to vindicate the reputation of his father who destroyed Babylon,

▸ Military vs. Diplomacy

International relations were realized through several means. (1) The most common for Israel was military contact, since Israel sat between the Mesopotamian and Egyptian empires, experiencing incursions as they campaigned through the region. Israel's neighbors were also part of the military threat to her during this period (see Isa. 7). In this case, power is the means by which international relations were wielded.[A-188]

(2) Diplomacy is a means of noncoercive cooperation. Pursued through intermediaries, ambassadors, or messengers, nations and rulers sought to win their cause through persuasion rather than through direct power. The Amarna letters between Canaanite city-state rulers and Egypt show the attempt by the former to woo the latter to address their plight, which might in turn involve Egyptian military intervention.[A-189]

Diplomacy is also evident in the various treaty documents between states. While earlier relationships between the parties may have been military, diplomacy was the preferred method of interaction.[A-190] The cult also at times furthered diplomatic contact, as in cases where rulers, in the name of providing service to deities, involved themselves in reconstruction and provision projects, not only of temples in their own territories, but also of those of other rulers.[A-191]

(3) Diplomacy at times included the exchange of goods in the form of diplomatic gift-giving (see comments on 1:23; 18:7; 39:1).[A-192] This is not far removed from the third means of international relations, commercial trade. Relative scarcity of important or valuable commodities in some areas and their availability in others drove their exchange. While on the national level, this could have precipitated military or diplomatic activity,[A-193] it often flourished at a subnational level of individual merchants driven by economic motives.[A-194] Trade flourished during most periods, joining Mesopotamia, Anatolia, Syria-Palestine, Egypt, and beyond.[A-195]

Isaiah 39 is an example of diplomatic contact between two powers. It exemplifies the overlap between the three areas discussed, since this is in the context of military alliances, ultimately resulting in Israel's annexation by the very nation here using diplomacy.

Eunuch on Neo-Assyrian relief
Marie-Lan Nguyen/Wikimedia Commons, courtesy of the Louvre

placed the blame for this on the god Marduk himself. He is said to have blamed his people from turning elsewhere than to him for aid: "The people who lived there … forsook their gods, they abandoned the worship of their goddesses.… The silver, gold and precious stones they squandered on Elam as payment for support."[939]

Received the envoys gladly (39:2). Joy at receiving good messages, in this case with gifts, is known also from Ugarit. When Athirat finally won permission from Il that Baal may have the palace he so desired, she delivered the message to him, and "mighty Baal rejoiced."[940] In turn, upon hearing the message that Baal will submit to him, "Mot, son of Il, rejoiced."[941]

Eunuchs (39:7). See 56:3–5. Some eunuchs occupied important bureaucratic positions in Assyria and Babylonia (Dan. 1:3, *sarîs*, equivalent to Akkadian *ša rēši*).[942] The important role of harem attendant, based on their neutered state, could have

▸ Road Building

Transportation and travel, especially by cart and chariot, needed relatively smooth roads.[A-196] In Nuzi texts, these are specifically called "wagon roads."[A-197] In the Gilgamesh Epic, Humbaba takes a path because "the paths were prepared, the road was good."[A-198] Few roads, except in towns, were paved.[A-199] A letter from Mari states that because of difficulty in travel on one road (or perhaps the road fee), "we will [instead] travel the road through the hinterland."[A-200]

Tiglath-pileser I wrote, "I improved the road for the passage of my heavy vehicles and my army."[A-201] Shalmaneser III describes part of a military campaign in which "I smashed out with copper picks rough paths in mighty mountains.... I moved chariots (and) troops over (those paths)."[A-202] Part of his self-laudatory introduction is that he is one "who opens paths above and below."[A-203] The well-prepared road here resembles the "king's highway" in various Akkadian texts from this period,[A-204] including preparing a "fair path" for a king's military advance.[A-205]

The Romans were not the first to value durable and smooth roads. This Roman road near Aleppo was built over the main international highway that ran through here for millennia.
Yasmin Bochi

led to other responsible positions, where physical castration might not have been necessary. They served in military and palace administrative roles, as well as being scribes and musicians.[943] Tiglath-pileser III appointed one as governor over Babylonia.[944] They are pictured as clean-shaven on Assyrian reliefs and seals.[945] From the context, this potential future is not desirable for Hezekiah's sons.

Yahweh Returns to Jerusalem (40)

Received ... double for all her sins (40:2). Multifold restitution is a strong deterrent from wrongdoing. One of Hammurabi's laws against theft states: "If a man stole either an ox, sheep, donkey, pig or wooden boat, if it was either divine or royal property, he shall pay thirtyfold. If it belongs to a poor man, he shall replace tenfold."[946] In the

Weighing tribute from obelisk from Nimrud, Ashurnasirpal II
Z. Radovan/www.BibleLand Pictures.com

Hittite plague prayer of Murshili, the king prays to avert a devastating, long-lasting plague that he suspects was caused by sin. He states that "Hattusha has made restitution through the plague ... twenty-fold."[947] Israel is getting off relatively lightly.

Every mountain and hill made low (40:4). A Hittite ritual prayer uses the same terminology when describing coming deities: "Let the mountains be leveled before you (O gods)!" An incantation to a goddess reads: "Before you let the valleys be leveled! Let the mountains betake themselves down to the vegetation!"[948]

Glory of the LORD (40:5). See comments on 2:10; 11:2; 35:2.

All men are like grass (40:6–7). On human mortality, see comments on 5:25; 26:19; 28:14; 38:10; 57:1; see sidebar on "Sheol and the Afterlife" at 14:9–11.

The word of our God stands forever (40:8). Unlike fickle humans, it is important that words spoken by the divine are unchanging. For Isaiah, this provides comfort, perhaps referring to God's word spoken at creation or to his promises of deliverance. The Lament over the Destruction of Sumer and Ur records that a city's decreed fate cannot even be altered by prayer, since "An is never to change his word, Enlil is never to alter the word he utters."[949]

Cylinder seal depicting shepherd with musical instrument leading sheep from pen
Werner Forman Archive/The British Museum

Theologically this seems to contrast a divine plan, with several options of how it might be fulfilled, and a divine decree, which is more univocal. This could also contrast the unalterable benevolence of Israel's God with the inability of Mesopotamian gods to exhibit grace once judgment has been proclaimed.

Bring good tidings ... with a shout (40:9). The good news bearer is feminine in Hebrew, like Anat, who brings good news to Baal in the Ugaritic Baal myth. She shouts: "You have good news, Baal. I bring you good news."[950] His long-awaited house may be built just as these long-exiled folks will be restored.

While messengers were generally men,[951] female messengers ("a daughter of the message") were also used in Mesopotamia.[952] Joy at the receipt of good news, shown here by the shout, is evident elsewhere. From an El-Amarna letter: "And when I heard the words of the king, my lord, when he wrote to his servant, then my heart rejoiced, and my head went high, and my eyes shone, at hearing the words of the king, my lord."[953]

Reward ... recompense (40:10). "Reward" elsewhere parallels booty (Ezek. 29:18–19). There Babylon is taking such from a captured Egypt; but here the tables are reversed, for captive Judah will be released, taking booty of her own. Recompense denotes results from doing some kind of action, as seen from the Aramaic text from Deir ʿAlla, where the same root is used to describe "the acts of the gods."[954]

Shepherd (40:11). Both rulers and deities were described as shepherds of their people in a rich and extensively used metaphor.[955] The early Egyptian prophecy of Ipuwer designates pharaoh as a "herdsman,"[956] and the Sumerian king Shulgi (2094–2047 B.C.) speaks of the god Enlil being a shepherd, who also appoints Shulgi himself to be one.[957] A Neo-Assyrian text describes a Kassite king as a "strong shepherd,"[958] while, much closer in time to Isaiah, Shalmaneser III, in the self-laudatory introduction on some of his inscriptions, designated himself as "faithful shepherd who leads in peace the population of Assyria."[959] The metaphor emphasizes powerful guardianship exercised with gentle care.

Measured the waters in the hollow of his hand (40:12). In the Akkadian creation epic *Enuma Elish*, Marduk, after defeating the salt-water goddess, Tiamat, also looks after the fresh-water god, Apsu: "As the lord measured the dimensions of Apsu."[960] He is praised in the Akkadian New Year's festival account as one "who measures the sea's waters,"[961] where also the Dog-Star, Sirius, is one "who measures the waters of the sea."[962]

Weighed the mountains on the scales and the hills in a balance (40:12). In the Egyptian tomb of Ay, a hymn speaks of "the itemization and counting of the mountains, weighed with the balance."[963] Balance scales had two metal pans suspended from a central beam to weigh something against an object of known weight.[964] Using such an instrument on these major elements of the earth shows the power and control of the deity over them. In the Babylonian New Year's festival, Marduk is described as one who "stretches out the heavens, piles up the earth, measures the sea's waters."[965]

Whom did the LORD consult? (40:13–14). The rhetorical questions in these verses are asked in such a way as to indicate that Yahweh acted alone in creation; he had no need for any outside consultants.[966] A Sumerian poem speaks similarly of Enlil, who "makes decisions himself . . . no god looks on."[967]

Usually, however, divine decisions were made in consultation with others in the divine council. This could be an individual, such as Apsu's vizier Mummu, who advised concerning noisy junior gods: "Put an end here and now, father, to their troublesome ways!"[968] It could be a group, such as Tiamat's divine schemers "convening and assembly, that they might cause hostilities."[969] Sometimes it is gods, such as those assembling to appoint Marduk as their champion and leader: "If indeed I am to champion you, subdue Tiamat and save your lives, convene the assembly, nominate me for supreme destiny! Take your place in the Assembly Place of the Gods."[970]

Right way (40:14). The Hebrew term *mišpāt* occurs most frequently with either a forensic ("judge, judgment") or procedural ("prescribed way") meaning. Here it moves beyond the realm of the court or the tabernacle courtyard to a wider understanding of "the way things are or should be," a connotation of worldview. In the Baal Epic, a goddess is told, speaking of the chief god El, "Surely he will pull up [the foundations of your] (royal) seat, overturn [the throne of] your kingship, break the staff of your rule (*thpt*, cognate with the Hebrew term)."[971] The whole order of rule is jeopardized.

A suggested semantic parallel in Akkadian involves a different verb (*šutēšuru*) concerning the right working in good order of things ranging from weaponry to ritual song.[972] Isaiah looks beyond a God who needs no advice in legal procedure to one who needs none in the entire structuring of how the universe should work.

As for an idol (40:18–19). Cultic statues were made from stone, metal, or wood (see comment on 2:8).[973] An Akkadian text describes the New Year festival at Babylon, which includes constructing several idols.

Ordering the Cosmos

The universe was not understood in the ancient Near East as random, but rather as organized and structured. The Sumerians developed the concept of the ME, a divine ordering of cosmic and cultural entities that led them perpetually to function according as their design.[A-206] Stored by Enki, the god of wisdom, in his temple in Eridu, the love goddess Inanna attempts to usurp them for herself through trickery. In Inanna and Enki, the list of ME is broken, but 94 remain. These include:

> Godship, the mighty legitimate crown, the throne of kingship ... shepherdship ... truth ... descending into the Netherworld ... sword and club ... love making, kissing, prostitution ... speech, slander ... the art of singing, the (wise) state of old age, heroism, possession of power, dishonesty, righteousness, plundering of cities, singing of lamentations, rejoicing, deceit ... the craft of the carpenter, coppersmith, scribe, smith, leather-worker, fuller, builder, mat weaver, understanding, knowledge ... triumph, counseling, deliberation, jurisdiction, decision-making.[A-207]

These are presented as being the way the universe works, without any moral judgments laid, since the gods themselves partook in activities from both the moral and immoral ends of the spectrum.

In Egypt, a similar concept was the *maʿat*, personified as a goddess with the same name, who is depicted wearing an ostrich feather in her crown.[A-208] Upon death, the heart of the deceased is placed on a balance against this feather, representing truth and the world order, so to judge the life of the departed; those not found fit are devoured, while those conforming to *maʿat* move on into the afterlife.[A-209]

In an Egyptian tomb text from a vizier under Thutmose III, the pharaoh

A relief from the mastaba of Niankhkhnum and Khnumhotep. The top register depicts two sculptors working on a statue. The lower shows metalworkers.
Werner Forman Archive

> Three hours after sun-up [he shall summon] a metalworker and he shall give him high quality stones and gold from Marduk's property in order to make two images. He summons a carpenter, giving him cedar and tamarisk wood. He summons a goldsmith, giving him gold.... The images, their height is seven fingers. One is of cedar and one of tamarisk. Their pedestal is a shekel of gold.... They wear red cloth.[974]

The dais or pedestal firmly holds the idol so it will not "topple." A text of Adad-Nirari I (early thirteenth century B.C.) describes a chapel "within which the dais of the god Ashur, my lord, was built and annually the god Ashur, my lord, proceeds to that dais to take up residence."[975] The tools

Maʿat stands to the right of the scales in the weighing of the heart judgment scene from the Book of the Dead.
Werner Forman Archive/E. Strouhal, Egyptian Museum, Turin

hopes that everything might be carried out according his goodwill, since "then Maat will rest in her place,"[A-210] with everything done decently and in order. Chapter 125 of the Book of the Dead contains the Negative Confession, where the writer disavows forty-two evil acts upon entering the presence of *Maʿat*: "I have not done crimes against people, mistreated cattle ... caused pain ... killed ... copulated nor defiled myself, ... taken milk from the mouth of children ... I am pure!"[A-211] Here the expectations are more morally positive than in Mesopotamia, more aligned with the "right way" envisioned by Isaiah.

of the artisans are ritually disposed of, and their hands are symbolically removed while they state that the image was in fact of divine rather than human origin.[976]

Craftsman casts it (40:19). Some metal idols were made by melting the metal and pouring it into a mold.[977] This used the lost wax process, where a figure would be designed from wax and covered with clay, which was then baked. This process melted the wax, which was then replaced by the molten metal that, when hardened, was revealed by breaking off the surrounding clay.[978]

An idol that will not topple (40:20). A fallen representation of a god shows its lack of power and is humiliating both to it and its worshipers. It would be held in place on its base by a metal peg remaining from the casting process. A third-century Aramaic text from Syene speaks of invaders throwing down and trampling various deities.[979] In contrast, an Egyptian ritual speaks of gods who are "firm on their seats."[980]

He sits enthroned above the circle of the earth (40:22). See 6:1. The common ancient Near Eastern perspective was of the heavens like an inverted bowl covering

Modern artistic reconstruction of an ancient Israelite view of the cosmos. The sky, supported by mountains at the edges, holds back the waters above as it arches over the flat, disk-shaped earth which is upheld by pillars. Numerous graves lead to the netherworld, Sheol, and the cosmos waters surround the earth on the horizontal plane, as well as the entire cosmos on the vertical plane. Lurking in the depths is mighty Leviathan (here more in Medieval design). The temple on earth is matched by the temple in heaven, the dwelling place of God. The skies are inhabited by birds as well as celestial bodies and rain is let through windows of heaven. Stars are engraved on the underside of the sky.
John H. Walton, drawing by Alva Steffler

the earth, itself above the primeval waters, which surmounted the underworld.[981] From the perspective of the eye looking at the curving horizon, the ancients viewed the earth as a circle. A late Babylonian map of the world shows a circular earth with its center in Babylon,[982] while a fourth-century Egyptian sarcophagus relief shows a circular earth enclosing a circular underworld and itself surrounded by the circular sea.[983]

The Shamash Hymn refers to "the circle of the lands you suspend in the midst of the heavens."[984] In the Erra and Ishum epic Shamash is also credited as being the one who "can see the rim of everything,"[985] seeing to the circle of the world's edge. Ramesses III, in his description of his war against the Sea People, describes their encroachment as laying "their hands on the lands as far as the circuit of the earth."[986]

He stretches out the heavens (40:22). This describes an aspect of creation found also among Israel's neighbors. An Aramaic text in Demotic script from the third century B.C. is a ritual of service to numerous gods, the chief of which is called Mar, "Lord." He is called to return, as "you stretched out the heavens, Mar, you set the stars in place."[987] This, like the Isaiah passage, celebrates the divine work of creation.

He ... brings out the starry host ... and calls them each by name (40:26). In *Enuma Elish*, it is said of Marduk: "He made positions for the great gods, he established in constellations the stars, their likenesses. He marked the year, describing its boundaries; he set up twelve months of three stars each."[988] Interest here lies in the stars as seasonal markers (see Gen. 1:16–18) rather than as independent objects.

Mesopotamians, through their interest in omens, developed a sophisticated understanding of lunar, solar, and astral cycles, including such things as eclipses, in lengthy tablet collections.[989] Stars and planets were seen to rise according to three different "paths" along which celestial bodies rose and set.[990] From the fifth century Aramaic

Words of Ahiqar found at Elephantine in Egypt comes a statement contrasting to this: "Many are the stars of heaven whose name a man does not know."[991]

He will not grow tired or weary, and his understanding no one can fathom (40:28). While Israel's God is portrayed as powerful and independent, their neighbors' gods are not always so, but rather are at times weak and dependent, even on humanity. In the Akkadian fable of the Tamarisk and the Palm, there is mention that "the gods became tired"[992] (but in a broken context where the exact significance is unclear). In the Erra epic, the warrior god Erra is called out to battle, but "Erra himself felt as weak as a man short of sleep."[993]

In the Gilgamesh Epic, the gods gather around Utnapishtim's sacrifice "like flies" because the destruction they had wrought left them without either food or drink.[994] In Egyptian and Mesopotamian texts, several gods are associated with wisdom, such as Bel, Ea/Enki, Ishtar, Marduk, Nabu, Thot, though none is beyond the ken of any other.[995]

Creator of the ends of the earth (40:28). The title for a god as creator is well-attested in the ancient Near East, reflecting a commonly understood divine undertaking. The Hebrew Jerusalem ostracon speaks of one who is "creator of the earth,"[996] but a break precludes knowing to whom it refers. The three visible names with Yahweh as one element could allow it to refer to him. Other Northwest Semitic texts refer to the god El with this epithet.[997]

In a Hittite myth, one of the protagonists is named Elkunirsha,[998] a derivation from the West Semitic "God (*el*) creates (*qnh*) the earth (*ʾrṣ*)."[999] Thutmoses III recorded in his military annals that "from Iursa to the outer ends of the earth had become rebellious against his majesty."[1000] Mesopotamian kings regularly described their rule as extending "to the four quarters/edges of the world"[1001] (see comments on 11:12).

God's Accusations (41:1–29)

One from the east (41:2). This must refer to Cyrus II, ruler of the Medes and Persians (see 44:28), the one who, in opposing Babylon, assists Israel.[1002]

He turns them ... to windblown chaff (41:2). During the threshing process of grain, the nutritious kernel was separated from the worthless chaff (33:11) by the wind (40:24). Since grain was so commonly raised in the region, this metaphor for something transitory came easily to mind. A Mesopotamian incantation against a headache wishes: "Like the chaff that the wind sweeps away, may it not come back."[1003] The insignificance of chaff highlights the note in the Kadesh battle inscription of Ramesses II: "He heeded not the foreign multitude; he regarded them as chaff."[1004]

Calling forth the generations from the beginning (41:4). God acts by guiding history from its beginning through its end. Occurring in cycles of good and ill, faith and apostasy (e.g., Judg. 2:10–19), for the ancients the past in some ways prefigured the future.[1005] Mesopotamian omen texts share somewhat in this view of history (see 8:18, 22). Another more closely related genre is the fictional Akkadian autobiography, some

Winnowing
Rob George

of which contain prophetic elements based on prior history.[1006]

Islands ... ends of the earth (41:5). Islands, possibly referring to Tyre (see 23:2, 6), or "coastlands" (see 20:6) indicate the Philistine and Phoenician territory to Israel's west and north. Those at the ends of the earth are those lying in the hinterlands to the north and east. A similar usage lauds the extensive power of the Sixth Dynasty Pepi I, as noted on his sarcophagus: "O Osiris Pepi, you are great and round like the ring that circles the islands," apparently referring to those in the Aegean.[1007] Piye, a pharaoh contemporary with Isaiah, on a victory stele speaks of far-flung places in a similar vein: "The west, the east, and the islands in the midst are in fear of him."[1008]

Nails down the idol (41:6–7). See comments on 40:18–19.

My friend (41:8). This phrase (lit., "my beloved") is used to describe numerous Mesopotamian rulers in relation to a deity. It was the name of several, including a ruler from the Dynasty of Akkad, Narām-Sin, "the beloved of the moon god,"[1009] and is part of the title and description of many others,[1010] including private individuals.[1011]

I ... have not rejected you (41:9). Abandonment by one's gods was a fearful prospect, since one was dependent for help, protection, and life itself upon one's personal god. A frightening possibility is found in a Babylonian extispicy text: "The prince's gods will abandon him."[1012] In contrast, Ishtar of Arbela, in an oracle to Esarhaddon, urges him not to give up hope because "I have not abandoned you."[1013] Yahweh's relationship with his people, stated in covenant terms, was different in that he could not abandon his promised relationship. While individuals or even a generation could experience separation from God as punishment, his covenant promise kept the relationship sure.

Hittite god Sharruma protecting King Tudhaliya IV with arm around him and holding him by the wrist to guide him
M. Willis Monroe

Do not fear (41:10). A similar word of encouragement is given several times to Esarhaddon from the goddess Ishtar of Arbela, and to Ashurbanipal by Ishtar and Ninurta, "Don't be afraid!"[1014] Naram-Sin similarly exhorted the readers of his stele not to fear.[1015] Such cases, like that of Isaiah, promise divine intervention on behalf of someone in trouble.

My righteous right hand (41:10). See comment on 9:12, 17, 21. Being the dominant hand, the right had special significance. In the Seleucid period, a property mark was inscribed on a slave's right hand.[1016] In an Egyptian Aramaic liturgical text, the chief god, Mar, says: "Be strong ...

your enemies I will destroy ... I shall support your right hand,"[1017] apparently the hand used in battle. Gods and other people took one's hand in order to assist them. "When my lord the king took my hands, he brought me back to life."[1018] In an early second millennium Babylonian seal, a minor deity takes with his right hand the hand of a supplicant, leading him before a major god.[1019]

Will be as nothing at all (41:12). Prophetic messages such as these were also received among Israel's neighbors. They included anticipations of both weal, as here, and woe. An undated Akkadian text anticipates both: "[A ruler will come] and reign 18 years. The land will live in safety and flourish and the people [will have] abundance.... A ruler will arise and rule for 13 years. There will be confusion, disturbance, and unhappy events in the land."[1020] From nineteenth-century Mari on the Euphrates, a letter to King Zimri-Lim states: "Although you neglect me, I will continue to love you. I will give your enemies into your hand."[1021] Most prophecies from Mari were self-serving pleas to renew provision for various temples.

I am the LORD (41:13). A prophetic letter to Ashurbanipal begins, "I am the lord (Bel)."[1022] The deity referred to is Marduk, whom the Assyrians considered as a personification of their chief god, Ashur, who brings peace and a release from fear.[1023] A similar call to cease worry was given in letters to his father, Esarhaddon: "I am Ishtar of Arbela."[1024] The depth of care for the king indicated here is shown when Ishtar also says, "I am your father and mother. Between my wings I brought you up."[1025]

Former things ... final outcome (41:22). Mesopotamia used similar terms for the past ("formerly, before") and future ("that which is behind, comes after"), showing the future in relation to what had already taken place.[1026] In a sense, history was cyclical, with what happened reappearing again, as seen by analogy in seasons or successive human generations. A god encouraged Esarhaddon in an oracle: "[Like a] skilled pilot [I will ste]er [the ship] into a good port. [The fu]ture [shall] be like the past; [I will go] around you and protect you."[1027]

He treads on rulers as if they were mortar, as if he were a potter treading the clay (41:25). This metaphor shows how malleable building materials were worked prior to use. These are worked with the feet for consistency and mixed in additives such as straw.[1028] These two terms indicate various types of clay.[1029] A Mesopotamian creation myth (see 42:5) gathers goddesses "to tread upon the clay," preparing it for creating humans.[1030]

Good tidings (41:27). See comment on 40:9.

Yahweh Works through His Servant, Blind and Deaf Israel (42:1–25)

My chosen one in whom I delight (42:1). Divine selection is significant in the ancient world. Akkadian texts from the first millennium also refer to those "chosen/selected by god X."[1031] It has the connotation of election, selecting from among others for a special purpose. The specific purpose of election is not specified, but the context of royal identifications suggests this is a claim to divine enthronement. For Isaiah, the election is national, with a servant rather than a king bringing about justice and righteousness.

A bruised reed he will not break (42:3). An Akkadian metaphor provides a contrast to that used here. Esarhaddon brags that "with the trustworthy support of Ashur, Shamash, Nabu and Marduk ... all those not subservient to him, kings not subservient to him, he snapped like a marsh-reed, he subdued them under his feet."[1032] Such harshness of Assyrian practice on the frail will not be evident with the servant of Yahweh.

Smoldering wick (42:3). The wick is literally flax, from whose broken fibers a wick is made.[1033] These fibers were braided together into a string or cord that trailed

Creator Gods

There is no unified view of the relationship between deity and creation in cultures of the ancient world, or even within a single geographic area.[A-212] Egypt, for example, had numerous political and religious centers over its long history, each with its own traditions. Some of its traditions linked creation with a single deity. In a hymn written in the New Kingdom to Aten, the sun god represented by the solar disk, he is praised: "Splendid you rise in heaven's lightland, O living Aten, creator of life,"[A-213] though no creative means are given.

Elephantine was the cultic center for Khnum who, in a hymn from the Roman period, is "God of the potter's wheel ... he has fashioned (from clay) gods and men, he has formed flocks and herds, he made birds as well as fishes, he created bulls, engendered cows."[A-214] The Memphite Theology, likely from the nineteenth Dynasty, states: "Great and important is Ptah, who gave life to all the [gods] ... through this heart and through this tongue."[A-215] He first conceptualized in his heart and then spoke into being through his tongue, not only the gods, but "every body and every mouth—of all the gods, all people, all animals, and all crawling things that live—planning and governing everything he wishes."

This is considered by those of Memphis as a vastly superior means of creation than the physical means used by Atum and Ra.[A-216] In their cases, creation is by sexual means, through masturbation. The sun god Ra states: "I copulated with my own fist, I masturbated with my own hand, I ejaculated into my own mouth. I exhaled Shu the wind, I spat Tefnut the rain."[A-217] The latter two

The Shabako stone is inscribed with the creation myth known as the Memphite Theology. Its poor condition results from the fact that it was used for a grinding stone. Lenka Peacock, courtesy of the British Museum

Detail from the painted sarcophagus of Butehamun from the Twenty-first Dynasty showing creation as a sexual act between the sky goddess Nut, and Geb, god of the earth
Werner Forman Archive/Museo Egizio, Turin, Italy

then procreated through regular sexual means, producing Geb (the earth) and Nu (the sky), who themselves then reproduced sexually, with Geb's virility clearly evident in some artistic renditions.[A-218]

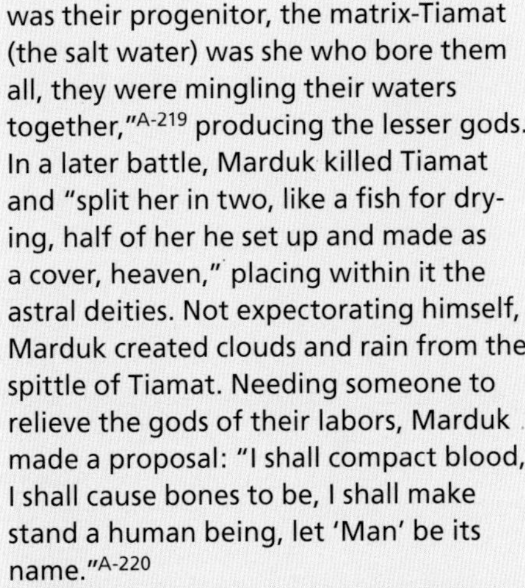

Sexual reproduction is also assumed, though not stated, in the Mesopotamian *Enuma Elish* epic: "Primeval Apsu (the fresh water) was their progenitor, the matrix-Tiamat (the salt water) was she who bore them all, they were mingling their waters together,"[A-219] producing the lesser gods. In a later battle, Marduk killed Tiamat and "split her in two, like a fish for drying, half of her he set up and made as a cover, heaven," placing within it the astral deities. Not expectorating himself, Marduk created clouds and rain from the spittle of Tiamat. Needing someone to relieve the gods of their labors, Marduk made a proposal: "I shall compact blood, I shall cause bones to be, I shall make stand a human being, let 'Man' be its name."[A-220]

Other means of creation are also known in Mesopotamia. In the Sumerian Song of the Hoe, Enlil "will make the seed of mankind rise from the ground.... Here, 'where the flesh sprouts,' he set his very hoe to work: he had it place the first model of mankind in the brickmold. And (according to this model) his people started to break through the soil."[A-221] An Old Babylonian text requests that "one god be slain, and let the gods be purified by immersion in his flesh and blood. Let Nintu (the mother goddess) mix clay, god and man, let them together be smeared with clay."[A-222]

Canaanite texts from Ugarit have not yielded a creation account per se, though Athirat is called "Progenitrix of the gods," and El is called "Creator of creatures,"[A-223] being mother and father deities respectively.

Isaiah highlights the person of the Creator and the purpose of the creation of his people rather than the means by which creation comes about or any stuff from which it is made. He is pictured as creating from without rather than within the creation itself.[A-224] While he is the key actor, the purpose of the account is ministry to creation rather than either the self-aggrandizement of the Creator or the service of him, as found in several neighboring creation accounts.

Election represented in the Egyptian gods participating in the coronation of Ramesses II
Manfred Näder, Gabana Studios, Germany

from the oil to the edge of the lamp, moving the oil to the lit end through osmosis. Since their purpose is to produce light, one that is smoldering is ordinarily quickly removed, discarded, and replaced, but not under the care of this gentle ruler.

This is what God the LORD says (42:5). See comments on 6:9 regarding his messengers.

Called you in righteousness (42:6). Righteousness or justice is to be a mark of one close to God, especially a ruler. In Akkadian, the corresponding term, *kīnu*, "reliable, righteous," also has the connotation of legitimacy, one with a right to position.[1034] Used as a royal name (Sargon = *Šarru-kīn*, "legitimate/righteous king"; so also Melchizedek, Gen. 14:18), it is also a description of Sargon II.[1035]

I will take hold of your hand (42:6). See comments on 40:10, 13.

I will keep you (42:6). Wishes for well-being are common blessings, especially at the beginning of letters. In a Canaanite letter between members of the royal family, a son writes to his mother using the traditional greeting: "May it be well with you. May the gods of Ugarit guard you, may they keep you well."[1036] Akkadian texts used a similar blessing.[1037] For Israel, this wish is being fulfilled.

Blind ... prison ... dungeon ... darkness (42:7). The chiastic literary structure points to the blinding darkness of imprisonment being eradicated. Sargon wrote: "Citizens of Sippar, Nippur, Babylon, and Borsippa, who, without their consent were detained in it [the captured city of Dur-Yakin], I destroyed their prison and I exposed them to light (i.e., I showed them the light of day by freeing them from captivity)."[1038] Marduk is praised: "The one thrown into prison you showed the light (of freedom)."[1039]

Prison (42:7). While prisoners, especially those captives taken in battle, are commonly mentioned in texts and depicted on reliefs, actual prisons are rarely encountered in Israel itself, though known among its neighbors. In Mesopotamia, only political crimes merited imprisonment by the state. Other wrongs were between citizens and thus civil cases, and any penalties were by means of financial payment or physical punishment.[1040] Some might also have been

Nungal Hymn
Kim Walton, courtesy of the Oriental Institute Museum

tection of family or citizenship who, in this enlightened period, will find family, citizenship, and freedom among God's people.

Free captives ... release (42:7). When captivity can take many forms (physical, social, or economic), freedom through release from such captivity is a valuable commodity. Physical release from prison is valued on a national rather than simply an individual scale. Marduk is praised since "you liberate him who was thrown into prison,"[1048] while the Egyptian document Instructions of Ankhsheshonq speaks of the way a new pharaoh tried to win the hearts of the people. "After this there occurred the accession-day of Pharaoh. Pharaoh released everyone who was in the prisons."[1049]

Manumission, or release from slavery (called in Akkadian *andurārum*) was possible during some periods for those who found themselves in this state temporarily because of economic hardship, having lost control over any means of production, such as their family fields. They or their family could become indentured servants (see 50:1).[1050] Manumission was regulated by law very early, as noted in this statement about King Urukagina from Lagash (2250 B.C.):[1051] "He cleared and cancelled obligations for those indentured families, citizens of Lagash living as debtors because of grain taxes, barley payments, theft or murder."[1052] One of Hammurabi's laws states that a debt slave and his family should work for three years, but "in the fourth year their release shall be arranged."[1053] It is not clear that the practice was widely done.[1054]

There were also financial obligations on people from commercial activities or in the form of taxes payable to the state or the temple. These could also be waived or remitted, using the same Akkadian term *andurārum* or others.[1055] Several Mesopotamian rulers mention among their feats being an "establisher of freedom."[1056] Up to the Old Babylonian period there were several *mēšarum*

imprisoned for debt (see comment on 42:7), but these would more likely be enslaved, allowing them to pay off their obligations.

Since punishment was more closely related to the crimes committed and were handled quickly, there was less need for places of confinement than in the contemporary West.[1041] One such was called the "house of confinement" (cognate with "prison" in 2 Kings 25:27).[1042] Marduk, after defeating Tiamat, took her allies: "They were bearing his punishment, to prison confined."[1043] The Sumerian Nungal Hymn describes a prison, with a female jailer, for holding those awaiting trial by the river ordeal.[1044]

In Egypt, prison does not seem to be the regular practice (see Gen. 39:20). A Middle Egyptian tale of a magician named Djedi states: ""Have brought to me a prisoner from the prison, that he be executed." Said Djedi: "But not to a human being, O king, my lord! Surely, it is not permitted to do such a thing."[1045] A later text (The Instruction of Papyrus Insinger) instructs: "The fool who has no protection sleeps in prison."[1046] A Hebrew seal reads "Belonging to Azariah, porter (2 Kings 7:10) of the prison."[1047]

Those being released here are not the violent felons found in contemporary prisons, since they would have been punished in other ways. These are those without pro-

God as a Warrior

Divine warriors are ubiquitous in the ancient Near East. The very creation of the world, according to the *Enuma Elish* account, is a result of battle between Marduk and Tiamat.[A-225] The Mesopotamian goddess Ishtar is known as "the one who wields weapons, the one who causes battle,"[A-226] and the god Nergal (2 Kings 17:30) is "the lord of weapons."[A-227] Nergal, or his Syrian equivalent Resheph, is mentioned in an Amarna letter that complains about the loss of copper workers, caused because "the hand of Nergal (or Resheph) is now in my country; he has slain all the men of my country."[A-228] Resheph is depicted holding a club in his upraised hand,[A-229] as is the Canaanite god Baal.

In the Baal epic, Baal battles Yam, the sea, with the use of two maces.[A-230] In the same Baal account, the goddess Anat, Baal's lover, is also a bloodthirsty warrior: "She attaches heads around her neck, ties hands to her waist. Up to her knees she wades in the blood of soldiers."[A-231] She is also found among the Egyptian pantheon, especially during the Nineteenth Dynasty, where she is shown holding shield and spear.[A-232]

While battle is not Yahweh's chief occupation, he does involve himself in it on behalf of his people.[A-233] In societies such as those of Israel and her neighbors, which were regularly under military threat, having a divine battle champion was psychologically and theologically important.

Ninth century relief found in Nimrud shows Ninurta as warrior god fighting a monster. Photo by Mark Borisuk/www.BiblePlaces.com. Sketch from Wikimedia Commons ("justice") edicts that, among other things, freed citizens from various debts.[1057]

I am the Lord (42:8). See comment on 41:13.

The former things have taken place, and new things I declare (42:9). Among Israel's neighbors, the past was predictive of the future in the form of omens and divination (see sidebar on "Superstitions and Divination" at 2:6; see also 7:11–14; 8:18). Rather than actual predictions of an unknown future, these prognostications were based on an understanding that the past would repeat itself.

There is indication that the gods were considered to know the future to some extent: "O Ashur, you know from the beginning to the end."[1058] A hymn to Shamash also indicates that the future of humanity is established by the gods: "Shamash ... you determine their future to the four winds,"[1059] that is, to the edges of the earth. Fate or destiny is in their hands, as in an epithet for Ea, Shamash, and Asaluhhi: "determiners of the order of things, planners of the way things work, assigners of destinies."[1060] While the gods seek to control the future, they do not choose to share it with humanity. This is in stark contrast with Isaiah's God, who does not act in secret but openly reveals his plans through his prophets.

Desert and its towns (42:11). The Arabian peninsula to the west of Mesopotamia was desert, as was the Negev in southern Judah, though both had some towns (e.g., Josh. 15:21–32). Nabonidus records a military campaign he took: "The Akkadian forces marched with him; he turned toward Tema in the west."[1061] Tema (see 21:14) was an oasis in northern Arabia (Job 6:19; Jer. 25:23).[1062]

Sela (42:11). See comment on 16:1. Associated here with mountaintops, this may refer to the Edomite Sela, known elsewhere in the Old Testament (Obad. 1, 3).[1063]

Servant of the Lord (42:19). To indicate the proper respect toward a superior, letter senders identified themselves as "your servant" in their relation with the recipient.[1064] Other texts use the term in a person's relation to a superior such as a king.[1065] "Servant of god X" is also common in the ancient Near East.[1066] A Northwest Semitic seal reads "Belonging to Mikneiah,[1067] servant of Yahweh."[1068] So far this mention of Yahweh in such a context outside the Old Testament is unique.

God the Merciful Creator (43:1–14)

He who formed you (43:1). See comment on 42:5. The verb connotes working and forming like a potter does the clay (e.g., Gen. 2:7). A Twelfth Dynasty stele of a royal treasurer of Egypt says that "he is the Khnum of everybody, begetter who makes mankind,"[1069] and the situation is so bad in the Admonitions of Ipuwer that "women are barren, none conceive, Khnum does not fashion because of the state of the land."[1070] In the Instructions of Amenemope, Khnum is called "The Potter"[1071] since he forms

Sela mountaintop
Todd Bolen/www.BiblePlaces.com

Oracles of Consolation and Hope

Israel needed hope following destruction and exile after God abandoned Zion as a result of Israel's sins (1:7–8). Likewise, Babylonia needed encouragement after Marduk departed from Esagila, his temple in Babylon,[A-234] when Assyria captured it under Sennacherib.[A-235] This loss was possibly due to the previous "Sin of Sargon."[A-236] It was his son, Esarhaddon, whose policy it was to restore the Babylonian capital, including the statues of the gods, under his own Assyrian control, uniting the two nations.[A-237] This is indicated by the statement that "Marduk, the king of the gods, is at peace with the king my lord,"[A-238] since his status was restored. Because the god's throne is secure, so is that of the king, and so hope is restored.

everyone on his wheel.[1072] He is depicted on a relief from Luxor fashioning Amenhotep III on a potter's wheel.[1073]

The *Enuma Elish* story speaks of "the black-headed people (i.e., humanity) whom his (Marduk's) hands have created,"[1074] a term used elsewhere of making figurines from metal or stone.[1075] Isaiah's concept moves beyond physical craftsmanship to an intimacy of relationship. Humanity is not simply formed and used, but made and cherished.

Khnum forming human on potter's wheel
Brian J. McMorrow

Fear not (43:1). See comment on 41:10.

I have summoned you by name (43:1). In Mesopotamia, from the early Dynastic to the Neo-Babylonian periods, kings received a divine call, legitimating them in office. For example, an inscription of Esarhaddon reads: "whom Assur, the father of the gods, called my name for the rule of the land of Assur and the governorship of the lands of Sumer and Akkad,"[1076] and "Nabu-apla-iddina, king of Babylon, called by Marduk," the god of Babylon.[1077] Here the entire nation of Israel is personally commissioned by God, not just her ruler, for service of him.

Pass through the water (43:2). Baal, the Canaanite storm god, is pictured as walking on flowing water, symbolizing his power over it.[1078] In the Baal Epic, he defeats the power of the water in the form of "Sea" and "River."[1079] Israel itself does not have such power and cannot on her own survive an encounter with overwhelming water. Survival can only come through the protection of her God. Water is controlled by him as its Creator.

I am the Lord (43:3, 11, 15). See comment on 41:13.

I love you (43:4). See comment on 41:8. Mesopotamian texts record several different objects of the love of the gods. The most common recipient of such divine favor is the king, with one, Narām-Sin, "beloved of the god Sin," having this as part of his name.[1080] Private individuals also have this as an element of their name.[1081] The gods are also said to love places, such as the temple Eanna that Esarhaddon describes as "beloved of my lady Ishtar."[1082] Israel's God, rather than loving an individual or place, loves an entire people, acting on that love on their behalf.

Bring in their witnesses (43:9). See sidebar on "Covenant Lawsuit" at 1:2.

Before me no god was formed, nor will there be one after me (43:10). God's uniqueness (see 46:9) is expressed in terms of relative time of formation. Ancient Near Eastern theogonies (accounts of the origins of the gods) are usually structured around generations of gods in family relationships or formed by some other physical means (see 42:5).[1083] Of Khnum, the Egyptian creator god (see 43:1), it is said that "he has fashioned gods and men; he has formed flocks and herds."[1084]

Gods come into being not simply on an ontological level, an understanding of whether they exist or not, but on a functional one, since they are tied with natural phenomena and thus have tasks in the physical world. Function and form came to be simultaneously. Receiving a function and a name brought a new deity into being.[1085] The latter is shown in the *Enuma Elish* story, which speaks of a time "when yet no gods were manifest, nor names pronounced, nor destinies decreed."[1086] Divine functions also related to spheres of influence, with some deities playing roles in heaven, others on earth, still others in the netherworld. The earthly sphere was also delineated by influence over distinct geographical areas, whether temples, towns, or nations.

Yahweh here starkly contrasts himself with other deities. He does not identify himself in cosmogonic terms of his own beginning or end, but places himself completely outside this temporal realm, unlike all other gods. This also contrasts his function (the unlimited in contrast

Baal stele shows Baal walking across the waters.
Erich Lessing/Art Resource, NY, courtesy of the Louvre

to the limited) and his realm to theirs (all of creation in contrast to a limited geographical sphere). He is therefore unique, unaffected by their bickering for power and position.

When I act, who can reverse it? (43:13). The irreversibility of God's acts is attributed to Marduk in *Enuma Elish*. He wished supreme authority over the gods: "Let me ordain destinies instead of you. Let nothing that I bring about be altered, nor what I say be revoked or changed."[1087] He is then told: "Your command is supreme! Henceforth your command cannot be changed."[1088] In the Gilgamesh Epic, the collective of the gods decided to destroy humanity, but their plans were thwarted by one of their own, Ea, who leaked the news.[1089] Yahweh, as sole God wielding unique divine authority, has no one who can sway him from his decisions.

Babylonians, in the ships in which they took pride (43:14). Both Egypt (e.g., Deut. 28:68) and Mesopotamia used ships in warfare and in trade much more than did the Israelites.[1090] A letter from Amarna uses this Hebrew word for "ships" (ʾ*nyh*) when speaking of Labayu from Megiddo: "I will send him to the king by boat."[1091] Sennacherib brags of such activity that the wood used by the boat builders "made tall trees in the forests rare."[1092] He used them for transporting captives: "I carried off the people of Bit-Iakin with their gods, and the people of Elam ... loaded them on boats,

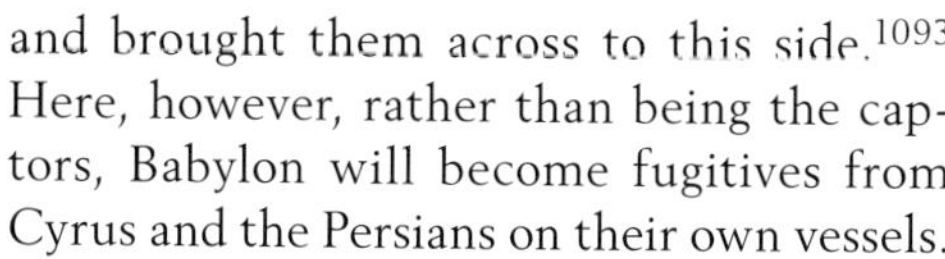

and brought them across to this side.[1093] Here, however, rather than being the captors, Babylon will become fugitives from Cyrus and the Persians on their own vessels.

The gods are represented by the natural phenomena with which they were associated.
Caryn Reeder, courtesy of the British Museum

Rebuffing God's Mercy (43:15–28)

The LORD ... your King (43:15). A deified king is foreign to Israelite understanding; the king receives the throne from God but never takes God's throne. No neighboring deity has a claim on them—only Yahweh who, being the sole Creator, wields universal authority.

In Egypt, kings were deified, especially upon their death.[1094] An Old Kingdom pyramid text speaks of the king (the "Unas") joining the sun god: "Re-Atum, this Unas comes to you, a spirit indestructible ... your son comes to you."[1095] Old Kingdom Memphite theology views kingship as being wielded by the gods—Seth over Upper Egypt and Horus over Lower Egypt.[1096] An early Egyptian creation account speaks of the sun god: "'Re, when he began to rule that which he had made' means that Re began to appear as king."[1097]

Royal deification in Mesopotamia lasted only for a short period during the Akkadian dynasty in Sumer (late third millennium), but soon disappeared.[1098] Later the king was seen as separate from the gods but closer to them than any other mortal—close enough to be their image. Several Neo-Assyrian texts speak of a king as "the image [*ṣalmu*]" of a god.[1099] The Akkadian Poem of the Righteous Sufferer speaks of "the king, the god's flesh, Shamash (the sun god) of his people,"[1100] and several people are named Sharru-Ilia, "the king is my god."[1101] A hymn of Nebuchadnezzar II says, "Enlil my god is the preeminent king."[1102] In Ugaritic literature, the god El is called "king, father of years,"[1103] and mighty Baal is described as "our king."[1104]

Chariots and hoses (43:17). See comment on 2:7.

Calamus
Itoaito

Fragrant calamus (43:24). This is an aromatic reed or cane (*qaneh*; Ex. 30:23); the same term in Akkadian is designated as "good, i.e., sweet reed" (cf. Jer. 6:20), an ingredient in recipes and rituals.[1105] This reed is burnt with other aromatics by Utnapishtim after he survived the flood in the Gilgamesh Epic: "I set up an offering stand ...

	Babylonian Kings	Persian Kings	Key Events
620	Nabopolassar 626-605	Cyaxares 625-585 (Mede)	Fall of Nineveh 612
610	Nebuchadnezzar 605-562		
600			
590		Astyages 585-550 (Mede)	Fall of Jerusalem 586
580			
570	Amel-Marduk 562-560		
560	Neriglissar 560-556		
	Labashi-Marduk 556	Cyrus 559-530	
550	Nabonidus 556-539		
540			Fall of Babylon 539
530		Cambyses 530-522	
520		Darius I 522-486	

I heaped reeds, cedar, and myrtle in their bowls. The gods smelled the savor; the gods smelled the sweet savor."[1106]

The Lord's Servant (44:1–5)

Formed you in womb (44:2). God is not only Creator on the cosmic level, but is also intimately involved in human conception and gestation. Formation and care in the uterus engender praise in the Hymn to the Aten, of whom it is written: "Who makes seed grow in women, who creates people from sperm; who feeds the son in his mother's womb, who soothes him to still his tears. Nurse in the womb, giver of breath, to nourish all that he made."[1107] This is in contrast to the asexual creation of the Egyptian god Shu, god of the air, who says, "I was not built in the womb ... I was not conceived by conception"[1108] Rather than the distance of self-sufficiency, Israel experiences an almost maternal intimacy from her Creator.

Write on his hand, "The LORD's" (44:5). In the Code of Hammurabi, Babylonian slaves had a distinguishing mark of some kind, apparently in their hair.[1109] The fifth-century Aramaic texts from Elephantine in Egypt mention a similar practice: "A slave has a 'yod' [the smallest Hebrew letter] on his right hand, a brand reading in Aramaic like this, 'Mibtahiah's [slave].'"[1110]

Terracotta relief of carpenter from Uruk
Erich Lessing/Art Resource, NY, courtesy of the Louvre

Rejecting Idols (44:6–23)

Who ... casts an idol (44:10). See comments on 40:18–19.

Tool (44:12). Elsewhere, this is a woodworking tool, usually taken as an axe or chisel of some kind (e.g., Jer. 10:3). In the Gezer Calendar the term is associated with flax harvest,[1111] which fits with the Ugaritic use of the word for sickle.[1112] In this context, it seems to be something that is forged.

Blacksmith ... carpenter ... he kindles a fire (44:12–15). These two craftsmen are mentioned in proximity in the Egyptian Satire of the Trades, an Eighteenth to Nineteenth Dynasty work deriding all trades but that of the scribe, with a sarcasm that parallels this passage:

> But I have seen the smith at work
> At the opening of his furnace;
> With fingers like claws of a crocodile
> He stinks more than fish roe.
> The carpenter who wields an adze,
> He is wearier than a field-laborer;
> His field is the timber, his hoe the adze.
> There is no end to his labor,
> He does more than his arms can do,
> Yet at night he kindles light.[1113]

Cedars ... cypress ... oak ... pine (44:14). The identity of two of these trees is certain, the cedar (see comment on 2:1) and the oak.[1114] The other two are more problematic. The word translated "cypress" (*tirzâ*) occurs only here and not in other cognate languages, so its interpretation is at best tentative. The fourth tree may be cognate with an Akkadian word for "cedar" (*erēnu*),[1115] though the exact meaning here is still uncertain.[1116]

Bakes bread (44:15). Bread is a staple of the ancient Near Eastern diet, so it is evidenced in text, art, and archaeology. It is so ubiquitous that the term for bread is used as a more general word for food in both Hebrew

Canaanite deity
Werner Forman Archive/Sold at Christie's, London

▸ Against Idols

The ideal and the real come into conflict in the area of physical representations of deity. The Ten Commandments clearly forbid for Israel the manufacture or worship of images in any form (Ex. 20:4–5; Deut. 5:8–9). It is also clear that Israelites possessed such things not only in the early, prenational period (e.g., Gen. 31:19–37), but also continued to do so throughout the monarchy (e.g., 2 Kings 18:4). This is evident from the repeated prophetic condemnations of the ongoing practice, as in Isaiah.

There is also archaeological[A-239] and textual evidence (see Isa. 10:10–11) for their use.[A-240] Sargon II describes taking Samaria in 721 B.C.: "I counted as spoil 27,800 people, together with their chariots, and gods in which they trusted."[A-241] This implies a physical reality rather than simply a theological construct, and some suggest they included representations of Yahweh himself.[A-242] While this is debated, their relative rarity, or nonexistence, is in striking contrast to the many representations of other deities in Israel and its vicinity.[A-243]

It is much more difficult to prove any aniconic practice in Israel since this is attempting to prove a negative—that is, that something (in this case images) did *not* exist.[A-244] A change has been noted in representations on seals late in the seventh century. Earlier in that century, seals depicted symbols of astral gods,[A-245] while two groups of later bullae contain none of these.[A-246] While the shift is noticeable, a lack of such evidence does not prove that images were not condemned much earlier. Every society shows a disconnect between policy and practice, which is one reason why Israelite prophets were never out of work.

and Akkadian.[1117] Bread could be baked as simply as on a smooth stone heated by a fire, after the fire was removed, or even in the ashes. The Epic of Erra and Ishum from first millennium Mesopotamia lauds military life on the march over a stay-at-home existence: "plenteous city bread a loaf baked on the coals."[1118] Beehive shaped ovens were also used, made from clay and straw.[1119]

Restored Jerusalem (44:24–28)

I am the LORD (44:24). See comment on 41:13.

Spread out the earth by myself (44:24). See 42:5; 43:10; 44:2. Yahweh is the sole God according to orthodox Israelite understanding, having no consort with whom he works and not being part of any pantheon. He is alone in creation and in sustaining creation (see sidebar on "Creation Gods" at 42:5; also comments on 40:13–14). Several texts from the monarchy period refer to "Yahweh and his asherah,"[1120] indicating that not everyone held to orthodoxy. This is one reason why prophets had a message to preach.

False prophets … diviners (44:25). See sidebar on "Superstitions and Divination" at 2:6. Oracular priests known as *bārû* were mentioned often in Akkadian sources,[1121] so many have proposed a textual emendation of the Hebrew term used here for "false prophet" (*bd*), since /*d*/ and /*r*/ look similar in Hebrew orthography of the period.[1122] But an official from Mari in north Syria is called a *baddum*,[1123] rendering this proposed emendation unnecessary. Diviners (*qsm*; see 3:1–3) consulted various types of oracles, seeking signs indicating the future (e.g., 8:18). King Zakkur of Hamath in Syria wrote in an Aramaic inscription of the eighth century, "I raised my hands to Baalshamayn and Baalshamayn answered me. Baalshamayn spoke to me through seers and diviners."[1124]

Cyrus (44:28). Cyrus II came to the Persian throne in 559 B.C.[1125] When he overthrew the Median king Astyages in 550 B.C., he instituted the Persian (Achaemenid) empire, which he ruled until his death in 530 B.C. He successfully moved against Lydia in Asia Minor in 547 B.C., and in 539/538 B.C. he defeated the Babylonian empire under Nabonidus, placing the whole of the Near East except Egypt under his control. Nabonidus's own chronicle records: "In the month Tishri when Cyrus did battle ... the people of Akkad retreated. On the fourteenth day ... Nabonidus fled. On the sixteenth day ... the army of Cyrus entered Babylon without a battle."[1126]

From his perspective, Cyrus wrote on a clay cylinder that the chief Babylonian god, Marduk, was incensed at the lack of proper worship by Nabonidus, so the god invited Cyrus to take the throne and reestablish legitimate worship.[1127] The conquered people welcomed him: "Green twigs were spread in front of him—the state of 'Peace' was imposed upon the city."[1128]

Among the policies Cyrus instituted was one that found a place in heart of the exiled Israelites. He decreed that exiles could return to their native lands and reestablish their religious practices. This is mentioned in the Bible (2 Chr. 36:22–23; Ezra 1:1–4) as well as in Cyrus's own document: "I returned the gods to the sacred centers [on the other side of] the Tigris whose sanctuaries had been abandoned for a long time.... I gathered all the inhabitants and returned their dwellings."[1129] The claim is validated by an inscribed brick, probably one from among many, from Uruk that reads: "I am Cyrus, the rebuilder of Esagila (the Marduk temple) and Ezida (the Nabu temple)."[1130]

Shepherd (44:28). See comment on 40:11.

Let its foundations be laid (44:28). Since deities lived and were cared for in their temples, it was important that they be well maintained. A well-cared-for god would be kindly disposed to the ruler who rebuilt his temple, so rulers regularly recorded rebuilding activities of numerous cities captured by them, alongside military exploits, as highlights of their reign. Sargon II describes rebuilding a temple: "The outer walls of the Eanna shrine ... he cleared its foundation. With fervent prayers and respectful gestures he laid its foundations on the breast of the underworld, founding it like a mountain."[1131]

This was a common practice.[1132] A ninth-century Phoenician building inscription from Byblos identifies a "temple ('house') which Yahimilk, the king of Byblos built. He rebuilt ('revivified') all the ruins of the

Cyrus cylinder
Caryn Reeder, courtesy of the British Museum

▸ Cyrus's Religion

Cyrus acknowledged that various gods were worshiped by different peoples, each having control over their own people and place. In the Cyrus Cylinder, even though Marduk is the chief Babylonian deity, Cyrus acknowledges his work in his own circumstances as well as that of Nabu, and also the existence of the "gods of Sumer and Akkad, whose sanctuaries he rebuilt."[A-247]

In a polytheistic system, adding deities is not a theological problem. In fact, in claiming support from a new god, the theologically neutral becomes an economic and political advantage. Cyrus thus had no problem in recognizing Yahweh, though he would not have personally worshiped him, since such recognition cost nothing but gained the support of Yahweh worshipers through their tribute and allegiance. Polytheistic priests of the newly recognized god would also likely expect royal support for their religious endeavors, so they also benefited.

Persia was also the geographical matrix for dualistic Zoroastrianism, with two supreme deities: Ahuramazda, creator of all good, and the evil Angra Mainyu.[A-248] It is strongly debated as to when this religion took root. Some suggest it began as early as Cyrus.[A-249] It saw two uncreated, opposing spirits, one good and one evil, with all of creation aligned with one or the other. Whichever interpretation is adopted, dualism or polytheism, both stand in contrast to Isaiah's strong monotheism (see 43:10; 44:24; 45:7).

Ahuramazda
Susanna Vagt

temples."[1133] Rulers sought by this means to curry and maintain divine favor.

Cyrus, a Messiah (45:1–25)

Anointed ... Cyrus (45:1). "Anointed" is the Hebrew term *māšîaḥ* ("Messiah"). The term developed an eschatological significance in Israel of a promised deliverer, but it is also used in its nominal and verbal forms of anointing a leader such as a priest or king (e.g., 1 Sam. 15:1).[1134] Considering a foreign ruler as Israel's deliverer is unique in the Old Testament, but it does fit into Persian royal practice. On his Persian period statue, the Egyptian court official Udjahorresnet writes of Cambyses, the first Persian emperor over Egypt: "The Great Chief of all foreign lands, Cambyses came to Egypt. . . . I composed his titulary, to wit his name of King of Upper and Lower Egypt."[1135]

Cyrus claims to have been placed on the Babylonian throne by the Babylonian god Marduk (see comment on 44:28). He says: "I returned the gods to the sacred centers . . . and I let them dwell in eternal abodes,"[1136] a duty of the Babylonian king.[1137] Here too the Persians see themselves assuming the role of the monarchs they replace. In the same way, Cyrus could be assuming aspects of the theology and role of the Davidic monarchy, at least to the extent of reestablishing the people in their land;[1138] this includes being the anointed Messiah. While not

King anointed by gods, relief from Esna
Brian J. McMorrow

Portions of Balawat gate
Michael Greenhalgh/ ArtServe, courtesy of the Istanbul Museum

the eschatological deliverer, Cyrus is God's deliverer of the moment from Babylonian exile.

Whose right hand I take hold of (45:1). See comment on 41:13. God is initiating a new relationship with Cyrus, offering him support. This is a well-known Akkadian idiom, indicating aid and guidance.[1139] In the Cyrus Cylinder, Cyrus is said to take Marduk's hand, restoring him to prominence in the cult.[1140] The blessing section of a Neo-Assyrian letter says, "The goddess Tashmetum, whom you revere, has indeed seized both your hands."[1141] Mesha, king of Moab, said: "I built this high place for Chemosh ... because he saved me from all the attackers."[1142]

Doors ... gates of bronze ... bars of iron (45:1–2). A city's fortifications were extensive and strong. Excavations in Balawat, near Kalhu (Nimrud) in Assyria, found a palace built by Shalmaneser III (859–824 B.C.). It had huge gates covered with strips of bronze embossed with battle and other scenes. Divine power over entry into a city is also described in similar terms in the Famine Stele from Ptolemaic Egypt. The god Khnum is described: "He holds the door bolt in his hand, opens the gate as he wishes."[1143] Iron is viewed as a special metal, called "metal from heaven" in the Egyptian Immortality of Writers,[1144] in the context indicating its durability, but also perhaps its source. Before iron-smelting technology, meteoric iron was used.

Set my exiles free (45:13). See comments on 11:11; 44:28.

Egypt ... Cush ... Sabaeans (45:14). Egypt and Cush (see comments on 18:1–7) clearly refer to Lower and Upper Egypt, respectively, while the location of the Sabaeans is less clear. Josephus (*Ant.* 2.10.2) looks to the tall Nubians of Ethiopia, geographi-

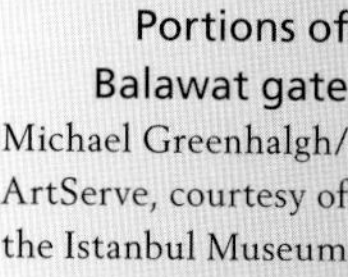

cally close to the others. The designation could also refer to one of two groups in the Arabian Peninsula, those from Sheba in the south (Yemen) or the Saba in northwest Arabia.

Darius I speaks of completing an east-west canal connecting the Nile and the Red Sea: "I am Persian; from Persia I seized Egypt; I gave the order to dig this canal from a river by name Nile which flows in Egypt to the sea which goes from Persia."[1145] This canal, shown in recent satellite images,[1146] made contact between African people and those in Arabia much closer.

God ... made the earth (45:18). See 40:28.

By myself I have sworn (45:23). Swearing an oath on the name of a god is not rare now, nor was it in the time of Isaiah. Tying an oath to a deity provides gravity to it by calling the god as witness and possible punisher if the oath were broken. Akkadian texts mention invoking a god's name in an oath,[1147] but more regularly designate an oath as "by the life of a god" (*nīš ilim*), or that of the king.[1148] Several letters from Lachish in Israel use as an oath formula "as Yahweh lives."[1149] But in no case does there seem to be god or king swearing by themselves as Yahweh, sole God and true King, does here.

Babylon's Gods vs. Israel's God (46:1–13)

Bel (46:1). In the Akkadian language, *bēlu* is the equivalent to English "lord, master."[1150] This is thus a title rather than a proper name for a god.[1151] The term is used as a substitute for the name of at least two Mesopotamian gods, Shamash and Marduk.[1152] The *Enuma Elish* describes how Marduk attained this position as head of the pantheon.[1153] The Babylonian king Nebuchadnezzar had a Marduk temple, named Esagila, near his great palace in Babylon.[1154] The esteem in which Marduk/Bel was held is demonstrated by the number of Neo-Assyrian and Neo-Babylonian personal names that bore "Bel" as one element, such as the last king of Babylon, Belshazzar (Dan. 5).[1155]

For a period Marduk/Bel lost his hegemony, since his statue was "kidnapped" by Sennacherib and taken to Assyria in 689 B.C. (see 36:7),[1156] where, according to the Esarhaddon Chronicle, "for 8 years of Sennacherib and 12 years of Esarhaddon, a total of 20 years, Bel dwelt in Baltil (Assur)."[1157] Marduk is probably the god referred to here (see Jer. 50:2; 51:44), since it was the Babylonians whom Cyrus defeated.

Nebo (46:1). Nebo is the Hebrew rendition of the Akkadian god Nabu, the son of Marduk. He was the god of writing and wisdom, was involved in determining fate,[1158] and was a major figure in the pantheon, as shown by the number of names in which it was included (e.g., Nabopolassar, Nebuchadnezzar, and Nabonidus).[1159] Marduk/Bel and Nabu are two of the deities mentioned in the mid-eighth-century Aramaic inscriptions found at Sefire in Syria,[1160] and they are even found in the salutation of a mid-fifth-century Aramaic ostracon written at Elephantine in Egypt.[1161] A ninth-century text from Kalah reads: "Trust in Nabu; do not trust in any other god."[1162]

Images that are carried about (46:1). Many gods were regularly associated with animals, which at times transported them. In Egypt, the goddess Qadesh is shown being carried while standing on a lion,[1163] as are Syrian and Mesopotamian deities, including the goddess Ishtar.[1164] Some also stood on a bull, a "beast of burden."[1165] One relief shows numerous gods each being transported on

Marduk on boundary stone
Z. Radovan/www.BibleLand Pictures.com

Tukulti-Ninurta I is shown both standing and kneeling before a cult stand bearing the stylus and the writing board which are symbols of the god Nabu.
Nathanael Shelley, courtesy of the Vorderasiatisches Museum, Berlin

different animals.[1166] Such a "divine journey" was time of lavish celebration.[1167]

While in the ancient Near East this transport seems at times a matter of honor, it can also be demeaning, as when the divine images are taken captive.[1168] Isaiah sees this as demeaning in that a lifeless, powerless idol cannot move on its own.

Even to your old age and gray hairs ... I will carry you (46:4). Mesopotamians referred to humans as "dark haired,"[1169] while the Akkadian term for the old is "grey-haired."[1170] Long life was a desired blessing, but its accompanying infirmities were the opposite. The enfeebled need care, as a prayer to Nabu indicates: "Old age has me bedridden prematurely.... My hands are outstretched ... I have entreated slaves and slave girls."[1171]

In an Aramaic slave manumission document, one of the obligations of the freed slave is "as a son or daughter provides for [lit., 'carries'] his/her father in your life and until your death."[1172] Attendance to one who is incapacitated is shown in the Canaanite story of the chief god El, who is inebriated after a drinking party. "Il walked home; he enters into his courtyard. They loaded the gods *thkmn* and *shnm* with him."[1173]

Images of gods carried off as plunder by soldiers of Tiglath-pileser III
Caryn Reeder, courtesy of the British Museum

Pour out gold ... weigh out silver ... to make it into a god (46:6). See comment on 30:22.

Weigh out silver on the scales (46:6). The scales probably refer to a balance, with the Hebrew term indicating the horizontal balance beam. Things were put on one side of the balance with a known weight on the other. An Egyptian wall painting shows a human heart being weighed in this way.[1174]

They ... carry it (46:7). After an idol is made, it must be carried to its shrine to be worshiped. In an Aramaic inscription in Demotic, the goddess Marah is described: "My wise one carries you; she carries your burden and your load."[1175] This sarcasm of Isaiah contrasts with the power of the true God, who supports his worshipers.

I am God, and there is no other (46:9). The Assyrians saw their god Ashur as being the god from whom all other gods derive. A proper name from the period of Isaiah is Gabbu-Ilani-Ashur: "Ashur is all the gods."[1176] In the Hymn to the Aten from New Kingdom Egypt, Aten is hailed as the "sole God beside whom there is none."[1177] In an environment where numerous other deities claimed power, Israel's God is not making an absolute statement of uniqueness, though he could, according to Israel's theology. He is rather saying that the readers know his uniqueness through past experience, and this will be confirmed through future fulfillment of God's plans.

My purpose will stand (46:10). Yahweh is portrayed as all-knowing, not bound by time, and all-powerful, not bound by ability or external circumstances. In Mesopotamia, gods did not have intrinsic knowledge and ability to control the world. Such power was derived from the Tablets of Destiny, which established the place of the gods in the universe. The Tablets controlling one's destiny could change hands, with their inherent power exercised by whoever possessed them.

Kingu was given the Tablets by Tiamat in the creation account: "She gave him the tablets of destiny, had him hold it to his chest, (saying) 'As for you, your command will not be changed, your utterance will be eternal. Now that Kingu is the highest ... and has [ordained] destinies for his divine children.'"[1178] The other gods promised Marduk that if he defeated Tiamat and her minions, "your destiny, O Lord, shall be foremost of the gods"; this took place when Marduk triumphed: "He took from him the tablet of destinies."[1179] The struggle for control of these tablets is also the main concern of the Mesopotamian Anzu epic.[1180] Israel's God is never portrayed as being bound by some external force; rather, he controls universal "destiny."

Babylon's Abasement (47:1–15)

Sit on the ground without a throne (47:1). Royal power was symbolized by a throne (cf. Isa. 6:1). Its symbolism was so powerful that Sennacherib took a portable throne along to receive homage from those whom he had captured. The loss of the throne thus indicated despair and powerlessness. When El heard of the death of his son Baal, "he descended from his throne sitting on the footstool, and from the footstool he sat on the ground."[1181] The Ugaritic text goes one step further, with El stating a wish: "I would go down to the underworld,"[1182] following Baal to death (see v. 5, "go into darkness").[1183] Isaiah thus sees Babylon not simply deposed but sent to the netherworld.

Virgin Daughter of Babylon (47:1). "Daughter" personifies either a country or city, here the nation's capital (see comment on 37:22). Ironically, the purity that should characterize Israel (e.g., Lam. 2:13) is replaced by profligacy with foreign gods (e.g., Jer. 6:1–3) and is applied to her Mesopotamian overlord, a land with many gods of her own. The Ugaritic goddess Anat is also entitled "Virgin," though she is associated with fertility and has a consort in Baal.[1184] The "virgin" Babylon, though the lover of many gods, will suffer the losses of war, when virgins are particularly vulnerable. She will move from a state of virginity to widowhood (v. 8) in short order.

Take millstones and grind flour (47:2). Grain was ground into flour by grinding it between a pair of stones (the Hebrew form indicates the instrument functions as a pair), a movable upper stone that "rides" (Deut. 24:6) on the fixed lower stone.[1185] This task for women or servants[1186] would be shameful for men (Lam. 5:13). The context suggests that there may be a sexual connotation to the activity, at least necessitating some loss of modesty in leaning over and grinding.

Veil (47:2). This rare term apparently indicates a veil-like covering. In Middle Assyrian and Hittite laws, a married woman was veiled at the wedding, apparently by the husband, and veiling publicly indicates that wedding.[1187] In the Gilgamesh Epic, Gilgamesh mourns his dead friend Enkidu: "He covered, like a bride, the face of his friend,"[1188] suggesting

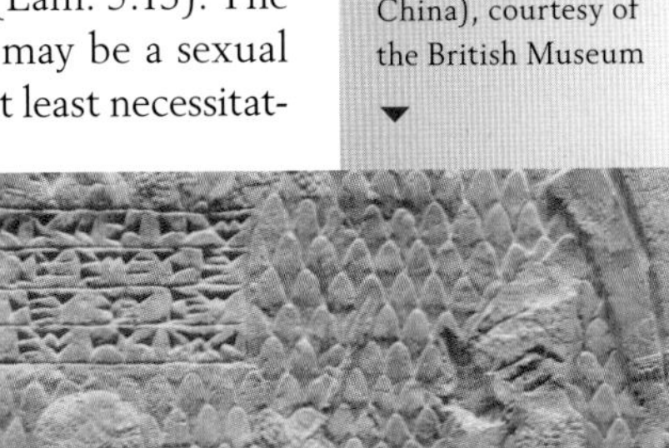

Sennacherib on portable throne receiving defeated enemies
LAO, Dong (Beijing, China), courtesy of the British Museum

a bride is the paradigmatic veiled person.[1189]

There is no indication from pictorial representations that veils were regularly worn in Israel or among her neighbors by married women subsequently, suggesting their use only by brides in conjunction with the ceremony itself.[1190] It is the veiling that turns the woman into a bride, according to a Middle Assyrian law: "If a man would veil his concubine, 5 (or) 6 of his companions he shall gather and he shall veil her in their presence. He shall say, 'She is (my) wife.'"[1191] This covering symbolizes the duty of care and provision.[1192]

Bread maker using grindstone
Kim Walton, courtesy of the Oriental Institute Museum
▲

The bride's unveiling by the groom in private symbolized the new intimate relationship. In contrast, "a harlot must not veil herself; her head must be uncovered."[1193] Unveiling such as this is the sign of an extramarital relationship, since the veil was neither placed nor removed by a husband but by the woman herself in the context of intimacy with others. Unveiling or uncovering such as this is the sign of a breach of relationship. In Old Babylonian texts from Nuzi and elsewhere, stripping and expulsion signified a divorce: "If X will live with (another) husband, they will strip her of clothes and make her go out naked."[1194]

Bare your legs ... nakedness (47:2–3). Respectable women are generally portrayed with long skirts, so uncovered legs were considered inappropriate.[1195] Nakedness was reserved for the poor, prisoners (see Isa. 20:2–4), dancing girls,[1196] or worse. Ishtar, the queen of heaven through marriage to the sky god, An, upon her descent to the netherworld, had to strip off all her jewelry. Then the gatekeeper "stripped off and took away the proud garment of her body,"[1197] leaving her humiliated like the naked dead who arrive there.[1198] As the goddess of love and fertility, she is the prostitutes' patroness[1199] and is at times portrayed in full frontal nudity.

At other times her robe is parted below the waist to display either her legs or her genitalia. This association may indicate that Babylon the great has fallen not only to the point of poverty, needing to engage in menial work, but even to prostitution. It was only the poor who might find themselves regularly unable to clothe themselves.

Daughter of the Babylonians (47:5). A citizen of a place is called in Akkadian and Ugaritic a "son/daughter of place X,"[1200] but here the term is demeaning, contrasting with queenship.

You showed them no mercy (47:6). Aggressive enemies deserve no quarter, as the boundary stele of the Egyptian king Sesostris III describes the king: "Considerate to clients, steady in mercy [cf. Isa 55:7], merciless to the foe who attacks him."[1201]

Yoke (47: 6). See comment on 9:4.

I am (47:8). While for Yahweh it is sufficient simply to state his existence (e.g., Ex. 3:14), ancient Near Eastern dignitaries provide lengthy self-adulations. The Old

Israelite women from Lachish with their long skirts
Caryn Reeder, courtesy of the British Museum
▶

▸ Occult Practices

Though banned from orthodox Israelite practice, practices wielding occult power continued to be used in Israel as they were among her neighbors. Their use for extraordinary situations rather than on a regular basis is one element that distinguishes occult witchcraft from formal cultic religious observance, though at times actual differences between "magic" and "religion" are difficult to determine objectively.

Incantations and magical spells were used frequently in Mesopotamia, often in close proximity with medical texts since they both concerned, among other things, the avoidance or amelioration of sickness.[A-250] In Egypt, magic was used in similar ways, but since special emphasis was placed on the afterlife and the well-being of the king in this life and the next, magical practices also dealt with these areas.[A-251] Ugaritic literature also includes incantations, such as one against snakebite.[A-252]

The occult involves what might be classified good or "white" magic, in contrast to harmful or "black" magic, which, though practiced, was not socially acceptable.[A-253] Isaiah condemns any such thing whatsoever, whether "black" or "white."

Block statue of Djedher, a fourth century official and sage, covered in texts of incantation against ailments
Werner Forman Archive/The Egyptian Museum, Cairo
▲

Kingdom autobiography of Ankhtifi has him not only saying that he is placed as king and blessed by Horus, but also "I am the vanguard of men and the rearguard of men. One who finds the solution where it is lacking. A leader of the land through active conduct. Strong in speech, collected in thought.... For I am a champion without peer."[1202]

The ninth-century Assyrian king Ashurnasirpal identifies himself : "I am king, I am lord, I am praiseworthy, I am exalted, I am important, I am magnificent, I am foremost, I am a hero, I am a warrior, I am a lion, and I am virile."[1203] Though Mesopotamian kings used laudatory epithets extensively,[1204] they did not always reflect reality. Babylon's self-aggrandizement here proves illusory.

Widow (47:8–9). Widowhood indicates vulnerability (see 1:17; 10:2). In the Ugaritic composition Dawn and Dusk the god Mutu-wa-sharru, whose name may derive from the god of death (*mutu*),[1205] holds in his hand the "rod of bereavement," also called "the rod of widowhood."[1206] The lack of progeny to care for one in old age and to continue the family is a well-known source of grief.

Astrologers ... stargazers (47:13). See comment on 13:10.

Stubborn Israel Accused (48:1–11)

The sinews of your neck were iron (48:4). King Sethos I campaigned in Canaan in the thirteenth century B.C. His frightening presence is explained as "valiant like a falcon and a strong bull wide-striding and sharp-horned ... and every limb as iron."[1207]

In Isaiah this symbolism of iron represents stubbornness rather than power.

My idols did them (48:5). Israel's claim that God acts in history was thought to distinguish it from its neighbors,[1208] but textual evidence shows this to be otherwise. Curses of the gods called on those who break treaties or who deface boundary stones indicate that gods are understood to work through history (see 5:25).[1209] Royal inscriptions of the gods bringing military victory through the Mesopotamian king indicate the same understanding.[1210]

Deities also played a role in the political realm, as when Ashurbanipal credits them with his throne: "The Queen-of-Nineveh, the merciful goddess, turned to my side and graciously set me on the throne of the father who begat me. The Mistress-of-Arbela, the great lady, granted regular acts of favour in the course of my kingship."[1211] Prayers, both individual and corporate, indicate that both Israel and her neighbors are open to, and even expect, their gods to be responsive in personal and national history.

Furnace (48:10). Smelting furnaces have been found at numerous archaeological sites.[1212] Though full metal workshops are less well known, two from the second millennium were found at Kanesh (Kültepe in Turkey) and another near Baghdad.[1213]

Some furnaces, like one from the Late Bronze site of Tel Zeror, have nozzles on them for bellows. These were necessary because the furnaces used for smelting needed to produce higher temperatures than furnaces with solely domestic functions. A Sixth Dynasty Egyptian tomb relief shows six men blowing air into a furnace through long pipes as part of the process of refining gold.[1214]

Refined you (48:10). See sidebar on "Silver and Dross" at 1:25.

God's Call of Love (48:12–22)

Chosen ally (48:14). See comment on 41:8.

His [Cyrus's] arm will be against the Babylonians (48:14). See comment on 44:28.

I have not spoken in secret (48:16). See comment on 45:19.

I am the LORD (48:17). See comment on 41:13.

Descendants ... name ... cut off (48:19). Losing the next generation and one's own honor was a serious thing. When deceased, only one's name or memory remains, and without descendants, one is soon

Detail of a relief in the tomb of Mereruka depicts metalworkers employed in the manufacture of jewelery. The detail shows the metalworkers using blowpipes to force the forge fire.
Werner Forman Archive

▸ The Servant and Royal Ideology

Several of the descriptions of the servant (42:1–9; 49:1–13; 50:4–11; 52:13–53:22) and his functions are also used of kings. Note the following chart:[A-254]

Description/role	King	Servant (* see comments)
Chosen (*bḥr*)	2 Sam. 21:6 (Saul); Ps. 89:3 (David)	42:1*
God accepts, delights (*rṣh*)	2 Sam. 24:23; 1 Chr. 28:4 (David)	42:1; 49:8
Bestowal of spirit	1 Sam. 10:10 (Saul); 16:13 (David)	42:1
Dispense justice	1 Kings 3:11, 28; 10:9 (Solomon)	42:1, 3, 4, 6*
Called (*qr*ʾ) by God	Isa. 22:20 (Eliakim)	42:6; 49:1*
Hold (*ḥzq*) the hand	Isa. 45:1 (Cyrus)	42:6
Establish (*ntn*) in a role	1 Kings 14:7 (Jeroboam); 16:2 (Jehu)	42:6; 49:6, 8
Release captives	Mesopotamia,[A-255] Egypt[A-256]	42:7*; 49:9
Victory (*yešua*ʿ) from God	2 Sam. 22:51	49:6, 8
Chosen (*bḥr*)	Mesopotamia[A-257]	49:7
Help (ʿ*zr*) from God	2 Chr. 28:23	49:8; 50:7, 9
Provide water	Mesopotamia[A-258]	49:10
Open to instruction for leadership	Solomon (1 Kings 3:4–15)	50:4, 9
Act wisely/succeed (*skl*)	1 Kings 2:2 (Solomon); 2 Kings 18:7 (Hezekiah)	52:13
Raised up (*rwm*)	Num. 24:7 (future king)	52:13
Lifted up (*ns*ʾ)	1 Chr. 14:2 (David); 2 Chr. 32:23 (Hezekiah)	52:13
Divide spoil (*šll*)	1 Sam. 30:20 (David)	53:12

forgotten (Jer. 11:19), the family line comes to an end, and, especially for those involved in a cult of the dead, there is no one to look after the interests of the departed. A Neo-Assyrian curse in a letter states: “May the name and seed of Sasî … be destroyed.”[1215]

The Servant of the Lord (49:1–7)

Before I was born the Lord called me (49:1). A prenatal call is not only important in the Old Testament, several Mesopotamian kings make mention of it too.[1216] Ashurbanipal writes: “I am Ashurbanipal, Ashur and Belet–[]'s creation, whose name … Il and Sin called for kingship, and formed him inside his mother in order to shepherd (see 40:11) the land of Assyria.”[1217]

Such kings are stating that they became rulers not just because of the mighty deeds they performed; rather, the gods recognized their uniqueness even before birth, seeing that they were intrinsically worthy before having proven themselves in any way. The servant in Isaiah 49 does not use this concept for self-aggrandizement, however, but to point out not only God's prenatal call, but God's prenatal preparation of the servant.

Made mention of my name (49:1). See comment on 43:1. This means more than just to recall someone. The same literal expression ("remember/invoke a name"), with a deity as the subject, also means "to recognize as king" in the Akkadian of this period. Of Nebuchadnezzar it is stated: "when Marduk named me permanently to kingship," and Cyrus claimed the same treatment (see 45:1).[1218]

The servant does not fulfill his office simply through chance or circumstance of birth. He is chosen by God and thus also equipped by him. By contrast, in Egypt a high god could be described as "Unas is master of cunning whose mother knows not his name,"[1219] which highlights his aloofness and inscrutability.

He made my mouth like a sharpened sword (49:2). The mouth or tongue piercing like a sword is not only a biblical metaphor (e.g., Job 5:15) but was also used among Israel's neighbors. In the Instructions to King Merikare from Egypt, "the tongue is a [king's] sword; speaking is stronger than fighting."[1220]

Who formed me in the womb (49:5). See comment on 44:2.

To bring Jacob back to him (49:5). Mesopotamian kings saw themselves as divinely appointed and so were delegated tasks by their deity. Often they list their achievements in the introductory section of official records. For example, Sennacherib starts the record of his first military campaign with: "Sennacherib, the great king ... prayerful shepherd, worshipper of the great gods; guardian of the right, lover of justice, who lends support, who comes to the aid of the needy, who turns to pious deeds."[1221] Restoration from exile was one of the duties of a good king (see 5:14; 11:11; 44:28).

Hammurabi, in describing his tasks in looking after Sumer and Akkad, states that he not only dug an irrigation canal, but also "gathered the scattered peoples of the land of Sumer and Akkad (and) provided them pastures and watering places";[1222] a similar claim is also made by his son, Shamshu-Iluna.[1223] Kings from Hammurabi through Merodach-Baladan II describe themselves as "gatherer of the dispersed."[1224]

Israel Restored (49:8–26)

Restore the land (49:8). Through neglect or war, destruction was common. Rebuilding and restoration efforts were not only necessary for the good of the country, but were also politically and theologically astute policies for Mesopotamian kings. The people benefited, but so did the gods when their temples were reestablished.[1225] Building inscriptions detailing such tasks are an important element of Akkadian literature. Tiglath-pileser I records that after establishing his control over the land,

> I rebuilt the temple of ... the gods of my city Ashur. I ... brought the great gods, my lords, inside. I rebuilt, completed the palaces ... of the great towns in ... my entire land which since the time of my forefathers during hard years had been abandoned and had fallen into ruin and decay. I repaired the weakened fortifications of my land.[1226]

This type of activity provided something of an economic circularity, according to the Mesopotamian view. A god helped the king conquer a city or territory, which filled the royal treasury. Some of this revenue was in turn used to rebuild and replenish the divine sanctuaries, benefiting the gods, who would then in the future be pleased to support further expansion.

Kings are even depicted as taking part in the building efforts personally, such as when Ashurbanipal carries a basket in rebuilding a Babylonian temple.[1227] Yehimilk, king of Byblos, in an early first millennium text dedicating a new building, describes himself as one "who also has restored all the ruins of the houses here."[1228] Isaiah presents the promise as one-sided, not circular. Yahweh offers his help with no explicit request for any *quid pro quo* from the people.

Say to the captives, "Come out" (49:9). See comment on 42:7.

Aswan (49:12). This location (Heb. "Sînîm," Syene, modern Aswan) is located at

Architect's drawing of the ground plan of the palace of Nur Adad in Larsa
The Schøyen Collection MS 3031, Oslo and London

the first cataract of the Nile in Egypt.[1229] The site was militarily and commercially important. Just opposite in an island in the middle of the Nile was Elephantine, the site where a group of Aramaic papyrus documents from the fifth century B.C. were found.[1230] One of these documents claims to have been written by a scribe in Syene.[1231]

Mother (49:15). See comment on 66:13.

I have engraved you on the palms of my hands; your walls are ever before me (49:16). The mention of walls suggests that what is signified is not a mark of ownership (see 44:5) but rather a town plan or blueprint for the reconstructed city.[1232] A palace plan from nineteenth-century Larsa shows details of walls, rooms, and courtyards, while the Sumerian king Gudea had a similar plan of a temple building inscribed on the lap of one of his statues, showing even the thickness of the walls.[1233]

As surely as I live (49:18). Solemnity is added to oaths when sworn in the name of a god (see comment on 45:23), but here God swears by himself, being unable to call a higher authority as witness. Egyptians used the same oath formula, placing themselves on the line if the oath should be broken. In Ramesses II's Kadesh battle inscription, an oath begins: "As I live, as Re loves me, as my father Atum favors me, everything that my majesty has told I did in truth"[1234] (swearing by himself and his gods).

Like a bride (49:18). Fine clothing and special treatment characterize a bride (Jer. 2:32). The last day of the celebration associated with installation of the high priestess at Emar in Syria says that "when the high priestess leaves the (family) house, they cover her head like a bride with a bright sash.... Her two maids embrace her like a bride."[1235] Bridal gifts included ornaments such as jewelry.[1236]

Born during your bereavement (49:20). The Hebrew term *škl* refers specifically to a loss of a child, a serious concern not only from the aspect of parental grief but also because of the economic loss of a future worker. A Ugaritic liturgy against snake bite, a common cause of death, has the protagonist turn to a dozen gods for help, only receiving aid from Horanu. "She turns her face to Horanu, for she has been bereaved of her offspring."[1237]

In this verse, decimation and loss will be replaced by abundant children. This not only reflects economic abundance but also hope for the future. Rather than the line and family name being wiped out, as Israel feared through the depredations of her neighbors, it will expand and flourish. Hopelessness has become hope.

I am the LORD (49:23). See comment on 41:13.

Kings ... foster fathers ... queens ... nursing mothers (49:23). As a mother brings life and nourishment to a baby, so foreign kings and queens metaphorically bring these to the nation of Israel. More often this nurturing is divine rather than royal. A Sumerian proverb speaks of "the palace—one day it is a mother who has given birth."[1238] More commonly, the suckling role is given to a goddess, as shown in Egyptian, Syro-Phoenician, Canaanite, and Hittite seal impressions of goddesses suckling humans.[1239]

A Ugaritic text speaks of gods "sucking the nipples of Athirat,"[1240] while Marduk's Ordeal speaks of "the milk, which they drew in front of Ishtar of Nineveh, because she brought him

Horus suckled by Isis in relief from the Edfu birth house
Todd Bolen/www.BiblePlaces.com

up and showed compassion to him";[1241] this shows the action's significance. In a prophecy to Ashurbanipal, "You whose nurse is the Lady of Arbela (the goddess Ishtar), have no fear! I will carry you on my hip like a nurse, I will put you between my breasts.... At night I will stay awake and guard you; in the daytime I will give you milk.... As for you, have no fear, my calf, who I rear."[1242]

The metaphor seems also to be expanded by showing depictions of calves feeding from their mothers.[1243] Here the nurture is provided by human royalty who, recognizing Israel's new, exalted position, provide care and support where previously they had brought destruction and loss.

Drunk on their own blood (49:26). The description is not of a savage conqueror, but rather of one who has been relegated to cannibalism in order to remain alive (see 2 Kings 6:28–29). One of the curses in a treaty between Assyria and Arpad calls on one who breaches the covenant "hunger, want and famine, so that they eat the flesh of their sons and daughters and it tastes as good to them as the flesh of spring lambs."[1244] One of Ashurbanipal's inscriptions describes a situation so dire that "they drank blood and dung-polluted water in their thirst,"[1245] and another in which the besieged Babylonians "ate each other's flesh in their ravenous hunger."[1246] On a metaphorical level, it speaks of a pharaoh as "a god who lives on his fathers, who feeds on his mothers."[1247]

Sin and Obedience (50:1–11)

To which of my creditors did I sell you? (50:1). See 42:7. There were two main sources of slaves in the ancient Near East: the imperialistic capture of foreigners through war, and economic or debt slavery with its supportive overtones. In the latter case, when someone became destitute, he could be forced to sell himself or family members into slavery in order to have the resources to survive.

This practice is also known elsewhere in the area.[1248] In a social system where there was no program of assistance for those in need, debt slavery provided a means of salvation from death in the face of starvation. The choice between enslaved life and freedom and death was not hard to make. Rib-Hadda, the governor of Byblos, complains to the pharaoh that, because of external attack, "we have no grain to eat.... Their sons, their daughters, the furnishings of their houses are gone, since they have been sold in the land of Yarimuta for provisions to keep us alive."[1249]

Zion's Comfort (51:1–16)

The rock from which you were cut (51:1). Stone was a common building material in Israel and was used in both dressed and undressed form. Limestone was common, shaped in the form of ashlar, which is dressed on all six sides after being hewn from a stone quarry.[1250] Quarried stone is

Rock quarry in City of David showing stones half-hewn
Daniel Frese/www.BiblePlaces.com

a matter of pride for Mesopotamian kings in their massive building projects, showing their power. Nebuchadnezzar writes of "a great wall from strong stones quarried from the great mountains."[1251] Zion's pride lies in the mighty foundation stones of their forefather and mother, Abraham and Sarah.

Cut Rahab to pieces (51:9). Complete domination is shown by dismemberment. In the Ugaritic Baal Epic, the goddess Anat acts similarly toward her opponents, described by the same verb (*ḥṣb*): "She 'cuts to pieces' the inhabitants of (or 'between') the two cities," cutting off heads and hands.[1252] A Neo-Assyrian prophecy has a similar statement: "I will cut them to pieces before his feet."[1253] The chaos monster subdued by God at creation is also the metaphorical representation of Egypt (see comment on 30:7).

This verse seems to employ both of these nuances in showing God's power, not only at creation but also in his defeat of Egypt, which led to Israel's exodus. Egypt itself had a myth of the confrontation between the sun god and a serpent/dragon during the former's daily journey.[1254]

You who dried up the sea (51:10). This verse clearly refers to God's control over the waters of the Red Sea at the time of the exodus (e.g., Ex. 14:21; 15:4). The original readers would also call to mind the Canaanite background of conflict with the sea. In the Baal Myth, Baal fights against Yam (the sea), killing him. "The mace whirls in Baal's hand ... strikes Prince [Yam] on the head, Ruler Naharu on the forehead. Yam goes groggy, falls to the ground.... Baal grabs Yam and sets about dismembering him, sets about finishing River Naharu off."[1255]

The ransomed of the LORD will return (51:11). The return of those dispersed through war, plague, or famine is important to a nation (see 10:21). An undated Akkadian prophecy states that "the city will prosper, (its) scattered will be reassembled."[1256] Numerous Mesopotamian kings, from Hammurabi through Merodach-Baladan II, claim restoration of the scattered as part of their legacy.[1257]

Prisoners ... dungeons (51:14). See comment on 42:7.

I am the LORD (51:15). See comment on 41:13.

Drunk on God's Wrath (51:17–23)

Cup of his wrath (51:17). Divine blessing was sought because divine wrath was terrible to behold and should be avoided at all costs. The Egyptian Instructions of Ani warn: "Offer to your god, beware of offending him ... be careful, help to protect him, let your eye watch out for his wrath."[1258] In the Mesopotamian creation story *Enuma Elish*, the goddess Tiamat is characterized by this emotion: "Tiamat our mother has grown angry ... furious with rage.... Tiamat whom you have enraged, where is one who can face her?"[1259] This frightening, death-delivering anger, which should be avoided at all costs, must be consumed by Israel.

None to take her by the hand (51:18). While those suffering from age and enfeeblement require care from others, the

King standing on neck of defeated enemy from relief found at Nimrud
Caryn Reeder, courtesy of the British Museum

Ugaritic legend of Aqhat indicates a more specific understanding of this action. In a list of duties that a son should perform for a parent is "to take his hand when (he is) drunk."[1260] It is not simply the inability of Jerusalem to care for itself that is envisaged here, but more specifically an incapacity as a result of becoming drunk on the cup of God's wrath.

Like antelope caught in a net (51:20). See comment on 8:14.

Your back ... like a street to be walked over (51:23). A victor could show the degradation of the vanquished by trampling them (41:25) or putting his foot on their necks (Josh. 10:24). An Akkadian ritual text notes that "Bel treads down on the neck of his uncooperative enemies."[1261] A third-century Aramaic text from Syene speaks words of assurance: "[Your foes] I shall destroy in front of you; [you shall place] your foot on their necks."[1262] Both Egyptian and Mesopotamian art show a ruler with his feet on subject people.[1263]

Zion's Enthronement (52:1–12)

The uncircumcised and defiled will not enter you again (52:1). The culturally or religiously different are often suspect and shunned. In Egypt at the time of the patriarchs, shepherds or those with facial hair were unacceptable. Egypt and Israel shared the practice of circumcision, the surgical removal of the foreskin from the male penis.[1264]

The reason for this practice in Egypt is unclear, but in Israel it was an outward covenantal sign. One who was uncircumcised was an outsider, whose entry into the holy city was unacceptable, running counter to the very idea of holiness and separation. They were unacceptable in Egyptian royal society as well, since an eighth-century monument, contemporaneous to Isaiah, reads: "Now the kings and counts of Lower Egypt ... could not enter the palace because they were uncircumcised ... which is an abomination to the palace."[1265] Esarhaddon, after building and dedicating the temple Esharra, says: "I excluded 'foreign seed' from its midst."[1266] All of these episodes could reflect xenophobia as regards the core of one's national identity.

The feet (52:7). While messengers often traveled by other means, some went on foot, a speedy means of transport over short distances (cf. 18:2). In Akkadian, couriers could also be called "runners" and were particularly used in military contexts.[1267]

Good tidings (52:7). See comment on 40:9.

When the LORD returns to Zion (52:8). When a god departs or is removed, it is a

The god Ashur as winged sun disk with bow accompanying the king
Caryn Reeder, courtesy of the British Museum

time of mourning (see sidebar on "Oracles of Consolation and Hope" at 43:1–7), but entry into a shrine is a time of celebration, since normality is restored. An Old Babylonian text records "that the gods Shamash and Aja should enter into their pure dwelling with celebrations."[1268] For Isaiah's audience, God is coming back home.

The LORD will go before (52:12). In the ancient Near East, one did not have to venture out alone but was preceded, guided, and aided by one's god. In the ninth century, Ashurnasirpal II went out to subdue a rebellion: "With the support of Ashur, the great lord, my lord, and the divine standard which goes before me … I mustered my weapons and troops and marched to the pass of the city."[1269] The great gods, including Ishtar, precede the royal army.[1270] An Aramaic Tel Dan inscription describes an unnamed ruler's confidence that even though Israel was advancing against him, he had been enthroned by his god Hadad, and "Hadad went before me."[1271]

God's Servant Suffers (52:13–53:12)

His appearance was so disfigured (52:14). Literal mutilation was generally reserved for punishment, as in the laws of Hammurabi. A symbolic assault takes place during the fifth day of the annual Mesopotamian New Year's *akītu*-festival. The king's royal emblems are removed and placed before Bel/Marduk; a priest "strikes the cheek of the king," the emblems are restored, and he is struck again. The blows are real in that they may produce tears and humiliation.[1272]

In Ishtar's Descent into the Netherworld, Ereshkigal curses Asushanimar to eat dirt and drink sewage, living as a homeless beggar. He also says: "May the drunk and thirsty strike your cheek."[1273] Such blows struck by the outcasts of the city humiliate a person. The servant is thus not just physically but also psychologically battered.

Substitutionary Rites

Israel and her neighbors provided substitutionary atonement for wrongs ordinarily through animal or plant sacrifice. Human substitution is much rarer. One example is the substitute king, known from Mesopotamian texts of the early second through late first millennia. This was precipitated by an omen that predicted the demise of the king. In order to save himself from this fate, he temporarily removed himself from the throne and enthroned an expendable substitute. The substitute heard recitation of the evil omens, attracting them to himself: "[Concerning the] signs ... [after] we had enthroned him, we had him hear them in front of Shamash. Furthermore, yesterday I had him hear them again, and I bent down and bound them in his hem."[A-259] On another occasion we read: "I made him recite the omen litanies before Shamash; he took all the celestial and terrestrial portents on himself,"[A-260] identifying himself with them.

Finally, he and his substitute queen were put to death, carrying the fate of the real king upon himself. "[Damqi], ... who had ruled Assyria, Babylonia, and all the countries, died with his queen ... as a substitute for the king, my lord.... He went to his fate for their redemption."[A-261] The substitute king and his queen were laid to rest in a royal tomb with appropriate accompanying ritual.[A-262]

While there are numerous parallels between the Servant in Isaiah 53:4–9 and the substitutionary king, the former is not royal, and the latter provides no service of any kind, much less redemptive, for the people as a whole, but only for the king.

Hittite substitute king text
Istanbul Archaeological Museum; © Dr. James C. Martin

Like a tender shoot, and like a root (53:2). Comparing people to plants is known in Egypt, where people are compared to trees who face defoliation and ultimate removal.[1274] The Akkadian language compares them to reeds and grass in their frailty and weakness.[1275]

Stricken by God (53:4). A blow by one's god is a serious matter. An Akkadian incantation against a witch states: "May the night-gods strike her because of her witchcraft,"[1276] while an Ashurbanipal inscription speaks of a man: "Nergal [the underworld and plague god] and Ishum struck him with an incurable wound."[1277] The threefold reiteration of the blow emphasizes its seriousness.

By his wounds we are healed (53:5). The gods aided in the healing process among Israel's neighbors. A truly international incident involved Nimmureya/Amenemophis III of Egypt, who had married the sister of the Mitannian king Tushratta and of Babylonia's Kassite king Kadashman-Enlil. He suffered greatly, including from abscessed teeth, and convinced his Mitannian brother to send a statue of Shaushka/Ishtar of Nineveh, since she possessed healing powers.[1278]

Numerous Mesopotamian deities, including Marduk, Nusku, Nabu, and Gula, were involved in healings and even resuscitations.[1279] In Egypt, Sekhmet was the goddess of healing,[1280] though others such as Hathor and the deified Imhotep could also heal.[1281] These all healed from their own power, but they did not assume the suffering upon themselves, as does the Servant of Isaiah 53.

Like a lamb to the slaughter (53:7). In addition to being slaughtered for domestic use, lambs were also slaughtered for ritual use in the Old Testament and among Israel's neighbors.[1282] In an Aramaic text, a man laments to his god that even though he was guiltless, "you made me a lamb in their flocks, a ram in their folds. They constantly feel me (saying): 'Let us kill him.... Let us eat his flesh.'"[1283] In an Egyptian text, an ox replaces the lamb as the slaughtered animal in a cry for mercy in the Book of the Dead: "Do not let my head be removed from me! For mine is an eye that sees, an ear that hears; for I am not an ox for slaughter, I shall not be an offering for those above! Let me pass by you, I am pure, Osiris has vanquished his foes!"[1284]

Sheep before her shearers is silent (53:7). Sheep shearing was a significant part of the agricultural year because of the importance of wool. An Aramaic text from Elephantine gives instructions: "The big ewe which is yours has arrived to shear the wool of hers before it can be torn by thorns.... On the day that you will wash her you should shear her."[1285] In a letter to his god, the Sumerian ruler Shulgi says: "I am like a sheep who has no reliable shepherd.... An unintelligent merchant transported me for trading purposes. With a vicious whip he [...] me cruelly.... I am noble (?) but do not utter a word."[1286]

Nor was any deceit in his mouth (53:9). Since truth was desirable (see 1:17), deceitfulness was not. In the Aramaic text in Demotic script, the writer laments to his god: "No evil is in my hands, my god; no duplicity in my mouth."[1287] By contrast, part of the wickedness of Tiamat in the Babylonian creation account was that "falsehood, lies she held ready on her lips."[1288]

He will see his offspring and prolong his days (53:10). With the average life expectancy of the common people probably less than forty years,[1289] a blessing would be to have a longer life (65:20) and offspring to provide support in one's infirmity. Esarhaddon wishes a similar blessing on any who might in the future repair the temple he rebuilt: "The gods will hear his prayer,

Sekhmet
Lenka Peacock, courtesy of the British Museum

Divine Mercy

While anger and punishment follow countering the will of a deity or king, permanent destruction or immediate death is counterproductive. That is, if death automatically followed every wrongdoing, there would soon be neither worshiper nor subject. Prayer commonly sought divine mercy, with an Akkadian verb (*enēnu*) combining the two.[A-263] A bilingual Sumerian-Akkadian text speaks of a prayer "by which I prayed to him, pleading for his mercy every day."

The same root in several Old Akkadian and Babylonian names is a constant cry for mercy, such as "Mercy-Baal!"[A-264] Two Amarna letters show the same root used in Canaanite, describing the desired mercy of city-state kings.[A-265] Two Hebrew inscriptions, one from ninth-century Kuntillet ʿAjrud and the other from seventh-century Khirbet Beit Lei, associate this mercy or grace with Yahweh.[A-266] A Nineteenth Dynasty Egyptian prayer gives thanks to Amon-Re:

> Though it may be that the servant is normal in doing wrong, still the Lord is normal in being merciful. The Lord of Thebes does not spend an entire day angry. As for his anger—in the completion of a moment there is no remnant, and the wind is turned about in mercy for us, and Amon has turned around with his breezes.[A-267]

Isaiah's picture of God differs from both of the situations noted above. There is no prayer for it to be given, and it does not show the apparently fickleness of mercy driven by the breeze. The mercy shown by God is here bracketed by his own will.

Si'gabbar funerary stele
Marie-Lan Nguyen/Wikimedia Commons, courtesy of the Louvre

he will extend his days, he will enlarge his family."[1290] The seventh-century Aramaic tomb inscription of the priest Siʾgabbar indicates that this blessing can be deserved: "Because of my righteousness in his (the Aramean moon god) presence, he gave me a good name and long life."[1291]

The colophon at the end of the Egyptian Tale of the Shipwrecked Sailor wishes well on its readers: "Life, prosperity, health!"[1292] An inscription on a statue of Nebneteru also combines blessing, life, and offspring: "I saw my sons as great priests, son after son who issued from me. I attained the age of ninety-six, being healthy, without illness. If one desires the length of my life, one must praise god for another in my name."[1293]

Barren Zion Vindicated (54)

Barren woman (54:1). Children ensured the continuity of the clan and family and provided support for aging parents. Fertility was a matter of pride, while a barren woman was of lower socioeconomic status and thus felt shame. Even though Israel was not to worship the dead (see sidebar on "Cult of the Dead" at 57:6), they were remembered and venerated by future generations, a legacy lost through barrenness.

Barrenness was also a serious economic problem in a society where labor-intensive agriculture placed a high demand on finding

Bedouin tent
David Bivin/www.LifeintheHolyLand.com

sufficient helpers. Where descendants were a blessing, their lack is a problem; no one was childless by choice. A Sumerian myth includes barrenness among other infirmities such as blindness, crippling, and incontinence.[1294] Some texts from Alalakh in Syria dating from the last half of the second century B.C. allow a man to remarry if his wife is barren.[1295]

Tent (54:2). Tents, as portable accommodation, were often used by nomads or people on the move, while settled folk dwelt in more permanent houses. The earliest listed kings in the Assyrian King List are designated as "those who live in tents."[1296] Here the tent does not symbolize transience and hardship, but rather that which is easily expandable, allowing gathered abundance. Such royal tents are mentioned in Mesopotamia as well. Speaking of Merodach-Baladan, Sargon writes: "I took away his royal tent and his golden royal umbrella."[1297]

Reproach of your widowhood (54:4). Widows were marginalized in ancient Near Eastern society, having no one to provide for and protect them and placing them low in the socioeconomic hierarchy.[1298] A Sumerian proverb acknowledges that "poverty is the widow's lot."[1299] One of Hammurabi's laws indicates that she is not entrusted with her late husband's property. "If a widow with small children has come to a decision to enter the house of a second man, she shall not enter without legal authority."[1300] Her rights are inferior to those of her children.[1301]

An early Hebrew text reflects a widow's concern for her lot, but also her ability to petition an official for protection: "My husband died childless, so may your hand be with me, and may you place into the control of your servant the inheritance of which you spoke."[1302]

Your Maker is your husband (54:5). God is metaphorically Israel's husband.[1303] The Hebrew term *baʿal* can mean "husband" but also "owner, master." Two separate words fulfill these functions in Akkadian. The cognate *bēlu* has the latter meaning only and is used of gods.[1304] "Husband" (*mutu*) rarely refers to a deity, though in an Old Akkadian text a king is designated "husband of (the goddess) Ishtar."[1305]

Israel's God Yahweh is the true "Baal" (1 Chr. 12:5), providing for the once widowed

Discontinuity between Gods and Humans

In the Old Testament, humanity is God's creation, which, while being in his image, shares no divinity with him. God is rather a spiritual being, though at times he is described in anthropomorphic terms. God is in every way superior to his creation.

This is not the picture painted among Israel's neighbors. Many of their myths about the origin of their gods are in human, sexual terms (see sidebar on "Creator Gods" at 42:5), and many gods are presented as showing jealousy and rivalry. The same epic shows blood lust, when Anat slaughters until "up to her knees she wades in the blood of soldiers, to her neck in the gore of fighters."

Sexual lust is a commonplace, for example in Enki and the World Order, where couplings play a prominent role.[A-268] The Egyptian goddess Hathor, called among other things "mistress of the vagina,"[A-269] and the god Min, often portrayed ichthyphallically,[A-270] are two deities especially linked with sexuality.

Gods are powerful, but they are affected by circumstances that seem to be beyond their control. The Atraḫasis Epic pictures the gods themselves suffering under the calamitous flood that Enlil brought on humanity: "As for Nintu the Great Mistress, her lips were encrusted with rime. The great gods, the Anunna, stayed parched and famished. The goddess watched and wept."[A-271] Regarding the same event in the Epic of Gilgamesh, "the gods were afraid of the flood weapon. They withdrew.... The gods cowered, like dogs crouched by an outside wall. Ishtar screamed like a woman giving birth."[A-272]

Ancient gods, while not mortal in the way humans are, can still die or be killed, as when Tiamat is killed in the *Enuma Elish* creation story,[A-273] Baal dies in the Canaanite Baal myth,[A-274] and divine death is implied in the Egyptian "Cannibal Hymn," where "Unas is he who eats men, feeds on gods."[A-275] In the Book of the Dead, a prayer for immortality to Osiris in the Papyrus of Nu reads: "I pray thee, let me not fall into rottenness, as thou lettest every god, and every goddess, and every animal, and every reptile, see corruption, when the soul hath gone out of them, after their death."[A-276]

Though there are numerous divine-human similarities, they are also recognized as different. Words similar to those used by Isaiah are found in the Egyptian Instructions of Ankhsheshonq: "The plans of the god are one thing, the thoughts of men are another."[A-277] A hymn to Amun-Re highlights how he is elevated not only above humanity, but even the other gods:

The pyramid of Unas, Saqqara. The interior walls are inscribed with the Pyramid Texts. These inscriptions can be divided among some 750 utterances and 2,300 shorter spells.
Werner Forman Archive

But One alone is the hidden God, who hides himself from them all, who conceals himself from gods, whose features cannot be known. He is farther above than heaven, deeper down than the world below and no gods at all can know his true nature.... He is mysterious to the depths of his majesty—great beyond any perception of him, mighty beyond comprehension.[A-278]

Babylonian wisdom recognized this distance as well: "The god's mind is as remote as the interior of heaven."[A-279] God in Isaiah highlights the strong contrast between himself and his creation.

wife, Israel. This intimate and exclusive metaphor does not seem to be used among Israel's neighbors. Though tongue in cheek, a Sumerian proverb shows the expectation of a husband's support for his family: "He who does not support a wife or child, his nose has not borne a nose-rope."[1306]

God of all the earth (54:5). A pyramid text of Pepi I praises the sky goddess: "You are strong and you are mighty, you fill every place with your beauty, the whole earth is beneath you, you possess it."[1307] Similarly, a hymn to the sun god Aten attests: "When you dawn, their eyes observe you as your rays light the whole earth; every heart acclaims your sight."[1308] The universality of the natural manifestation of these deities supported their universal sovereignty.

A Hebrew cave inscription from Khirbet Beit Lei, probably from the sixth century, shows what apparently an Israelite layperson's theology is: "Yahweh is the god of the whole earth."[1309] Even though he is not tied to a universal natural phenomenon such as the sun or moon with their global manifestations as are many of the gods of Israel's neighbors, Yahweh still reigns over all.

Servants of the LORD (54:17). See comment on 42:19.

Compassion for the Oppressed (55:1–13)

Milk (55:1). Milk, usually from goats, was a staple of Israel's diet (e.g., Gen. 18:8; Deut. 32:14; Judg. 4:19). It was also consumed in Mesopotamia. It was a food and was also used in religious rituals (e.g., "you shall pour [as a libation offering] milk, beer, and [wine]").[1310] Milking scenes are depicted in ancient Near Eastern art from both Mesopotamia and Egypt.[1311]

He will have mercy (55:7). In Akkadian, the same root (Heb. *rḥm*; Akk. *rēmu*) is used of gods. An Old Babylonian text speaks of repaying a loan to Shamash "when Shamash acted mercifully."[1312] In the Egyptian Instructions of Merikare, a deity is called "he who is merciful."[1313] Sinuhe found this on his journeys as well: "It was the god who acted, so as to show mercy to one with whom he had been angry."[1314]

A seventh-century Hebrew text from Yavneh-Yam is an appeal from a farmer to an official since he has been mistreated: "[Please return] my garment. If the official

Milking scene from the tomb of Kagemni in Saqqara
Leandro César

Gebel el-Arak knife handle with variety of wild beasts
Rama/Wikimedia Commons, courtesy of the Louvre

does not consider it an obligation to return [your servant's garment, then have] pity upon him and [return] your servant's [garment] from that motivation."[1315] This is a trait desired for anyone in authority, whether king or god.

My word ... will not return to me empty (55:11). See comment on 40:8.

Clap their hands (55:12). Clapping the hands is a sign of joy done either literally by people (Ezek. 25:6) or figuratively, as here, by elements of nature (Ps. 98:8). A Canaanite king also seems to clap in the annual celebration of the new grape harvest.[1316]

Outsiders Made Insiders (56:1–8)

Sabbath (56:2). See comment on 1:13.

Eunuchs (56:3–5). See comment on 39:7. Eunuchs (i.e., males who have lost their testicles for some reason) are maimed and cannot enter God's presence (Deut. 23:1). In the messianic kingdom, God will bless them with a special place. The Hebrew term *sarîs* is cognate to the Akkadian *šareši*, Mesopotamian court officials who may or may not be eunuchs.[1317] Some suggest that the beardless men found in many reliefs could be eunuchs (see 8:1).[1318] The Myth of Enki and Ninmah describes that a person without male or female genitalia cannot "stand in attendance before the king."[1319]

Memorial (56:5). Literally this is a "hand," though "memorial" fits the context best. Excavations at Hazor in northern Israel have found a stone stele with hands carved on it,[1320] which, while not clearly understood, gives this verse a literal rather than a figurative meaning.

Accusing the Wicked (56:9–57:13)

Beasts of the field ... beasts of the forest (56:9). One purpose of effective government is protecting citizens from danger, whether natural or human. Here the two are combined, using the metaphor of ravenous beasts to indicate rapacious humans. On the divine level, several aggressive deities are presented as animals, such as the leonine war god Apedamak of southern Egypt,[1321] Pakhet from Middle Egypt,[1322] and Sekhmet, who combines fearsome and protective attributes.[1323]

Kings also liken themselves to lions in their ferocity (see comment on 5:29).[1324] A Mari text describes a ferocious attack: "I have attacked you like a wolf, I have spewed my saliva on you like a lion." An Old Babylonian incantation reads: "like a lion, moving quickly, like a wolf, full of rage."[1325]

Mute dogs (56:10–11). In Israel dogs were held in contempt (e.g., 1 Sam. 17:43), possibly because of their eating habits (e.g., Ex. 22:30).[1326] Here they are even more useless, being unable even to warn by barking. Dogs are connected more positively with the Akkadian goddess Gula, who is associated with healing.[1327] Several Sargonic period seals depict dogs flanking people or even supplying protection.[1328] This positive relationship is suggested as the reason why more than 1,500 dogs were buried in a fifth-century cemetery in Ashkelon.[1329]

Ponders it in his heart (57:1). Cognition and emotions are metaphorically associated with different body parts in various cultures. In Israel, strong affections are often associated with the kidneys and fear with the bowels, while particularly serious reflection and rumination take place in the heart. Such reflection and meditation are associated metaphorically with the heart in Mesopotamia as well. Esarhaddon said, "I spoke repeatedly with my heart and pondered mightily."[1330]

A person's essence, the emotional and intellectual center, was the heart in Egyptian belief. After death it was weighed on a balance opposite the feather of truth and righteousness to determine whether the deceased deserved eternal life.[1331] For Isaiah, no serious consideration is being given to the death of the just.

The righteous are taken away (57:1). When times are difficult, death can be a release, as here for the righteous. In Mesopotamia, death was viewed less as a benefit than as a natural part of life reserved for humanity, since, in the Old Babylonian version of the Gilgamesh Epic, the gods "allotted death to mankind, but life they kept for themselves."[1332] However, Gilgamesh sought immortality for himself after facing the death of his friend Enkidu.[1333]

Egypt, with its developed theology of the afterlife, still did not seek death, since the journey to the blessing of the afterlife could be treacherous. The netherworld is painted with bleaker strokes during the Sumerian period in Mesopotamia: "To the dark house ... to the house which those who enter cannot leave ... to the house where those who enter are deprived of light, where soil is their sustenance, clay their food."[1334] None of Israel's neighbors saw death as something sought with anticipation of great benefit.

Death (57:2). See sidebar on "Sheol and the Afterlife" at 14:9.

Sorceress ... adulterers ... prostitutes (57:3). See sidebars on "Superstitions and Divination" at 2:6; "Occult Practices" at 47:9; "Cult of the Dead" at 57:8.

Oaks ... every spreading tree (57:5). Trees, valuable for shade, wood, and fruit, also played a role in pagan cultic practices (see comment on 1:29–30). Asherah, Canaanite fertility goddess, was associated with wood and trees (17:8). In Mesopotamia, several deities are tree gods: Lugal-asar/Bel-sarbi, god of the poplar tree; Lugal-shinig/Bel-bin, god of the tamarisk tree; Lugal-gishammar, god of the date palm.[1335] These three are equated with Nergal, god of the underworld, in some god lists.[1336] Some Egyptian deities also had associations with trees.[1337]

You sacrifice your children (57:5). Human sacrifice of any kind was unacceptable for Israel, though some, including King Ahaz, took part in it anyway (2 Kings 16:1).[1338] Child sacrifice is particularly associated with the Ammonite god Molech (see

Egyptian tree goddess giving provision
Werner Forman Archive/E. Strouhal
◀

57:9).[1339] Texts from Ebla provide the first evidence of the worship of "Malik," though with no child sacrifice evident,[1340] nor is there any at Mari[1341] or in Ammonite territory,[1342] where the name is also evident. Nuzi may provide examples of child sacrifice in the case of infants buried within buildings rather than in tombs.[1343] An underworld connection for the Ugaritic god *mlk* is debated,[1344] though it is clear in this Isaiah passage that he is found in Sheol (v. 9).[1345]

The strongest ties of the deity to child sacrifice come from later Punic material. The textual evidence for the connection is ambiguous,[1346] but a stone relief with Phoenician/Punic influences found at Pozo Moro in Spain and dating from c. 500 B.C. shows what may be a sacrificial scene of a child.[1347] Archaeology has confirmed the practice in several Punic sites through urns found in cultic contexts contain children's bones.[1348] Molek, in his association with the dead, is the underworld's counterpart of Baal, god of life and fertility.[1349]

You have poured out drink offerings (57:6). In Israel, while blood and grain sacrifices were most common, there were also offerings of poured-out water and wine called libations. Such liquids were dedicated to deities for their use, including pagan deities such as those being condemned here. Libations are also apparent in Mesopotamia and Egypt.[1350] The Egyptian treasurer Tjetji speaks of "an offering which the king gives: an offering of a thousand of bread and beer."[1351] A small wine decanter from eighth- to seventh-century Judah is inscribed: "Belonging to Mattanyahu, libation wine, ¼ (measure)."[1352] From the owner's name, one assumes the libation is directed to Yahweh.

Forsaking me, you uncovered your bed (57:8). Pagan worship is imbued with strong sexual overtones, as are clear here. Some suggest that sacred prostitutes, female and more rarely male, served as part of the fertility cult in the ancient Near East, particularly among Canaanites, or that there was a sexual component as part of the "sacred marriage" ceremony in Mesopotamia.[1353]

Physical intercourse with a temple prostitute was intended, through sympathetic magic, to induce the deities to bring fertility to the fields, divine semen in the form of rain impregnating "mother earth." The sacred marriage concerned a physical relationship between the love goddess Inanna/Ishtar or her representative and the king.[1354] A term possibly referring to the sexual cultic functionaries (*qdš[h]*) occurs in Hebrew, Ugaritic, and Akkadian, though it is not used in this Isaiah passage.[1355]

Recent studies have suggested that cultic prostitution is not as ubiquitous as previously suggested[1356] and that the physical act might better be understood metaphorically. In either case, neither is acceptable for Israel, who is here condemned for directing her desires toward someone other than her God.[1357]

Looked on their nakedness (57:8). Literally, it is the "hand" (*yād*) that is looked upon, with that word as a euphemism for "penis" (cf. Ugaritic).[1358] This is a fitting interpreta-

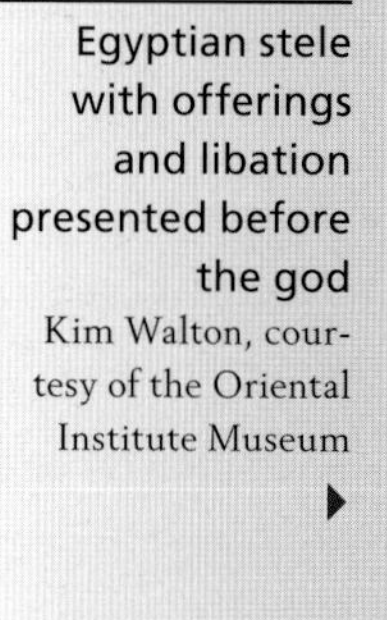

Egyptian stele with offerings and libation presented before the god

Kim Walton, courtesy of the Oriental Institute Museum

▸ Cult of the Dead

Among the religious practices of Israel's neighbors were various manifestations of worship of the dead in order for them to deliver blessings to the offerer. The dead also depended on the living to provide their sustenance, so it served the living well to practice what they would soon need themselves.[A-280]

The Egyptians had an elaborate understanding of the netherworld, providing documents such as the Book of the Dead, which contained instructions and spells to help the departed reach divinity.[A-281] Some priests were required regularly to provide offerings of food and drink to the dead. As time passed, these became symbolic, with only libations of water being offered.[A-282] Among the instructions in the Book of the Dead is one where the departed is to say: "O you Sycamore of Nut, give me the water and air in you."[A-283]

A Mesopotamian funerary text directed to dead ancestors asks, "Come, eat this, drink this and bless Ammisaduqa, son of Ammiditana, the king of Babylon."[A-284] Another mentions some specific needs for which funerary offerings are brought: "You perform funerary offerings for fallow fields, you perform funerary offerings for waterways which carry no water."[A-285] An Old Babylonian texts states that "milk and ghee will be required for the funerary offering,"[A-286] liquids poured out for the gods (57:6).

Similar funerary drink offerings to the dead are evident among the Canaanites at Ugarit.[A-287] Many funeral vaults there had channels and pipes directing the libations from the surface into the vaults themselves.[A-288]

Israel is not to worship the dead, but there is archaeological evidence from tombs that libations may have been performed at least until the decomposition of the body.[A-289] Prophetic condemnation of cultic practices such as this by Isaiah show that orthodox religion was not universally kept.[A-290]

Offerings presented to the dead
Werner Forman Archive
◂

Egyptian gods Hathor, Isis, and Amun
Frederick J. Mabie

tion in the context of the sexual debauchery noted here, but it could also indicate the stone memorial mentioned in 56:5 (also *yād*).[1359]

Molech (57:9). See comment on 57:5.

Collection of idols (57:13). Israel's neighbors were polytheists, and two of their many gods, Baal and Molech, have already been encountered in this chapter. Shrines and temples were ubiquitous, serving as worship centers for one or a number of deities.[1360] Plurality among Egyptian gods is shown by several groups of deities often associated with each other, in groups ranging from pairs to groups of twelve.[1361]

The fourteenth-century monotheistic attempt by Akhenaten was short-lived, since polytheism was so firmly entrenched.[1362] The Mesopotamian Poem of Erra and Ishum also speaks of a group of gods: "When Anu, king of the gods, impregnated Earth, she bore the Seven Gods for him and he named them Sebitti."[1363] We have encountered numerous other Mesopotamian and Ugaritic deities. Israel itself was not immune, repeatedly turning to other gods besides Yahweh.[1364]

The Contrite Revived (57:14–21)

Prepare the road (57:14). See comment on 40:3–4.

High and lofty One (57:15). See comments on 33:5, 16.

Mire (57:20). The term is used only here in the Old Testament. In Akkadian the term designates "excrement, spittle, vomit,"[1365] making the results of the work of the wicked even more abhorrent.

Fasting: The Good and the Bad (58:1–14)

Seek me out (58:2). Messages from the gods (see comment on 1:1) were sought through oracles (see 44:25), which could come about through dreams or divination (see sidebar on "Superstitions and Divination" at 2:6). These will come for Israel when they live justly.

Fasting (58:4). Fasting (abstention from food) is a much rarer practice as religious ritual in ancient Near Eastern texts than in the Old Testament.[1366] The Old Kingdom

▸ Caring for the Needy as an Act of Piety

Special kindness is expected toward the destitute who have no means of looking after themselves. Those unable even to clothe themselves are in a state of shame (47:2–3). One who has been blessed should bless those less fortunate. The Old Babylonian Man and his God adjures the one so blessed: "As for you, do not tarry to anoint the parched, feed the hungry, give the thirsty water to drink; may he who sits down with feverish eyes see your food, suckle, receive it and be pleased with you."[A-291]

A Sixth Dynasty inscription from a tomb lauds its inhabitant: "I rescued the weak from one stronger than he as much as was in my power. I gave bread to the hungry, clothes to the naked; I brought the boatless to land. I buried him who had no son, I made a boat for him who lacked one."[A-292] A good Assyrian king will do what a prophecy concerning Ashurbanipal says concerning his good reign: "The naked have been clothed with garments."[A-293] It is insufficient simply to believe in the gods; one must practically serve them and others in their name.[A-294]

prophecies of Neferti associate it with grief; as a result of turmoil in a land, "none will weep over death, none will wake fasting for death."[1367] Zoroastrianism goes as far as to condemn fasting as sinful since it weakens the body.[1368] Isaiah here condemns its misuse, not the practice per se.

The pointing finger and malicious talk (58:9). Evil talk and insinuating actions are known among Israel's neighbors. A bilingual Sumerian-Akkadian Hymn to Ninurta lists numerous evildoers, including "he who inseminates a man's wife, a slanderer, one who points an evil finger at a colleague," spreading unfounded rumors about him.[1369]

He will satisfy your needs (58:11). In contrast to idols, for which their makers must provide food and lodging (see comment on 2:8), Yahweh is Israel's provider. Ashurbanipal makes this claim for himself: "His people, who had fled to me from famine and starvation, settled in my own land, and I satisfied their hunger."[1370] The Ugaritic Baal myth places this provision ironically in the mouth of Mot, the god of death: "Mot is always proclaiming ... I am the only one ... who fattens gods and men, who satisfies the hordes of the earth."[1371]

Rebuild the ancient ruins (58:12). See comments on 44:28; 49:8.

Ride on the heights of the land (58:14). Whether in a hilly landscape such as in Israel and Canaan or in flatter terrain such as that

Heights of the land represented here in the Eastern mountains of Samaria
Todd Bolen/www.BiblePlaces.com

of Egypt and some of Mesopotamia, height found on a ridge or hill provides strategic advantages of easier protection from enemies and the ability to observe those approaching from afar. Height also signifies superiority (see comment on 2:2), as when Baal is indicated to be superior to others by being "the cloud rider" (see 19:1). The Egyptian building inscription of Sesostris I boasts: "My power reaches heaven's heights."[1372]

The specific word used in this verse (*bmh*) sometimes designates the high place shrines, such as the one mentioned by King Mesha: "I reigned after my father, (who) made this high place for Chemosh."[1373] This may imply Israelite superiority over those worshiped at these places.

Sin, Separation, and Redemption (59:1–21)

Breastplace ... helmet (59:17). Yahweh the warrior takes a stand against his people's enemies. This metaphor plays on his clothing, which was also worn by a warrior for both battle and covering. Such garments are richly portrayed in reliefs and other iconography from the ancient Near East. They are also mentioned in texts.

The first term (*širyôn*) can be a breastplate, guarding the chest, or a more encompassing coat of mail.[1374] The New Kingdom story The Egyptians and the Amazons, while broken, speaks of an army of women "bearing armor ... helmets with bull's faces ... breastplates."[1375] Somewhat earlier, the annals of Thutmose III present him joining battle in his finery: "His majesty set out on a chariot of fine gold, decked in his shining armor like strong-armed Horus."[1376]

Erra, an Akkadian war god, is told: "Yours is warlike armor,"[1377] while Marduk's battle against Tiamat is described with considerable sound play: "He was garbed in a ghastly armored garment, on his head he was covered with terrifying auras."[1378] Here God's passions serve as Israel's defense rather than actual, physical garments.

Assyrian soldiers wearing scale armor vests, ninth century, Nimrud
Z. Radovan/www.BibleLandPictures.com

Jerusalem's Glory Restored (60:1–22)

Arise, shine, for your light has come (60:1). While darkness signifies despair, light signifies hope (see comments on 9:2; 42:7). Mesopotamian literature credits light to Enlil ("the life-giving light"[1379]) and Shamash, the sun god, or to kings (see 10:16). Egypt also credits it to manifestations of the sun god. In the northern Sinai site of Kuntillet ʿAjrud, a Hebrew text, probably from the eighth century, speaks of a day of battle "when God (El) shone forth,"[1380] bringing victory (as he does in Isaiah).

To you the riches of the nations will come (60:5). When the Assyrians and Babylonians conquered nations, they exacted tribute that was brought to them, as is described in texts (see comments on 7:1, 6; 13:17; 18:7) and pictured by laden people shown on palace reliefs.[1381] Now the tables are turned, with the erstwhile captives now receiving tribute gifts.

Herds of camels ... young camels (60:6). Camels were part of the tribute

Camels in the Negev
Copyright 1995–2009 Phoenix Data Systems

brought to Mesopotamian kings. Tiglath-pileser III states: "I received she camels along with their young camels [the same term, *bkr*, as is used here]."[1382] Here they will be returned to Israel, a one-time tribute payer herself.

Incense (60:6). See comments on 1:13; 17:8.

Kedar ... Nebaioth (60:7). Inhabited by descendants of Ishmael (Gen. 25:13; 1 Chron. 1:29), the area probably lies in the northwest Arabian peninsula.[1383] Kedar (Qedar) and Nebaioth (Nabayatu) are mentioned in Akkadian texts from the Neo-Assyrian and Neo-Babylonian periods.[1384] Ashurbanipal mentions both towns in descriptions of his campaigns,[1385] and Kedar's king joined the Persians to attack Egypt during the Persian period.[1386]

Fly along like ... doves to their nests (60:8). Doves are among the clean animals used for sacrifice (Lev.1:14). Here they are a sign of hope and settledness, returning to the window ledges[1387] from which they had previously departed. A Sumerian lament from the second millennium sheds light on the importance of this bird. There the dove is symbolic of a deity (cf. Matt. 3:16), whose departure from the temple symbolizes her abandonment of her people: "Like a frightened dove, I spend the day (huddled) against the rafters.... The window where I focus attention has been destroyed. Its dove flies away. The dove of the window has abandoned her nest."[1388] What looks like a dove is pictured on an Israelite jar-handle seal.[1389]

Ships of Tarshish ... with their silver (60:9). Though the exact location of Tarshish is uncertain,[1390] it is also associated with silver in the seventh-century Hebrew Temple of the Lord ostracon: "As Ashyahu the king commanded (you) to give into the hand of Zechariah three sh(eqels) of silver of Tarshish."[1391]

Glory of Lebanon (60:13). On Lebanon's trees, see comment on 2:13.

Pine (60:13). Most likely juniper, this was a fragrant wood used in Mesopotamian building. Sargon roofed his royal palace "with juniper beams and made it smell sweet."[1392] An Egyptian text directed to King Merikare describes a military campaign: "I pacified the entire West as far as the coast of the sea. It pays taxes, it gives cedar wood, one sees juniper wood which they give us."[1393] This reflects the same Isaianic context of tribute.

Bow down at your feet (60:14). A person abasing himself before another often associates himself with that person's feet. The writer of an Amarna letter describes himself as "[the dust] under the sandals of the king, my lord; I fall at the king's feet,"[1394] while a god approaches two other gods, "his

Courtiers kneeling
Werner Forman Archive/Schimmel Collection, New York

▸ Year of the Lord's Favor

Happiness and plenty are the goal of an ideal reign. A letter containing a prophecy addressed to Ashurbanipal foretells blessings from Shamash and Adad. These gods establish

> a happy reign: days of justice, years of equity, heavy rains, water in full flood, a thriving commerce.... Old men dance, young men sing, women and maidens are glad and make merry.... Whom his crime has condemned to death, the king my lord has let live; who has been held prisoner many years, is set free; who were sick many days have recovered. The hungry have been sated; the lice-infested have been anointed; the naked have been clad in garments.[A-295]

Many of these same elements characterize the anticipated messianic reign in Israel. Since justice and righteousness are the ideal (61:3, 8, 10, 11; see sidebars on "Unjust Laws" at 10:1, "The Ideal King" at 11:1), they are anticipated. An Amarna letter indicates much the same understanding of the terms involved here when Rib-hadda asks that his case be heard "and give me my due"[A-296]—that which is rightfully and equitably his. The Egyptian Instruction of Ptahhotep indicates the importance of justice in Egypt: "Great is justice, lasting in effect, unchallenged since the time of Osiris.... In the end it is justice that lasts."[A-297]

The poor benefit from increased commerce; trade brings prosperity from faraway places. It was an important part of the economy of the entire region (see sidebar on "Military vs. Diplomacy" at 39:1). Jubilation will replace a downcast heart, freedom will replace captivity, and clothing, nakedness. Poverty is equated to bondage in a Prayer to Atum in Papyrus Anastasi: "Amun, lend your ear to the lonely in court, he is poor.... Let the poor go free; might the poor appear as the justified."[A-298]

ancestors. He prostrated (himself), kissed the ground before them."[1395] The great gods "kiss the ground" before the goddess Inanna in the Sumerian Exaltation of Inanna.[1396]

You have been forsaken (60:15). Divine abandonment explained the fall of cities or nations. When the deity is with the people, they flourish, but when the god leaves, they fall. Mesopotamian examples begin with third millennium Sumerian texts and continue with second millennium Akkadian ones.[1397] Esarhaddon, in a building description, recounts his rebuilding of Babylon, which had been destroyed because of evil within. It was precipitated because "the gods and goddesses, who dwelt therein, went up to heaven,"[1398] leaving the city to fend for itself.[1399]

Abandonment by the Moabite god Kemosh is implied in the Mesha Inscription, since "Omri was the king of Israel, and he oppressed Moab for many days, for Kemosh was angry with his land,"[1400] leaving it to its own devices. But abandonment is not permanent, since Kemosh, and Esarhaddon's gods, return, as does the God of Israel, as the end of this verse indicates.

Nursed at royal breasts (60:16). See comment on 49:23.

The LORD will be your everlasting light (60:19). See comment on 60:1.

I am the LORD (60:22). See comment on 41:13.

God's Good Favor (61:1–11)

Release from darkness (61:1). Literally "eye-opening"; see comment on 42:7.

Who mourn ... who grieve (61:2–3). See sidebar on "Mourning Rites" at 15:2.

Procession of soldiers with standards from Deir el Bahri
Manfred Näder, Gabana Studios, Germany

Oil of gladness (61:3). Anointing with oil was not only a sign of consecration for a task (v. 1); it was also part of joyful feasting that took place when messengers brought good news.[1401] In the incantation series Maqlu speaks of "oil that soothes men's muscles."[1402] The state of the destitute will be reversed. Instead of being outcasts, they will be welcomed.

As a bride (61:10). See comment on 49:18.

Zion's Coming Salvation (62:1–12)

Crown of splendor in the LORD's hand (62:3). Deities are regularly depicted wearing crowns. Marduk's crown is described in lavish terms: "a crown with mighty horns, a lordly crown befitting a god, full of splendor, of lapis lazuli and gold. On the top of his crown I put (various precious) stones, and I also studded the outer surface of the crown with (various precious) stones."[1403] An Akkadian text addressed to Bel (Marduk) says, "Borsippa (a city south of Babylon) is your crown,"[1404] with the city metaphorically representing the crown's finery. Israel's capital city is here equated to a divine crown with its beautiful fittings.

Your land will be married (62:4). A deity marrying a land will protect and provide for it. Lack of such care is found in an Amarna proverb used by Rib-Hadda, "For lack of a cultivator, my field is like a woman without a husband."[1405] Akkadian deities can "marry" a king, as when an Old Akkadian king is called "husband of Ishtar,"[1406] or when the same goddess calls to Gilgamesh, "You can be my husband and I can be your wife."[1407] But nowhere else besides Isaiah is the country itself being married to a god.

Raise a banner (62:10). A banner or ensign was a visible symbol that could be elevated to identify a person or group (see 5:26; 11:12). While "banner" connotes some sort of flag, this more likely indicates a staff topped by an identifying emblem. Akkadian texts mention these topped by

Pharaoh presented by gods with crown, Kom Ombo
Frederick J. Mabie

divine symbols. Sargon wrote that "the ensign of Ashur my lord I installed [in the city]" under his control.[1408] Isaiah's banner will show Yahweh's control and summon all to him.

God's Angry Vengeance (63:1–6)

Edom ... Bozrah (63:1). See comments on 21:11–12; 34:6.

Trodden ... trampled ... stained (63:3–6). See sidebar on "God as a Warrior" at 42:13.

Prayer for God's Love and Mercy (63:7–64:12)

You, O LORD, are our Father (63:16). God as Father highlights his watchful care over his offspring. In addition to Mesopotamian and Egyptian examples of a god being called "father" (see comments on 41:13; 49:18), the Zukru festival at Emar in Syria describes ritual activities, including "they bring out in procession Dagan the very father."[1409]

No one has seen any God besides you (64:4). See comments on 37:20; 40:28–29; 46:9.

O LORD, you are our Father (64:8). See comment on 63:16.

Dispensing Judgment and Salvation (65:1–16)

Offering sacrifices in gardens (65:3). See comments on 1:29–20.

Who sit among the graves, and spend their nights keeping secret vigil (65:4). An Aramaic text in Demotic script also associates a grave with a vigil. As is said in a description of a sacred marriage ceremony, "Harps keep you awake in the evening; in the grave of my ancestor, a dirge. A sound of lyres from the grave keeps you awake in the evening."[1410] Night vigils were accompanied by music. The vigil mentioned here appears to hold some sacred function, beyond simply mourning by a grave. The Hebrew shows it is being done inside the grave. Secrecy indicates that it is not a generally acceptable practice, probably part of a funerary cult (see sidebar on "Cult of the Dead" at 57:6).[1411]

Eat the flesh of pigs (65:4). A distinctive element of orthodox Israelite religious practice was avoiding pork; thus, eating pork shows the people's religious deterioration. Even though banned, archaeological evidence indicates numerous Israelite sites with a small amount of pig remains.[1412] Pigs are rarely depicted in the ancient Near East, though there is a fourth millennium seal from Luristan showing a wild pig.[1413] There is textual evidence for Egyptian abomination of pork, even for the gods,[1414] but it was by no means universally followed.

Even in Egypt and Mesopotamia, where pigs were raised and eaten, they were not part of the regular offerings.[1415] An eighth-century Assyrian wisdom saying collection states: "The pig is not fit for a temple ... an abomination to the gods, and abhorrence, accursed by Shamash."[1416]

It stands written before me ... I will pay it back into their laps (65:6). Economic texts are frequent in the ancient Near East, among them numerous loan documents. Akkadian loan documents may contain any of several elements: repayment date, repayment medium, interest rate.[1417] Usually such records are written in the third person, but some are in the first person. A letter to a Kassite king reads: "Let us settle our accounts with each other and I will collect and pay you in full."[1418] Hebrew ostraca from Arad concerning supply allocations order that the transaction be written down.[1419]

Spread a table (65:11). A table is prepared for honored guests (2 Sam.9:7).[1420] Ptah-Hotep is instructed on how to behave in such a situation: "If you are one among guests at the table of one greater than you, take what he gives."[1421] This is unacceptable for Israel since here they are entertaining pagan deities. Part of the ritual for installing the high priestess at Emar involved table preparation: "They set four tables before the gods. They set one table for the storm god, one table for (. . .), and (two tables) on the ground for the underworld gods."[1422]

Fortune . . . Destiny (65:11). "Fortune" or "luck" (*gad*) is the name of a Syrian deity worshiped widely. The term appears often in Ugaritic and Phoenician names, though whether having in mind the deity or simply good fortune is not clear.[1423] A common Israelite name is "Gad/Fortune is Yahweh."[1424] "Destiny" or "Fate" (*menî*) is another deity.[1425] Several Egyptian stele and papyri combine Egyptian and Canaanite deities, including a list "to the Ennead (nine-gods) of the House of Ptah, to Baalat, to Qedesh, to Meni, Baal-Zaphon, to Sodpu."[1426]

Egyptian god Min
Manfred Näder, Gabana Studios, Germany

In Egypt, Min is a fertility and creation god. The root meaning of the Hebrew term is "assign, determine, destine," a play here, since God will "destine" the sword for Israel (v. 12). In the Gilgamesh Epic, Enlil is snubbed from feasting at a sacrifice because "my people he destined for catastrophe."[1427] Both gods are rivaling Yahweh, the one who truly determines Israel's fate. It appears that a banquet is held here in honor of them, ignoring the rightful God.

God of truth (65:16). An important attribute for the divine, "truth" is also a personal name found on several seals: "Hananiah (son of) Truth"[1428] and "Belonging to 'the true one.'"[1429] Koole suggests a wordplay here on truth (*ʾmn*) and the god Meni (65:11).[1430]

Heaven and Earth Renewed (65:17–25)

Come to mind (65:17). Literally "go up to the heart," the equivalent clause is also found in the Aramaic Sefire inscriptions: "If it should cross your mind, and if it should come upon your lips to kill me," you will have broken this treaty.[1431]

God Repays Good and Ill (66:1–6)

Heaven is my throne and the earth is my footstool. Where is the house you will build for me? (66:1). The house of the deity is a temple. Since deities inhabited the cosmos, their earthly residences were only emblematic of their cosmic habitations. Divine houses in Mesopotamia were associated with the cosmic mountain that lay at the center of the universe, providing it orientation: "The great house, it is a mountain great" (see comment on 2:2).[1432]

In Egypt, the primeval hill emerging from the waters at creation was the equivalent of this cosmic mountain.[1433] Heaven, earth, and even the underworld reach cosmic union in the temple as Esarhaddon describes in a building inscription: "I raised to heaven the head of Esarra, my lord Assur's dwelling. Above, heavenward, I raised its head,

▸ Utopian Paradise (65:17–25)

Looking beyond his present situation, Isaiah envisages a renewed paradise of peace and plenty. Similar renewal language is found in the Akkadian Marduk prophecy at the coming of a new Babylonian king: "He will renew the house of announcement, the Ekur-Sagil (shrine). He will draw the plans of heaven and earth in the Ekur-Sagil [implying their renewal].... The fields and plans will be full of yield.... The harvest of the land will thrive.... Brother will love his brother."[A-299] Here, as well as in Isaiah, both human and divine benefit from the anticipated situation, though Isaiah portrays paradise coming from divine, rather than royal, initiative.

A similar utopian motif appears in Enki and Ninhursag, a Sumerian myth whose setting is Dilmun, probably identified with modern Bahrain.[A-300] It is a "pure, virginal, pristine" land where "the lion slew not, the wolf was not carrying off the lamb," there is no widowhood, suggesting lack of death, nor sickness or aging.[A-301] Originally lacking water, the gods supply it so there grows plentiful grain and fruit.[A-302] The nature of this description is under dispute, but it does refer to a mythological period in the past. It could be a previous, desirable paradise,[A-303] or the initial uninhabitable world state prior to creation of the functioning world as we know it.[A-304] While sharing motifs with Isaiah, the latter clearly anticipates a future time of blessing and plenty.

Such positive renewal is usually associated with the earthly realm, not the afterlife (see sidebar on "Cult of the Dead" at 57:7). The latter, according to Egyptian understanding, would be blessed for some, but they had to make a dangerous and arduous passage between the world of life and the underworld and were dependent for a high standard of living there either on items interred with them or on offerings for them made by those yet alive (see comment on 5:25). The afterlife does not appear intrinsically paradisiacal.[A-305]

below, in the underworld, I made firm its foundations, Ehursaggula (meaning) House of the Great Mountain."[1434] *Enuma Elish* also stresses the cosmic earthly tie of the temple when speaking of Marduk's temple: "He shall make on earth the counterpart of what he brought to pass in heaven."[1435]

The tie between the temple and its deity was close, which was a major concern for Israel when Yahweh's temple was destroyed by the Babylonians in 586 B.C. God chided the returning Israelites for not taking his temple rebuilding seriously after their return to the land under the Persians (e.g., Hag. 1:4–11). In Mesopotamia, if a god's temple was uninhabitable, it made the god "arise from his seat" in the temple and leave it.[1436]

The Canaanite gods Yam and Baal also sought a new temple/palace for themselves. The chief god Il commands: "Build a house for Yam, raise up a palace for judge River."[1437] Later Baal complains: "Baal has no house like the gods, nor courtyard like Athirat's son, dwelling like Il's,"[1438] and he wants this situation put right. Assyrian texts also contained complaints from the gods that their temples were in ruins and needed rebuilding. Cyrus uses this as the excuse to take over their capital from the Babylonians: "The lord of the gods became very angry ... that the sanctuaries of all of their settlements were in ruins."[1439]

My resting place (66:1). This term denotes a place where work and wandering is over, not unlike Marduk resting in

Shamash enthroned over heavens
Z. Radovan/www.BibleLand Pictures.com

the temple after it was built in honor of his newly won primacy over the gods.[1440]

Their souls delight in their abominations (66:3). In this verse, three acceptable ritual activities—bull, lamb, and grain offerings—are turned on their head, contrasted to unacceptable pagan practices. Killing a man at the least refers to manslaughter, but apparently here refers to human sacrifice, not of a child, but of an adult man (*ʾîš*). Such sacrifices are rare in Mesopotamia, only found when the consort and retainers were buried as part of the ritual of the substitute king (see sidebar on "Substitutionary Rites" at 53:4).[1441] During the First Dynasty in Egypt, a king was joined in his death by a retinue to serve him, though the practice was soon replaced by providing model figures and even representations of them painted on tomb wall.[1442]

Animals, including puppy dogs (see 56:10–11), were killed to seal a covenant. A letter from Mari concerns making such a covenant: "I went to Ashlakka to 'kill a donkey' (i.e., 'make a covenant') between the Hanaeans [a West Semitic people[1443]] and Idamaraz. They brought a puppy and a goat, but I served my lord by not offering the puppy or the goat. The donkey, offspring of a she-ass, I had sacrificed."[1444]

Excavations at Tel Haror, just south of Ashkelon, have found puppy burials with the skeletons having broken necks; their significance, while suggestive, is unclear.[1445] Puppies also played a role in Hittite ritual.[1446] One reads: "When the army is defeated by an enemy, then the following sacrifice is prepared ... a man, a kid, a puppy-dog, and a suckling pig are cut in half,"[1447] combining all three of the sacrificial elements in the Isaiah passage.

Pig bones unearthed at Tell es-Safi
Joshua Walton, courtesy of the Tell es-Safi excavations

Pigs, as unclean animals, were unacceptable for sacrifice in orthodox Israelite worship (see comment on 65:4).[1448] A Middle Kingdom coffin text explains how, through a declaration of Re, pork is unclean in Egypt: "That is how the pig became an abomination to the gods."[1449] This attitude was apparently shared by the Phoenicians, whose sites leave no pig remains.[1450]

Mother Zion Rejoices (66:7–14)

Before she goes into labor, she gives birth (66:7). Because of its ubiquitous nature, birth is a common metaphor. The literal process is accompanied by magical-medical ritual to aid the process and to protect those involved.[1451] One text found in several versions over a number of centuries is A Cow of Sîn, in which the god Sîn impregnates his beloved cow. This mythological tale, entitled an "incantation," includes a wish: "Just as Geme-Sîn gave birth normally, may also this girl in labor give birth. Let the midwife not tarry, let the pregnant one be all right."[1452]

You will nurse and be satisfied (66:11). See comment on 49:23. A blessing for those returning to Mother Jerusalem will be sufficiency of nourishment. The intimacy of a suckling child makes the imagery even more evocative. An Aramaic curse from the ninth century expresses the opposite: "100 mothers who just bore, may they not satisfy one baby!"[1453]

As a mother (66:13). Unlike the gods of Israel's neighbors, Yahweh is not understood as a sexual being and does not, in orthodox Israelite religious belief, have a consort (see comments on 1:29–30; 44:24). He is described metaphorically, however, using both male and female terms. God is called Father (see comments on 9:6; 63:16). More rarely is Yahweh described using feminine metaphors (see 16:11; 46:3–4; 49:15; 54:14; 63:15–16).

A relief from the temple of Hathor at Dendera shows a squatting woman giving birth assisted by two goddesses Hathor. Hathor with Taweret was invoked during childbearing.
Werner Forman Archive/The Egyptian Museum, Cairo

Judgment and Hope (66:15–24)

His chariots (66:15). See comment on 2:7. Marduk rides a chariot in his violent conflict with Tiamat in the *Enuma Elish* epic. "He mounted the terrible chariot, the unopposable Storm Demon, he hitched to it the four-steed team, he tied them at his side: 'Slaughterer,' 'Merciless,' 'Overwhelmer,' 'Soaring.'"[1454] Sennacherib, speaking of himself in the context of Ashur's association with battle, says: "I am the conqueror, installed in Ashur's chariot."[1455] Baal used clouds as his chariot (see 19:1), being called "charioteer of the clouds" in battle contexts.[1456] In a cultic context, Mesopotamian gods rode on chariots or carts in some festival processions.[1457]

On horses, in chariots and wagons, and on mules and camels (66:20). See comment on 21:7. On a Neo-Assyrian seal from about 700 B.C., a god stands on the back of a horse.[1458] Horses are rare on Hebrew seals, though one is found on a number of jar handles.[1459] Sennacherib speaks of "chariots, wagons, horses, mules,[1460] camels, and Bactrian camels."[1461] That the Akkadian list closes with two terms for camel lends support to reading Isaiah thus here, for this word occurs only here.[1462]

From one New Moon to another and from one Sabbath to another (66:23). See comment on 1:13–14. Israel celebrated a cycle of sacrifices and festivals. In addition to the daily morning and evening sacrifices, there

Defeated people bowing before ruler
Todd Bolen/www.BiblePlaces.com

were weekly Sabbath celebrations, as well as the New Moon every twenty-eight days. They also seem at times to have pagan connotations (e.g., Hos. 5:7), with iconographic evidence that the moon was worshiped about this time in Syria and Israel.[1463] An ostracon from Arad mentions an occasion of giving supplies to some soldiers "on the first of the month ['new moon'] to the sixth of the month," which could indicate an extended festival[1464] or simply provisions for an expedition.

Bow down (66:23). To show honor and servitude, it was customary to bow down before a superior such as a king or a god. An Egyptian Hymn to Osiris, god of fertility and the netherworld, shows the esteem with which he was regarded: "whom the great powers fear, for whom the great rise from their mats … to whom the Two Assemblies come bowing down, for great is fear of him, strong is awe of him."[1465] Such submission could be beneficial. An Akkadian precept in the Counsels of a Pessimist urges: "Bow down to your city goddess that she may grant you offspring."[1466]

Bibliography

Beuken, Willem A. M. *Isaiah: Part 2.* Volume 2: *Isaiah 28–39.* Historical Commentary on the Old Testament. Leuven: Peeters, 2000. An excellent commentary series for historical and linguistic information.

Cornelius, Izak. *The Iconography of the Canaanite Gods Reshef and Baʿal: Late Bronze and Iron Age I Periods (c 1500–1000 B.C.E.).* OBO 140. Göttingen: Vandenhoeck & Ruprecht, 1995. A description of depictions of two of the chief Canaanite deities.

Dick, Michael B., ed. *Born in Heaven, Made on Earth: The Making of the Cult Image in the Ancient Near East.* Winona Lake, Ind.: Eisenbrauns, 1999. Studies of the phenomenon as practiced in the Bible, Mesopotamia, Egypt, and contemporary south India.

Keel, Othmar. *Goddesses and Trees, New Moon and Yahweh: Ancient Near Eastern Art and the Hebrew Bible.* JSOTSup 261; Sheffield: Sheffield Academic Press, 1998. A work by one of the leading iconographers of the ancient Near Eastern world, touching on several important areas.

_____. *Studien zu den Stempelsiegeln aus Palästina /Israel* IV. OBO 135. Göttingen: Vandenhoeck & Ruprecht, 1994. These are important studies of the most common textual artifacts from the area of Israel, stamp seals.

_____, Hildi Keel-Leu, and Silvia Schroer. *Studien zu den Stempelsiegeln aus Palästina / Israel* II. OBO 88. Göttingen: Vandenhoeck & Ruprecht, 1989.

_____, and Silvia Schroer. *Studien zu den Stempelsiegeln aus Palästina /Israel.* OBO 67. Göttingen: Vandenhoeck & Ruprecht, 1985.

_____, Menakhem Shuval, and Christoph Uehlinger. *Studien zu den Stempelsiegeln aus Palästina /Israel* III. OBO 100. Göttingen: Vandenhoeck & Ruprecht, 1990.

Koole, Jan L. *Isaiah:* Volume 1: *Isaiah 40–48;* Volume 2: *Isaiah 49–55;* Volume 3: *Isaiah 56–66.* Historical Commentary on the Old Testament. Kampen: Kok Pharos, 1997, 1998, 2001. An excellent commentary series for historical and linguistic information.

MacDonald, Burton. *"East of the Jordan": Territories and Sites of the Hebrew Scriptures.* Boston: ASOR, 2000. A useful study of Transjordan and its relevance for Old Testament studies.

Oswalt, John N. *The Book of Isaiah: Chapters 1–39,* and *Chapters 40–66.* Grand Rapids: Eerdmans, 1986 and 1998. A commentary from a conservative perspective with good historical and background information.

Seibert, Ilse. *Women in the Ancient Near East.* New York: Abner Schram, 1974. Brief studies with lavish illustrations from the sixth millennium B.C. through sixth century A.D.

Uehlinger, Christoph, ed. *Images as Media: Sources for the Cultural History of the Near East and the Eastern Mediterranean (1st millennium B.C.E.).* OBO 175. Göttingen: Vandenhoeck & Ruprecht, 2000. A study of various aspects of ancient Near Eastern iconography.

Walker, Christopher, and Michael Dick. *The Induction of the Cult Image in Ancient Mesopotamia: The Mesopotamian* Mīs Pî *Ritual.* Helsinki: The Neo-Assyrian Text Corpus Project, 2001. A helpful discussion of making and installing cultic images.

Wildberger, Hans. *Isaiah 1–12: A Commentary,* and *Isaiah 13–27: A Commentary.* OTL. Minneapolis: Fortress, 1991, 1997. Helpful commentaries with some ancient Near Eastern background information.

Winter, Urs. *Frau und Göttin: Exegetische und ikonographische Studien zum weiblichen Gottesbild im Alten Israel und in dessen Umwelt.* OBO 53. Göttingen: Vandenhoeck & Ruprecht, 1983. A massive study of the feminine and the divine.

Main Text Notes

1. Dates in parentheses indicate a period of coregency, when a king shared the throne with his predecessor.
2. In addition to commentary introductions, see, e.g., L. J. Liebreich, "The Compilation of the Book of Isaiah," *JQR* 46 (1955/1956): 259–77; 47 (1956): 114–38; S. Erlandsson, *The Burden of Babylon: A Study of Isaiah 13:2–14:23* (ConBOT 4; Lund: Gleerup, 1970); Y. Radday, *The Unity of Isaiah in the Light of Statistical Linguistics* (Hildesheim: Gerstenberg, 1973); W. L. Holladay, *Isaiah: Scroll of a Prophetic Heritage* (Grand Rapids: Eerdmans, 1978); R. E. Clements, "The Unity of the Book of Isaiah," *Int* 36 (1982): 117–29; R. Rendtorff, "Zur Komposition des Buches Jesaja, *VT* 34 (1984): 295–320; S. Erlandsson, "The Unity of Isaiah: A New Solution?" in *A Lively Legacy: Essays in Honor of Robert Preus*, ed. K. E. Marquart, J. R. Stephenson, B. W. TeiGen (Fort Wayne, Ind.: Concordia Theological Seminary, 1985), 33–39; C. E. Evans, "On the Unity and Parallel Structure of Isaiah," *VT* 38 (1988): 129–47; H. G. M. Williamson, *The Book Called Isaiah: Deutero-Isaiah's Role in Composition and Redaction* (Oxford: Clarendon, 1994); C. C. Broyles and C. E. Evans, ed., *Writing and Reading the Scroll of Isaiah: Studies of an Interpretive Tradition* (VTSup; Formation and Interpretation of Old Testament Literature 1; Leiden: Brill, 1997); J. van Ruiten and M. Vervenne, ed., *Studies in the Book of Isaiah: Festschrift Willem A. M. Beuken* (BETL 132; Louvain: Leuven Univ. Press, 1997).
3. On the Syro-Ephraimite war, see, e.g., S. A. Irvine, *Isaiah, Ahaz, and the Syro-Ephraimitic Crisis* (SBLDS 123: Atlanta: Scholars, 1980); M. E. W. Thompson, *Situation and Theology: Old Testament Interpretations of the Syro-Ephraimite War* (Prophets and Historians 1; Sheffield: Almond Press, 1982); B. Becking, *The Fall of Samaria: An Historical and Archaeological Study* (SHANE 2; Leiden: Brill, 1992); H. Cazelles, "Syro-Ephraimite War," *ABD*, 6:282–85.
4. See E. Vogt, "Jesaja und die drohende Eroberung Palästinas durch Tiglath-Pilizer," *FB* 2 (1972): 249–55; H. Donner, "The Syro-Ephraimite War and the End of the Kingdom of Israel," in *Israelite and Judean History*, ed. J. H. Hayes and J. M. Miller (OTL; Philadelphia: Westminster, 1977), 421–34; M. Weippert, "Zur Syrienpolitik Tiglathpilesers III," in *Mesopotamien und seine Nachbarn: Politische und kulturelle Wechselbeziehungen im Alten Orient vom 4. bis 1. Jahrtausend v. Chr.*, ed. H. Kühne, H.-J. Nissen, and J. Renger (Berliner Beiträge zum Vorderen Orient 1; Berlin: Reimer, 1982), 1:395–408; G. Galil, *Israel and Assyria* (Heb.) (Haifa: Univ. of Haifa Press, 2001); N. Na'aman, "Tiglath-pileser III's Campaigns against Tyre and Israel (734–732 B.C.E.)," in *Ancient Israel and Its Neighbors: Interaction and Counteraction: Collected Essays*, ed. N. Na'aman (Winona Lake, Ind.: Eisenbrauns, 2005), 56–67; P. Dubovský, "Tiglath-pileser III's Campaigns in 734–732 B.C.: Historical Background of Isa 7; 2 Kgs 15–16 and 2 Chr 27–28," *Bib* 87 (2006): 153–70.
5. *ANET*, 284–85.
6. Younger, "Recent Study on Sargon II," in M. Chavales and K. L. Younger Jr., *Mesopotamia and the Bible*, 312–13.
7. E. Vogt, *Der Aufstand Hiskias und der Belagerung Jerusalems 701 v. Chr.* (AnBib 106; Rome: Biblical Institute, 1986); N. Na'aman, "Hezekiah and the Kings of Assyria," *TA* 21 (1994): 235–56; J. Bright, *A History of Israel*, 4th ed. (Louisville: Westminster John Knox, 2000), 285–86. See D. Ussishkin, *The Conquest of Lachish by Sennacherib* (Tel Aviv: Tel Aviv Univ., Institute of Archaeology, 1982); L. L. Grabbe, ed., *"Like a Bird in a Cage": The Invasion of Sennacherib in 701 B.C.E.* (JSOTSup 363; Sheffield: Sheffield Academic Press, 2003); J. K. Hoffmeier, "Egypt's Role in the Events of 701 B.C. in Jerusalem," in A. G. Vaughn and A. E. Killebrew, *Jerusalem in Bible and Archaeology: the First Temple Period* (Symposium Series 18; Atlanta: Society of Biblical Literature, 2003), 219–34; J. J. M. Roberts, "Egypt, Assyria, Isaiah, and the Ashdod Affair: An Alternative Proposal," in ibid., 265–83; J. K. Hoffmeier, "Egypt's Role in the Events of 701 B.C.: A Rejoinder to J. J. M. Roberts," in ibid., 285–89.
8. COS, 2.119B.
9. *ANET*, 291, 294.
10. A. Kuhrt, *Ancient Near East (c. 3000–330 BC)* (New York: Routledge, 1995), 589–622.
11. COS, 2.27:1.
12. *ANET*, 632; A. L. Oppenheim, *The Interpretation of Dreams in the Ancient Near East with a Translation of an Assyrian Dream-Book* (Philadelphia: American Philosophical Society, 1956); M. Bonechi, "Oniromancie et magie à Mari à l'époque d'Ébla," in *Literature and Literary Language at Ebla*, ed. P. Fronzaroli (Quaderni di Semitistika 18; Firenze: Univ. of Firenze Press, 1992), 151–59; K. van der Toorn, *From her Cradle to her Grave: The Role of Religion in the Life of the Israelite and the Babylonian Woman* (Sheffield: Sheffield Academic Press, 1994), 127–28.
13. See A. R. Millard, *The Eponyms of the Assyrian Empire 910–612 B.C.* (SAAS 2; Helsinki: Neo-Assyrian Text Corpus Project, 1994).
14. The bibliography on ancient Near Eastern covenants is vast, but see D. J. McCarthy, *Treaty and Covenant*, new ed. (Rome: Pontifical Biblical Institute, 1981); K. A. Kitchen, *On the Reliability of the Old Testament* (Grand Rapids: Eerdmans), 283–94.
15. *ANET*, 200–201, 205–6, 533–35.
16. COS, 2.17B, A iv:19–20; 2.18 iv:1–4; Gary Beckman, *Hittite Diplomatic Texts* (Atlanta: Scholars, 1996), 43 §13 end.
17. COS, 1.47 XXVI:6–7.

18. Ibid., 1.82 II:1–17.
19. Ibid., 1.113 II:61′–62′.
20. Ibid., IV:73–74: "The people abandoned justice and took to atrocities. They deserted righteousness and planned wickedness."
21. M. Lichtheim, *Ancient Egyptian Literature*, 3 vols. (Berkeley : Univ. of California Press, 1973, 1975, 2006), 2:27. On Hatshepsut, see C. Roehrig, "When a Woman Ruled Egypt," *BAR* 32/2 (2006): 64–70.
22. Roehrig, "When a Woman Ruled Egypt," 75.
23. *COS*, 3.42B:6–7.
24. P. J. King and L. E. Stager, *Life in Biblical Israel* (Louisville: Westminster John Knox, 2001), 97.
25. Lev. 13–14; see the massive compendium by J. Scurlock and B. R. Andersen, *Diagnoses in Assyrian and Babylonian Medicine* (Urbana: Univ. of Illinois Press, 2005); I. L. Finkel and M. J. Geller, *Disease in Babylonia* (Leiden: Brill, 2006); also E. K. Ritter, "Magical-Expert (=*āšipu*) and Physician (=*asû*): Notes on Two Complementary Professions in Babylonian Medicine," in *Studies in Honor of Benno Landsberger on His Seventy-Fifth Birthday, April 21, 1965*, ed. H. G. Güterbock and T. Jacobsen (AS 16; Chicago: Univ. of Chicago Press, 1965), 299–321; M. Stol, *Epilepsy in Babylonia* (Leiden: Brill, 1993); H. Avalos, *Illness and Healthcare in the Ancient Near East: The Role of the Temple in Greece, Mesopotamia, and Israel* (HSM 54; Atlanta: Scholars, 1995); *CANE*, 1787–98 (Egypt), 1911–24 (Mesopotamia); I. L. Finkel, "On Late Babylonian Medical Training," in *Wisdom, Gods and Literature: Studies in Assyriology in Honour of W. G. Lambert*, ed. A. R. George and I. L. Finkel (Winona Lake, Ind.: Eisenbrauns, 2000), 137–223.
26. *CAD*, 17/1, 327, with other examples 327–28.
27. Ibid., 14, 114.
28. E.g., A. Mazar and G. L. Kelm, "Matashi, Tell El-," *ABD*, 1:626; F. Brandon, "Beth-Shemesh," *ABD*, 1:697; W. G. Dever, "Gezer," *ABD*, 2:1000; J. S. Holladday Jr., "Maskhuta, Tell El-," *ABD*, 4:590; D. Ussishkin, "Megiddo," *ABD*, 4:673; L. T. Geraty and L. G. Herr, "ʿUmeiri, Tell El-," *ABD*, 6:723.
29. S. Dalley, *Myths From Mesopotamia*, "Erra and Ishum" (Oxford: Oxford Univ. Press, 1991), 297–98; cf. *COS*, 1.113. Burning is common in Akkadian royal inscriptions; *AHw*, 1185; *COS*, 2.113A, C.
30. M. Hasel, *Military Practice and Polemic: Laws of Warfare in Near Eastern Perspective* (Berrien Springs, Mich.: Andrews Univ. Press, 2005), 61; *COS*, 2.113C, 115B.
31. A. K. Grayson, *Assyrian Rulers of the Early First Millennium II (858–745 B.C.)* (Toronto: Univ. of Toronto Press, 1996), 2:29, 30; see Hasel, *Military Practice*, 60–61. For a study of this ruler, see S. Yamada, *The Construction of the Assyrian Empire: A Historical Study of the Inscriptions of Shalmaneser III (859–824 B.C.) Relating to His Campaigns to the West* (Leiden: Brill, 2000).
32. *COS*, 1.166.
33. J. T. Strong, "Zion, Theology of," *NIDOTTE*, 4:1314–21; W. H. Mare, "Zion," *ABD*, 6:1096–97; E. R. Follis, "Zion, Daughter of," *ABD*, 6:1103.
34. *ANET*, 295. The Assyrians in the time of Isaiah used the same tactic; cf. *COS*, 2.117A (Rezin of Syria; cf. Isa. 7:1, 4, 8); 2.119B (Hezekiah; cf. 2 Kings 18:17–37); I. Ephʾal, "Ways and Means to Conquer a City, Based on Assyrian Queries to the Sungod," in *Assyria 1995: Proceedings of the 10th Anniversary Symposium of the Neo-Assyrian Text Corpus Project, Helsinki, September 7–11, 1995*, ed. S. Parpola and R. M. Whiting (Helsinki: Neo-Assyrian Text Corpus Project, 1997), 49–53; Hasel, *Military Practice*, 51–93; *CANE*, 1533–37.
35. W. L. Moran, *The Amarna Letters* (Baltimore: Johns Hopkins Univ. Press, 1992), 298, also 236, 238.
36. Hasel, *Military Practice*, 100–13.
37. *COS*, 1.111 vi:1–8 (servants; Mesopotamia, see H. W. F. Saggs, *The Encounter with the Divine in Mesopotamia and Israel* [London: Athlone, 1978]); *COS*, 1.35:131 (cattle; Egypt).
38. *CAD*, 10/I, 124 *mākālu* b; cf. starving gods in *COS*, 1.132:159–161. In Israel, see Lev. 21:6, 8, 17, 21, 22; 22:25; cf. Ezek. 44:7.
39. *CAD*, 12, 264; see 263–64.
40. K. Nielsen, *Incense in Ancient Israel* (VTSup 38; Leiden: Brill, 1986); King and Stager, *Life*, 346–48.
41. See S. E. Loewenstamm, "Ostraca 7 from Arad, Attesting the Observance of the New-Moon Day?" in *From Babylon to Canaan: Studies in the Bible and its Oriental Background* (Jerusalem: Magnes, 1976/1992), 131–35.
42. *COS*, 1.130. The last of these days is called a *shapattu* in Akkadian, possibly related to the Hebrew term *Shabbat*/sabbath (*COS*, 1, 451, n. 5).
43. *COS*, 1.124, 438; D. E. Fleming, "New Moon Celebrations Once a Year: Emar's HIDAŠU of Dagan," in *Immigration and Emigration within the Ancient Near East*, ed. K. Vanlerberghe and A. Schoors (OLA 65; Leuven: Peeters, 1995), 57–63. See also O. Keel, "The New Moon in the Hebrew Bible," in *Goddesses and Trees, New Moon and Yahweh: Ancient Near Eastern Art and the Hebrew Bible*, ed. O. Keel (JSOTSup 261; Sheffield: Sheffield Academic Press, 1998), 102–9.
44. *CAD*, 11/II, 85.
45. Ibid., 4, 214.
46. *COS*, 1.102.
47. See, e.g., M. I. Gruber, *Aspects of Nonverbal Communication in the Ancient Near East* (Studia Pohl 12; Rome: Pontifical Biblical Institute, 1980); Å. Viberg, *Symbols of the Law: A Contextual Analysis of Legal Symbolic Acts in the Old Testament* (ConBOT 34; Stockholm: Almqvist & Wicksell, 1992); M. Nissinen and S. Parpola, "Marduk's Return and Reconciliation in a Prophetic Letter from Arbela," *StudOr* 99 (2004): 209.
48. *CAD*, 17/II, 284.
49. *ANET*, 391–92.
50. *CTU*, 1.14 III 52–57, IV 5–6. See also J. Laessøe, *Studies on the Assyrian Ritual and Series bît rimki* (Copenhagen: Munksgaard, 1955), 45–46.
51. G. Frame, *Rulers of Babylonia: From the Second Dynasty of Isin to the End of the Assyrian Domina-*

tion (1157–612 B.C.) (Toronto: Univ. of Toronto Press, 1995), 140.
52. COS, 2.107A.
53. Ibid., 1.155.
54. A. Livingstone, *Mystical and Mythological Explanatory Works of Assyrian and Babylonian Scholars* (Oxford: Clarendon, 1986), 127; see also 129; *CAD*, 14, 113.
55. M. Weinfeld, *Social Justice in Ancient Israel and in the Ancient Near East* (Minneapolis: Fortress, 1995).
56. COS, 2.131 V 14–25.
57. Ibid., 1.102 VI 46–49.0. See F. C. Fensham, "Widow, Orphan, and the Poor in Ancient Near Eastern Legal and Wisdom Literature," *JNES* 21 (1962): 129–39; L. Epsztein, *Social Justice in the Ancient Near East and the People of the Bible* (London: SCM, 1986); Weinfeld, *Social Justice in Ancient Israel*.
58. *CAD*, 1, 364; A. A. Tavares, "L'*Almanah* hébraïque et l'*Almattu* des textes akkadiens," in *La femme dans le Proche-Orient antique: compte rendu de la XXXIIIe Rencontre Assyriologique Internationale (Paris, 7–10 Juillet 1986)*, ed. J.-M. Durand and D. Charpin (Paris: Éditions recherche sur les civilisations, 1987), 155–62; M. T. Roth, "The Neo-Babylonian Widow," *JCS* 43–45 (1991–1993): 1–26.
59. *AHw*, 857 *peṣû I*.
60. Livingstone, *Mystical and Mythological Explanatory Works*, 219.
61. J. Scurlock, "Animals in Mesopotamian Religion," in *A History of the Animal World in the Ancient Near East*, ed. B. J. Collins (Leiden: Brill, 2002), 379.
62. *AEL*, 1:142-43; cf. COS, 1.45:43–45, 54–56.
63. M. Dayagi-Mendeles, *Drink and Be Merry: Wine and Beer in Ancient Times* (Jerusalem: Israel Museum, 1999); J. Geller, "From Prehistory to History: Beer in Egypt," in *The Followers of Horus: Studies Dedicated to Michael Allen Hoffman*, ed. R. Friedman and B. Adams (Oxford: Oxbow, 2000), 19–26; D. Samuel, "Brewing and Baking," in *Ancient Egyptian Materials and Technology*, ed. P. T. Nicholson and I. Shaw (Cambridge: Cambridge Univ. Press, 2000), 537–70; R. I. Curtis, *Ancient Food Technology* (Leiden: Brill, 2001); M. M. Homan, "Beer and Its Drinkers: An Ancient Near Eastern Love Song," *NEA* 67 (2004): 84–95.
64. G. Hadas, "Beer Barrels from Tel Goren, Ein Gedi," *RB* 111 (2004): 409–18.
65. M. V. Fox, "Egyptian Literature (Love Songs)," *ABD*, 2:394.
66. M. Civil, "A Hymn to the Beer Goddess and a Drinking Song," in *Studies Presented to A. Leo Oppenheim, June 7, 1964* (Chicago: Oriental Institute, 1964), 67–89, cited in Homan, "Beer and Its Drinkers," 84.
67. COS, 1.173:150–154.
68. J. P. Brown, "The Mediterranean Vocabulary of the Vine," *VT* 19 (1969): 146–70; J. M. Sasson, "The Blood of Grapes: Viticulture and Intoxication in the Hebrew Bible," in *Drinking in Ancient Societies: History and Culture of Drinks in the Ancient Near East*, ed. L. Milano (Padova: Sargon, 1994), 399–419; C. E. Walsh, *The Fruit of the Vine: Viticulture in Ancient Israel* (Winona Lake, Ind.: Eisenbrauns, 2000); P. McGovern, *Ancient Wine: The Search for the Origins of Viniculture* (Princeton: Princeton Univ. Press, 2003); Hadas, "Beer Barrels," 414–16.
69. A. R. Millard, "Ezekiel XVII.19: The Wine Trade of Damascus," *JSS* 7 (1962): 201–3.
70. COS, 3.83, 84, 110.
71. Ibid., 3.94, a text in Akkadian found at Aphek in Israel.
72. *CAD*, 17/3, 246–47.
73. J. J. Finkelstein, "The Middle Assyrian *Šulmānu*-Texts," *JAOS* 72 (1952): 77–80.
74. In Akkadian, see *ARM*, II 131:35.
75. *ANET*, 328–29.
76. Ibid., 559.
77. D. J. Wiseman, *Nebuchadrezzar and Babylon* (Oxford: Oxford Univ. Press, 1985), 56–58; idem, "Palace and Temple Gardens in the Ancient Near East," 37–43, in *Monarchies and Socio-Religious Traditions in the Ancient Near East*, ed. T. Mikasa (Wiesbaden: Otto Harrassowitz, 1984).
78. G. del Olmo Lete, *Canaanite Religion according to the Liturgical Texts of Ugarit* (Winona Lake, Ind.: Eisenbrauns, 2004), 224. See also Baal and an unidentified goddess ascending to a garden in an Aramaic lament for Nineveh dating possibly from the third century B.C., COS, 1.99 XVII.
79. T. Ornan, *The Triumph of the Symbol: Pictorial Representation of Deities in Mesopotamia and the Biblical Image Ban* (OBO 213; Göttingen: Vandenhoeck & Ruprecht, 2005), 153–59.
80. Keel, *Goddesses and Trees*, fig. 53.
81. Ibid., fig. 54.
82. J. E. Taylor, "The Asherah, the Menorah and the Sacred Tree," *JSOT* 66 (1995): 29–54.
83. COS, 1.86, *CTA*, 4 v 106–119. See H. Niehr, "Zaphon," *DDD*, 927–29; R. Stadelmann, *Syrisch-palästinensische Gottheiten in Ägypten* (Probleme der Ägyptologie 5; Leiden: Brill, 1967), 32–47; Z. Robertson, "Zion and Saphon," *VT* 24 (1974): 118–23; M. Astour, "Place Names," in *Ras Shamra Parallels: The Texts from Ugarit and the Hebrew Bible* II (AnOr 50; Rome: Pontifical Biblical Institute, 1975), 318–42.
84. M. H. Pope, *El in the Ugaritic Texts* (VTSup 2; Leiden: Brill, 1955), 61–72; R. J. Clifford, *The Cosmic Mountain in Canaan and the Old Testament* (HSM 4; Cambridge, Mass.: Harvard Univ. Press, 1972), 34–57; M. S. Smith, "Mt. *ll* in *KTU* 1.2.I.19–20," *UF* 14 (1986): 458.
85. COS, 2.155 Cyl. A xxi 19–23.
86. Ibid., 1.138—the Weidner Chronicle, purporting to record events from the nineteenth century B.C.
87. Ibid., 2.155, Cyl. A ix 16–18. See also people coming to Nippur, the city of Enlil in *ANET*, 574.
88. S. Parpola, *Assyrian Prophecies* (SAA 9; Helsinki: Helsinki Univ. Press, 1997), 38.
89. M. Liverani, "The Ideology of the Assyrian Empire," in *Power and Propoganda: A Symposium*

on Ancient Empires, ed. M. T. Larsen (Mesopotamia 7; Copenhagen: Akademisk Forlag, 1979), 301; B. A. Levine, "Assyrian Ideology and Israelite Monotheism," in Collon and George, ed., *Nineveh*, 1:412.

90. Saggs, *Might*, 195–97.
91. C. Cohen and D. Sivan, *The Ugaritic Hippiatric Texts: A Critical Edition* (New Haven, Conn.: Yale Univ. Press, 1983).
92. *ANEP*, 465, 482; W. G. Dever, "Temples and Sanctuaries," *ABD*, 6:378.
93. *ANEP*, 478, 495, 497; C. Clamer, "A Gold Plaque from Tel Lachish," *Tel* Aviv 7 (1960): 152–62; Lewis, "Syro-Palestinian Iconography," 85–87.
94. *ANEP*, 481; *AEL*, 1:114, 119 (and often, referring to Horus), 123; 2:198 (referring to the elderly Re); Moran, *Amarna Letters*, 128 (see 85, 87).
95. E. M. Curtis, "Idol, Idolatry," *ABD*, 3:376. A Sumerian goddess is said to be "robbed ... of her precious metal" and thrown away.
96. *ANEP*, 483, 484; M.-L. Buhl, "Hamath," *ABD*, 3:35.
97. Oppenheim, *Ancient Mesopotamia*, 184.
98. *CTU*, 4.168, 4.182; see T. J. Lewis, "Syro-Palestinian Iconography and Divine Images," in *Cult Images and Divine Representation in the Ancient Near East*, ed. N. H. Walls (Boston: American Schools of Oriental Research, 2005), 92.
99. *CAD*, 9, 61–65.
100. See T. Jacobsen, "The Graven Image," in *Ancient Israelite Religion: Essays in Honor of Frank Moore Cross*, ed. P. D. Miller Jr. et al. (Philadelphia: Fortress, 1987), 23–28; A. Berlejung, "Washing the Mouth: The Consecration of Divine Images in Mesopotamia," in *The Image and the Book: Iconic Cults, Aniconism, and the Rise of Book Religion in Israel and the Ancient Near East*, ed. K. van der Toorn (Leuven: Peeters, 1997), 45–72; idem, *Die Theologie der Bilder: Herstellung und Einweihung von Kultbildern in Mesopotamien und die alttestamentliche Bilderpolemik* (OBO 162; Göttingen: Vandenhoeck & Ruprecht, 1998), 178–283, 422–73; M. B. Dick, ed., *Born in Heaven, Made on Earth: The Making of the Cult Image in the Ancient Near East* (Winona Lake, Ind.: Eisenbrauns, 1999), especially 55–121; idem, "The Mesopotamian Cult Statue: A Sacramental Encounter with the Divine," in *Cult Image and Divine Representation in the Ancient Near East* (Boston: American Schools of Oriental Research, 2005), 58–65; C. Walker and M. B. Dick, *The Induction of the Cult Image in Ancient Mesopotamia: The Mesopotamian Mis Pî Ritual* (Helsinki: Neo-Assyrian Text Corpus Project, Univ. of Helsinki, 2001).
101. Oppenheim, *Ancient Mesopotamia*, 183–86.
102. E.g., *COS*, 1.132:156–69.
103. *CAD*, 19/II, 9–12; A. L. Oppenheim, "Akkadian *pul(u)h(t)u* and *melammu*," *JAOS* 63 (1943): 31–34; M. Weinfeld, "Divine Intervention in War in Ancient Israel and in the Ancient Near East" in *History, Historiography and Interpretation: Studies in Biblical and Cuneiform Literatures*, ed. H. Tadmor and M. Weinfeld (Jerusalem: Magnes, 1983), 121–47, for Egypt, 125–27; M. Weinfeld, "The Day of the Lord: Aspirations for the Kingdom of God in the Bible and Jewish Liturgy" in *Studies in Bible*, ed. S. Japhet (ScrHeir 31; Jerusalem: Magnes, 1986), 364; idem, "כָּבוֹד (*kābôd*)," *TDOT*, 7:29–31.
104. G. Colbow, *Die kriegerische Ištar: Zu den Erscheinungsformen bewaffeneter Gottheiten zwischen der Mitte 2 Jahrtausends* (Munich: Profil, 1991); Z. Bahrani, *Women of Babylon: Gender and Representation in Mesopotamia* (New York: Routledge, 2001), 131–34.
105. *COS*, 2.114E.
106. Ibid., 1.86 v: 70.
107. Grayson, *Early First Millennium*, 2:18, 25, etc.
108. *ANET*, 268–69; V. Hurowitz, *I Have Built an Exalted House: Temple Building in the Bible in Light of Mesopotamian and Northwest Semitic Writings* (JSOTSup 115; Sheffield: Sheffield Academic Press, 1992), 205–6; J. N. Postgate, "Trees and Timber in the Assyrian Texts," *Bulletin on Sumerian Agriculture* 6 (1992): 188; S. Sherwin, "In Search of Trees: Isaiah XLIV 14 and its Implications," *VT* 53 (2003): 516–18.
109. B. MacDonald, *"East of the Jordan": Territories and Sites of the Hebrew Scriptures* (ASOR Books 6; Boston: American Schools of Oriental Research, 2000), 128–31.
110. Based on *COS*, 3.2, 12.
111. King and Stager, *Life*, 108.
112. G. del Olmo Lete and J. Sanmartín, *A Dictionary of the Ugaritic Language in the Alphabetic Tradition* (Leiden: Brill, 2004), 59; *CAD*, 1/1, 354–55.
113. *COS*, 2.31.
114. King and Stager, *Life*, 232.
115. *NEAEHL*, 906.
116. *OEANE*, 3, 295; see *CANE*, 1532–33.
117. *OEANE*, 4, 146; D. Stronach, "Notes on the Fall of Nineveh," in Parpola and Whiting, *Assyria 1995*, 307–24, especially 311.
118. M. De Odorico, *The Use of Numbers and Quantifications in the Assyrian Royal Inscriptions* (Helsinki: Neo-Assyrian Text Corpus Project, 1995), 16, 62.
119. *COS*, 3.5.
120. *OEANE*, 4, 365–66; *NEAEHL*, 843–46.
121. D. Pardee and P. Bordreuil, "Ugarit," *ABD*, 6:713.
122. K. A. Kitchen, "The Exodus," *ABD*, 2:704.
123. *COS*, 1.39; see Ps. 48:7; Acts 27:27–44.
124. E.g., King and Stager, *Life*, 180–81, a Phoenician wreck from the period of Isaiah with a cargo of wine.
125. D. W. Baker, "Tarshish (Place)," *ABD*, 6:332.
126. *COS*, 2.86.
127. Grayson, *Early First Millennium*, 2:13.
128. *COS*, 1.160:34–37.
129. E.g., R. Harris, *Ancient Sippar: A Demographic Study of an Old Babylonian City (1894–1595 B.C.)* (Leiden: Nederlands Historisch-Archaeologisch Instituut te Istanbul, 1975), 57–86; *CANE*, 273–87, 395–411, 587–603; M. van de Mieroop, "The Government of an Ancient Mesopotamian City: What We Know and Why We

Know so Little," in *Priests and Officials in the Ancient Near East*, ed. K. Watanabe (Heidelberg: Winter, 1999), 139–61; R. Mattila, *The King's Magnates: A Study of the Highest Officials of the Neo-Assyrian Empire* (SAA XI; Helsinki: Neo-Assyrian Text Corpus Project, 2000).
130. *CANE*, 289–301, 413–22, 545–54.
131. Mattila, *King's Magnates*, 77–90, 164.
132. J. Lust, "On Wizards and Prophets," in *Studies on Prophecy: A Collection of Twelve Papers* (VTSup 26; Leiden: Brill, 1974), 133–42; H. W. F. Saggs, *The Encounter with the Divine in Mesopotamia and Israel* (London: Athlone, 1978); H. Ringgren, "Prophecy in the Ancient Near East," in *Israel's Prophetic Tradition: Essays in Honour of Peter R. Ackroyd* (Cambridge: Cambridge Univ. Press, 1982), 1–11; *CANE*, 2083–94; D. W. Baker, "Israelite Prophets and Prophecy," in *The Face of Old Testament Study: A Survey of Contemporary Approaches* (Grand Rapids: Baker, 1999), 271–75.
133. *COS*, 2.86.
134. E. A. W. Budge and L. W. King, *Annals of the Kings of Assyria* (London: Trustees of the British Museum, 1902), 1:224; M.-J. Seux, *Épithètes royales akkadiennes et sumériennes* (Paris: Letouzey, 1967), 187.
135. *CAD*, 11/1, 286.
136. *COS*, 2.131, §226.
137. See O. Keel and C. Uehlinger, *Gods, Goddesses, and Images of God in Ancient Israel* (Minneapolis: Fortress, 1998), 248ff.
138. This word is derived from the Ugaritic deity *šahar*; see Keel and Uehlinger, *Gods, Goddesses*, 298ff.; U. Seidl, "Babylonische und assyrische Kultbilder in den Massenmedien des 1. Jahrtausends v. Chr.," in *Images as Media: Sources for the Cultural History of the Near East and the Eastern Mediterranean (1st millennium B.C.E.)*, ed. C. Uehlinger (OBO 175; Göttingen: Vandenhoeck & Ruprecht, 2000), 90–96.
139. E. E. Platt, "Jewelry, Ancient Israelite," *ABD*, 3:826.
140. *ANEP*, 7–9.
141. Ibid., 439–51 (Mesopotamia); 378, 394, 397–99, 415 (Egypt).
142. *CAD*, 17/2, 126.
143. Moran, *Amarna Letters*, 31.
144. Gilgamesh Epic 9.136 (pers. trans.).
145. R. Labat, *Manuel d'épigraphie akkadienne*, 6th ed. (Paris: Paul Geuthner, 1988), 247:598c.
146. G. Cunningham, *"Deliver Me from Evil": Mesopotamian Incantations 2500–1500 B.C.* (Studia Pohl: Series Maior 17; Rome: Pontifical Biblical Institute, 1997), 26; *CAD*, 15, 204.
147. *COS*, 1.160.
148. S. M. Paul, "Heavenly Tablets and the Book of Life," *JANESCU* 5 (1973): 345–53.
149. *COS*, 1.111:155–160.
150. Ibid., 2.122.
151. W. G. Lambert, *Babylonian Wisdom Literature* (Oxford: Clarendon, 1960), 61.
152. *CAD*, 10, 10.
153. Del Olmo Lete, *Dictionary*, 170.
154. S. M. Paul, "A Lover's Garden of Verse: Literal and Metaphorical Imagery in Ancient Near Eastern Love Poetry," in *Tehillah le-Mosheh: Biblical and Judaic Studies in Honor of Moshe Greenberg*, ed. M. Cogan (Winona Lake, Ind.: Eisenbrauns, 1997), 105, see 100–105.
155. *ANET*, 413:330.
156. Moran, *Amarna Letters*, 143, 145, 151, 163.
157. King and Stager, *Life*, 98–101; C. Walsh, *The Fruit of the Vine: Viticulture in Ancient Israel* (Winona Lake, Ind.: Eisenbrauns, 2000).
158. M. E. J. Richardson, *Hammurabi's Laws* (Sheffield: Sheffield Academic Press, 2000), 87, laws 142–143; Paul, "A Lover's Garden," 109–10.
159. H. W. F. Saggs, *The Might That Was Assyria* (New York: St. Martin's, 1990), 131–34.
160. G. R. Driver and J. C. Miles, *The Assyrian Laws* (Oxford: Clarendon, 1935), 429.
161. Ibid., 435.
162. R. H. Wilkinson, *The Complete Gods and Goddesses of Ancient Egypt* (London: Thames & Hudson, 2003), 106–8.
163. B. B. Williams, "Nile (Geography)," *ABD*, 4:1113.
164. V. Loret and A. Moret, "La grande inscription des Mes," *Zeitschrift für Aegyptische Sprache* 39 (1901): 1–39; A. H. Gardiner, *The Inscription of Mes: A Contribution to the Study of Egyptian Judicial Procedure* (Untersuchungen zur Geschichte und Altertumsurkunde Ägyptens, IV, 3; Leipzig: Hinrichs, 1905); G. A. Gaballa, *The Memphite Tomb-Chapel of Mose* (Warminster: Aris & Phillips, 1977); S. L. D. Katary, *Land Tenure in the Ramesside Period* (London: Kegan Paul International, 1989), 220–22.
165. M. A. Powell, "Weights and Measures," *ABD*, 6:901–5.
166. *COS*, 1.46.
167. Ibid., 1.111 III: 133–136.
168. J. Braun, *Music in Ancient Israel/Palestine* (Grand Rapids: Eerdmans, 2002), 135–43.
169. Gordon, *Sumerian Proverbs*, 211.
170. E.g., *COS*, 2.89, 243; 2.113A, 263; A. K. Grayson, *Assyrian and Babylonian Chronicles* (Locust Valley, N.Y.: Augustin, 1975), 77:28; 78:42; 79:3–5, and *passim*; cf.; R. Zadok, *The Jews in Babylonia during the Chaldean and Achaemenian Periods* (Haifa: Haifa Univ. Press, 1979); N. Na'aman and R. Zadoq, "Sargon II's Deportations to Israel and Philistia (716–708)," *JCS* 40 (1988): 36–46; B. Oded, "The Settlements of the Israelite and Judean Exiles in Mesopotamia in the 8th–6th Centuries B.C.E.," VTSup 81 (2000): 91–103; S. W. Holloway, *Aššur is King! Aššur is King! Religion in the Exercise of Power in the Neo-Assyrian Empire* (Leiden: Brill, 2002), 109–10.
171. B. Oded, *Mass Deportations and Deportees in the Neo-Assyrian Empire* (Wiesbaden: Ludwig Reichert, 1979), 20. Some of the exiles are designated as "slaves," which could support deportation from among all levels of society (ibid., 22)
172. K. L. Younger Jr., "Israelites in Exile: Their Names Appear at All Levels of Assyrian Society," *BAR* 29/6 (2003): 36–45, 65–66.

173. Oded, *Mass Deportations*, 43–45. For several other reasons for deportation, see 41–74.
174. Ibid., 23–25.
175. N. Naʾaman, "Population Changes in Palestine Following Assyrian Deportations," *Tel Aviv* 20 (1993): 104–24.
176. Oded, *Mass Deportations*, 6–11.
177. Ibid., 11–16. See Z. Gal, "Israel in Exile: Deserted Galilee Testifies to Assyrian Conquest of the Northern Kingdom," *BAR* 24/3 (1998): 48–53.
178. S. Parker, *Ugaritic Narrative Poetry* (SBLWAW 9; Atlanta: SBL, 1997), 142; cf. *COS*, 1.86; *CTA* 5 i:4–7.
179. King and Stager, *Life*, 104.
180. Homan, "Beer and Its Drinkers," 86.
181. Law 5 (pers. trans.).
182. J. Klein, "The God Martu in Sumerian Literature," in *Sumerian Gods and Their Representations*, ed. I. L. Finkel and M. J. Geller (Cuneiform Monographs 7; Groningen: Styx, 1997), 116.
183. Moran, *Amarna Letters*, 241.
184. T. Abusch, "Ghost and God: Some Observations on a Babylonian Understanding of Human Nature," in *Self, Soul and Body in Religious Experience*, ed. A. I. Baumgarten et al. (Leiden: Brill, 1998), 363–83, especially 373; J. Scurlock, "Soul Emplacements in Ancient Mesopotamian Funerary Rituals," in Ciraolo and Seidel, *Magic and Divination*, 1–6.
185. B. R. Foster, *Before the Muses: An Anthology of Akkadian Literature*, (Bethesda, Md.: CDL, 1996), 783.
186. Driver and Miles, *The Assyrian Laws*, 420–21.
187. *ANET*, 538–39; D. R. Hillers, *Treaty-Curses and the Old Testament Prophets* (BibOr 16; Rome: Pontifical Biblical Institute, 1964), 68–69.
188. *AEL*, 2:172.
189. Ibid., 2:208.
190. E.g.,B. Sass, "The Pre-Exilic Hebrew Seals: Iconism vs. Aniconism," *Studies in the Iconography*, 232–33:136; 248:12, 13223:109, 110. See B. A. Strawn, *What Is Stronger Than a Lion? Leonine Image and Metaphor in the Hebrew Bible and the Ancient Near East* (OBO 212; Göttingen: Vandenhoeck & Ruprecht, 2005).
191. E.g., R. D. Barnett and D. J. Wiseman, *Fifty Pieces of Ancient Near Eastern Art in the Department of Western Asiatic Antiquities of The British Museum* (London: Trustees of the British Museum, 1969), 42, 58, 60.
192. Frame, *Rulers of Babylonia*, 18.
193. A. K. Grayson, *Assyrian Royal Inscriptions* II (Wiesbaden: Harrassowitz, 1976), 121, 540; C. E. Watanabe, *Animal Symbolism in Mesopotamia: A Contextual Approach* (Vienna: Institut für Orientalistik der Universität Wien, 2002), 42–56, 89–91.
194. *ANET*, 282.
195. H. Tadmor, "Azriyau of Yaudi," in *Studies on the Bible*, ed. C. Rabin (ScrHier, 8; Jerusalem: Magnes Press, 1961), 232–71; J. J. M. Roberts, *Understanding the Word: Essays in Honour of Bernard W. Anderson*, ed. J. T. Butler et al. (JSOTSup 37; Sheffield: Sheffield Academic Press, 1985), 155–66; Bright, *History*, 270. However see N. Naʾaman, "Sennacherib's 'Letter to God' on his Campaign to Judah," *BASOR* 214 (1974): 25–39; idem, "Tiglath-pileser III's Campaigns against Tyre and Israel (734–732 B.C.E.)," *TA* 22 (1995): 276–77.
196. For example, Livingstone, *Mystical and Mythological Explanatory Works*, 173, 177–87.
197. *ANET*, 83–84.
198. *CAD*, 3, 23.
199. Lambert, *Babylonian Wisdom Literature*, 71:21; *CAD*, 11/2, 123, translation mine.
200. *CAD*, 3, 24.
201. H. Niehr, "In Search of YHWH's Cult Statue in the First Temple," in *The Image and the Book*, ed. van der Toorn, 73–95; see H. G. M. Williamson, "Temple and Temple Worship in Isaiah 6," in *Temple and Worship in Biblical Israel*, ed. J. Day (London: T. & T. Clark, 2005), 129.
202. A. Abū ʿAssāf, *Der Tempel von ʿAin Dārā* (Damaszener Forschungen 3; Mainz: von Zabern, 1990), 14 and pl. 11; J. Monson, "The New ʿAin Dara Temple: Closest Solomonic Parallel," *BAR* 26/3 (2000): 23, 26, 27; Williamson, "Temple and Temple Worship," 125.
203. See "God, Names of," *Dictionary of the Old Testament: Pentateuch*, ed. T. D. Alexander and D. W. Baker (Downers Grove, Ill.: InterVarsity Press, 2003), 362–65.
204. *RlA*, 1, 353.
205. *CAD*, 13, 83–84; 15, 323b, c.
206. "And he held the hem of his lord, the Assyrian king" (*KAI* 215:11); J. C. Greenfield, "Two Proverbs of Ahiqar," in *Lingering over Words: Studies in Ancient Near Eastern Literature in Honor of William L. Moran*, ed. T. Abusch et al. (HSS 37; Atlanta: Scholars, 1990), 197.
207. J. Day, "Echoes of Baal's Seven Thunders and Lightnings in Psalm XXIX and Habakkuk III 9 and the Identity of the Seraphim in Isaiah VI," *VT* 29 (1979): 149.
208. COS, 2.101B, 252, protective genii, Warad-sin; see pictures in O. Keel, *Yahweh—Visioner und Siegelkunst* (SBS 84/85; Stuttgart: Verlag Katholisches Bibelwerk, 1977), 72–115; cf. *ANEP*, 669.
209. Jacobsen, "The Graven Image," 21 and n. 23.
210. J. De Savignac, "Les 'Seraphim,'" *VT* 22 (1972): 320–25; K. R. Joines, *Serpent Symbolism in the Old Testament: A Linguistic, Archaeological, and Literary Study* (Haddonfield, N.J.: Haddonfield, 1974), 42–60; A. Schoors, "Isaiah, the Minister of Royal Anointment?" in *Instruction and Interpretation: Studies in Hebrew Language, Palestinian Archaeology and Biblical Exegesis* (OTS 20; Leiden: Brill, 1977), 95–99; Keel, *Gods, Goddesses*, 272–75; Williamson, *Temple and Worship*, 130–31.
211. T. N. D. Mettinger, "Seraphim," *DDD*, 742–44; O. Keel and C. Uehlinger, *Altorientalische Miniaturkunst* (Mainz am Rhein: Philipp von Zabern, 1990), 20–22.
212. *IBHS*, 116, 233 n. 15.
213. E.g., G. Meier, *Die assyrische Beschwörungssammlung Maqlû* (Osnabruck: Biblio-Verlag, 1961

rep. from 1937), 8, I:37, "earth, earth, earth"; I:42–43, "my city Zabban, my city Zabban, my city Zabban"; III:158–59, "Hand, hand, hand"; cf. also E. Reiner, *Šurpu: Collection of Sumerian and Akkadian Incantations* (Graz: Weidner, 1958), 48, IX:88–89; R. D. Briggs, *ŠA.ZI.GA: Ancient Mesopotamian Potency Incantations* (Locust Valley, N.Y.: Augustin, 1967), 28:7; 40:13; 70:9, 20.

214. C. Walker and M. Dick, *The Induction of the Cult Image in Ancient Mesopotamia: The Akkadian* Mīs Pî *Ritual* (Helsinki: Neo-Assyrian Text Corpus Project, 2001), 53:8; 56:52; 57:59a, etc.
215. E.g., "mighty Baal," COS, 1.86, 249; "warrior Erra," 1.113, 406; "warrior Marduk," 1.114, 416.
216. E.g., "noble Atum," COS, 1.29, 47; "ruler Naharu," 1.86, 246, "prince Yammu," 1.86, 248.
217. Ibid., 1.103.
218. F. Thureau-Dangin, *Une relation de la huitième campagne de Sargon* (Paris: Paul Geuthner, 1912), 35:213. Sumerian laments were also used in Akkadian rituals; cf. F. Thureau-Dangin, *Rituels accadiens* (Paris: Ernest Leroux, 1921), 35:6, where the title of one is given using a cognate of the Hebrew term used here.
219. V. Hurowitz, "Isaiah's Impure Lips and their Purification in Light of Mouth Purification and Mouth Purity in Akkadian Sources," *HUCA* 60 (1989): 39–89; Gregory Yuri Glazov, *The Bridling of the Tongue and the Opening of the Mouth in Biblical Prophecy* (JSOTSup 311: Sheffield: Sheffield Academic Press, 2001).
220. Walker and Dick, *Induction of the Cult Image*, 53:8; 54:19, etc.
221. Glazov, *The Bridling of the Tongue*, 377; V. A. Hurowitz, "Isaiah's Impure Lips and Their Purification in Light of Akkadian Sources, *HUCA* 60 (1990): 64–70.
222. Glazov, *The Bridling of the Tongue*, 121, 368–70.
223. *CAD, K* 178–179.
224. Reiner, *Šurpu*, 11.
225. Cunningham, *"Deliver Me from Evil,"* 122.
226. E.g., the Baal myth, COS, 1.86, 246, n. 37; Kirtu, COS, 1.102, 341; see del Olmo Lete, *Dictionary*, 669–70.
227. E.g., COS, 2.29.
228. *Enuma Elish*: COS, 1.111, 392, 400–401; Gilgamesh: COS, 1.132, 458–59; Reiner, *Šurpu*, 43:78.
229. See S. A. Meier, *The Messenger in the Ancient Semitic World* (Atlanta: Scholars, 1988); various discussions among the essays in R. Cohen and R. Westbrook, *Amarna Diplomacy: The Beginnings of International Relations* (Baltimore: Johns Hopkins Univ. Press, 2000); N. Na'aman, "The Distribution of Messages in the Kingdom of Judah in Light of the Lachish Ostraca," *VT* 53 (2003): 169–80.
230. From the instructions of Ptah: "If you are a man of trust, sent by one great man to another, adhere to the nature of him who sent you. Give his message as he sent it.... Keep to the truth, don't exceed it.... Do not malign anyone" (*AEL*, 1:65; cf. Prov. 25:13).
231. E.g., 1 Sam. 11:9; 25:5–9; 2 Sam. 11:19–21, 25.
232. *ANET*, 623; a common Akkadian letter heading reads: "Say to the king, my lord: Message of X, your servant/ thus X, your servant"; COS, 3.92A-F.
233. *ANET*, 25–29, especially 29.
234. M. E. Polley, "Hebrew Prophecy within the Council of Yahweh, Examined in its Ancient Near Eastern Setting, in *Scripture in Context: Essays on the Comparative Method*, ed. C. D. Evans et al. (Pittsburgh: Pickwick, 1980), 148–51 and bibliography there; M. Nissinen, "Prophets and the Divine Council," in *Kein Land für sich allein: Studien zum Kulturkontakt in Kanaan, Israel/Palästina und Ebirnâri für Manfred Weippert zum 65. Geburtstag*, ed. U. Hübner and E. A. Knauf (OBO 186; Göttingen: Vandenhoeck & Ruprecht, 2002), 4–19.
235. COS, 1.111:32 and elsewhere in the text.
236. Meier, *The Messenger*, 119–22 (Mesopotamia), 124–28 (Ugarit).
237. E.g., Ugaritic—COS, 1.86:243–46, 255; Akkadian—W. G. Lambert and A. R. Millard, *Atraḫasis: The Babylonian Story of the Flood* (Oxford: Clarendon, 1969), 51:118–24; COS, 1.109–11.
238. E.g., in an incantation: G. Meier, *Maqlû* 9:52–53.
239. COS, 1.153, II:73–74.
240. W. W. Hallo, "Individual Prayer in Sumerian: The Continuity of a Tradition," *JAOS* 88 (1968): 85 v:26.
241. G. K. Beale, "Isaiah VI 9–13: A Retributive Taunt against Idolatry," *VT* 41 (1991): 257–78. Beale sees the idolatry theme strengthened through reference to pagan cultic practices in v. 13, referring back to 1:29–31, and reference to a stump, which elsewhere in Scripture is understood as a sacred stone pillar (Lev. 26:1; Deut. 16:22), and condemned.
242. E.g., M. Burrows, "The Conduit of the Upper Pool," *ZAW* 70 (1958): 221–27; R. Amiran, "The Water Supply of Israelite Jerusalem," in *Jerusalem Revealed: Archaeology in the Holy City, 1968–1974*, ed. Y. Yadin (Jerusalem: Israel Exploration Society, 1975), 75–78; A. Mazar, "The Aqueducts of Jerusalem," ibid., 79–84 (concerning later water systems); J. Simons, *Jerusalem in the Old Testament* (Leiden: Brill, 1952), 334–37; D. Bahat, "The Fuller's Field and the 'Conduit of the Upper Pool,'" in A. Ben-Tor et al., *ErIsr* 20 (1989): 253–55 [Eng. 203*–204*]; R. Reich and E. Shukron, "Light at the End of the Tunnel," *BAR* 25/1 (1999): 22–33, 72; A. Faust, "Warren's Shaft: Yes, It Really Was Used to Draw Water," *BAR* 29/5 (2003): 70–76; A. Shimron, "Warren's Shaft: No, It Really Was Not Used to Draw Water," *BAR* 30/4 (2004): 14–15.
243. King and Stager, *Life*, 158–59.
244. COS, 3.423B.
245. Ibid., 3, 79, n. 14.
246. Wildberger, *Isaiah 1–12*, 284.
247. COS, 2.117B; ibid., 287, n. 5; cf. J. K. Kuan, *Neo-Assyrian Historical Inscriptions and Syria-Palestine*

(Hong Kong: Alliance Bible Seminary, 1995), 153.

248. *CAD*, 2, 193–94.
249. *COS*, 1.111 IV:1–21; T. Abusch, "Marduk," *DDD*, 543.
250. P. J. van Zijl, *Baal: A Study of Texts in Connexion with Baal in the Ugaritic Epics* (AOAT 10; Neukirchen-Vluyn: Neukirchener Verlag, 1972); I. Cornelius, *The Iconography of the Canaanite Gods Reshef and Baᶜal : Late Bronze and Iron Age I Periods (C. 1500–1000 B.C.E.)* (Göttingen: Vandenhoeck & Ruprecht, 1994); W. Herrmann, "Baal," *DDD*, 132–39; J. Day, *Yahweh and the Gods and Goddesses of Canaan* (JSOTSup 265; Sheffield: Sheffield Academic Press, 2002).
251. *COS*, 2.33.
252. *ANET*, 290. See also 293 regarding a raid into Egypt.
253. Ibid., 295–96.
254. Ibid., 301.
255. Pers. trans.; *CAD*, 7, 306.
256. Parpola, *Assyrian Prophecies*, 9.
257. M. Nissinen, *References to Prophecy in Neo-Assyrian Sources* (SAA, 7; Helsinki: The Neo-Assyrian Text Corpus Project, 1998), 35.
258. Among the many examples, see E. Reiner, *Babylonian Planetary Omens* (Malibu: Undena, 1975); W. H. van Soldt, *Solar Omens of Enuma Anu Enlil: Tablets 23 (24)–29 (30)* (Istanbul: Nederlands Historisch-Archaeologisch Instituut Te Istanbul, 1995); E. Reiner, *Babylonian Planetary Omens: Part Three* (Leiden: Brill, 1998); E. Reiner, "Early Zodiologia and Related Matters," in George and Finkel, *Wisdom, Gods and Literature*, 421–28; Guinan, "A Severed Head Laughed"; E. Reiner, *Babylonian Planetary Omens: Part Four* (Leiden: Brill, 2005).
259. A. Biran and J. Naveh, "An Aramaic Stele Fragment from Tel Dan," *IEJ* 43 (1993): 81–98; E. Ben Zvi, "On the Reading "*bytdwd* in the Aramaic Stele from Tel Dan," *JSOT* 64 (1994): 25–32; anonymous, "'David" Found at Dan," *BAR* 20/2 (1994): 26–39; B. I. Demsky, "On Reading Ancient Inscriptions: The Monumental Aramaic Stele Fragment from Tel Dan," *JANES* 23 (1995): 29–35; É. Puech, "Le stele araméenne de Dan: Bar Hadad II et la coalition des Omrides et de la maison de David," *RB* 101 (1994): 215–241; A. Biran and J. Naveh, "The Tel Dan Inscription: A New Fragment," *IEJ* 45 (1995): 1–18; P. E. Dion, "The Tel Dan Stele and its Historical Significance," in *Michael: Historical, Epigraphical and Biblical Studies in Honor of Prof. Michael Heltzer*, ed. Y. Avishur and R. Deutsch (Tel Aviv: Archaeological Center Publications, 1999): 145–56. J. T. Willis suggests that it comes from a destruction level caused by Tiglath-pileser III in 733 B.C., "The Newly Discovered Fragmentary Aramaic Inscription from Tel Dan," *Restoration Quarterly* 37 (1995): 219–26.
260. E.g., F. H. Cryer, "On the Recently Discovered 'House of David' Inscription," *SJOT* 8 (1994): 3–19; idem, "A 'Betdawd' Miscellany: *Dwd, Dwd*ʾ or *Dwdh?*" *SJOT* 9 (1995): 52–58; idem, "King Hadad," *SJOT* 9 (1995): 223–35; idem, "Of Epistemology, Northwest-Semitic Epigraphy and Irony: The 'BYTDWD/House of David' Inscription Revisited," *JSOT* 69 (1996): 3–17; N. P. Lemche and T. L. Thompson, "Did Biran Kill David? The Bible in the Light Of Archaeology," *JSOT* 64 (1994): 3–22; William M. Schniedewind, "Tel Dan Stela: New Light on Aramaic and Jehu's Revolt," *BASOR* 302 (May 1996): 75–90; T. L. Thompson, "'House of David': An Eponymic Referent to Yahweh as Godfather," *SJOT* 9 (1995): 59–74; idem, "Dissonance and Disconnections: Notes on the *bytdwd* and *hmlk.hdd* Fragments from Tel Dan," *SJOT* 9 (1995): 236–40.
261. A. Lemaire, "Le dynastie davidique (*byt dwd*) dans les deux inscriptions ouest-sémitiques de ixe s. av. J.-C.," *Studi Epigrafici e Linguistici* 11 (1994): 17–19; idem, "'House of David' Restored in Moabite Inscription," *BAR* 20/3 (1994): 30–37; B. Routledge, *Moab in the Iron Age: Hegemony, Polity, Archaeology* (Philadelphia: Univ. of Pennsylvania Press, 2004), 133–53; K. A. Kitchen, "A Possible Mention of David in the Late Tenth Century B.C.E., and Deity *Dod as Dead as a Dodo?" *JSOT* 76 (1997): 29–44; A. F. Rainey, "Syntax, Hermeneutics and History," *IEJ* 48 (1998): 239–51; L. J. Mykytiuk, *Identifying Biblical Persons in Northwest Semitic Inscriptions of 1200–539 B.C.E.* (Atlanta: Society of Biblical Literature, 2004), 265–77.
262. *COS*, 2.23, 113F, 118G, H, etc.
263. See, for the Hebrew Bible, R. W. Neff, *The Announcement in Old Testament Birth Stories* (New Haven, Conn.: Yale Univ. Press, 1969); T. D. Finley, *The Birth Report Genre in the Hebrew Bible* (FAT 2.12; Tübingen: Mohr Siebeck, 2005).
264. Foster, *Before the Muses*, 231.
265. *CAT*, 1.24:7; translated in N. Wyatt, *Religious Texts from Ugarit*, 2nd ed. (Sheffield: Sheffield Academic Press, 2002), 337 in the past tense.
266. N. Avigad and B. Sass, *Corpus of West Semitic Stamp Seals* (Jerusalem: Israel Academy of Sciences and Humanities, 1997), 65:42. Another name with the same meaning but a slightly different Hebrew term is found in ibid., 64:40–41. Several seals show the name "Yahweh is with me": ibid., 64:40, 41; 222:590; perhaps 226:605.
267. King and Stager, *Life*, 103; *CAD*, 6, 189.
268. King and Stager, *Life*, 190.
269. Ibid., 104; I. Jacob and W. Jacob, "Flora," *ABD*, 2:807.
270. A Sumero-Akkadian lexical list terms a bee as a "honey fly"; Hh. XIV 325–6 (*CAD*, 3, 161).
271. Keel and Uehlinger, *Altorientalische Miniaturkunst*, 88:116.
272. Frame, *Rulers of Babylonia*, 281.
273. *CAD*, 3, 161–63.
274. *CAD*, 1, 43.
275. J. N. Postgate, *Fifty Neo-Assyrian Legal Documents* (Warminster: Aris & Phillips, 1976), 9.
276. Ibid., 138.
277. *COS*, 3.86:8.
278. Called "a man's wife" (*ANET*, 624d), an *apiltum* ("answerer"; ibid., 625h); van der Toorn, *From her Cradle*, 128–29.

279. Ibid., 129–30; *ANET*, 450.
280. The Akkadian terms for "watering pipes" and "water canal" are from the same Semitic root (*shlh*) as Shiloah; Wildberger, *Isaiah 1–12*, 343.
281. D. Tarler and J. M. Cahill, "David, City of," *ABD*, 2:62.
282. *ANET*, 649.
283. J. G. Westenholz, *Legends of the Kings of Akkade: The Texts* (Winona Lake, Ind.: Eisenbrauns, 1997), 277.
284. Seux, *Épithètes royales*, 34.
285. J. C. Greenfield, "Hadad," *DDD*, 378–79. See also the Babylonian ruler Nabonidus (556–539 B.C.), who describes an enemy who "swept in like a flood storm" (*ANET*, 309).
286. Ibid., 377; see also Grayson, *Early First Millennium*, 2:28, 35, 51, etc.
287. COS, 2.86.
288. Syria-Palestine: *ANEP*, 486, 493; U. Winter, *Frau und Göttin: Exegetische und ikonographische Studien zum weiblichen Gottesbild im alten Israel und in dessen Umwelt* (OBO 53; Göttingen: Vandenhoeck & Ruprecht, 1983), 277, 288; T. Ornan, "A Complex System of Religious Symbols," in *Crafts and Images in Contact: Studies on Eastern Mediterranean Art of the First Millennium* B.C.E., ed. C. E. Suter and C. Uehlinger (OBO 210; Göttingen: Vandenhoeck & Ruprecht, 2005), 207–41; Assyria: *ANEP* 534, 536; J. Black and A. Green, *Gods, Demons and Symbols: An Illustrated Dictionary* (Austin: Univ. of Texas Press, 2003), 185–86.
289. Black and Green, *Gods, Demons and Symbols*, 186. See also *ANEP*, 536, with Ashur shooting a bow superimposed on a winged disk with flames.
290. Wilkinson, *Complete Gods and Goddesses*, 24–25.
291. Ibid., 150–52.
292. Ibid., 160–63.
293. Black and Green, *Gods, Demons and Symbols*, 49.
294. Ibid., 50.
295. E.g., *ANET*, 289, Esarhaddon (680–669 B.C.). See P. D. Miller and J. J. M. Roberts. *The Hand of the Lord: A Reassessment of the Ark Narrative of 1 Samuel* (Baltimore: Johns Hopkins Univ. Press, 1977), 10–11, 92; Holloway, *Aššur is King!*
296. COS, 2.124.
297. Ibid., 2.37.
298. *SSI*, 2, 83.
299. COS, 1.131.
300. Ibid., 1.172.
301. Leichty, *The Omen Series Šumma Izbu*; D. B. Weisberg, "An Old Babylonian Forerunner to Šumma Ālu," *HUCA* 40–41 (1969): 83–104; R. C. Bailey, "Prophetic Use of Omen Motifs: A Preliminary Study" in *The Biblical Canon in Comparative Perspective*, ed. K. L. Younger Jr. et al. (Lewiston, N.Y.: Mellen, 1991), 203–11.
302. J. Tropper, "Spirit of the Dead," *DDD*, 806–9.
303. *ANET*, 98:79–80; see C. J. Gadd, *Ideas of Divine Rule in the Ancient East* (London: Oxford Univ. Press, 1948), 88–89; H. A. Hoffner, "אוֹב (*ʾôbh*)," *TDOT*, 1:133.
304. I. L. Finkel, "Necromancy in Ancient Mesopotamia," *AfO* 29–30 (1983–1984): 1–17; J. Tropper, *Nekromantie: Totenbefragung im Alten Orient und im Alten Testament* (Neukirchen-Vluyn: Neukirchener Verlag, 1989); van der Toorn, *From her Cradle*, 123–24.
305. Gordon, *Sumerian Proverbs*, 59.
306. J. Tropper, "Wizard," *DDD*, 907–8. See P. S. Johnston, *Shades of Sheol: Death and Afterlife in the Old Testament* (Downers Grove, Ill.: InterVarsity Press, 2002), 150–51.
307. COS, 1.90:19.
308. Y. Aharoni et al., *The Macmillan Bible Atlas*, 3rd ed. (New York: Macmillan, 1993), 10, 59.
309. See *ANET*, 284.
310. *OEANE*, 2:170; *NEAEHL*, 357–68.
311. A. F. Rainey and R. S. Notley, *The Sacred Bridge* (Jerusalem: Carta), 231; E. Stern, "Dor," *ABD*, 2:223–25.
312. D. Ussishkin, "Megiddo," *ABD*, 4:666–79; *OEANE*, 3:467–68; *NEAEHL*, 1003–24.
313. M. Ottosson, "Gilead (Place)," *ABD*, 2:1020–22.
314. Aharoni, *Macmillan Bible Atlas*, 146, 148; Rainey and Notley, *Sacred Bridge*, 231.
315. D. Frayne, *Old Babylonian Period (2003-1595)* (RIME 4; Toronto: Univ. of Toronto Press, 1990), 334; cf. COS, 2.107[a].
316. Ibid., 2.131.
317. E. Lipiński, "Shemesh," *DDD*, 764–68.
318. *ANEP*, 166–67.
319. Ibid., 85.
320. Moran, *Amarna Letters*, 297.
321. *CAD*, 11/2, 263.
322. Lambert and Millard, *Atraḫasis*, 44:2.
323. Lambert, *Babylonian Wisdom Literature*, 84:240.
324. COS, 1.73.
325. *CAD*, 10/2, 38; *AHw*, 1213–14.
326. *ANEP*, 205
327. COS, 1.86 ii:13–15.
328. COS, 2.36:15b f.
329. *ANET*, 534–41.
330. *ʾbʿd*; Avigad and Sass, *Corpus*, 270:724.
331. Foster, *Before the Muses*, 303–4.
332. Frame, *Rulers of Babylonia*, 26.
333. Moran, *Amarna Letters*, 114.
334. Parpola, *Assyrian Prophecies*, 7–8; Nissinen, *References*, 29; *CAD*, 3, 111.
335. Moran, *Amarna Letters*, 50, 143; a perpetual promise, 48, 242–44; *CAD*, 3, 107–8, 111–18.
336. See A. Tomasino, "עוֹלָם," *NIDOTTE*, 3:345–51.
337. King and Stager, *Life*, 22–23.
338. A. K. Grayson, "Assyria: Tiglath-pileser III to Sargon II (744–705 B.C.)," in *CAH*, III^2,77–79.
339. *ANET*, 282.
340. Ibid., 283.
341. Ibid.
342. Foster, *Before the Muses*, 814; see *CAD*, 7, 122.
343. D. L. Lyon, *Keilschrifttexte Sargon's Königs von Assyrien (722–705 v. Chr.)* (Leipzig: Hinrichs, 1883), 8; *CAD*, 1/2, 522.
344. A. George, *The Epic of Gilgamesh* (London: Penguin, 1999), 24.
345. *CAD*, 7, 12.
346. COS, 1.87; Wyatt, *Religious Texts*, 334.

347. *AEL*, 1:36–37.
348. Lambert and Millard, *Atraḫasis*, 113.
349. *ANET*, 538–39; cf. *CAD*, 1/1, 250 for further examples.
350. Ibid., 524.
351. *COS*, 1.102.
352. See ibid., 1.43 B1:62–63.
353. Moran, *Amarna Letters*, 158.
354. Ibid., 178.
355. Ibid., 143, 145, 148.
356. Ibid., 138.
357. *CTA*, 2.61:3–11, pers. trans.
358. Avigad and Sass, *Corpus*, 51:4.
359. R. Deutsch, *Messages from the Past: Hebrew Bullae from the Time of Isaiah through the Destruction of the First Temple. Shlomo Moussaieff Collection and an Up to Date Corpus* (Heb.) (Tel Aviv: Archaeological Center Publications, 1997), 49–51.
360. Avigad and Sass, *Corpus*, 51:5.
361. R. Deutsch, "New Bullae Reveal Egyptian-Style Emblems of Judah's Royal Seals," *BAR* 28/4 (July/August 2002): 4.
362. E.g., Avigad and Sass, *Corpus*, 62:34; 81:97; 86:115.
363. Grayson, *Assyrian Royal Inscriptions*, 2:119–21.
364. Ibid., 149.
365. *COS*, 2.5A.
366. K. E. Slansky, *The Babylonian Entitlement* Narûs *(Kudurrus)* (ASOR Books 9; Boston: American Schools of Oriental Research, 2003).
367. E.g., L. W. King, *Babylonian Boundary-Stones and Memorial Tablets in the British Museum* (London: British Museum, 1912), 22–23.
368. Slansky, *Babylonian Entitlement* Narûs, 176–79, and *passim*.
369. *ANET*, 283; Machinist, "Assyria and Its Image," 725.
370. M. E. J. Richardson, *Hammurabi's Laws* (Sheffield: Sheffield Academic Press, 2000), 133–35.
371. Moran, *Amarna Letters*, 218.
372. Seux, *Epithètes royales*, 284.
373. Richardson, *Hammurabi's Laws*, 63:59.
374. *CAD*, 7, 215. See S. W. Cole, "The Destruction of Orchards in Assyrian Warfare," in Parpola and Whiting, *Assyria 1995*, 29–40.
375. Lambert and Millard, *Atraḫasis*, 67, 73.
376. *ANET*, 458.
377. B. T. Arnold, "The Weidner Chronicle and the Idea of History in Israel and Mesopotamia," in *Faith Tradition and History: Old Testament Historiography in its Near Eastern Context*, ed. A. R. Millard, J. K. Hoffmeier, and D. W. Baker (Winona Lake, Ind.: Eisenbrauns, 1994), 136–37.
378. *COS*, 1.113 iv:61–62.
379. *AHw*, 1413; see, more generally, E. Noort, *Untersuchungen zum Gottesbeschied in Mari: Die "Mariprophetie" in der alttestamentlichen Forschung* (AOAT 202; Neukirchen-Vluyn: Neukirchener Verlag, 1977), 30–32; F. Ellermeier, *Prophetie in Mari und Israel*, 2nd ed. (Göttingen: Friedich Ellermeier, 1977), 111–13.
380. *ANET*, 285. For the extent of the Assyrian empire at this time, see Aharoni, *Macmillan Bible Atlas*, 147.
381. D. Dorsey, *The Roads and Highways of Ancient Israel* (Baltimore: Johns Hopkins Univ. Press, 1991), 136–40.
382. Rainey and Notley, *Sacred Bridge*, 234–38, especially 235.
383. *ANET*, 286; H. Tadmor, "The Campaigns of Sargon II of Assur," *JCS* 12 (1958): 79–80.
384. J. Sudilowsky, "Assyrians in Ashdod: Palace Uncovered near Israel's Coast," *BAR* 30/6 (2004): 12. See also N. Naʾaman, "The Brook of Egypt and Assyrian Policy on the Border of Egypt," *Tel Aviv* 6 (1979): 68–90; N. Franklin, "A Room with a View: Images from Room V at Khorsabad, Samaria, Nubians, the Brook of Egypt and Ashdod," in *Studies in the Archaeology of the Iron Age in Israel and Jordan*, ed. A. Mazar (JSOTSup 331: Sheffield: Sheffield Academic Press, 2001), 257–77, especially 259–61.
385. *COS*, 2.119B.
386. U. Winter, *Frau und Göttin*, 543.
387. *CAT*, 1.17 I:18–21.
388. *COS*, 2.31.
389. Pers. trans.; see *COS*, 2.119B. For an account of a site overrun by Sennacherib, see O. Borowski, "Tel Halif: In the Path of Sennacherib," *BAR* 31/3 (2005): 24–35.
390. E.g., *ANEP*, 501, 522; Black and Green, *Gods, Demons and Symbols*, 31.
391. Ibid., 518.
392. F. J. Stephens, *Votive and Historical Texts from Babylonia and Assyria* (YOS 9; New Haven, Conn.: Yale Univ. Press, 1937), text 62; *CAD*, 3, 30.
393. *CAT*, 2.81, pers. trans.
394. *CAD*, 3, 32.
395. *AEL*, 1:164; E. A. W. Budge, *The Gods of the Egyptians* (London: Methuen, 1904), 1:401.
396. *AEL*, 1:17.
397. M. Krebernik, "Mesopotamian Myths at Ebla: *ARET* 5, 6 and *ARET* 5,7," in Fronzaroli, *Literature and Literary Language*, 91.
398. *AEL*, 1:64, 68.
399. Ibid., 2:38.
400. Ibid., 2:3.
401. Ibid., 1:45 and n. 36.
402. Seux, *Epithètes royales*, 305–8; W. Horowitz, *Mesopotamian Cosmic Geography* (Winona Lake, Ind.: Eisenbrauns, 1998), 25, 40.
403. Ibid., 298–330.
404. W. Horowitz, "The Babylonian Map of the World," *Iraq* 50 (1989): 147–65.
405. *CAT*, 1.3 III:38–42; pers. trans.
406. *ANEP*, 691.
407. Pers. trans.; *CAD*, 15, 204.
408. Pers. trans; cf. *ANET*, 321.
409. Ibid., 275.
410. Ibid., 279.
411. Ibid., 285.
412. *CAD*, 21, 37.
413. Ibid., 36.
414. Gordon, *Sumerian Proverbs*, 201; see Black, *Concise Dictionary*, 255.
415. Ibid., 204.
416. A. R. George, "Studies in Cultic Topography and Ideology," *BO* 53 (1996): 364–65; idem, *Babylo-*

nian Topographical Texts* (OLA 40; Leuven: Peeters, 1992), 83–98.

417. D. J. Wiseman, "Babylonia 605–539 B.C.," *CAH*[3], III/2, 236–39.
418. *AEL*, 3:51.
419. E.g., H. Lutzky, "Shadday as a Goddess Epithet," *VT* 48 (1998): 15–36.
420. *AHw*, 1125.
421. *COS*, 2.27.
422. Lipiński, "Shemesh," 764–68; Black and Green, *Gods, Demons and Symbols*, 182–84; for depictions on Hebrew seals, see Sass, "Pre-Exilic Hebrew Seals," 238, 241:147–52.
423. B. B. Schmidt, "Moon," *DDD*, 585–93; on Hebrew seals, see Sass, "Pre-Exilic Hebrew Seals," 239–40:153–56.
424. On Hebrew seals, see Sass, "Pre-Exilic Hebrew Seals," 240–41:157–58.
425. J. Oates, *Babylon* (London: Thames & Hudson, 1979), 112.
426. Cf. Isa. 2:6; H. Hunger, *Astrological Reports to Assyrian Kings* (SAA 8; Helsinki: Helsinki Univ. Press, 1992); E. Reiner, *Astral Magic in Babylon* (Philadelphia: American Philosophical Society, 1995); U. Koch-Westenholz, *Mesopotamian Astrology* (CNI 19; Copenhagen: Museum Tusculanum, Univ. of Copenhagen, 1995).
427. *COS*, 2.27.
428. J. G. Westenholz, *The Legends of the Kings of Akkade: The Texts* (Winona Lake, Ind.: Eisenbrauns, 1997), 71:60–62.
429. D. J. Wiseman, *The Vassal-Treaties of Esarhaddon* (London: British School of Archaeology in Iraq, 1958), 60:423–24, pers. trans.
430. *CAD*, 7, 61.
431. *COS*, 1.132; Malul, *Knowledge, Control and Sex*, 261–62.
432. Saggs, *Might*, 248–50.
433. Holloway, *Aššur is King!* 80–216.
434. Saggs, *Might*, 249.
435. See E. Yamauchi, "Metal Sources and Metallurgy in the Biblical World," *Perspectives on Science and Christian Faith* 45 (1993): 256–57.
436. *CAT*, 1.4 vii:29–32; pers. trans.
437. *ANET*, 560.
438. E. Firmage, "Zoology (Animal Profiles)," *ABD*, 6:1141–42.
439. Sass, "Pre-Exilic Hebrew Seals," 223–24:111–13.
440. Herodotus 7.62; Strabo 15.2.8.
441. E. Yamauchi, "Persians," in *Peoples of the Old Testament World*, ed. A. J. Hoerth et al. (Grand Rapids: Baker, 1994), 107–10.
442. *CAD*, 2, 235.
443. Ibid., 234–36 for further examples.
444. P. Vargyas, "Silver and Money in Achaemenid and Hellenistic Babylonia," in *Assyriologica et Semitica: Festschrift für Joachim Oelsner anlässlich seines 65. Geburtstages am 18. Februar 1997* (AOAT 252; Münster: Ugarit-Verlag, 2000), 513–21.
445. J. A. Fitzmyer, *The Aramaic Inscriptions of Sefire* (BibOr 19; Rome: Pontifical Biblical Institute, 1967), 14:36; pers. trans.
446. *ANET*, 300.
447. Fitzmyer, *Aramaic Inscriptions*, 14:32–33.
448. Wildberger, *Isaiah 1–11*, 52–53.
449. A. K. Grayson, *Assyrian Rulers of the Third and Second Millennia B.C. (to 1115 B.C.)* (RIM A1; Toronto: Univ. of Toronto Press, 1987), 183.
450. *COS*, 1.35.
451. Ibid., 2.91; L. Marfoe, "Cedar Forest to Silver Mountain: Social Change and the Development of Long-Distance Trade," in *Center and Periphery in the Ancient World*, ed. M. Rowlands, M. Larsen, and K. Kristiansen (Cambridge: Cambridge Univ. Press, 1987), 25–35.
452. George, *Epic of Gilgamesh*, 39.
453. Ibid., 44–46.
454. *ANET*, 307.
455. Del Olmo Lete, *Dictionary*, 743; J. C. de Moor, "*Rāpiʾūma*—Rephaim," *ZAW* 88 (1976): 323–45; W. Pitard, "A New Edition of the '*Rāpiʾūma*' Texts: KTU 1.20–22," *BASOR* 285 (1992): 33–77; idem, "The Rpum Texts," in *Handbook of Ugaritic Studies*, ed. W. G. E. Watson and N. Wyatt (HO 39; Leiden: Brill, 1999), 259–69; H. Rouillard, "Rephaim," *DDD*, 692–700; O. Loretz, *Götter–Ahnen–Könige als gerechte Richter: Der "Rechtsfall" des Menschen vor Gott nach altorientalischen und biblischen Texten* (AOAT 290; Münster: Ugarit-Verlag, 2003), 211–336.
456. J. C. de Moor, *The Rise of Yahwism: The Roots of Israelite Monotheism*, 2nd ed. (BETL 91; Leuven: Univ. Press, 1997), 75, 336, 355; M. L. Brown, "Was there a West Semitic Asklepios?" *UF* 30 (1998): 133–54; Loretz, *Götter–Ahnen–Könige*, 221–38; P. J. Williams, "Are the Biblical Rephaim and the Ugaritic RPUM Healers?" in Gordon and de Moor, *The Old Testament in Its World*, 366–75.
457. *COS*, 1.105.
458. Ibid., 2.57.
459. Swerdlow, *Ancient Astronomy*, 23.
460. *COS*, 1.91.
461. Ibid., 1.339.
462. Ibid., 1.274.
463. Ibid., 1.111.
464. J. Day, "Baal (Deity)," *ABD*, 1:546.
465. *COS*, 1.86.
466. Ibid., 1.251.
467. Niehr, "Zaphon," 928.
468. E.g., Keel and Uehlinger, *Gods, Goddesses and Images*, 256, 311.
469. *CAD*, 4, 111.
470. *ANET*, 659; H. Niehr, *Der höchste Gott: Alttestamentlicher JHWJ-Glaube im Kontext syrisch-kanaanäischer Religion des 1. Jahrtausends v. Chr.* (BZAW 190; Berlin: de Gruyter, 1990); F. W. Schmidt, "Most High," *ABD*, 4:922; E. E. Elnes and P. D. Miller, "Elyon," *DDD*, 293–99.
471. *CAD*, 2, 342; *HALOT*, 116.
472. E. M. Meyers, "Secondary Burials in Palestine," *BA* 33 (1970): 2–29; Johnston, *Shades of Sheol*, 81–82.
473. *CAD*, 13, 202–4.
474. Ibid., 3, 110; Lambert, *Babylonian Wisdom Literature*, 87.
475. *COS*, 1.111.

476. M. Chavalas, *The Ancient Near East* (Oxford: Blackwell, 2006), 428, text 157; cf. COS, 2.124.
477. T. Dothan, *The Philistines and their Material Culture* (New Haven, Conn.: Yale Univ. Press, 1982); W. F. Albright, "Syria, the Philistines, and Phoenicia," in *CAH*[3], II/2, 507–36; R. D. Barnett, "The Sea Peoples," in ibid., 371–78; T. Dothan and M. Dothan, *People of the Sea: The Search for the Philistines* (New York: MacMillan, 1992); H. J. Katzenstein, "Philistines (History)," *ABD*, 5:326.
478. C. S. Ehrlich, *The Philistines in Transition: A History from c.a. 1000–730 B.C.E.* (SHCANE 10; Leiden: Brill, 1996), 1–21.
479. Ibid., 23–77.
480. Ibid., 85–104; Katzenstein, "Philistines (History)," *ABD*, 5:327–28; Grayson, "Assyria: Tiglath-pileser III," 77–78, 88–89.
481. Millard, *Eponyms*, 59.
482. H. Tadmor, *The Inscriptions of Tiglath-pileser III* (Jerusalem: Israel Academy of Sciences and Humanities, 1994), 83.
483. Ehrlich, *Philistines in Transition*, 94–98, 181–82, 185–89.
484. Katzenstein, "Philistines (History)," 327; Grayson, "Assyria: Tiglath-pileser III," 88–89.
485. Katzenstein, "Philistines (History)," 327.
486. Grayson, *Early First Millennium*, 2:190, cf. 193.
487. Gordon, *Sumerian Proverbs*, 281.
488. MacDonald, *"East of the Jordan,"* 84–86.
489. COS, 2.23:1.
490. P. H. Vaughn, *The Meaning of Bāmâ in the Old Testament: A Study of Etymological, Textual and Archaeological Evidence* (London: Cambridge Univ. Press, 1974); J. T. Whitney, "Bamoth in the Old Testament," *TynBul* 30 (1979): 125–47; M. D. Fowler, "The Israelite *bāmâ*: A Question of Interpretation," *ZAW* 94 (1982): 203–13; J. M. Grintz, "Some Observations on the 'High Place' in the History of Israel," *VT* 27 (1977): 111–13; E. C. LaRocca-Pitts, *Of Wood and Stone* (HSM 61, Winona Lake, Ind.: Eisenbrauns, 2001), 127–59; J. E. Catron, "Temple and *Bamah*: Some Considerations," in *The Pitcher Is Broken: Memorial Essays for Gösta W. Ahlström*, ed. S. W. Holloway and L. K. Handy (JSOTSup 190; Sheffield: Sheffield Academic Press, 1995), 150–65; A. Biran, "Sacred Spaces: Of Standing Stones, High Places and Cult Objects at Tel Dan," *BAR* 24/5 (1998): 38–45, 70; B. Nakhai, *Archaeology and the Religions of Canaan and Israel* (Boston: ASOR, 2001), 161–200; A. Biran, "The High Places of Biblical Dan," in Mazar, ed., *Studies in the Archaeology*, 148–55; Z. Zevit, *The Religions of Ancient Israel: A Synthesis of Parallactic Approaches* (London: Continuum, 2001), 262–63.
491. COS, 2.23: 3b–4.
492. *ANET*, 457.
493. Nissinen, *References to Prophecy*, 26; pers. trans.
494. See also A. K. Grayson, *Assyrian Rulers of the Early First Millennium B.C. I* (Toronto: Univ. of Toronto, 1991), 1:209, 211.
495. MacDonald, *"East of the Jordan,"* 182.
496. COS, 2.138.
497. Aharoni, *Macmillan Bible Atlas*, 9.
498. COS, 1.87.
499. G. L. Mattingly, "Aroer," *ABD*, 1:399; E. Olávarri, "Sondages à ʿArôʿer sur l'Arnon," *RB* 72 (1965): 77–94.
500. COS, 2.23.
501. Ibid., 1.90:7.
502. G. Edelstein, "Rephaim, Valley of," *ABD*, 5:676.
503. J. Day, "Asherah," *ABD*, 1:483–87; N. Wyatt, "Asherah," *DDD*, 99–105; C. Frevel, *Aschera und der Ausschliesslichkeitsanspruch YHWHs: Beiträge zu literarischen, religionsgeschichtlichen und ikonographischen Aspekten der Ascheradiskussion* (BBB 94, 1–1; Weinheim: Beltz Athenäum, 1995); T. Binger, *Asherah: Goddesses in Ugarit, Israel and the Old Testament* (JSOTSup 232; Sheffield: Sheffield Academic Press, 1997); Judith M. Hadley, *The Cult of Asherah in Ancient Israel and Judah: Evidence for a Hebrew Goddess* (Cambridge: Cambridge Univ. Press, 2000); M. S. Smith, *The Early History of God: Yahweh and the Other Deities in Ancient Israel*, 2nd ed. (Grand Rapids: Eerdmans, 2002), xxx–xxxvi, 108–47.
504. M. D. Fowler, "Incense Altars," *ABD*, 3:409–10; Zevit, *Religions*, 310, n. 104, 314.
505. A Goetze, "An Old Babylonian Prayer of the Divination Priest," *JCS* 22 (1968): 26; *CAD*, 13, 324.
506. *CAD*, 13, 321.
507. A study of the verbs associated with the practice was undertaken by A. M. Kitz, "The Hebrew Terminology of Lot Casting and Its Ancient Near Eastern Context," *CBQ* 62 (2000): 207–14.
508. Pers. trans.; *CAD*, 7, 201.
509. Ibid., 7, 198–201; A. M. Kitz, "Undivided Inheritance and Lot Casting in the Book of Joshua," *JBL* 119 (2000): 601–18.
510. Kitz, "Undivided Inheritance," 604, n. 11.
511. COS, 3.55.
512. B. Trigger, "Nubian, Negro, Black, or Nilotic?" in *Africa in Antiquity: The Arts of Ancient Nubia and Sudan*, Vol. 1, *The Essays*, ed. S. Wenig (Brooklyn: The Brooklyn Museum, 1978), 26–35; J. D. Hays, *From Every People and Nation: A Biblical Theology of Race* (Downers Grove, Ill.: InterVarsity Press, 2003), 36–39. On the Negroid features of Cushites in art, see P. Albenda, "Observations on Egyptians in Assyrian Art," *Bulletin of the Egyptological Seminar* (1982): 8; J. E. Reade, "Sargon's Campaigns of 720, 716, and 715 B.C.: Evidence from the Sculptures," *JNES* 35 (1976): 100.
513. R. H. Smith, "Ethiopia," *ABD*, 2:665; F. J. Yurco, "Egypt and Nubia: Old, Middle, and New Kingdom Eras," in *Africa and Africans in Antiquity*, ed. E. M. Yamauchi (East Lansing: Michigan State Univ. Press, 2001), 28–112; D. B. Redford, *From Slave to Pharaoh: The Black Experience of Ancient Egypt* (Baltimore: Johns Hopkins Univ. Press, 2004).
514. K. A. Kitchen, *The Third Intermediate Period in Egypt, 1100–650 B.C.*, 2nd ed. (Warminster: Aris & Philips, 1986), 362–98; E. M. Yamauchi, *Africa and the Bible* (Grand Rapids: Baker, 2004), 107–48.

515. K. Lawson Younger Jr., "Recent Study on Sargon II, King of Assyria: Implication for Biblical Studies," in Chavalas and Younger, *Mesopotamia and the Bible*, 288–329.
516. COS, 2.118E and n. 9; Oppenheim, *Ancient Mesopotamia*, 64, 398.
517. *ANEP*, 33.
518. Ibid., 109; A. Niwiński, "Iconography of the 21st Dynasty: Its Main Features, Levels of Attestation, the Media and their Diffusion," in Uehlinger, *Images as Media*, 24, 40.
519. D. Collon, "Moon, Boats and Battle," in Finkel and Geller, *Sumerian Gods*, 11–16; P. Steinkeller, "Early Semitic Literature and Third Millennium Seals with Mythological Motifs," in Fronzaroli, ed., *Literature and Literary Language at Ebla*, 256–67, pl. 4–5; see B. Pomgratz-Lesiten, *Ina Šulmi Īrub: Die kulttopographische und ideologische Programmatik der* akītu-*Prozession in Babylon und Assyrien in I. Jahrtausend v. Chr.* (Baghdader Forschungen 16; Mainz am Rhein: Philip von Zabern, 1994), 196–98.
520. Sass, "The Pre-Exilic Hebrew Seals," 232–33:136; 248:12, 13.
521. Pers. trans.; G. Dossin, *Correspondance de Šamši-Addu et de ses fils* (ARM I; Paris: Imprimerie nationale, 1950), 178–80; *CAD*, 13, 62; Meier, *Messengers*, 25.
522. *CAD*, 6, 71.
523. *ANEP*, 3, 45–47.
524. Ibid., 432, 439–51.
525. Ibid., 376–426.
526. Herodotus 3.20.
527. E.g., A. Niccacci, "Isaiah XVIII–XX from an Egyptological Perspective," *VT* 48 (1998): 216.
528. *HALOT*, 1081.
529. P. E. McGovern et al., ed., *The Origins and Ancient History of Wine* (Philadelphia: Gordon & Breach, 1995); C. A. Walsh, *The Fruit of the Vine: Viticulture in Ancient Israel* (HSM 60; Winona Lake, Ind.: Eisenbrauns, 2000).
530. Sass, "Pre-Exilic Hebrew Seals," 219:98–100.
531. Wiseman, *Vassal-Treaties*, 62:426–27.
532. The same word as used in our passage.
533. COS, 2.37.
534. Ibid., 2.2B.
535. N. Wyatt, "The Titles of the Ugaritic Storm-God," *UF* 24 (1992): 420–22; S. B. Parker, ed., *Ugaritic Narrative Poetry* (Atlanta: Society of Biblical Literature, 1997), 103.
536. A. R. W. Green, *The Storm-God in the Ancient Near East* (Winona Lake, Ind.: Eisenbrauns, 2003), 193.
537. Ibid., 56. For other references to Adad's association with clouds (*erpetu*), see *CAD*, 4, 302–4.
538. The Assyrian Adad is also associated with lightning; Ornan, *Triumph of the Symbol*, 23–26.
539. See further J. Goldingay, *Daniel* (WBC 30; Waco, Tex.: Word, 1989), 151.
540. George, *Epic of Gilgamesh*, 92; pers. trans.
541. COS, 1.45:38–40.
542. *ANET*, 443.
543. Gordon, *Sumerian Proverbs*, 110.
544. *AEL*, 1:155.
545. A. H. Gardner and K. Sethe, *Egyptian Letters to the Dead: Mainly from the Old and Middle Kingdoms* (London: Egypt Exploration Society, 1928); S. R. Keller, "Egyptian Letters to the Dead in Relation to the Old Testament and Other Near Eastern Sources" (PhD diss., New York Univ., 1989); E. F. Wente, "Correspondence," *The Oxford Encyclopedia of Ancient Egypt*, 1:313–14; Johnston, "Death in Israel and Egypt: A Theological Reflection," in *The Old Testament in Its World*, 95–98.
546. E. F. Wente, *Letters from Ancient Egypt* (Atlanta: Scholars Press, 1990), 215; see 215–19. On dream oracles in Egypt, see S. Sauneron, "Les songes et leur interpretation dans l'Égypte ancienne," in *Les songes et leur interpretation*, ed. S. Sauneron (Sources oreintales 2; Paris: Éditions de Seuil, 1959), 17–61.
547. Johnston, "Death in Israel and Egypt," 97–98.
548. *AEL*, 3:70.
549. *ANET*, 294; Spalinger, "Egypt, History of (Dyn. 21–26)," *ABD*, 2:360; M. H. Feldman, "Nineveh to Thebes and Back: Art and Politics between Assyria and Egypt in the Seventh Century B.C.E.," in Collon and George, ed., *Nineveh*, 1:141–50.
550. *ANET*, 295.
551. *AEL*, 1:106.
552. Ibid., 1:159.
553. *CAD*, 2, 3, 31–32.
554. Borger, *Inschriften Asarhaddons*, 114; *CAD*, 2, 32.
555. A. de Groot and D. T. Ariel, ed., *City of David Excavations Final Report III* (Jerusalem: Institute of Archaeology, Hebrew University, 1992), 131–48; King and Stager, *Life*, 121–22.
556. Sass, "Pre-Exilic Hebrew Seals," 218–19:94–97; a neo-Assyrian seal from the mid-ninth century, Keel and Uehlinger, *Altorientalische Miniaturkunst*, 44:48.
557. *CAD*, 2, 32.
558. COS, 1.45.
559. J. Baines and J. Malek, *Cultural Atlas of Ancient Egypt*, rev. ed. (New York: Checkmark Books, 2000), 47.
560. Kitchen, *Third Intermediate Period*, 268, 426–30; *OEANE*, 3, 384.
561. I. Shaw, *Exploring Ancient Egypt* (Oxford: Oxford Univ. Press, 2003), 223–32.
562. Seux, *Épithète royales*, 159–60.
563. Among numerous examples, see *AEL*, 1:58–59, 61–81; 2:135–65.
564. Baines and Malek, *Cultural Atlas*, 134–35.
565. D. B. Redford, "Memphis," *ABD*, 4:689–91; *OEANE*, 3, 470–71.
566. Kitchen, *Third Intermediate Period*, 348–77.
567. *ANET*, 293.
568. *AEL*, 3:73, 80; see Niccacci, "Isaiah XVIII–XX," 220.
569. *ANET*, 533.
570. Ibid., 259.
571. Ibid., 243.
572. Raabe, "Baal-Zephon," *ABD*, 1:554; R. N. Jones and Z. T. Fiema, "Tahpanhes," *ABD*, 6:308–9.
573. Redford, "Memphis," *ABD*, 4:689–91; Baines and Malek, *Cultural Atlas*, 134–35.

574. *ANET*, 293–96.
575. Ibid., 290; D. B. Redford, "Pathros," *ABD*, 5:178.
576. A. E. Cowley, *Aramaic Papyri of the Fifth Century B.C.* (Oxford: Clarendon, 1932); B. Porten and A. Yardeni, *Textbook of Aramaic Documents from Ancient Egypt* (Jerusalem: Hebrew Univ., 1986-).
577. E. Lipiński, *Semitic Languages: Outline of a Comparative Grammar* (Leuven: Peeters, 1997), 56–61.
578. *ANET*, 248, Syrians in Thebes; 553–54, "Asiatics" (Canaanites) in service in Egypt.
579. *COS*, 1.38.
580. See Watts, *Isaiah 1–33*, 259, for sources regarding Jewish populations in Egypt.
581. *ANET*, 492.
582. E. M. Yamauchi, *Persia and the Bible* (Grand Rapids: Baker, 1996), 93–128.
583. D. Ben-Ami, "Mysterious Standing Stones: What Do These Ubiquitous Things Mean?" *BAR* 32/2 (2006): 38–45.
584. C. F. Graesser, "Standing Stones in Ancient Palestine," *BA* 35/2 (1972): 34–63.
585. Tel Dan: A. Biran, "Sacred Spaces: Of Standing Stones, High Places and Cult Objects at Tel Dan," *BAR* 24/5 (1998): 38–45, 70; Arad: Y. Aharoni, "The Israelite Sanctuary at Arad," in *New Directions in Biblical Archaeology*, ed. D. N. Freedman and J. C. Greenfield (New York: Doubleday, 1971), 28–44.
586. Ben-Ami, "Mysterious Standing Stones," 44.
587. *KAI*, 2,203–204; *COS*, 2.33; pers. trans. Hadad is the Canaanite storm god, often designated as Baal, and Melqart is the chief god of Phoenician Tyre.
588. E.g., Richardson, *Hammurabi's Laws*, 49 (Law 23), 79 (Law 120), 81 (Law 126), 111 (Law 240); *CAD*, 2, 127–29; 4, 7, 135, 214.
589. Borger, *Inschriften Asarhaddons*, 40; *CAD*, 21, 116.
590. *CAD*, 10/I, 190.
591. *COS*, 1.86; pers. trans. See Japhet, *Studies in Bible*, 161–62, for a discussion and other examples.
592. J. Black, A. George, and N. Postgate, *A Concise Dictionary of Akkadian*, 2nd ed. (Wiesbaden: Harrassowitz, 2000), 401.
593. *COS*, 2.115A.
594. Ibid., 2.119.
595. Mattila, *The King's Magnates*, 107–25, 153–54; Millard, *Eponyms*, 88, 90, 91, 101, etc.
596. H. Hoffner, "Some Contributions of Hittitology to Old Testament Study," *TynBul* 20 (1969): 44.
597. See Bahrani, *Women of Babylon*, 59–65, for a discussion and representations of nudity, death, and defeat.
598. G. Davies, "Some Uses of Writing in Ancient Israel in the Light of Recently Published Inscriptions," in *Writing and Ancient Near Eastern Society: Papers in Honour of Alan R. Millard* (New York: T. & T. Clark, 2005), 158.
599. *ANEP*, 7–10, 55, 57, 332, etc.
600. Grayson, *Assyrian Rulers of the Third and Second Millennia*, 236; see also *CAD*, 9, 223.
601. F. Vallat, "Elam," *ABD*, 2:424–29.
602. T. C. Young Jr., "Media," *ABD*, 4:658–59; Yamauchi, "Persians," 107–10; idem, *Persia and the Bible*, 31–63.
603. T. S. Philip, *Menstruation and Childbirth in the Bible: Fertility and Impurity* (New York: Peter Lang, 2006), 81–110, especially 96–101.
604. *COS*, 1.132; pers. trans.
605. Ibid., 1.44.
606. King and Stager, *Life*, 63–64, 353–57.
607. *COS*, 1.86; pers. trans.
608. *ANEP*, 637, possibly eighth century; also 846, 849.
609. A. Kempinski, "From Death to Resurrection: The Early Evidence [Punic funerary monument, Pozo Moro, Spain]," *BAR* 21/5 (1995): 63.
610. *ANEP*, 375; cf. 374.
611. Ibid., 351–55.
612. Ibid., 3.
613. Bright, *History*, 360.
614. *COS*, 3.51; pers. trans.
615. B. Rothenberg, *Timnaʿ: Valley of the Biblical Copper Mines* (London: Thames & Hudson, 1972); MacDonald, *"East of the Jordan,"* 185–94; *OEANE*, 5:217–18.
616. Baker, *Joel*, 150–51.
617. J. R. Bartlett, "Edom," *ABD*, 2:287–95; idem, *Edom and the Edomites* (JSOTSup 77; Sheffield: Sheffield Academic Press, 1989), especially 157–61; Hoerth, ed., *Peoples*, 335–47.
618. Aharoni, *Macmillan Bible Atlas*, 141, 147.
619. *COS*, 1.38
620. Ibid., 2.113A.
621. Ibid., 2.117B.
622. See D. W. Baker, "Further Examples of the *Waw Explicativum*," *VT* 30 (1980): 129–36.
623. *COS*, 2, 287, n. 3.
624. Aharoni, *Macmillan Bible Atlas*, 147. Further, see D. J. Wiseman, ed., *Peoples of Old Testament Times* (London: Oxford Univ. Press, 1973), 287–311.
625. *SSI*, 2, 25:1.
626. Ibid., 2, 148–51.
627. R. H. Smith, "Arabia," *ABD*, 1:325; J. Taylor, *Petra and the Lost Kingdom of the Nabataeans* (Cambridge, Mass.: Harvard Univ. Press, 2002); G. Markoe, ed., *Petra Rediscovered: The Lost City of the Nabataeans* (New York: Abrams, 2003); G. A. Crawford, *Petra and the Nabataeans: A Bibliography* (Lanham, Md.: Scarecrow, 2003).
628. Del Olmo Lete, *Dictionary*, 296; *COS*, 1.102.
629. *CAD*, 14, 404.
630. *COS*, 2.119B; pers. trans.
631. Ibid., 2.24; *SSI*, 1.16:21; pers. trans.
632. *SSI*, 1, 81.
633. *COS*, 1.147; *CAD*, M/2, 245–46; pers. trans.
634. *ANET*, 425.
635. *SSI*, 1, 18.
636. Ibid., 3, 15; cf. also 67–68.
637. H. J. Katzenstein, "The Royal Steward," *IEJ* 10 (1960): 149–54; T. N. D. Mettinger, *Solomonic State Officials: A Study of the Civil Government Officials of the Israelite Monarchy* (ConBOT 5; Lund: Gleerup, 1971), 70–110.
638. King and Stager, *Life*, 370–72.

639. A longer form of Shebna; Neh. 9:4, 5; 10:5, 11, 13.
640. *COS*, 2.54; pers. trans.
641. D. Pararye, "À propos des sceaux oust-sémitiques: le rôle de l'iconographie dans l'attribution d'un sceau à une aire culturelle et à un atelier," in *Studies in the Iconography*, 45:27.
642. Ibid, 44:23; Ornan, "Mesopotamian Influence," 69:68.
643. *COS*, 1.86; pers. trans.
644. Ibid., 3.87J and n. 2.
645. A. Böckler, *Gott als Vater im Alten Testament: Traditionsgeschichtliche Untersuchungen zur Entstehung und Entwicklung eines Gottesbildes* (Gütersloh: Gütersloher Verlagshaus, 2000).
646. *SSI*, 3, 35, 38; see also 47, Ai3; *COS*, 2.21, 2.31 for Hittite and Phoenician inscriptions respectively, where the king is father and mother.
647. For other references to keys, see Judg. 3:25; 1 Chr. 9:27; Matt. 16:19; Rev. 1:18. See King and Stager, *Life*, 31–33.
648. See B. Peckham, "Phoenicia, History of," *ABD*, 5:355–56, for a chronology of the Phoenician kings.
649. Ibid.; *ANET*, 275.
650. *ANET*, 283.
651. Ibid., 287.
652. Baker, "Tarshish," 6:332–33.
653. S. Moscati, *The World of the Phoenicians* (London: Weidenfeld & Nicolson, 1968), 103.
654. *SSI*, 1, 51–52.
655. *ANET*, 284.
656. Ibid., 285; cf. Hayes and Irvine, *Isaiah*, 287–90.
657. *COS*, 1.102; pers. trans.
658. *ANET*, 477 (Egypt), 290 (Assyria).
659. D. R. Edwards, "Tyre," *ABD*, 6:686–92; H. J. Katzenstein, *The History of Tyre: From the Beginning of the Second Millennium B.C.E. until the Fall of the Neo-Babylonian Empire in 538 B.C.E*, 2nd ed. (Jerusalem: Ben Gurion Univ. of the Negev Press, 1997); M. E. Aubet, *The Phoenicians and the West: Politics, Colonies and Trade*, 2nd ed. (Cambridge: Cambridge Univ. Press, 2001).
660. *ANEP*, 356, 357.
661. *ANET*, 282.
662. M. Nissinen, "City as Lofty as Heaven: Arbela and Other Cities in Neo-Assyrian Prophecy," in *"Every City Shall Be Forsaken": Urbanism and Prophecy in Ancient Israel and the Near East*, ed. L. L. Grabbe and R. D. Haak (JSOTSup 330; Sheffield: Sheffield Academic Press, 2001), 177.
663. *ANEP*, 356–57.
664. Ibid., 490, 491, 493, 498; Ornan, *Triumph of the Symbol*, 13, 56.
665. M. Leuchter, "Tyre's '70 Years' in Isaiah 23,15–18," *Bib* 87 (2006): 412–17.
666. Pers. trans.; Borger, *Inschriften Asarhaddons*, 15; Leuchter, "70 Years," 414.
667. Leuchter, "70 Years," 416.
668. G. Leick, *Sex and Eroticism in Mesopotamian Literature* (London: Routledge, 2003), 61.
669. Ibid., 152–53; see 162–69; W. G. Lambert, "Prostitution," in *Aussenseiter und Randgruppen: Beiträge zu einer Sozialgeschichte des Alten Orients*, ed. V. Haas (Konstanz: Universitätsverlag Konstanz, 1992), 127–57.
670. *COS*, 1.94.
671. Homan, "Beer and its Drinkers," 84–95.
672. Winter, *Frau und Göttin*, 346–48, pictures 342, 346, 347, 348.
673. T. Jacobsen, "Two ba-bal-e Dialogues," in *Love and Death in the Ancient Near East: Essays on Honor of Marvin H. Pope*, ed. J. H. Marks and R. M. Good (Guildford: Four Quarters, 1987), 60.
674. Gordon, *Sumerian Proverbs*, 264.
675. *COS*, 1.132; pers. trans.
676. See, e.g., N. Sarna, *Understanding Genesis: The Heritage of Biblical Israel* (New York: Schocken, 1966), 5; O. Keel, *The Symbolism of the Biblical World: Ancient Near Eastern Iconography and the Book of Psalms* (New York: Seabury, 1978), 35–47; Walton, *Ancient Near Eastern Thought*, 168–70.
677. *COS*, 2.124.
678. Watts, *Isaiah 1–33*, 325–26.
679. *COS*, 1.111, especially tablets 5–7; 1.138; 1.149; 2.122B; D. I. Block, *The Gods of the Nations*, 2nd ed. (ETS Studies; Grand Rapids: Baker, 2000), 54.
680. P. D. Stern, *The Biblical Ḥerem: A Window on Israel's Religious Experience* (Brown Judaic Studies 211; Atlanta: Scholars, 1991).
681. Ibid., 39. For further examples of this use of the Akkadian verb, see *CAD*, 13, 46.
682. *COS*, 2.23. He did the same to Nebo.
683. Ibid., 1.72.
684. I. J. Gelb, "Prisoners of War in Ancient Mesopotamia," *JNES* 32 (1973): 71–72.
685. King and Stager, *Life*, 354–57.
686. *COS*, 1.111, III 130–36; pers. trans.; see also III 8; VI 35.
687. Grayson, *Early First Millennium*, 1:292–93; see A. K. Thomason, "From Sennacherib's Bronzes to Taharqa's Feet: Conceptions of the Material World at Nineveh," in Collon and George, ed., *Nineveh*, 1:153–55.
688. *CAD*, 317.
689. Green, *Storm-God*, 196–98, especially n. 206.
690. *COS*, 1.86, pers. trans.
691. King and Stager, *Life*, 231.
692. G. F. Hasel, "Resurrection in the Theology of Old Testament Apocalyptic," *ZAW* 92 (1980): 267–84.
693. Illustrating the elaborate burial practices, see, e.g., Hornung, *Ancient Egyptian Books*; Johnston, *Shades of Sheol*, 230–32; E. Hornung and B. M. Bryan, ed., *The Quest for Immortality: Treasures of Ancient Egypt* (Washington, D.C.: National Gallery of Art; 2002); Z. Hawass, *The Royal Tombs of Egypt* (New York: Thames & Hudson, 2006).
694. E. Yamauchi, "Life, Death, and the Afterlife in the Ancient Near East," in *Life in the Face of Death: The Resurrection Message of the New Testament*, ed. R. N. Longenecker (Grand Rapids: Eerdmans, 1998), 21–29.
695. Johnson, *Shades*, 232–33.
696. See *ANET*, 90.
697. George, *Epic of Gilgamesh*, 187.

698. Foster, *Before the Muses*, 499–504.
699. *COS*, 1.86.
700. Johnston, *Shades of Sheol*, 232–34.
701. *COS*, 1.103; pers. trans.
702. Ibid., 1.111.
703. See Black and Green, *Gods, Demons and Symbols*, 166–68.
704. *ANEP*, 671; see Keel, *Symbolism of the Biblical World*, 52–55; C. Uehllinger, "Leviathan," *DDD*, 511–15, and mention in a later Aramaic text, J. A. Montgomery, *Aramaic Incantation Texts from Nippur* (Philadelphia: Univ. Museum, 1913), 121.
705. *COS*, 1.86, pers. trans.
706. See A. Caquot, "Le Léviathan de Job 40,25–41,26," *RB* 99 (1992): 40–69. Anat also claims this conquest for herself; Uehllinger, "Leviathan," 512.
707. C. H. Gordon, "Leviathan: Symbol of Evil," in *Biblical Motifs: Origins and Transformations*, ed. A. Altmann (Cambridge, Mass.: Harvard Univ. Press, 1966), 4; M. K. Wakeman, *God's Battle with the Monster: A Study in Biblical Imagery* (Leiden: Brill, 1973); E. Williams-Forte, "The Snake and the Tree in the Iconography and Texts of Syria during the Bronze Age," *Ancient Seals and the Bible*, ed. L. Gorelick and E. Williams-Forte (Malibu: Undena, 1983), 18–43; J. Day, *God's Conflict with the Dragon and the Sea: Echoes of a Canaanite Myth in the Old Testament* (Cambridge: Cambridge Univ. Press, 1985).
708. H. Keel-Leu and B. Teissier, *Die vorderasiatischen Rollsiegel der Sammlung "Bibel+Orient" der Universität Freiburg Schweiz* (OBO 200; Göttingen: Vandenhoeck & Ruprecht, 2004), 405:179.
709. T. Ornan, "The Mesopotamian Influence on West Semitic Inscribed Seals: A Preference for the Depiction of Mortals," in Sass and Uehlinger, ed., *Studies in the Iconography*, 55:1.
710. O. Keel, et al., *Studien zu den Stempelsiegeln aus Palästina/Israel* (OBO 100; Göttingen: Vandenhoeck & Ruprecht, 1990), 235.
711. Wilkinson, *Complete Gods and Goddesses*, 16–19, 78–79; L. H. Lesko, "Ancient Egyptian Cosmogonies and Cosmology," in Shafer, *Religion in Ancient Egypt*, 90–115, who states that "most political and social crises were understood in terms of mythology and were resolved with the use of mythology" (97).
712. *COS*, 1.86; F. Stolz, "Sea," *DDD*, 739–40.
713. *COS*, 1.35.
714. Ibid., 1.111.
715. Ibid., 1.283; pers. trans.
716. Del Olmo Lete, *Dictionary*, 625.
717. King and Stage, *Life*, 21–22.
718. E.g., R. D. Haak, "Altar," *ABD*, 1:165.
719. D. Ussishkin, "Lachish," *ABD*, 4:117.
720. *CAD*, 11/1, 125; 2 Kings 24:7.
721. Ibid., 15, 165–66.
722. Ibid., 13, 138–39; in Ugarit, see del Olmo Lete, *Dictionary*, 711.
723. Ibid., 8, 358.
724. Ibid.
725. Ibid., 8, 357.
726. Ibid., 1.284; pers. trans.
727. *AEL*, 1:160, see 195.
728. Ibid., 2:137.
729. J. F. Healey, "Mot," *DDD*, 598–603.
730. M. H. van Voss, "Osiris," *DDD*, 649–51.
731. R. S. Ellis, *Foundation Deposits in Ancient Mesopotamia* (New Haven, Conn.: Yale Univ. Press, 1968), 177, see 31–32.
732. Ibid., 94–125.
733. R. G. Boling, "Gibeon," *ABD*, 2:1010–13.
734. King and Stage, *Life*, 92.
735. More likely two strains of cumin; O. Borowski, "Agriculture," *ABD*, 1:96; Jacob and Jacob, "Flora," 2:811.
736. H. Gruber et al., "Der zerbrechende Pflug: Methoden der Bibldverarbeitung bei der Analyse von Rollsiegelbildern," *Assyriologica et Semitica: Festschrift für Joachim Oelsner*, ed. J. Marzahn and H. Neumann (Münster: Ugarit-Verlag, 2000), 98, 100.
737. S. N. Kramer, *The Sumerians: Their History, Culture, and Character* (Chicago: Univ. of Chicago Press, 1963), 340–42.
738. *NBD*[2], 158.
739. *COS*, 2.23.
740. *RlA*, 1, 22–26; Black and Green, *Gods, Demons and Symbols*, 110–11.
741. Greenfield, "Hadad," 377–82.
742. Grayson, *Third and Second*, 184.
743. Livingstone, *Mystical and Mythological Explanatory Works*, 127.
744. See *COS*, 1.14.
745. Heidel, *Gilgamesh Epic*, 33–42.
746. *COS*, 1.41.
747. *COS*, 3.92B.
748. *CAD*, 16, 190.
749. A. L. Oppenheim, *Letters from Mesopotamia: Official, Business, and Private Letters on Clay Tablets from Two Millennia* (Chicago: Univ. of Chicago Press, 1967), 152. See M. S. Odell, "An Exploratory Study of Shame and Dependence in the Bible and Selected Near Eastern Parallels" in Younger, *The Biblical Canon*, 217–33.
750. D. B. Redford, "Zoan," *ABD*, 6:1106.
751. On flying lizards and snakes, the latter not from this geographical region, see A. Azuma, *The Biokinetics of Flying and Swimming*, 2nd ed. (Reston, Va.: American Institute of Aeronautics and Astronautics, 2006), 103.
752. *ANET*, 292.
753. K. van der Toorn, "Rahab," *DDD*, 684–86; Keel, *Symbolism*, figures 46–52.
754. G. C. Heider, "Tannin," *DDD*, 835.
755. *COS*, 2.27.
756. Nissinen, *References to Prophecy*, 9; J.-M. Durand, *Archives épistolaires de Mari* I/1 (ARM 26; Paris: Éditions Recherche sur les civilisations, 1988), 386–88; A. Malamat, "Prophecy at Mari," in *The Place is Too Small for Us: The Israelite Prophets in Recent Scholarship*, ed. R. P. Gordon (Sources for Biblical and Theological Study 5; Winona Lake, Ind.: Eisenbrauns, 1995), 57–58; Noort, *Untersuchungen*, 24–25, 71; J.-M. Durand, "Les prophéties des texts de Mari," in *Oracles et prophéties dans l'antiguité: Actes du colloque de*

Strasbourg 15–17 juin 1995, ed. J.-G. Heintz (Paris: De Boccard, 1997), 123–24.
757. Malamat, "Prophecy at Mari," 58–59; *CAD*, 1/II, 170; Noort, *Untersuchungen*, 69–70.
758. Nissinen, *References to Prophecy*, 9.
759. *CAD*, 17/I, 15.
760. Ibid., 17/I, 109–12.
761. Nissinen, *References to Prophecy*, 56–57.
762. Shafer, *Religion*, 170 and n. 129.
763. D. B. Redford, "Execration and Execration Texts," *ABD*, 2:681–82.
764. *COS*, 1.96; pers. trans.
765. Pers. trans.; *CAD*, 7, 209; Dick, "Mesopotamian Cult Statue," 57 (though there is a typo in the Akkadian).
766. Pers. trans.; M. Streck, *Assurbanipal und die letzten assyrischen Könige bis zum Untergange Ninivehs* (Leipzig: Hinrichs, 1966), 54; Dick, "Mesopotamian Cult Statue," 57.
767. Holloway, *Aššur is King!* 123–44 for a list of 55 examples.
768. J. Braun, *Music in Ancient Israel/Palestine: Archaeological, Written, and Comparative Sources* (Grand Rapids: Eerdmans, 2002), 29–31.
769. Ibid., 16–19; Del Olmo Lete, *Dictionary*, 450–51; *CAD*, 8, 387.
770. Gordon, *Sumerian Proverbs*, 129.
771. L. Stager, "Carthage: A View from the Tophet," in *Phönizier im Westen*, ed. H. G. Niemeyer (Madrider Beiträge 8: Mainz am Rhein: Zabern, 1982), 159–60; J. Day, *Molech: A God of Human Sacrifice in the Old Testament* (Cambridge: Cambridge Univ. Press, 1989), 24–28.
772. Sass, "Pre-Exilic Seals," 223:111; see Strawn, *What Is Stronger*, 405, 412–13.
773. Keel and Uehlinger, *Altorientalische Miniaturkunst*, 36:29.
774. Strawn, *What Is Stronger*, 392.
775. Ibid., 382, 394, 405.
776. Mesopotamia: ibid., 422–25, 428–31, 434; Egypt: ibid., 434–36, 446; Syro-Palestine: ibid., 425–26.
777. *AEL*, 1:137.
778. *ANEP*, 184.
779. M. Dick, "The Neo-Assyrian Royal Lion Hunt and Yahweh's Answer to Job," *JBL* 125 (2006): 243–70.
780. See J. Oates, "The Fall of Assyria (635–609 B.C.)," in *CAH*[2] III/2, 162–93; Kuhrt, *Ancient Near East*, 540–46, 589–97.
781. *ANET*, 62.
782. *CAD*, 12, 67–68; see 6, 127; *AHw*, 816; Malul, *Knowledge, Control and Sex*, 145.
783. George, *Epic of Gilgamesh*, 8; B. Foster, "Gilgamesh: Sex, Love and the Ascent of Knowledge," in *Love and Death in the Ancient Near East: Essays in Honor of Marvin H. Pope*, ed. J. H. Marks and R. M. Good (Guilford, Conn.: Four Quarters, 1987), 21–42, especially 25; Malul, *Knowledge, Control and Sex*, 290–93.
784. *COS*, 1.166; see Niehaus, *God at Sinai*, 136–40.
785. P. J. King, "Jerusalem," *ABD*, 3:751.
786. Pers. trans.; *COS*, 2.23; Gibson, *SSI*, 1, 76:22 (cf. p. 81); cf. King and Stager, *Life*, 128.
787. A. Mazar, "Giloh," *ABD*, 2:1027.
788. *NEAEHL*, 98.
789. A. Kempinski, "Joshua's Altar—An Iron Age I Watchtower," *BAR* 12/1 (1986): 42, 44–46, 48–49.
790. B. MacDonald, "Edom," *ABD*, 2:296–97.
791. See Baker, *Joel*, 21, 40–43.
792. *COS*, 1.141; V. A. Hurowitz, "Joel's Locust Plague in Light of Sargon II's Hymn to Nanaya," *JBL* 112 (1993): 598–600; pers. trans.
793. *COS*, 1.10; pers. trans.; see 1.86.
794. J. L. Crenshaw, *Joel* (AB; New York: Doubleday, 1995), 93.
795. Avigad and Sass, *Corpus*, 140:310.
796. Pers. trans.; Lambert, *Babylonian Wisdom Literature*, 105.
797. Dalley, *Myths from Mesopotamia*, 266; see *CAD* 12, 41–45.
798. Nissinen, *References to Prophecy*, 44; pers. trans.
799. *COS*, 2.82.
800. Black, *Concise Dictionary*, 423.
801. D. Hillers, "A Hebrew Cognate of *unuššu/unt* in Is. 33:8," *HTR* 64 (1971): 257–59.
802. See A. F. Rainey and R. S. Notley, *The Sacred Bridge: Carta's Atlas of the Biblical World* (Jerusalem: Carta, 2006), 37–42.
803. *COS*, 2.3.
804. Ibid., 1.166.
805. See, e.g., *CANE*, 273–329 (Egypt); 395–454 (Mesopotamia); 529–54 (Anatolia); 587–614 (Canaan and Israel); Watanabe, *Priests and Officials*; Mattila, *King's Magnates*; S. Sauneron, *The Priests of Ancient Egypt*, new ed. (Ithaca: Cornell Univ. Press, 2000).
806. A. Abou-Assaf et al., *La statue de Tell Fekheriye et son inscription bilingue Assyro-araméenne* (Paris: Éditions recherché sur les civilsations, 1982); S. A. Kaufman, "Reflections on the Assyrian-Aramaic Bilingual from Tell Fakhariyeh," *Maarav* 3 (1982): 137–75; A. R. Millard and P. Bordreuil, "A Statue from Syria with Assyrian and Aramaic Inscriptions," *BA* 45 (1982): 135–41; T. Muraoka, "The Tell-Fekherye Bilingual Inscription and Early Aramaic," *AbrN* 22 (1983–1984): 79–117; F. M. Fales, "La double bilingualisme de la statue de Tell Fekherye," *Syria* 40 (1983): 233–50; D. M. Gropp and T. J. Lewis, "Notes on problems in the Aramaic Text of the Hadd-Yithi Bilingual," *BASOR* 259 (1985): 45–61; J. Naveh, "Proto-Canaanite, Archaic Greek, and the Script of the Tell Fakhariyah Statue," in Miller, *Ancient Israelite Religion*, 101–13; A. R. Millard, "The Tell Fekheriyeh Inscriptions," in *Biblical Archaeology Today, 1990: Proceedings of the Second International Congress on Biblical Archaeology, Jerusalem, June-July, 1990*, ed. A Biran and J. Aviram (Jerusalem: Israel Exploration Society, 1993), 518–24; G. Sauer, "Die assyrische Zeit und die Bilingue von Tell Fekherije," in *Religionsgeschichte Syriens* (Stuttgart: Kohlhammer, 1996), 122–27, 377, 436.
807. J. Naveh, "Aramaic Script," *ABD*, 1:343; G. R. Driver, *Semitic Writing: From Pictograph to Alphabet*, 2nd ed. (London: Oxford Univ. Press, 1976), 119–23. For the Ashur Ostracon, see J. M.

Lindenberger, *Ancient Aramaic and Hebrew Letters* (SBLWAW 4; Atlanta: Scholars, 1994), 18–20.

808. See the story in 2 Kings 5 where Naaman, an Aramaic speaker, was able to be understood by an Israelite servant.
809. *ANEP*, 41–42, 111.
810. Ibid., 103–8.
811. N. Avigad, "A Hebrew Seal Depicting a Sailing Ship," *BASOR* 246 (1982): 59–62.
812. COS, 1.86; *CTA*, 4:2.
813. A. W. Bowes, "The Basilmorphic Conception of Deity in Israel and Mesopotamia," in Younger, ed., *The Biblical Canon*, 235–75.
814. E.g., *CAD*, 3, 32–33.
815. Meier, *Maqlû*, 7; *CAD*, 3, 100–102.
816. Richardson, *Hammurabi's Laws*, 41.
817. *ANET*, 388.
818. T. L. Mafico, "Ethics (OT)," *ABD*, 2:647.
819. *ANEP*, 158, 493, 514, 518–20, 529; Black and Green, *Gods, Demons and Symbols*, 169–70.
820. N. Sarna, *Understanding Genesis: The Heritage of Biblical Israel* (New York: Schocken, 1966), 5.
821. Foster, *Before the Muses*, 462. "Hide" is variously read; see Horowitz, *Mesopotamian Cosmic Geography*, 262; *CAD*, 17/I, 22, "skin"; *CAD*, 10/I, 342, "dividing line." The difference arises from two possible readings of the same Akkadian sign.
822. Black and Green, *Gods, Demons and Symbols*, 30; M. Hutter, "Heaven," *DDD*, 388–89.
823. Ebeling and Meissner, *RlA*, 2, 379.
824. Ibid., 387–90.
825. Ebeling and Meissner, *RlA*, 2, 379–81.
826. *ANET*, 259.
827. Ibid., 282.
828. J. R. Bartlett, "The Rise and Fall of the Kingdom of Edom," *PEQ* 104 (1972): 31–35.
829. *ANET*, 287.
830. Bartlett, "Edom," 2:287–95, here 292.
831. MacDonald, *"East of the Jordan,"* 186, 189–90.
832. Aharoni, *Macmillan Bible Atlas*, 10.
833. *NEAEHL*, 1, 264–66; U. Hübner, "Bozrah," *ABD*, 1:774–75.
834. Seux, *Épithètes royals*, 250; see Watanabe, *Animal Symbolism*, 57–68.
835. R. O. Faulkner, *A Concise Dictionary of Middle Egyptian* (Oxford: Griffith Institute, 1981), 90; del Olmo Lete, *Dictionary*, 678.
836. *CAD*, 4, 150; 8, 180, 554.
837. COS, 2.155.
838. Ibid., 1.43.
839. Ibid., 1.166.
840. Possibly referring to foreign Asiatics moving into the area; ibid., 1, 108, n. 19.
841. Ibid., 1.45.
842. *CAD*, 2, 241–42; 9, 190, where she is designated a "demon."
843. M. Hutter, "Lilith," *DDD*, 520–51.
844. *Reallexikon der Assyriologie* 7, 23–25; Frankfort, *Art and Architecture*, pl. 56. For the development of Jewish and Christian interpretations, see Watts, *Isaiah 34–66*, 13–14.
845. COS, 2.86. Association with the night in this translation, and other understandings of her, derive from a similarity with the word for "night" (*laylâ*).
846. E. Cassin, *La splendeur divin* (Paris: Mouton, 1968).
847. Foster, *Before the Muses*, 459.
848. George, *Gilgamesh*, 71.
849. G. Mendenhall, *The Tenth Generation: The Origins of the Biblical Tradition* (Baltimore: Johns Hopkins Univ. Press, 1973), 52–53.
850. *CAD*, 10/II, 12.
851. D. Baly, *The Geography of the Bible*, 2nd ed. (New York: Harper & Row, 1974), 58.
852. H. O. Thompson, "Carmel, Mount of," *ABD*, 1:875.
853. Grayson, *Assyrian Rulers of the First Millennium* B.C., 2:54–55; Rainey, *Sacred Bridge*, 208; *ANET*, 280.
854. H. R. Weeks, "Sharon," *ABD*, 5:1161.
855. *ANET*, 243, 246.
856. Ibid., 320.
857. Ibid., 662.
858. *CAD*, 2, 46–47.
859. Ibid., 2, 58.
860. Ibid., 17/I, 219.
861. *AEL*, 2:219.
862. Ibid., 3:194.
863. *CAD*, 12, 292.
864. *CAD*, 17, 30–32.
865. Mattila, *King's Magnates*, 45–60, 155; Millard, *Eponyms*, 83, 88, 105, 110, 116.
866. Clines, *Dictionary*, 1:292.
867. Ibid., 2:162; Avigad and Sass, *Corpus*, 171–72:403–406.
868. Mettinger, *Solomonic State Officials*, 52–62.
869. A. Lemaire, "Les critères non-iconographiques de la classification des sceaux nord-ouest sémitiques inscrits," in *Studies in the Iconography of Northwest Semitic Inscribed Seals*, ed. B. Sass and C. Uehlinger (OBO 125; Göttingen: Vandenhoeck & Ruprecht, 1993), 23:1.
870. COS, 1.136; Millard, *Eponyms*, 44, 90; Mattila, *King's Magnates*, 29–43, 155; see Watts, *Isaiah 1–33*, 26.
871. Seux, *Épithètes royales*, 300; S. M. Paul, "Hosea 8:8–10 and Ancient Near Eastern Royal Epithets," in Japhet, ed., *Studies in Bible*, 200–201; C. Cohen, "Neo-Assyrian Elements in the First Speech of the Biblical Rab-Šāqê," *Israel Oriental Studies* 9 (1979): 38–39; P. Artzi and A. Malamat, "The Great King: A Preeminent Royal Title in Cuneiform Sources and the Bible," in *The Tablet and the Scroll: Near Eastern Studies in Honor of William W. Hallo*, ed. M. Cohen, D. Snell and D. Weisberg (Bethesda, Md.: CDL, 1993), 28–38.
872. Seux, *Épithètes royales*, 301.
873. Pers. trans.; Cohen, "Neo-Assyrian Elements," 40–41.
874. COS, 1.111; see T. Jacobsen, "The Battle between Marduk and Tiamat," in *Essays in Memory of E. A. Speiser*, ed. W. W. Hallo (AOS 53; New Haven, Conn.: American Oriental Society, 1968), 104–8 for another earthly interpretation of these celestial events.
875. Pers. trans.; *ANET*, 287; Cohen, "Neo-Assyrian Elements," 43.

876. Lewis, "Syro-Palestinian Iconography," 101 and nn. 114–115, with further bibliography. In 689 B.C., Sennacherib destroyed Babylon and removed the Marduk statue to Assur; Nissinen and Parpola, "Marduk's Return," 212–13.
877. *COS*, 1.72.
878. Ibid., 2.124.
879. See E. Ullendorff, "The Knowledge of Languages in the Old Testament," *BJRL* 44 (1962): 455–65.
880. J. Huehnergard, "Northwest Semitic Vocabulary in Akkadian Texts," *JAOS* 107 (1987): 713–25; A. F. Rainey, *Canaanite in the Amarna Tablets: A Linguistic Analysis of the Mixed Dialect Used by Scribes from Canaan*, 4. vols. (Leiden: Brill, 1996).
881. A. Caubet, *The Louvre: Near Eastern Antiquities* (London: Scala, 1991), 62.
882. *COS*, 1.97; pers. trans.
883. King and Stager, *Life*, 126–27; *NEAEHL*, 1, 45. See *ANEP*, 725 with cisterns in several private houses.
884. *CAD*, 15, 169.
885. Kitchen, *Third Intermediate Period*, 387–93; D. B. Redford, "Tirhakah," *ABD*, 6:572–73; Yamauchi, *Africa and the Bible*, 125–39.
886. *COS*, 1.136.
887. George and Finkel, *Wisdom, Gods and Literature*, 302.
888. *CAD*, 10, 260–65.
889. Ibid., 8, 559; Keel and Uehlinger, *Gods, Goddesses, and Images*, 168–69.
890. *COS*, 2.101B.
891. Ibid., 2.82.
892. *CAD*, 12, 351.
893. A. L. Oppenheim, "The Eyes of the Lord," in Hallo, *Essays*, 173–80.
894. Grayson, *Assyrian Rulers of the Third and Second Millennia*, 184–85; pers. trans.
895. Rainey and Notley, *Sacred Bridge*, 42.
896. Pers. trans.; *ANET*, 278; P. Machinist, "Assyria and Its Image in the First Isaiah," *JAOS* 103 (1983): 723.
897. Ibid., 236, 244.
898. *ANEP*, 447, 524,
899. *COS*, 2.57; pers. trans.
900. *ANET*, 288.
901. Ibid., 299–300.
902. *COS*, 1.60; H. J. Houwink ten Cate, "Hittite Royal Prayers," *Numen* 16 (1969): 81–98.
903. *COS*, 1.62–63.
904. *ANET*, 289.
905. *COS*, 1.137; pers. trans.; Grayson, *Assyrian and Babylonian Chronicles*, 81. For additional Akkadian references to the event, see S. Parpola, "The Murderer of Sennacherib," in *Death in Mesopotamia: XXVI[e] Rencontre assyriologique internationale*, ed. B. Alster (Mesopotamia 8; Copenhagen: Akademisk Forlag, 1980), 171–82, especially 171, n. 4, and E. Leichty, "Esarhaddon's 'Letter to the Gods,'" in *Ah Assyria—Studies in Assyrian History and Ancient Near Eastern Historiography Presented to Hayim Tadmor*, ed. M. Cogan and I. Ephʾal (ScrHier 33; Jerusalem: Magnes, 1991), 52–57.
906. *COS*, 3.95, perhaps the biblical Adrammelech. On the alternate reading Arad-Ninlil, see Parpola, "Murderer of Sennacherib."
907. *COS*, 1.134, where his name is abbreviated to "Esarha."
908. Wiseman, *Vassal-Treaties*, 5; Parpola, "Murderer of Sennacherib," 175.
909. *ANET*, 289–90; F. Reynolds, *The Babylonian Correspondence of Esarhaddon and Letters to Assurbanipal and Sin–Šarru-Iškun from Northern and Central Babylonia* (SAA XVIII; Helsinki: Helsinki Univ. Press, 2003), xx.
910. A. K. Grayson, "Esarhaddon," *ABD*, 2:574.
911. E. M. Yamauchi, *Foes from the Northern Frontier: Invading Hordes from the Russian Steppes* (Grand Rapids: Baker Book House, 1982), 29–40.
912. G. McMahon, "Anatolia," *ABD*, 1:234; L. R. Bailey, "Ararat," *ABD*, 1:351–52.
913. E.g., Reiner, *Šurpu*; T. J. Collins, "Natural Illness in Babylonian Medical Incantations" (PhD diss.; University of Chicago, 1999).
914. Grayson, *Assyrian Rulers*, 2:61.
915. H. Hunger, *Babylonische und assyrische Kolophone* (Neukirchen-Vluyn: Neukirchener Verlag, 1968); H. M. I. Gevaryahu, "Biblical Colophons: A Source for the 'Bibliography' of Authors, Texts and Books" (VTSup 28; Leiden: Brill, 1975), 42–59; D. W. Baker, "Biblical Colophons: Gevaryahu and Beyond," in *Studies in the Succession Narrative: OTWSA 27 (1984) and OTWSA 28 (1985): Old Testament Essays*, ed. W. C. van Wyk (Pretoria: OTWSA, 1986), 29–61.
916. George, *Epic of Gilgamesh*, 183.
917. *ANET*, 107–8.
918. *COS*, 2.27.
919. See, e.g., Katz, *Image of the Netherworld*, especially 192–96.
920. See Taylor, *Death*, 32–35; Hornung and Bryan, *Quest for Immortality*, 27–33; Johnston, *Shades of Sheol*, 76.
921. *COS*, 1.48.
922. This verb applies to David in 1 Sam. 16:16–23; 18:10; 19:9.
923. *ANET*, 585–86.
924. D. W. Baker, "Scribes as Transmitters of Tradition," in *Faith, Tradition, and History: Old Testament Historiography in Its Near Eastern Context*, ed. A. R. Millard, J. K. Hoffmeier, and D. W. Baker (Winona Lake, Ind.: Eisenbrauns, 1994), 69; R. Harris, *Gender and Aging in Mesopotamia: The Gilgamesh Epic and Other Ancient Literature* (Norman: Univ. of Oklahoma Press, 2000), 151–52.
925. *COS*, 1.106; pers. trans.
926. Watts, *Isaiah 34–66*, 52.
927. *COS*, 1, 467, n. 4; J. A. Brinkman, "Merodach-Baladan II," in *Studies Presented to A. L. Oppenheim* (Chicago: Oriental Institute, 1964), 6–53; Frame, *Rulers of Babylonia*, 135.
928. *COS*, 1.137.
929. Ibid., 2.118.
930. R. S. Hess, "Chaldea," *ABD*, 1:886–87.
931. Grayson, "Assyria," 97–100.
932. R. H. Sack, "Merodach-Baladan," *ABD*, 4:704; J. A. Brinkman, "Babylonia in the Shadow of

Assyria," in *CAH*, III/2, 13–19, 25–31; Grayson, "Assyria," 98.

933. Bright, *History of Israel*, 284–86; A. K. Grayson, "Assyria: Sennacherib and Esarhaddon (704–669 B.C.)," *CAH*, III/2, 105–9.
934. Brinkman, "Merodach-baladan II," 31–33. For an alternative proposal, placing the illness and envoy to 712/711, see J. N. Oswalt, *The Book of Isaiah: Chapters 1–39* (NICOT; Grand Rapids: Eerdmans, 1986), 693.
935. *COS*, 3.92A; see Moran, *Amarna Letters*, for many similar examples.
936. K. Avruch, "Reciprocity, Equality, and Status-Anxiety in the Amarna Letters," *Amarna Diplomacy: The Beginnings of International Relations*, ed. R. Cohen and R. Westbrook (Baltimore: Johns Hopkins Univ. Press, 2000), 154–64; N. Na'aman, "Armana Letters," *ABD*, 1:175–76.
937. *ANET*, 286; K. A. Kitchen, *The Third Intermediate Period in Egypt (1100–650 B.C.)* (Warminster: Aris & Phillips, 1973), 376.
938. J. A. Brinkman, "Merodach-Baladan II," *Studies Presented to A. Leo Oppenheim: June 7, 1964* (Chicago: Oriental Institute, 1964), 19.
939. M. van de Mieroop, "Revenge, Assyrian Style," *Past & Present* 179 (May, 2003): 17–18, from R. Borger, *Die Inschriften Asarhaddons Königs von Assyrien* (AfO Beihefte 9; Graz; Self-published, 1956), 12–15.
940. *COS*, 1.86; pers. trans.
941. Ibid., 1.86; pers. trans.
942. A. K. Grayson, "Eunuchs in Power: Their Role in the Assyrian Bureaucracy," in *Vom Alten Orient zum Alten Testament: Festschrift für Wolfram Freiherrn von Soden*, ed. M. Dietrich and O. Loretz (AOAT 240; Neukirchen-Vluyn: Neukirchener Verlag, 1995), 85–98; K. Deller, "The Assyrian Eunuchs and Their Predecessors," in Watanabe, *Priests and Officials*, 303–11; Mattila, *King's Magnates*, 61–76, 131–36.
943. P. Bienkowski and A. R. Millard, ed., *Dictionary of the Ancient Near East* (Philadelphia: Univ. of Pennsylvania, 2000), 110.
944. Nemet-Nejat, *Daily Life*, 37–38.
945. I. J. Winter, "*Le Palais imaginaire*: Scale and Meaning in the Iconography of the Neo-Assyrian Cylinder Seals" in Uehlinger, *Images as Media*, 70–71.
946. Richardson, *Hammurabi's Laws*, 45; pers. trans.
947. *COS*, 1.60.
948. H. A. Hoffner, "The Hittites and the Hurrians," in Wiseman, *Peoples of Old Testament Times*, 215.
949. *COS*, 1.166.
950. Ibid., 1.86.
951. *CAD*, 10/I, 260–65.
952. Meier, *Messenger*, 16–17; 2 Sam. 17:17.
953. Moran, *Amarna Letters*, 230; 87; Meier, *Messenger*, 213–18.
954. *COS*, 2.27.
955. See P. A. Porter, *Metaphors and Monsters: A Literary-Critical Study of Daniel 7 and 8* (ConBOT 20; Lund: Gleerup, 1983), 61–120; B. Willmes, *Die sogenannte Hirtenallegorie Ez 34: Studien zum Bild des Hirten im Alten Testament* (BBET 19; Frankfurt: Lang, 1984).
956. *ANET*, 440. See D. Müller, "Der gute Hirt: Ein Beitrag zur Geschichte ägyptischer Bildrede," *ZÄS* 86 (1961): 126–44; E. Bosetti, "Le terminologia del pastore in Egitto e nella Bibbia," *BeO* 140 (1984): 75–102; P. J. P. Van Hecke, "Pastoral Metaphors in the Hebrew Bible and in Its Ancient Near Eastern Context," in *Old Testament in Its World*, 210; Porter, *Metaphors*, 87.
957. *COS*, 1.172; Porter, *Metaphors*, 85, 90.
958. Longman, *Fictional Akkadian Autobiography*, 85.
959. Grayson, *Early First Millennium*, 2:7, 14. See Seux, *Épithètes royales*, 244–50, 441–46; Paul, "Deutero-Isaiah," 181. See I. Seibert, *Hirt–Herde–König: Zur Herausbildung des Königtums in Mesopotamien* (SSA 53; Berlin: Akademie-Verlag, 1969); Van Hecke, "Pastoral Metaphors," 210–17.
960. *ANET*, 67.
961. Ibid., 332.
962. Ibid., 333.
963. *COS*, 2.14. See Couroyer, "Isaïe XL, 12," 191–92.
964. King and Stager, *Life*, 195–96.
965. Thureau-Dangin, *Rituels accadiens*, 134, cf. 138; F. Stummer, "Einige keilschriftliche Parallelen zu Jes. 40–66," *JBL* 45 (1926): 173–74. See the Babylonian Creation Myth, where he "measures the dimensions of Apsu," *ANET*, 67.
966. On the topic of the Divine Council in Israel, see, e.g., E. T. Mullen Jr., *The Assembly of the Gods: The Divine Council in Canaanite and Early Hebrew Literature* (HSM 24; Chico, Calif.: Society of Biblical Literature, 1980); C. R. Seitz, "The Divine Council: Temporal Transition and New Prophecy in the Book of Isaiah," *JBL* 109 (1990): 229–47; R. P. Gordon, "'Comparatism' and the God of Israel," in *Old Testament in Its World*, 62–66.
967. T. Jacobsen, *The Harps That Once*, 107.
968. *COS*, 1.111, I:48. Also Nudimmud, counselor of his father Anshar, ibid., II: 57–59.
969. Ibid., I:132.
970. Foster, *Before the Muses*, 451; cf. *COS*, II:157–60.
971. *COS*, 1.86.
972. *CAD*, 4, 359–60; see S. H. Scholnick, "The Meaning of *mišpat* in the Book of Job," *JBL* 101 (1982): 521–29; idem, "Poetry in the Courtroom: Job 38–41," in *Directions in Hebrew Poetry*, ed. E. Follis (Sheffield: Sheffield Academic Press, 1987), 185–204; M. B. Dick, "The Neo-Assyrian Royal Lion Hunt and Yahweh's Answer to Job," *JBL* 125 (2006): 268.
973. Lewis, "Syro-Palestinian Iconography," 85–90.
974. *ANET*, 331; pers. trans.
975. A. K. Grayson, *Assyrian Royal Inscriptions I; From the Beginning to Ashur-resha-ishi I* (Wiesbaden: Harrassowitz, 1972), 69–70.
976. M. B. Dick, "Prophetic Parodies of Making the Cult Image," *Born in Heaven*, 40.
977. See A. Fitzgerald, "The Technology of Isaiah 40:19–20 + 41:6–7," *CBQ* 51 (1989): 426–46; P. M. McNutt, *The Forging of Israel: Iron Technology, Symbolism, and Tradition in Ancient Society* (JSOTSup 108; Sheffield: Sheffield Academic Press, 1990); M. C. A. Korpel, "Soldering in Isaiah

40:19–20 and 1 Kings 6:21," *UF* 23 (1991): 219–22; K. R. Baltzer, "The Polemic against the Gods and its Relevance for Second Isaiah's Conception of the New Jerusalem," in *Second Temple Studies 2. Temple Community in the Persian Period*, ed. T. C. Eskenazi and K. H. Richards (JSOTSup 175; Sheffield: Sheffield Academic Press, 1994), 53–54; K. Holter, *Second Isaiah's Idol-Fabrication Passages* (BBET, 28; Frankfurt am Main: Peter Lang, 1995).

978. Platt, "Jewelry, Ancient Israelite," *ABD*, 3:823; Dietrich and Loretz, *Cuneiform Texts from Ugarit*, 122; *COS*, 1.99.
979. *COS*, 1.99 XIII.9–17.
980. D. Lorton, "The Theology of Cult Statues in Ancient Egypt," in Dick, *Born in Heaven*, 139.
981. See N. Sarna, *Understanding Genesis: The Heritage of Biblical Israel* (New York: Schocken, 1966), 5.
982. Horowitz, "The Babylonian Map," 147–65; Horowitz, *Mesopotamian Cosmic Geography*, 334.
983. Keel, *Symbolism*, 37–42, fig. 33.
984. Pers. trans.; Lambert, *Babylonian Wisdom Literature*, 127.
985. *COS*, 1.113.
986. *ANET*, 262.
987. *COS*, 1.99.
988. Ibid., 1.111.
989. See Hunger and Pingree, *Astral Sciences*, on Enuma Anu Enlil and MUL.APIN in particular.
990. Ibid., 50–57.
991. *ANET*, 429; B. Porten and A. Yardeni, *Textbook of Aramaic Documents from Ancient Egypt* (Jerusalem: Hebrew Univ., 1993), 3, 47.
992. *CAD*, 1/II, 102.
993. *COS*, 1.113.
994. Ibid., 1.132.
995. *CAD*, 6, 127; R. L. Vos, "Toth," *DDD*, 861–64.
996. *COS*, 2.49.
997. P. D. Miller, "El, Creator of the Earth," *BASOR* 239 (1980): 43–46; Hoftijzer and Jongeling, *Dictionary*, 1015–16.
998. *COS*, 1.55.
999. G. McMahon, "Anatolia," *ABD*, 1:238; Day, "Asherah," *ABD*, 1:484.
1000. *ANET*, 235.
1001. Seux, *Épithètes royales*, 248, 266, 273, 305–8, 313, 323, 421; *CAD* 8, 331–32.
1002. Yamauchi, *Persia and the Bible*, 68–92.
1003. Pers. trans.; *CAD*, 7, 90.
1004. *AEL*, 2:62; see 69; *COS*, 1.99.
1005. M. Dijkstra, "'He Calls the Eras from the Beginning' (Isa 41:4): From History to Eschatology in Second Isaiah," in *The New Things: Eschatology in Old Testament Prophecy: Festschrift for Henk Leene*, ed. F. Postma, K. Spronk, and E. Talstra (ACEBT 3; Maastricht: Shaker, 2002), 65–69.
1006. Longman, *Fictional Akkadian Autobiography*, 131–90; Dijkstra, "'He Who Calls,'" 69–76.
1007. *AEL*, 1:46 and n. 1.
1008. Ibid., 3:80.
1009. K. L. Tallqvist, *Assyrian Personal Names* (Hildesheim: Georg Olms, 1966; 1914 original), 167–68.
1010. Seux, *Épithètes royales*, 189–97; *CAD*, 11/1, 344.
1011. *CAD*, 11/1, 345.
1012. Ibid., 4, 417.
1013. *ANET*, 450.
1014. Ibid., 449–51.
1015. O. R. Gurney, "The Cuthaean Legend of Naram-Sin," *Anatolian Studies* 5 (1955): 107:55.
1016. *CAD*, 13, 186.
1017. *COS*, 1.99.
1018. *CAD*, 16, 31, see 30–32; Stummer, "Einige Keilschriftliche Parallelen," 177–78; B. Pongratz-Leisten, *Ina Šulmi Īrub: Die kulttopographische und ideologische Programmatik der* akītu-*Prozession in Babylonien und Assyrien im I. Jahrtausend v. Chr.* (Baghdader Forschungen 16; Mainz: von Zabern, 1994), 171–74.
1019. Keel and Uehlinger, *Altorientalische Miniaturkunst*, 38.
1020. *ANET*, 606; Grayson and Lambert, "Akkadian Prophecies," 7–14.
1021. W. Beyerlin, ed., *Near Eastern Religious Texts Relating to the Old Testament* (Philadelphia: Westminster, 1978), 125; *ANET*, 630.
1022. Nissinen and Parpola, "Marduk's Return," 200; the clause repeats on line 6; Parpola, *Assyrian Prophecies*, 6.
1023. Ibid., 201.
1024. Parpola, *Assyrian Prophecies*, 4, 5, 7; cf. 9, 10, 15.
1025. Ibid., 18; pers. trans.
1026. J.-J. Glassner, *Mesopotamian Chronicles* (SBLWAW 19; Atlanta: Society of Biblical Literature, 2004), 7. See idem, "Historical Times in Mesopotamia," in *Israel Constructs its History: Deuteronomistic Historiography in Recent Research*, ed. A. de Pury et al. (JSOTSup 306; Sheffield: Sheffield Academic Press, 2000), 189–211.
1027. Parpola, *Assyrian Prophecies*, 14; cf. 6; Stummer, "Einige keilschriftliche Parallelen," 178–79. For the concept of recurrence in biblical historiography, see G. W. Trompf, "Notions of Historical Recurrence in Classical Hebrew Historiography," in *Studies in the Historical Books of the Old Testament*, ed. J. A. Emerton (VTSup 30; Leiden: Brill, 1979), 213–29.
1028. H. J. Franken, "Pottery," *ABD*, 5:429.
1029. R. H. Johnson, "The Biblical Potter," *BA* 37 (1974): 86–106; Franken, "Pottery," 5:429–33; King and Stager, *Life*, 133.
1030. *ANET*, 100.
1031. Seux, *Épithètes royales*, 121–22; *CAD*, 7, 317; Paul, "Deutero-Isaiah," 181.
1032. Pers. trans.; Cohen, "Neo-Assyrian Elements," 42–43; *CAD*, 6, 131.
1033. King and Stager, *Life*, 150.
1034. *CAD*, 8, 389–93, especially 392–93.
1035. Seux, *Épithètes royales*, 297 and n. 181; Paul, "Deutero-Isaiah," 192.
1036. *COS*, 3.45A and n. 4; also many of the following letters; del Olmo Lete, *Dictionary*, 818.
1037. *CAD*, 17/I, 219–20.
1038. H. Winkler, *Die Keilschrifttexte Sargons* I (Leipzig: Engelmann, 1889), 122–24; see 58–60; Paul, "Deutero-Isaiah," 182; *CAD*, 16, 156.

1039. W. G. Lambert, "Three Literary Prayers of the Babylonians," *AfO* 19 (1959–1960): 66; *CAD*, 16, 157.
1040. See, for example, the various penalties spelled out in Hammurabi's laws: Richardson, *Hammurabi's Laws*.
1041. A. K. Grayson, "Mesopotamia, History of (Babylonia)," *ABD*, 4:769; K. van der Toorn, "Prison," *ABD*, 5:468–69.
1042. *CAD*, 8, 360–361. See also 8, 450–451; 16, 155–157.
1043. *COS*, 1.111; *CAD*, 8, 465.
1044. Translation: http://etcsl.orinst.ox.ac.uk/section4/tr4281.htm; M. Civil, "On Mesopotamian Jails and Their Lady Warden," in *The Tablet and the Scroll: Near Eastern Studies in Honor of William W. Hallo*, ed. M. E. Cohen et al. (Bethesda, Md.: CDL, 1993), 72–78.
1045. *AEL*, 1:219.
1046. Ibid., 3, 193.
1047. Avigad and Sass, *Corpus*, 176:418.
1048. *CAD*, 16, 157.
1049. *AEL*, 3:163.
1050. C. Chirichigno, *Debt-Slavery in Israel and the Ancient Near East* (JSOTSup 141; Sheffield: Sheffield Academic Press, 1993); S. Greengus, "Law," *ABD*, 4:250–51.
1051. J. J. Finkelstein, "Ammisaduqa's Edict and the Babylonian 'Law Codes,'" *JCS* 15 (1961): 103–4.
1052. D. C. Snell, *Flight and Freedom in the Ancient Near East* (CHANE 8; Leiden: Brill, 2001), 64.
1053. Pers. trans.; Richardson, *Hammurabi's Laws*, 79, 95, 119; *CAD*, 1/II, 115–116; see Ex. 21:2; A. K. Grayson, "Mesopotamia, History of (Assyria)," *ABD*, 4:751.
1054. Snell, *Flight and Freedom*, 21, 26–27; W. W. Hallo, "Slave Release in the Biblical World in Light of a New Text," in *Solving Riddles and Untying Knots: Biblical, Epigraphic, and Semitic Studies in Honor of Jonas C. Greenfield*, ed. Z. Zevit et al. (Winona Lake, Ind.: Eisenbrauns, 1995), 79–93; E. Otto, "Soziale Restitution und Vertragsrecht. *Mīšaru(m), (an)durāru(m), kirenzi, parā tarnumar, šemitta* und *dᵉrōr* in Mesopotamien, Syrien, in der hebräischen Bible und die Frage des Rechtstransfers im alten Orient," *RA* 92 (1998): 125–60.
1055. *Kidinnu* and *šubarrû*; Snell, *Flight and Freedom*, 24–26.
1056. Seux, *Épithètes royales*, 270; *CAD*, 1/2, 116–17.
1057. Kraus, *Ein Edikt des Königs Ammi-Saduqa von Babylon* (SDOAP 5; Leiden: Brill, 1958); idem, *Königliche Verfügungen in altbabylonischer Zeit* (SDOAP 11; Leiden: Brill, 1984); Chirichigno, *Debt-Slavery*, 85–92.
1058. *CAD*, 1/2, 282.
1059. Lambert, *Babylonian Wisdom Literature*, 135, but see *CAD*, 12, 174.
1060. *CAD*, 7, 201; see also 17/3, 12–18.
1061. *ANET*, 313.
1062. E. A. Knauf, "Tema," *ABD*, 6:346–47.
1063. MacDonald, *"East of the Jordan,"* 192.
1064. *CAD*, 1/2, 251.
1065. Ibid., 247–51; Hoftijzer and Jongeling, *Dictionary*, 816–19.
1066. Cross, "Seal," 61–62; M. Silverman, "Servant (*ʿebed*) Names in Aramaic and in Other Semitic Languages," *JAOS* 101 (1981): 361–66.
1067. "Property of Yahweh"; see 1 Chron. 15:18.
1068. F. M. Cross, "The Seal of Miqnêyaw, Servant of Yahweh," in *Ancient Seals and the Bible*, ed. L. Gorelick and E. Williams-Forte (Malibu: Undena, 1983), 55–63, pl. IX; Lemaire, "Les critères," 23:8.
1069. *AEL*, 1:128; see 3:111.
1070. Ibid., 3:151.
1071. Ibid., 2:154.
1072. Ibid., 3:112–15, where he is "God of the potter's wheel."
1073. *ANEP*, 569.
1074. Foster, *Before the Muses*, 392.
1075. *CAD*, 2, 86.
1076. Seux, *Épithètes royales*, 176–77, see 175–79, 370–71; Paul, "Deutero-Isaiah," 181.
1077. *COS*, 2.135.
1078. Winter, *Frau und Göttin*, pict. 202, 205.
1079. *COS*, 1.86.
1080. Seux, *Épithètes royales*, 189–97; *CAD* 11/I, 344.
1081. *CAD*, 11/I, 345.
1082. Borger, *Inschriften Asarhaddons*, 74. See *CAD*, 11/I, 345; Nissinen, *References to Prophecy*, 53.
1083. *COS*, 1.111, tablet I; Stummer, "Einige keilschriftliche Parallelen," 180–81; J. Bottéro, *Religion in Ancient Mesopotamia* (Chicago: University of Chicago Press, 2001), 72–77; Walton, *Ancient Near Eastern Thought*, 87–92.
1084. *AEL*, 3:112.
1085. Walton, *Ancient Near Eastern Thought*, 97.
1086. S. Dalley, *Myths from Mesopotamia: Creation, the Flood, Gilgamesh, and Others* (Oxford World Classics; Oxford: Oxford Univ. Press, 1989), 233.
1087. *CAD*, 11/1, 170–71.
1088. *COS*, 1.111; Stummer, "Einige keilschriftliche Parallelen," 182–83.
1089. *COS*, 1.136.
1090. See a description of an Egyptian voyage in *COS*, 1.39. See K. R. Veenhof, "Militaire Strategie en Water in het Oude Mesopotamie," *Phoenix* 20 (1974): 371–82.
1091. Moran, *Amarna Letters*, 245.
1092. Pers. trans.; D. D. Luckenbill, *The Annals of Sennacherib* (OIP 2; Chicago: Univ. of Chicago Press, 1924), 104; *CAD*, 4, 93.
1093. Pers. trans.; Luckenbill, *Annals of Sennacherib*, 38.
1094. D. Wildung, *Egyptian Saints: Deification in Pharaonic Egypt* (New York: New York Univ. Press, 1977); D. P. Silverman, "Divinity and Deities in Ancient Egypt," in Shafer, *Religion in Ancient Egypt*, 55–73; J. Baines, "Ancient Egyptian Kingship; Official Forms, Rhetoric, Context," in *King and Messiah in Israel and the Ancient Near East: Proceedings of the Oxford Old Testament Seminar*, ed. J. Day (JSOTSup 270; Sheffield: Sheffield Academic Press, 1998), 28–41.
1095. *AEL*, 1:30.
1096. Ibid., 1:52; on Seth and Horus, see Lurker, *Illustrated Dictionary*, 109–10 and 65–67 respectively.
1097. *ANET*, 4.
1098. W. W. Hallo, "Texts, Statues and the Cult of the Divine King," in *Congress Volume: Jerusalem 1986*

(VTSup 40; Leiden: Brill, 1986), 58–62; I. J. Winter, "'Idols of the King': Royal Images as Recipients of Ritual Action in Ancient Mesopotamia," *Journal of Ritual Studies* 6/1 (1992): 13–42; W. G. Lambert, "Kingship in Mesopotamia," in Day, ed., *King and Messiah*, 58–59.

1099. Holloway, *Aššur Is King*, 181–86, especially 182, n. 343; P. Jones, "Divine and Non-Divine Kingship," in *Companion to the Ancient Near East*, ed. D. Snell (Oxford: Blackwell, 2005), 330–42.
1100. Pers. trans.; Lambert, *Babylonian Wisdom Literature*, 33.
1101. Tallqvist, *Assyrian Personal Names*, 217; *CAD*, 17/2, 86.
1102. S. A. Strong, "A Hymn of Nebuchadnezzar," *Proceedings of the Society of Biblical Archaeology* 20 (1898): 156; *CAD*, 10/1, 168.
1103. COS, 1.86; del Olmo Lete and Sanmartín, *Dictionary*, 552.
1104. COS, 1, 86; see Niehaus, *God at Sinai*, 86–91.
1105. *CAD*, 13, 88–89.
1106. COS, 1.132.
1107. *AEL*, 2:97–98.
1108. COS, 1.6.
1109. Richardson, *Hammurabi's Laws*, 87:146; 107:226, 227.
1110. B. Porten and A. Yardeni, *Textbook of Aramaic Documents from Ancient* Egypt (Jerusalem: Hebrew Univ. Press, 1989), 2, 51.
1111. COS, 2.85.
1112. Del Olmo Lete, *Dictionary*, 523.
1113. *AEL*, 1:186.
1114. S. J. Sherwin, "In Search of Trees: Isaiah 44:14 and its Implications," *VT* 53 (2003): 519–21.
1115. Dick, "Prophetic Parodies," 43.
1116. Sherwin, "In Search of Trees," 521–25.
1117. Heb. *leḥem*; Akk. *akalu*, derived from the verb "to eat," *akālu*, *CAD*, 1/1, 238–245.
1118. COS, 1.113.
1119. King and Stager, *Life*, 65–67.
1120. See 1:29–30; 17:8; A. Lemaire, "Les inscriptions de Khirbet el-Qôm et L'Ashérah de YHWH," *RB* 84 (1977): 595–608; Z. Meshel, *Kuntillet ʿAjrud: A Religious Centre from the Time of the Judaean Monarchy on the Border of Sinai* (Catalogue 175; Jerusalem: Israel Museum, 1978), unnumbered pages; idem, "Did Yahweh have a Consort? The New Religious Inscriptions from the Sinai," *BAR* 5 (1979): 24–34; F. Stolz, "Monotheismus in Israel," in *Monotheismus im alten Israel und seiner Umwelt*, ed. O. Keel (Biblische Beiträge 14; Fribourg: Verlag Schweizerisches Katholisches Bibelwerk, 1980), 167–72; M. Weinfeld, "Kuntillet ʿAjrud: A Sacred Site of the Monarchic Period," *Shnaton* 4 (1980): 280–84 (Hebrew); A. Lemaire, *Les écoles et la formation de la Bible dans l'ancien Israël* (Göttingen: Vandenhoeck & Ruprecht, 1981), 25–33; J. A. Emerton, "New Light on Israelite Religion: The Implications of the Inscriptions from Kuntillet Ajrud," *ZAW* 94 (1982): 2–29; D. Chase, "A Note on an Inscription from Kuntillet ʿAjrud," *BASOR* 246 (1982): 63–67; W. G. Dever, "Recent Archaeological Confirmation of the Cult of Asherah in Ancient Israel," *Hebrew Studies* 23 (1982): 37–44; idem, "Asherah, Consort of Yahweh? New Evidence from Kuntillet ʿAjrud," *BASOR* 255 (1984), 21–27; A. Lemaire, "Who or What Was Yahweh's Asherah?" *BAR* 10 (1984): 42–51; Z. Zevit, "The Khirbet el-Qôm Inscription Mentioning a Goddess," *BASOR* 255 (1984): 39–47; J. Day, "Asherah in the Hebrew Bible and Northwest Semitic Literature," *JBL* 105 (1986): 385–408; D. N. Freedman, "Yahweh of Samaria and his Asherah," *BA* 50 (1987): 241–49; J. Hadley, "The Khirbet el-Qom Inscription," *VT* 37 (1987): 50–62; M. Gilula, "To Yahweh Shomron and His Asherah," *Shnaton* 3 (1978–1979): 129–37 (Hebrew); R. North, "Yahweh's Asherah," in *To Touch the Text: Biblical and Related Studies in Honor of Joseph A. Fitzmyer, S. J.*, ed. M. P. Horgan and P. Kobelski (New York: Crossroad, 1989), 118–37; B. Margalit, "Some Observations on the Inscription and Drawing from Khirbet El-Qom," *VT* 39 (1989): 371–78; R. Pattai, *The Hebrew Goddess*, 3rd ed. (Detroit: Wayne State Univ. Press, 1990); Binger, *Asherah*; Keel and Uehlinger, *Gods, Goddesses*, 210–48; K. van der Toorn, "Goddesses in Early Israelite Religion," in *Ancient Goddesses: The Myths and the Evidence*, ed. L. Goodison and C. Morris (Madison: Univ. of Wisconsin Press, 1998), 83–97, especially 89–90; W. G. Dever, "Archaeology and the Ancient Israelite Cult: How the Kh. el-Qôm and Kuntillet ʿAjrud 'Asherah' Texts Have Changed the Picture," *ErIsr* 26 (1999): 9–15; B. Becking, *Only One God?: Monotheism in Ancient Israel and the Veneration of the Goddess Asherah* (Biblical Seminar 77; London: Sheffield Academic Press, 2001).
1121. *CAD*, 2, 121–25.
1122. J. L. Koole, *Isaiah III/I* (HCOT; Leuven: Peeters, 1997), 418.
1123. *AHw*, 95.
1124. COS, 2.35.
1125. Yamauchi, *Persia and the Bible*, 68–92.
1126. Grayson, *Assyrian and Babylonian Chronicles*, 109–10.
1127. COS, 2.124.
1128. *ANET*, 306.
1129. Ibid.
1130. W. Eiler, "Der Keilschrifttext des Kyros-Zylinders," in *Festgabe deutscher Iranisten zur 2500-Jahrfeier Irans*, ed. W. Eiler (Stuttgart: Hochwacht, 1971), 156; Yamauchi, *Persia and the Bible*, 76.
1131. Frame, *Rulers of Babylonia*, 148.
1132. Holloway, *Aššur Is King!*, 238–54, lists 54 such cases.
1133. *KAI*, 1, text 4; COS, 2.29.
1134. Among those considering Cyrus here simply designated in his royal role, see A. Laato, *The Servant of YHWH and Cyrus: A Reinterpretation of the Exilic Messianic Programme in Isaiah 40–55* (ConBOT, 35; Stockholm: Almqvist & Wiksell, 1992); B. S. Childs, *Isaiah* (OTL; Louisville: Westminster John Knox, 2001), 353–54.
1135. *AEL*, 3:37; on Udjahorresnet, see Yamauchi, *Persia and the Bible*, 105–8.
1136. COS, 2.124.

1137. Restoration of the gods of captured people is a common practice; see Holloway, *Aššur Is King!* 277–83 for 21 examples.

1138. L. S. Fried, "Cyrus the Messiah? The Historical Background of Isaiah 45:1," *HTR* 95 (2002): 373–93.

1139. See *CAD*, 16, 30–32; J. A. Black, "The New Year Ceremonies in Ancient Babylon: 'Taking Bel by the Hand' and a Cultic Picnic," *Religion* 11 (1981): 39–59.

1140. *ANET*, 315.

1141. R. H. Pfeiffer, *State Letters of Assyria* (New Haven, Conn.: American Oriental Society, 1935), 164–65; pers. trans.

1142. Pers. trans.; *COS*, 2.23; H. M. Barstad, "On the So-Called Babylonian Literary Influence in Second Isaiah," *SJOT* 2 (1987): 97–98.

1143. *AEL*, 3:97.

1144. Ibid., 2:176.

1145. R. G. Kent, *Old Persian*, 2nd ed. (New Haven, Conn. American Oriental Society, 1953), 147; Yamauchi, *Persia and the Bible*, 153.

1146. W. H. Shea, "A Date for the Recently Discovered Eastern Canal of Egypt," *BASOR* 226 (1977): 31–38.

1147. *CAD*, 17/III, 287.

1148. Ibid., 11/II, 290–92; 21, 19–20.

1149. *ANET*, 322.

1150. *CAD*, 2,191–98.

1151. In this it parallels the Canaanite/Hebrew *baʿal*, which also means "lord, master" and is used of the Canaanite storm god (e.g., 1 Kings 18:26), as well as of Yahweh, the God of Israel (e.g., Hos. 2:18; cf. Bealiah, "Baal = Yahweh," 1 Chron. 12:5).

1152. *CAD*, 2, 193:2'; see Nissinen and Parpola, "Marduk's Return," 201–2.

1153. See A. Heidel, *The Babylonian Genesis: The Story of Creation*, 2nd ed. (Chicago: Univ. of Chicago Press, 1963); *COS*, 1.111.

1154. J.-C. Margueron, "Babylon," *ABD*, 1:564.

1155. Tallqvist, *Assyrian Personal Names*, 53–63.

1156. Livingstone, *Mystical and Mythological Explanatory Works*, 209, 215.

1157. Grayson, *Assyrian and Babylonian Chronicles*, 127; Dick, "Mesopotamian Cult Statue," 53.

1158. A. R. Millard, "Nabû," *DDD*, 607–10; Koole, *Isaiah III/1*, 496.

1159. Tallqvist, *Assyrian Personal Names*, 142–65.

1160. *COS*, 2.82.

1161. B. Porten and A. Yardeni, *Textbook of Aramaic Documents from Ancient Egypt* (Jerusalem: Hebrew Univ., 1999) 4, 178: D7.30; *COS*, 3.87E.

1162. Millard, "Nabû," 607.

1163. *ANEP*, 470–74. An Akkadian seal has a god standing with one foot on a lion, and in another, holding a lion over his head; Watanabe, *Animal Symbolism*, fig. 19, 69.

1164. *ANEP*, 486, 522; T. Ornan, "Ištar as Depicted in Finds from Israel," in Mazar, *Studies in the Archaeology*, 235–56.

1165. *ANEP*, 500–501, 531; Watanabe, *Animal Symbolism*, fig. 64–66. See also W. Orthmann, *Die Alte Welt* (Berlin: Propyläen, 1975), 234, where the large *lamassu* statues are being transported.

1166. *ANEP*, 537. See Lewis, "Syro-Palestinian Iconography," 93–97.

1167. Oppenheim, *Ancient Mesopotamia*, 187; T. W. Mann, *Divine Presence and Guidance in Israelite Traditions: The Typology of Exaltation* (Baltimore: Johns Hopkins Univ. Press, 1977), 76–89; Berlejung, "Washing the Mouth," 67–68.

1168. *ANEP*, 538.

1169. *CAD*, 16, 75–76.

1170. Ibid., 17/2, 390–92; Harris, *Gender and Aging*, 50–51.

1171. Foster, *Before the Muses*, 604.

1172. Dated 427 B.C.; E. Kraeling, *The Brooklyn Museum Aramaic Papyri* (New Haven, Conn.: Yale Univ. Press for the Brooklyn Museum, 1953), 180–81; *COS*, 3.74; see J. Rabinowitz, "A Note on Isa 46:4," *JBL* 73 (1954): 237.

1173. *CAT*, 1.114:17–19; *COS*, 1.97.

1174. Pritchard, *Ancient Near East*, 1, 161.

1175. *COS*, 1.99.

1176. See S. Parpola, "The Assyrian Cabinet," in *Vom Alten Orient Zum Alten Testament: Festschrift für Wolfram Freiherrn von Soden zum 85. Geburtstag am 19. Juni 1993*, ed. M. Dietrich and O. Loretz (AOAT 240; Neukirchen-Vluyn: Neukirchener Verlag, 1995), 385, n. 17.

1177. *COS*, 1.28.

1178. Ibid., 1.111.

1179. Ibid.

1180. Dalley, *Myths*, 203–21.

1181. *CAT*, 1.5 vi:12–14; *COS*, 1.86, pers. trans.

1182. Ibid.

1183. G. A. Anderson, *A Time to Mourn, a Time to Dance* (University Park: Pennsylvania State Univ. Press, 1991), 60–69, where he also mentions other deities descending in mourning into the underworld. See C. A. Franke, "Reversals of Fortune in the Ancient Near East: A Study of the Babylon Oracles in the Book of Isaiah," in *New Visions of Isaiah*, ed. R. F. Melugin and M. A. Sweeney (JSOTSup 214; Atlanta: Society of Biblical Literature, 2006), 111.

1184. P. L. Day, "Anat," *DDD*, 36–43; N. H. Walls, *The Goddess Anat in Ugaritic Myth* (Atlanta: Scholars, 1992).

1185. King and Stager, *Life*, 94–95.

1186. *ANEP*, 149.

1187. M. Tsevat, "The Husband Veils a Wife (Hittite Laws §§ 197–98)," *JCS* 27 (1975): 235–40; K. van der Toorn, *Family Religion in Babylonia, Syria and Israel: Continuity and Change in the Forms of Religious Life* (SHCANE 7; Leiden: Brill, 1996), 43–45; V. H. Matthews, "Marriage and Family in the Ancient Near East," in *Marriage and Family in the Biblical World*, ed. K. M. Campbell (Downers Grove, Ill.: InterVarsity Press, 2003), 11–12.

1188. George, *Epic of Gilgamesh*, 65.

1189. See also the last day's rituals of the installation ceremony for the high priestess at Emar; *COS*, 1.122.

1190. Tsevat, "Husband Veils," 237, n. 12; K. van der Toorn, "The Significance of the Veil in the

Ancient Near East," in *Pomegranates and Golden Bells: Studies in Biblical, Jewish, and Near Eastern Ritual, Law, and Literature in Honor of Jacob Milgrom*, ed. D. P. Wright et al. (Winona Lake, Ind.: Eisenbrauns, 1995), 327–39.

1191. Pers. trans.; Driver and Miles, *The Assyrian Laws*, 408–11.
1192. Van der Toorn, *Family Religion*, 42–45.
1193. *ANET*, 183; *CAD*, 12, 218.
1194. *CAD*, 4, 320.
1195. *ANEP*, 3, 187.
1196. Ibid., 208, 209.
1197. *COS*, 1.108.
1198. R. Bauckham, "Descent to the Underworld," *ABD*, 2:146.
1199. T. Abusch, "Ishtar," *DDD*, 453.
1200. *CAD*, 10/1, 304, 315; del Olmo Lete and Sanmartín, *Dictionary*, 227, 245.
1201. *AEL*, 1:119.
1202. Ibid., 1:86.
1203. Grayson, *ARI* II, 121. See also his lengthy paean of self-praise in S. M. Paley, *King of the World: Ashur-nasir-pal II of Assyria 883–859* B.C. (New York: The Brooklyn Museum, 1976), 125–26.
1204. See Seux, *Épithètes royales*; W. W. Hallo, *Early Mesopotamian Royal Titles: A Philological and Historical Analysis* (New Haven, Conn.: American Oriental Society, 1957).
1205. *COS*, 1, 276, n. 13.
1206. Ibid., 1.87.
1207. *COS*, 2.4D.
1208. B. Albrektson, *History and the Gods: An Essay on the Idea of Historical Events as Divine Manifestations in the Ancient Near East and Israel* (ConBOT 1; Lund: Gleerup, 1967), 11–12. See the review by W. G. Lambert in *Or* 39 (1970): 170–77.
1209. Ibid., 17–22.
1210. Among many examples, see *COS*, 2.89, 91, 113, 114E, 118D, 118F, 119B, 124. See Weinfeld, "Divine Intervention in War," 121–47.
1211. W. G. Lambert, "Ištar of Nineveh," in Collon and George, ed., *Nineveh*, 1:35. See also B. N. Porter, "Ishtar of Nineveh and Her Collaborator, Ishtar of Arbela, in the Reign of Assurbanipal," in ibid., 41–44.
1212. E.g., Acco: M. Dothan, "Acco," *ABD*, 1:51; Mahanaim: D. V. Edelman, "Mahanaim," *ABD*, 4:473; Tel ed-Dibai: C. J. Davey, "Tell edh-Dhibaʾi and the Southern Near Eastern Tradition," in *The Beginning of the Use of Metals and Alloys: Paper from the Second International Conference on the Beginnings of the Use of Metals and Alloys, Zhengzhou, China, 21–26 October 1986*, ed. R. Maddin (Cambridge, Mass.: MIT Press, 1988), 63–68.
1213. T. Özgüç, *Kültepe/Kaneš* II (Ankara: Türk Tarih Kurumu Basimev, 1986), 39–51; J. N. Postgate, *Early Mesopotamia: Society and Economy at the Dawn of History* (New York: Routledge, 1992), 228–29; P. R. S. Moorey, *Ancient Mesopotamian Materials and Industries: The Archaeological Evidence* (New York: Oxford Univ. Press, 1994), 216–301; idem, *Metals and Metalwork, Glazed Materials and Glass* (International Series 237; Oxford: British Archaeological Reports, 1985); Nemet-Nejat, *Daily Life*, 291–95.
1214. *ANEP*, 133; *OEANE*, 4, 12.
1215. Nissinen, *References to Prophecy*, 111; pers. trans.; see 118, 122.
1216. Paul, "Deutero-Isaiah," 184–85, lists seven ranging in date from the twelfth through the sixth centuries; also *CAD*, 1/1, 146.
1217. Pers. trans.; cf. Paul, "Deutero-Isaiah," 185.
1218. *CAD*, 21, 18.
1219. *AEL*, 1:36.
1220. *AEL*, 1:99.
1221. Luckenbill, *Annals of Sennacherib*, 48.
1222. *COS*, 2.107B.
1223. Ibid., 2.108.
1224. Seux, *Épithètes royales*, 210–12; *CAD*, 12, 30.
1225. See M. Rivaroli, "Nineveh: From Ideology to Topography," in Collon and George, ed., *Nineveh*, 1:199–205.
1226. Grayson, *Early First Millennium*, 1:26.
1227. *ANEP*, 450.
1228. *ANET*, 653.
1229. G. Lambert, "Le livre d'Isaïe parle-t'il des Chinois?" *La nouvelle revue théologique* 85 (1953): 967–72 ; A. Betz, "Syene," *ABD*, 6:250.
1230. Baltzer, *Deutero-Isaiah*, 316 ; B. Porten, "Elephantine Papyri," *ABD*, 2:445–55.
1231. *COS*, 3.60.
1232. J. Blenkinsopp, *Isaiah 40–55* (AB; New York: Doubleday, 2002), 311.
1233. *ANEP*, 749; J. Aruz, *Art of the First Cities: The Third Millennium* B.C. *from the Mediterranean to the Indus* (New York: Metropolitan Museum of Art, 2003), 427; J. J. Coulton, *Ancient Greek Architects at Work* (Ithaca, N.Y.: Cornell Univ. Press, 1977), 52.
1234. *AEL*, 2:62; see ibid., 1:104.
1235. *COS*, 1.122.
1236. E.g., Moran, *Amarna Letters*, 93; King and Stager, *Life*, 55, 278.
1237. *COS*, 1.94, using the same word; *CTU*, 1.100:61.
1238. Gordon, *Sumerian Proverbs*, 281.
1239. Winter, *Frau und Göttin*, 397–404, pict. 404–12.
1240. *CTU*, 68–69; see Lewis, "Syro-Palestinian Iconography," 98.
1241. Livingstone, *Mystical and Mythological Explanatory Works*, 217.
1242. Parpola, *Assyrian Prophecies*, 39.
1243. Livingstone, *Mystical and Mythological Explanatory Works*, 404–13, pict. 413–19.
1244. *ANET*, 533; see also the Vassal Treaty of Esarhaddon, ibid, 538; *CAD*, 1/I, 250.
1245. M. Streck, *Assurbanipal und die letzten assyrischen Konige bis zum Untergange Ninivehs. II. Teil: Texte. Die Inschriften Assurbanipals und der letzten assyrischen Könige* (Vorderasiatische Bibliothek 7/2; Leipzig:, 1916), 74; *CAD*, 3, 78; pers. trans.
1246. *ANET*, 298.
1247. *AEL*, 1:36.
1248. M. A. Dandamayev, "Slavery (ANE and OT)," *ABD*, 6:58–65.

1249. Moran, *Amarna Letters*, 156. See M. A. Dandamaev, *Slavery in Babylonia from Nabopolassar to Alexander the Great (626–331 B.C.)* (DeKalb: Northern Illinois Univ. Press, 1984); Chirichigno, *Debt Slavery*.
1250. King and Stager, *Life*, 20–23.
1251. *CAD*, 1/I, 56.
1252. COS, 1.86; pers. trans. See P. D. Miller Jr. and J. J. M. Roberts, *The Hand of the Lord: A Reassessment of the "Ark Narrative" of 1 Samuel* (Baltimore: Johns Hopkins Univ. Press, 1977), 45–46; D. Bonatz, "Ashurbanipal's Headhunt: An Anthropological Perspective," in Collon and George, ed. *Nineveh* 1:93–101; C. E. Watanabe, "The Continuous Style in the Narrative Scheme of Assurbanipal's Reliefs," in ibid., 109–14, fig. 9–17; R. Dolce, "The 'Head of the Enemy' in the Sculptures from the Palaces of Nineveh: An Example of Cultural Migration?" in ibid., 121–32.
1253. Nissinen, *References to Prophecy*, 23; pers. trans.
1254. COS, 1.21. See van der Toorn, "Rahab," 684–86.
1255. COS, 1.86. See J. Day, *God's Conflict with the Dragon*; C. Kloos, *Yhwh's Combat with the Sea: A Canaanite Tradition in the Religion of Ancient Israel* (Leiden: Brill, 1986); Stolz, "Sea," 737–42.
1256. Grayson and Lambert, "Akkadian Prophecies," 22.
1257. Seux, *Épithètes royales*, 210–11; *CAD*, 15, 163.
1258. *AEL*, 2:141.
1259. COS, 1.111.
1260. Ibid., 1.103.
1261. Pers. trans.; Livingstone, *Mystical and Mythological Explanatory Works*, 117, see 119.
1262. COS, 1.99.
1263. Keel, *Symbolism of the Biblical World*, fig. 342; *ANEP*, 524.
1264. See what appears to be a circumcision ritual for Egyptian boys, *ANEP*, 629, and the description of a circumcision of 120 in *ANET*, 326. See R. G. Hall, "Circumcision," *ABD*, 1:1025–31.
1265. COS, 2.7.
1266. R. Border, *Die Inscriften Asarhaddons Königs von Assyrien*, AfOB. 9 1956 (reprinted Osnabrück: Biblio Verlag, 1967), 5.
1267. *CAD*, 9, 104–7; Meier, *Messenger*, 83.
1268. Pers. trans.; *CAD*, 4, 260.
1269. Grayson, *Assyrian Royal Inscriptions* 2, 128, 130, 140; see COS, 2, 161, n. 5.
1270. *CAD*, 1, 317.
1271. COS, 2.39.
1272. Thureau-Dangin, *Rituels accadiens*, 144–45. See Abusch, *Babylonian Witchcraft Literature*, 92, n. 13.
1273. Pers. trans.; Dalley, *Myths from Mesopotamia*, 159.
1274. *ANET*, 422.
1275. Ibid., 435.
1276. Pers. trans.; Meier, *Die assyrische Beschwörungssammlung Maqlû* 8; *CAD* 10/I, 75.
1277. Ibid.
1278. Moran, *Amarna Letters*, 61–62; "Egypt: Internal Affairs from Thuthmosis I to the Death of Amenophis III," in *CAH*, II/1, 345–46.
1279. *CAD*, 2, 58; Black and Green, *Gods, Demons and Symbols*, 101.
1280. Wilkinson, *Complete Gods and Goddesses*, 181–82.
1281. *AEL*, 2:219, where Hathor heals Horus; ibid., 3:104–5.
1282. *CAD*, 1/2, 336.
1283. COS, 1.99.
1284. *AEL*, 2:123.
1285. COS, 3.87B.
1286. Van Hecke, "Pastoral Metaphors," 216.
1287. COS, 1.99.
1288. Ibid., 1.111.
1289. King and Stager, *Life*, 37.
1290. Borger, *Die Inschriften Asarhaddons*, 75; *CAD*, 1/2, 225–26. For Ugaritic, see *CTA*, 1.10 II:20.
1291. COS, 2.59.
1292. *AEL*, 1:215; see 2:221, 223.
1293. Ibid., 3:19.
1294. COS, 1.159.
1295. COS, 3.101B, C.
1296. *ANET*, 564.
1297. A. G. Lie, *The Inscriptions of Sargon II, King of Assyria I, The Annals* (Paris: Geuthner, 1929), 413; *CAD*, 8, 601.
1298. King and Stager, *Life*, 53; H. A. Hoffner, "אַלְמָנָה (*ʾlmānâ*)," *TDOT*, 1:288–89.
1299. Gordon, *Sumerian Proverbs*, 197.
1300. Richardson, *Hammurabi's Laws*, 98.
1301. Driver and Miles, *Babylonian Laws*, 1:356–58.
1302. COS, 3.44; pers. trans.
1303. See Winter, *Frau und Göttin*, 630–39.
1304. *CAD*, 2, 191–94.
1305. Ibid., 10/II, 314.
1306. Gordon, *Sumerian Proverbs*, 120.
1307. *AEL*, 1:44.
1308. Ibid., 1:91.
1309. COS, 2.53.
1310. *CAD*, 17, 149, pers. trans.
1311. *ANEP*, 97–100.
1312. G. Boyer, *Contribution à l'histoire juridique de la 1re dynastie babylonienne* (Paris: Geuthner, 1928), 147; *CAD*, 14, 260–63; Nissinen, *Prophets and Prophecy*, 168; Nissinen and Parpola, "Marduk's Return," 206.
1313. *AEL*, 1:100.
1314. Ibid., 1:228.
1315. COS, 3.42.
1316. COS, 1.95.
1317. *CAD*, 14, 292–96.
1318. J. Reade, *Assyrian Sculpture* (Cambridge, Mass.: Harvard Univ. Press, 1983), 31.
1319. COS, 1.159.
1320. Y. Yadin, *Hazor* I (1958), fig. 29:1; *ANEP*, 871; M. Delcor, "Two Special Meanings of the Word *yd* in Biblical Hebrew," *JSS* 12 (1967): 230–34.
1321. Wilkinson, *Complete Gods and Goddesses*, 176–77.
1322. Ibid., 180.
1323. Ibid., 181–82.
1324. Dick, "Neo-Assyrian Royal Lion Hunt," 244–45.
1325. *CAD*, 1, 109.
1326. King and Stager, *Life*, 118–19.

1327. Ornan, *The Triumph of the Symbol*, 49–50, 121; M. Gibson, "Nippur, 1990: Gula, Goddess of Healing and an Akkadian Tomb," available at http://oi.uchicago.edu/research/pubs/nn/sep90_nip.html; *OEANE*, 2, 166.
1328. Steinkeller, "Early Semitic Literature," 248–58, pl. 1–2.
1329. L. E. Stager, "Why Were Hundreds of Dogs Buried at Ashkelon?" *BAR* 17 (1991): 26–42; P. Wapnish and B. Hesse, "Pampered Pooches or Plain Pariahs? The Ashkelon Dog Burials," *BA* 56/2 (1993): 55–80.
1330. A. K. Grayson, "Murmuring in Mesopotamia" in *Wisdom, Gods and Literature*, 305.
1331. R. O Faulkner, *The Book of the Dead* (New York: Macmillan, 1972); Currid, *Ancient Egypt*, 96–103.
1332. Dalley, *Myths from Mesopotamia*, 150. For other examples, see *CAD*, 10/II, 317.
1333. COS, 1.132.
1334. Katz, *Image of the Netherworld*, 227.
1335. See *RIA*, 7/1–2, 115, 151, 139–40 respectively.
1336. Steinkeller, "Early Semitic Literature," 269–72 and pl. 6. Steinkeller (p. 269) suggests all three are of Semitic origin.
1337. *AEL*, 2:122, 124, 216, 219; 3:81; Wilkinson, *Complete Gods and Goddesses*, 168–69.
1338. A. R. W. Green, *The Role of Human Sacrifice in the Ancient Near East* (ASOR Dissertation Series 1; Missoula, Mont.: Scholars, 1975).
1339. O. Eissfeldt understands *mlk* not as a personal or divine name, but rather a technical Phoenician/Punic word for a child-sacrifice cult; O. Eissfeldt, *Molk als Opferbegriff im Punischen und Hebräischen und das Ende des Gottes Moloch* (Beiträge zur Religionsgeschichte des Altertums 3; Halle: Niemeyer, 1935); P. G. Mosca, "Child Sacrifice in Canaanite and Israelite Religion: A Study of *Mulk* and *mlk*" (PhD diss., Harvard University, 1975); Day, *Molech*, 4–14; K. A. D. Smelik, "Moloch, Molech or Molk-Sacrifice?" *SJOT* 9 (1995): 133–92; G. C. Heider, "Molech," *DDD*, 581–82.
1340. Listed as an element of several names; G. C. Heider, *The Cult of Molek: A Reassessment* (JSOTSup 43; Sheffield: Sheffield Academic Press, 1985), 94–101, 409–15; see M. Dahood, "Are the Ebla Tablets Relevant to Biblical Research?" *BAR* 6/5 (1980): 56.
1341. Heider, *Cult of Molek*, 102–13, 416–17.
1342. S. H. Horn, "The Ammān Citadel Inscription," *BASOR* 193 (1969): 8; Heider, *Cult of Molek*, 169–70.
1343. Green, *Role of Human Sacrifice*, 59–65.
1344. Pro: M. H. Poe, "Notes on the Ugaritic Rephaim Texts," in *Essays on the Ancient Near East in Memory of Jacob Joel Finkelstein*, M. de Jong Ellis, ed. (Hamden: Archon Books, 1977), 169–72; con: Day, *Molech*, 50–51.
1345. Day, *Molech*, 50–52. See also M. Weinfeld, "The Worship of Molech and the Queen of Heaven," *UF* 4 (1972): 133–54; D. Edelman, "Biblical Molek Reassessed," *JAOS* 107 (1987): 727–31.
1346. Heider, *Cult of Molek*, 185–88.
1347. M. Almagro-Gorbea, "Les reliefs orientalisants de Pozo Moro (Albacete, Espagne)," in *Mythe et personification: actes du Colloque du Grand Palais (Paris), 7–8 mai, 1977*, ed. J. Duchemin (Paris: Belles lettres, 1980): 123–36 and 8 plates; C. A. Kennedy, "The Mythological Reliefs of Pozo Moro, Spain," *SBLSP* 20 (1981): 209–16; Heider, *Cult of Molek*, 189–92; Kempinski, "From Death to Resurrection," 56–65, 82, especially 63.
1348. S. Moscati, "Il sacrificio dei fanciulli: Nuove scoperte su un celebre rito cartaginese," *Rendiconti: Atti delle pontificia Accademia romana di Archeologia* 38 (1965–1966): 68, translated in Mosca, "Child Sacrifice," 39; see L. E. Stager, "The Rite of Child Sacrifice at Carthage," in *New Light on Ancient Carthage: Papers of a Symposium*, ed. J. G. Pedley (Ann Arbor: Univ. of Michigan Press, 1980), 1–11; L. E. Stager and S. R. Wolff, "Child Sacrifice at Carthage—Religious Rite or Population Control?" *BAR* 10/1 (1984): 30–51; Heider, *Cult of Molek*, 196–97; S. S. Brown, *Late Carthaginian Child Sacrifice and Sacrificial Monuments in their Mediterranean Context* (JSOT/ASOR Monograph Series 3; Sheffield: Sheffield Academic Press Press, 1991); M. H. Fantar, L. E. Stager, and J. A. Greene, "An Odyssey Debate: Were Living Children Sacrificed to the Gods in Punic Carthage?" *Archaeology Odyssey* 3/6 (2000): 28–31.
1349. K. Spronk, *Beatific Afterlife in Ancient Israel* (AOAT 219; Neukirchen-Vluyn: Neukirchener Verlag, 1986), 233.
1350. Mesopotamia: *ANEP*, 525, 600, 626, 689; Egypt, ibid., 640.
1351. *AEL*, 1:92.
1352. R. Deutsch and M. Heltzer, *Forty New West Semitic Inscriptions* (Tel Aviv: Archaeological Center Publications, 1994), 23–26; Zevit, *Religions of Ancient Israel*, 298.
1353. H. G. May, "The Fertility Cult in Hosea," *AJSL* 48 (1931–1932): 73–98; W. F. Albright, "The High Place in Ancient Palestine," *Volume de Congrès: Strassbourg, 1956* (VTSup 4; Leiden: Brill, 1957): 242–58; E. Yamauchi, "Cultic Prostitution: A Case Study in Cultural Diffusion," in *Orient and Occident: Essays Presented to Cyrus H. Gordon on the Occasion of his Sixty-fifth Birthday*, ed. H. A. Hoffner Jr. (Neukirchen-Vluyn: Neukirchener Verlag, 1973), 213–22; Oswalt, *Isaiah: Chapters 40–66*, 478–80; see J. Renger, "Heilige Hochzeit. A. Philologisch," *RlA* 4 (1972–1975), 251–59; R. A. Henshaw, *Female and Male: The Cultic Personnel: The Bible and the Rest of the Ancient Near East* (Princeton Theological Monograph Series 31; Allison Park: Pickwick, 1994), 120–233; J. Assante, "The *kar.kid/[kh]arimtu*, Prostitute or Single Woman? A Reconsideration of the Evidence," *UF* 30 (1998): 5–96.
1354. COS, 1.173; S. N. Kramer, *The Sacred Marriage Rite: Aspects of Faith, Myth, and Ritual in Ancient Sumer* (Bloomington, Ind.: Indiana Univ. Press, 1969); M. Wakeman, "Sacred Marriage," *JSOT* 22 (1982): 21–31; J. S. Cooper, "Sacred Marriage and Popular Cult in Ancient Mesopotamia," in

Official Cult and Popular Religion in the Ancient Near East, ed. E. Matsushima (Heidelberg: Winter, 1993), 81–96; P. Lapinkivi, *The Sumerian Sacred Marriage in the Light of Comparative Evidence* (SAAS XV; Helsinki: The Neo-Assyrian Text Corpus, 2004).

1355. Not everyone is agreed that the term refers either to cultic functionaries or to prostitutes; see M. I. Gruber, "Hebrew *Qĕdēšāh* and her Canaanite and Akkadian Cognates," *UF* 18 (1986): 133–48.

1356. Henshaw, *Female and Male*, 228–33; J. Assante, "From Whores to Hierodules: The Historiographic Invention of Mesopotamian Female Sex Professionals," in *Ancient Art and Its Historiography*, ed. A. A. Donahue and M. D. Fullerton (Cambridge: Cambridge Univ. Press, 2003), 13–47.

1357. See P. Bird, "'To Play the Harlot': An Inquiry into an Old Testament Metaphor," in *Gender and Difference in Ancient Israel*, ed. P. L. Day (Minneapolis: Fortress, 1989), 75–94.

1358. Gordon, *Ugaritic Textbook*, §19:1072; Delcor, "Two Special Meanings," 234.

1359. Delcor, "Two Special Meanings," 230–34; J. L. Koole, *Isaiah III/3: Isaiah Chapters 56–66* (HCOT; Leuven: Peeters, 2001), 71.

1360. See H. Ringgren, *Religions of the Ancient Near East* (Philadelphia: Westminster, 1973); also note the entire dictionary on deities, *Dictionary of Deities and Demons in the Bible* (abbreviated *DDD*).

1361. Wilkinson, *Complete Gods and Goddesses*, 74–79.

1362. See D. B. Redford, *Akhenaten, the Heretic King* (Princeton, N.J.: Princeton Univ. Press, 1984); J. Assmann, *Egyptian Solar Religion in the New Kingdom: Re, Amun and the Crisis of Polytheism* (London: Kegan Paul, 1995); E. Hornung, *Akhenaten and the Religion of Light* (Ithaca, N.Y.: Cornell Univ. Press, 1999); D. P. Silverman et al., *Akhenaten and Tutankhamun: Revolution and Restoration* (Philadelphia: Univ. of Pennsylvania Museum of Archaeology and Anthropology, 2006).

1363. COS, 1.113.

1364. Zevit, *Religions of Ancient Israel*, 648–58.

1365. *AHw*, 994; *CAD* 14, 414–415.

1366. J. Muddiman, "Fast, Fasting," *ABD*, 2:773–74; see S. Parpola, *Letters from Assyrian Scholars to the Kings Esarhaddon and Assurbanipal: Part 2A: Commentary and Appendices* (AOAT 5/2; Neukirchen-Vluyn: Butzon & Bercker, 1971), 58–59.

1367. *AEL*, 1:142.

1368. M. Boyce, "Zoroaster, Zoroastrianism," *ABD*, 6:1171.

1369. Lambert, *Babylonian Wisdom Literature*, 119; *AHw*, 1326.

1370. *CAD*, 2, 213.

1371. COS, 1.86.

1372. *AEL*, 1:117.

1373. *ANET*, 320.

1374. M. J. Fretz, "Weapons and Implements of Warfare," *ABD*, 6:894.

1375. *AEL*, 3:153.

1376. Ibid., 2:32. See ibid., 2:61, where Ramesses II's armor makes him look like powerful Seth.

1377. *CAD*, 1/II, 177.

1378. COS, 1.111; *CAD*, 1/II, 177.

1379. Ibid., 1.72.

1380. Ibid., 2.47B.

1381. See also P. Grelot, "Un parallèle babylonien d'Isaïe LX et du Psaume LXXII," *VT* 7 (1957): 319–21.

1382. *CAD*, 2, 35; *ANET*, 283; cf. 286; Paul, "Deutero-Isaiah," 184.

1383. F. V. Winnett, "The Arabian Genealogies in the Book of Genesis," in *Translating and Understanding the Old Testament: Essay in Honor of Herbert Gordon May*, ed. H. T. Frank and W. L. Reed (Nashville: Abingdon, 1970), 194; Smith, "Arabia," *ABD*, 1:326; E. A. Knauf, "Kedar," *ABD*, 4:9–10.

1384. S. Parpola, *Neo-Assyrian Toponyms* (Neukirchen-Vluyn: Neukirchener Verlag, 1970), 285–86, 254–55.

1385. *ANET*, 298–300.

1386. D. W. Manor and G. A. Herion, "Arad," *ABD*, 1:335; W. J. Dumbrell, "The Tell el-Maskhuṭa Bowls and the 'Kingdom' of Qedar in the Persian Period," *BASOR* 203 (1971): 33–44.

1387. NRSV—a translation preferable to the "nests" of the NIV; see Gen.7:8; 8:2, where the same term is used.

1388. See W. C. Bouzard III, "Doves in the Windows: Isaiah 60:8 in Light of Ancient Mesopotamian Lament Traditions," in *David and Zion: Biblical Studies in Honor of J. J. M. Roberts*, ed. B. Batto and K. L. Roberts (Winona Lake, Ind.: Eisenbrauns, 2004), 307–18; quote from 311.

1389. Sass, "Pre-Exilic Hebrew Seals," 218–19:101, though the owner, interestingly enough, is named "Raven." See also Keel and Uehlinger, *Altorientalische Miniaturkunst*, 126–27.

1390. Baker, "Tarshish (Place)," *ABD*, 6:331; King and Stager, *Life*, 183–84.

1391. Pers. trans.; H. Shanks, "The 'Three Shekels' and 'Widow's Plea' Ostraca: Real or Fake?" *BAR* 29/3 (2003): 40–44; COS, 2.50.

1392. *CAD*, 2, 327; Paul, "Deutero-Isaiah," 183, where he also suggests identifications of the next two trees as well, based on Akkadian and Talmudic usage.

1393. *AEL*, 1:103

1394. Moran, *Amarna Letters*, 337; see also e.g., COS, 3.92A-C, F, G.

1395. COS, 1.111. See *CAD*, 17/1, 470–473; 17/2, 297–98.

1396. COS, 1.160.

1397. See D. I. Block, "Divine Abandonment: Ezekiel's Adaptation of an Ancient Near Eastern Motif," in *The Book of Ezekiel: Theological and Anthropological Perspectives*, ed. M. S. Odell and J. T. Strong (SBLSymS 9; Atlanta: Society of Biblical Literature, 2000), 18–24.

1398. Luckenbill, *Ancient Records*, 2:243.

1399. See M. Cogan, *Imperialism and Religion: Assyria, Judah and Israel in the Eighth and Seventh Centuries B.C.E.* (SBLMS 19; Missoula, Mont.: Society of Biblical Literature, 1974), 9–15; H. Tadmor, "Sennacherib's Campaign in Judah" (Heb), *Zion* 50 (1986): 66–80; J. A. Dearman and G. L. Mattingly, "Mesha Stele," *ABD*, 4:708–9; Levine, "Assyrian Ideology and Israelite Monotheism," 422; Block, "Divine Abandonment," 24–34.

1400. COS, 2.23.
1401. *CAD*, 17/I, 327–328; Meier, *Messenger*, 222–29; Anderson, *A Time to Mourn*, 45–47.
1402. *CAD*, 17/I, 325.
1403. Ibid., 1/I, 154.
1404. Stummer, "Einige keilschriftliche Parallelen," 186.
1405. Moran, *Amarna Letters*, 143, 145, 151.
1406. *CAD*, 10/2, 314.
1407. Dalley, *Myths from Mesopotamia*, 77.
1408. *CAD*, 8, 56, see 55–56.
1409. COS, 1.123.
1410. Ibid., 1.99.
1411. T. J. Lewis, "Death Cult Imagery in Isaiah 57," *HAR* 11 (1987): 267–84; idem, *Cults of the Dead*, 143–60.
1412. W. Houston, *Purity and Monotheism: Clean and Unclean Animals in Biblical Law* (JSOTSup 140; Sheffield: Sheffield Academic Press, 1993), 136–40; see U. Hübner, "Schweine, Schweineknochen und ein Speiseverbot im alten Testament," *VT* 39 (1989): 225–36.
1413. Keel and Oehlinger, *Altorientalische Miniaturkunst*, 32.
1414. COS, 1.19.
1415. Houston, *Purity and Monotheism*, 149–50, 176. There is inconclusive evidence of their use in offerings to the dead; ibid., 161–65.
1416. Lambert, *Babylonian Wisdom Literature*, 215.
1417. Postgate, *Fifty Neo-Assyrian Legal Documents*, 37–43.
1418. *CAD*, 17/1, 226–227.
1419. COS, 3.43A, 43F.
1420. See Moran, *Amarna Letters*, 5.
1421. *AEL*, 1:65.
1422. COS, 1.122.
1423. S. Rabichini, "Gad," *DDD*, 339–41; O. Keel, "La glyptique du Tell Keisan (1971–1976)," *Studien zu den Stempsiegeln aus Palästina/Israel* III, *Die frühe Eisenzeit: Ein Workshop* (OBO 100; Göttingen: Vandenhoeck & Ruprecht, 1990), 248–52.
1424. Avigad and Sass, *Corpus*, 54:12; 87:117, 118; 188:454; 191:467; 232:628, 629; 238:649. Also Arad ostracon 71:3; Samaritan ostracon 2.
1425. K. Van der Toorn, "Min," *DDD*, 577; R. H. Wilkinson, *The Complete Gods and Goddesses of Ancient Egypt* (London: Thames & Hudson, 2003), 115–17. For both, see Koole, *Isaiah III/3*, 435–36.
1426. *ANET*, 249–50; see the discussion there.
1427. COS, 1.132; pers. trans.
1428. Avigad and Sass, *Corpus*, 100:163; they take it as a hypocoristic form.
1429. Ibid, 431:1138.
1430. Koole, *Isaiah III/3*, 443.
1431. Pers. trans.; J. A. Fitzmyer, *The Aramaic Inscriptions of Sefire* (BibOr 19; Rome: Pontifical Biblical Institute, 1967), 98–99; COS, 2.82.
1432. *ANET*, 582–83; J. D. Levenson "The Temple and the World," *JR* 64 (1984): 282–91.
1433. J. M. Lundquist, "What Is a Temple: A Preliminary Typology," in *The Quest For the Kingdom of God: Studies in Honor of George E. Mendenhall*, ed. H. Huffmon, F. Spina. and A. R. W. Green (Winona Lake, Ind.: Eisenbrauns, 1983), 208; Walton, *Ancient Near Eastern Thought*, 123–24.
1434. Hurowitz, *I Have Built*, 245; Walton, *Ancient Near Eastern Thought*, 126.
1435. COS, 1.111. See G. K. Beale, "Cosmic Symbolism of Temples in the Old Testament," in his *The Temple and the Church's Mission: A Biblical Theology of the Dwelling Place of God* (New Studies in Biblical Theology 17; Downers Grove, Ill.: InterVarsity Press, 2004), 29–80.
1436. *CAD*, 3, 125.
1437. COS, 1.86; *CTA*, 2 iii: 7; pers. trans.
1438. COS, 1.86; *CTA*, 4 v:38–39.
1439. *ANET*, 315.
1440. COS, 1.111 vi:65–75; see Hurowitz, *I Have Built*, 93–96.
1441. Green, *Role of Human Sacrifice*, 88–91; *CANE*, 1885.
1442. Taylor, *Death and the Afterlife*, 99–100.
1443. J. M. Sasson, "Isaiah lxvi 3–4a," *VT* 26 (1976): 204.
1444. Pers. trans.; C.-F. Jean, *Lettres diverses* (ARM II; Paris: Imprimerie national, 1950), 82; *ANET*, 482; G. E. Mendenhall, "Puppy and Lettuce in Northwest-Semitic Covenant Making," *BASOR* 133 (1954): 26–30.
1445. E. D. Oren, "The Kingdom of Sharuhen and the Hyksos Kingdom," in *The Hyksos: New Historical and Archaeological Perspectives*, ed. E. D. Oren (Philadelphia: Univ. Museum, Univ. of Pennsylvania, 1997), 264 and figure 8.14; King and Stager, *Life*, 44.
1446. J. C. Moyer, "Hittite and Israelite Cultic Practices: A Selected Comparison," in *Scripture in Context* II: *More Essays on the Comparative Method* (Winona Lake, Ind.: Eisenbrauns, 1983), 31–33; B. J. Collins, "The Puppy in Hittite Rituals," *JCS* 42 (1990): 211–26.
1447. Sasson, "Isaiah lxvi 3–4a," 205.
1448. R. de Vaux, "Les sacrifices de porcs en Palestine et dans l'Ancient Orient," in *Von Ugarit nach Qumran : Beiträge zur alttestamentlichen und altorientalischen Forschung: Otto Eissfeldt zum 1. September 1957 dargebracht von Freunden und Schülern*, ed. J. Hempel and L. Rost (BZAW 77; Berlin: de Gruyter, 1958), 250–65.
1449. *ANET*, 10.
1450. P. C. Schmitz, "Phoenician Religion," *ABD*, 5:360.
1451. E.g., G. Beckman, *Hittite Birth Rituals: An Introduction* (Malibu: Undena, 1978); K. van der Toorn, "The Prestige of Motherhood: Pregnancy and Birth," in van der Toorn, ed., *From her Cradle*, 77–92; M. Stol, *Birth in Babylonia and the Bible: Its Mediterranean Setting* (Groningen: Styx, 2000); R. D. Biggs, "Conception, Contraception, and Abortion in Ancient Mesopotamia," in George and Finkel, ed., *Wisdom, Gods and Literature*, 1–13.

1452. N. Veldhuis, *A Cow of Sîn* (Groningen: Styx, 1991), 9.
1453. COS, 2.34; A. Abou-Assaf et al., *La statue de Tell-Fekherye et son inscription bilingue assyro-araméenne* (Paris: Éditions Recherche sur les civilisations, 1982), 14.
1454. COS, 1.111.
1455. Pers. trans.; Luckenbill, *Annals of Sennacherib*, 142.
1456. COS, 1.86; del Olmo Lete, *Dictionary*, 739–40.
1457. *CAD*, 11/I, 357.
1458. Keel and Uehlinger, *Altorientalische Miniaturkunst*, 45:50.
1459. Sass, "Pre-Exilic Hebrew Seals," 225–26:119.
1460. The Hebrew term (*prd*) is not cognate to the Akkadian (*parû*), but is semantically synonymous; Paul, "Deutero-Isaiah," 184, n. 45.
1461. Pers. trans.; ibid., 183–84, n. 44.
1462. See Paul, "Deutero-Isaiah," 184.
1463. See Keel, *Goddesses and Trees*, 104–9; fig. 9, 10; Lewis, "Syro-Palestinian Iconography," 75 and fig. 4.9.
1464. Y. Aharoni, *Arad Inscriptions* (Jerusalem: Israel Exploration Society, 1981), 22; Keel, *Goddesses and Trees*, 105; S. E. Loewenstamm, *From Babylon to Canaan: Studies in the Bible and its Oriental Background* (Jerusalem: Magnes, 1992), 131–35.
1465. *AEL*, 1:203.
1466. Lambert, *Babylonian Wisdom Literature*, 109; see *CAD*, 8, 144–148.

Sidebar and Chart Notes

A-1. G. E. Wright, "The Lawsuit of God: A Form-Critical Study of Deuteronomy 32," in *Israel's Prophetic Heritage: Essays on Honor of James Muilenburg*, ed. B. Anderson and W. Harrelson (New York: Harper, 1962), 26–67; J. Limburg, "The Root *riv* and the Prophetic Lawsuit Speeches," *JBL* 88 (1969): 291–304; K. Nielsen, *Yahweh as Prosecutor and Judge: An Investigation of the Prophetic Lawsuit (Rib-Pattern)* (JSOTSup 9; Sheffield: Sheffield Academic Press, 1978); J. C. Laney, "The Role of the Prophets in God's Case against Israel," *BSac* 138 (1981): 313–24. See also H. J. Boecker, *Law and the Administration of Justice in the Old Testament and Ancient East* (Minneapolis: Augsburg, 1980); R. R. Wilson, "Israel's Judicial System in the Pre-exilic Period," *JQR* 74 (1983): 229–48; H. Niehr, *Rechtsprechung in Israel: Untersuchungen.zur Geschichte der Gerichtsorganisation im Alten Testament* (SBS 130; Stuttgart: Katholisches Bibelwerk, 1987).
A-2. For the religion of Egypt, see, e.g., S. Morenz, *Egyptian Religion* (Ithaca, N.Y.: Cornell Univ. Press, 1973); A. R. David, *The Ancient Egyptians: Religious Beliefs and Practices* (New York/London: Routledge & Kegan Paul, 1982); A. I. Sadek, *Popular Religion in Egypt during the New Kingdom* (Hildesheim: Gerstenberg, 1987); B. E. Shafer, ed., *Religion in Ancient Egypt: Gods, Myths, and Personal Practice* (Ithaca, N.Y.: Cornell Univ. Press, 1991). For Mesopotamia, see É. Dhorme and R. Dussaud, *Les religions de Babylone et d'Assyrie* (Paris: Presses universitaires de France, 1949); G. van Driel, *The Cult of Aššur* (Assen: Van Gorcum, 1969); T. Jakobsen, *The Treasures of Darkness: A History of Mesopotamian Religion* (New Haven, Conn.: Yale University Press, 1976). For the entire ancient Near Eastern area, see, e.g., H. Ringgren, *Religions of the Ancient Near East* (Philadelphia: Westminster, 1973); *CANE*, 1685–2094.
A-3. E.g., K. R. Nemet-Nejat, *Daily Life in Ancient Mesopotamia* (Westport, Conn.: Greenwood, 1998), 186–89.
A-4. Ibid., 189–90.
A-5. Ibid., 194–96.
A-6. Ibid., 190–94, 196–212; R. A. Henshaw, *Female and Male: The Cultic Personnel: The Bible and the Rest of the Ancient Near East* (Princeton Theological Monograph Series 31; Allison Park, Pa.: Pickwick, 1994).
A-7. F. E. Deist, *The Material Culture of the Bible: An Introduction* (Sheffield: Sheffield Academic Press, 2000), 217.
A-8. King and Stager, *Life*, 172–76.
A-9. U. K. Westenholz, *Babylonian Liver Omens* (CNI 25; Copenhagen: Museum Tusculanum, Univ. of Copenhagen, 2000); U. Jeyes, "A Compendium of Gall-Bladder Omens Extant in Middle Babylonian, Nineveh, and Seleucid Versions," in George and Finkel, *Wisdom, Gods and Literature*, 345–74; W. Hallo, "Before Tea Leaves: Divination in Ancient Babylonia," *BAR* 31/2 (2005): 32–39.
A-10. For a discussion of various different sorts of divination, see the proceedings of the 14th Rencontre assyriologique internationale (Strasbourg), *La divination en Mésopotamie ancienne et dans les régions voisines* (Paris: Presses universitaires de France, 1966); A. Caquot, *La divination: études recueilles par André Caquot et Marcel Leibovici* (Paris: Presses universitaires de France, 1968); A. L. Oppenheim, *Ancient Mesopotamia: Portrait of a Dead Civilization* (Chicago: Univ. of Chicago Press, 1964), 207; F. H. Cryer, *Divination in Ancient Israel and its Near Eastern Environment* (Sheffield: Sheffield Academic Press, 1994); for divination among the Egyptians, Mesopotamians, Hittites, Canaanites, and Israelites, see *CANE*, 1775–85, 1895–909, 2007–19, 2071–81 respectively; A. K. Guinan, "A Severed Head Laughed: Stories of Divinatory Interpretation," in *Magic and Divination in the Ancient World*, ed. L. Ciraolo and J. Seidel (Leiden: Brill, 2002), 7–40; for Egypt, J. Gee, "Oracle by Image: Coffin Text 103 in Context," ibid., 83–88.
A-11. R. K. Ritner, "Necromancy in Ancient Egypt," in *Magic and Divination in the Ancient World*, 89–96.
A-12. J. Seidel, "Necromantic Praxis in the Midrash on the Séance at En Dor," in *Magic and Divination in the Ancient World*, 97–106.
A-13. O. Neugebauer, *Astronomical Cuneiform Texts: Babylonian Ephemerides of the Seleucid Period*

for the Motion of the Sun, the Moon, and the Planets (London: Lund Humphries, 1955); A. L. Oppenheim, "Divination and Celestial Observation in the Late Assyrian Empire," *Centaurus* 14 (1969): 97–135; F. Rochberg-Halton, *Aspects of Babylonian Celestial Divination: The Lunar Eclipse Tablets of Enuma Anu Enlil* (Horn: Ferdinand Berger & Söhne, 1988); N. M. Swerdlow, *The Babylonian Theory of the Planets* (Princeton: Princeton Univ. Press, 1998); Cryer, *Divination*, 142–44; N. M. Swerdlow, *Ancient Astronomy and Celestial Divination* (Cambridge, Mass.: MIT Press, 1999); H. Hunger and D. Pingree, *Astral Sciences in Mesopotamia* (Leiden: Brill, 1999); D. Brown, *Mesopotamian Planetary Astronomy/Astrology* (Groningen: Styx, 2000); F. Rochberg, *The Heavenly Writing: Divination, Horoscopy, and Astronomy in Mesopotamian Culture* (Cambridge: Cambridge Univ. Press, 2004).

A-14. Cryer, *Divination*, 145–47.

A-15. See E. Leichty, *The Omen Series Šumma Izbu* (Locust Valley, N.Y.: Augustin, 1970); Oppenheim, *Ancient Mesopotamia*, 206–27; S. M. Moren, "Šumma Izbu XIX: New Light on the Animal Omens," *AfO* 27 (1980): 53–70; R. R. Wilson, *Prophecy and Society in Ancient Israel* (Philadelphia: Fortress, 1980), 90–98; Cryer, *Divination*, 148–54; also from Ugarit, M. Dietrich et al., "Der keilalphabetische Šumma Izbu-Text RS 24.247+265+268+328," *UF* 7 (1979): 134–40; M. Dietrich et al., *Mantik in Ugarit: Keilalphabetische Texte der Opferscha—Omensammlungen.-Necromantie* (Münster: Ugarit Verlag, 1990), 87–165; COS, 1.90

A-16. *ANET*, 328.

A-17. *ANET*, 592–93.

A-18. S. Dalley, *Myths From Mesopotamia*, "Erra and Ishum" (Oxford: Oxford Univ. Press, 1991), 304; cf. COS, 1.113 IV:40–42, 44.

A-19. After E. W. Bullinger, *Figures of Speech Used in the Bible* (Grand Rapids: Baker, 1968 [1898]), 313. More recent discussion of Hebrew wordplay is found in S. B. Noegel, ed. *Puns and Pundits: Word Play in the Hebrew Bible and Ancient Near Eastern Literature* (Bethesda, Md.: CDL Press, 2000), 137–248.

A-20. V. A. Hurowitz, "Alliterative Allusions, Rebus Writing, and Paronomastic Punishment: Some Aspects of Word Play in Akkadian Literature" in Noegel, ed., *Puns and Pundits*, 68. Further on Akkadian see A. D. Kilmer, "More Word Play in Akkadian Poetic Texts," in Noegel, ed., *Puns and Pundits*, 89–102; S. W. Greaves, "Ominous Homophony and Portentous Puns in Akkadian Omens," in Noegel, ed., *Puns and Pundits*, 103–13.

A-21. A. Loprieno, "Puns and Word Play in Ancient Egyptian" in Noegel, ed., *Puns and Pundits*, 3–20.

A-22. J. Klein and Y. Sefati, "Word Play in Sumerian Literature" in Noegel, ed., *Puns and Pundits*, 23–61.

A-23. W. G. E. Watson, "Puns Ugaritic Newly Surveyed" in Noegel, ed., *Puns and Pundits*, 117–34.

A-24. COS, 2.285.

A-25. Millard, *Eponyms*.

A-26. J.-J. Glassner, *Mesopotamian Chronicles* (SBLWAW 19; Atlanta: Society of Biblical Literature, 2004), 171.

A-27. COS, 2.117A, along with Menahem, an earlier Israelite king.

A-28. Ibid., 2.117C; "[I/they killed] Pekah, their king, and I installed Hoshea."

A-29. Dubovský, "Tiglath-pileser III's Campaigns," 154–56.

A-30. COS, 1.136.

A-31. Ibid., 2.117D.

A-32. Dubovský, "Tiglath-pileser III's Campaigns," 153–70, see 163.

A-33. M. E. W. Thompson, *Situation and Theology: Old Testament Interpretations of the Syro-Ephraimite War* (Sheffield: Sheffield Academic Press, 1982).

A-34. For a discussion of the meaning of the term and related ones, see J. H. Walton, "בְּתוּלָה," *NIDOTTE*, 1:781–84; "עֲלוּמִים," 3:415–19.

A-35. *CAT*, 1.15 II:22 (Wyatt, *Religious Texts*, 209); 1.14 IV:41 (ibid., 201); in both cases the girl in question is introduced in marriage into the king's house.

A-36. COS, 2.117B; cf. 2.117A; an incident recorded in 2 Kings 15:19.

A-37. *ANET*, 283.

A-38. Tiglath-pileser III Summary Inscription 4 lines 15'-19', H. Tadmor, *The Inscriptions of Tiglath-pileser III, King of Assyria* (Jerusalem: Israel Academy of Sciences and Humanities, 1994), 141; cf. COS 2.117C. Who killed Pekah is missing in the Akkadian fragment, but the biblical text attributes it to "them," i.e., his fellow Israelites.

A-39. Ibid., 2.117; *ANET*, 282–84.

A-40. COS, 2.118; *ANET*, 284–87.

A-41. COS, 2.119; *ANET*, 287–88.

A-42. COS, 2.120; *ANET*, 289–94.

A-43. *ANET*, 294–301.

A-44. Grayson, *Early First Millennium*, 2:14, also 8, 9, 10, etc.

A-45. J. C. Trever, *Scrolls from Qumran Cave I: The Great Isaiah Scroll, The Order of the Community, The Pesher to Habakkuk* (Jerusalem: Albright Institute/ Shrine of the Book, 1974), 6–63.

A-46. The form could also indicate a past tense; N. Wyatt, *Religious Texts from Ugarit*, 2nd ed. (London: Sheffield Academic Press, 2002), 264 n. 57.

A-47. COS, 1.103 ii:8 ff.

A-48. Wildberger, *Isaiah 1–12*, 400.

A-49. See also M. Malul, *Knowledge, Control and Sex: Studies in Biblical Thought, Culture and Worldview* (Tel Aviv-Jaffa: Archaeological Center Publications, 2002), 278–312.

A-50. J. M. Myers, *Ezra, Nehemiah* (AB 14; Garden City, N.Y.: Doubleday, 1965), 149, though others take the two names as linguistic variants, e.g., H. G. M. Williamson, *1 and 2 Chronicles* (NCBC; Grand Rapids: Eerdmans, 1982), 333–34.

A-51. Heb. *geber*; cf. Isa. 9:6 "mighty (*gibbor*) God."

A-52. Using the Qal prefix indicative, "he will call his name."

A-53. Supported by the Niphal, passive reading proposed in *BHS*.

A-54. Wildberger, *Isaiah 1–12*, 402.

A-55. *CAT*, 7, 63:4–7; del Olmo Lete, *Canaanite Religion*, 176.

A-56. Seux, *Épithètes royales*, 156.

A-57. Ibid., 67–70, 96. See a much earlier, late third-millennium inscription of Shar-kali-sharri, designating him as "heroic god" (ibid., 106).

A-58. Ibid., 229–31, *qarrādu*, cf. the Hebrew *gibbor*.

A-59. Ibid., 297, expressed as a wish or desire, "may the king be eternal."

A-60. This term is surprisingly rare and could indicate an official in a position lower than king; *CAD*, 1/1, 72–73.

A-61. Seux, *Épithètes royales*, 91, 161.

A-62. Ibid., 182–83, 281–82.

A-63. *ANET*, 165.

A-64. Ibid., 177.

A-65. Ibid., 523.

A-66. Ibid., 159.

A-67. Ibid., 526.

A-68. *COS*, 1.136.

A-69. *ANET*, 241.

A-70. Ibid., 262.

A-71. Ibid., 275.

A-72. Ibid., 277–79.

A-73. Ibid., 283.

A-74. Ibid., 285.

A-75. Ibid., 242, 253.

A-76. Ibid., 278–80.

A-77. Ibid., 282.

A-78. Ibid., 284.

A-79. See the treaty entered into between Assyria and Arpad at this time; ibid., 532–33.

A-80. *COS*, 1.136.

A-81. Wildberger, *Isaiah 1–12*, 419.

A-82. *ANET*, 242, 248.

A-83. Ibid., 278–81.

A-84. Ibid., 285; *COS*, 1.136, where Damascus is mentioned in the eponyms of 733 and 732 B.C.

A-85. A. K. Grayson and W. G. Lambert, "Akkadian Prophecies," *JCS* 18 (1964): 13–14; cf. T. Longman III, *Fictional Akkadian Autobiography: A Generic and Comparative Study* (Winona Lake, Ind.: Eisenbrauns, 1991), 149–63, for a study of the text. A similar rule is described in the Marduk prophecy, see 9:7.

A-86. Grayson and Lambert ("Akkadian Prophecies," 10) suggest that this type of text was written because of the Akkadian cyclical view of history, that what goes around will again come around. Thus, a description of the past is also ipso facto a prediction of the future.

A-87. *ANET*, 627.

A-88. *ANET*, 38.

A-89. http://www-etcsl.orient.ox.ac.uk/section1/tr1823.htm.

A-90. B. Batto, "Paradise Reexamined," in Younger, *The Biblical Canon*, 58. See S. N. Kramer, *Enki and Ninhursag: A Sumerian "Paradise" Myth* (New Haven, Conn.: American Schools of Oriental Research, 1945); B. Alster, "Dilmun, Bahrain, and the Alleged Paradise," in *Dilmun: New Studies in the Archaeology and Early History of Bahrain*, ed. D. T. Potts (Berlin: Dietrich Reimer, 1983), 39–74; T. Jacobsen, *The Harps that Once...: Sumerian Poetry in Translation* (New Haven, Conn.: Yale Univ. Press, 1987), 182.

A-91. See M. Eliade, *The Myth of the Eternal Return* (New York: Pantheon, 1954).

A-92. *COS*, 1.46.

A-93. *ANET*, 329.

A-94. See the map of the extent of its empire in Aharoni, *Macmillan Bible Atlas*, 147.

A-95. A question might be why the more minor power of Babylon is mentioned in Isaiah prior to the more major Assyria (14:24–27). There is no evidence that the oracles are uniformly placed in chronological order, and at the time of subsequent editors of the text, Babylon could have attained superiority. Assyrian kings held the throne of Babylon from the time of Tiglath-pileser III (B. T. Arnold, *Who Were the Babylonians?* [Atlanta: Society of Biblical Literature, 2004], 89), so at the time of Isaiah, the two could have been coterminous (see K. L. Younger Jr., "Recent Study on Sargon II, King of Assyria: Implications for Biblical Studies," in Chavalas and Younger, *Mesopotamia and the Bible*, 319 n. 94. Assyria's fall has already been described by Isaiah (10:5–19).

A-96. *NBD*², 180.

A-97. J. A Brinkman, "Notes on Arameans and Chaldeans in Southern Babylonia in the Early Seventh Century B.C.," *Or* 46 (1977): 306–7; CAH³, 288–90; *RLA*, 5, 291–92; M. van de Mieroop, *A History of the Ancient Near East: ca. 3000–323 B.C.* (Malden: Blackwell, 2004), 198–99.

A-98. Arnold, *Who Were the Babylonians?* 87–91.

A-99. See J. H. Hayes and S. A. Irvine, *Isaiah The Eighth Century Prophet: His Life and Times* (Nashville: Abingdon, 1987), 24.

A-100. J. A. Brinkman, *A Political History of Post-Kassite Babylonia, 1158–722 B.C.* (AnOr 43; Rome: Pontifical Biblical Institute, 168), 260–85.

A-101. B. T. Arnold, "Babylonians," in Hoerth, *Peoples*, 58–59.

A-102. Ibid., 60–66; P.-A. Beaulieu, "King Nabonidus and the Neo-Babylonian Empire," *CANE*, 969–79.

A-103. See Johnston, *Shades of Sheol*, 69–124; *CANE*, 2068–70; J. H. Walton, *Ancient Near Eastern Thought and the Old Testament: Introducing the Conceptual World of the Hebrew Bible* (Grand Rapids: Baker, 2006), 314–29, especially 320–21.

A-104. *CANE*, 1763–74.

A-105. COS, 2.8–12; R. O. Faulkner, *The Ancient Egyptian Pyramid Texts* (Oxford: Clarendon, 1969); idem, *The Ancient Egyptian Coffin Texts*, 3 vols. (Warminster: Aris & Phillips, 1973–1978); idem, *The Ancient Egyptian Book of the Dead* (Austin: Univ. of Texas Press, 1990); D. Meeks and C. Favard-Meeks, *Daily Life of the Egyptian Gods* (Ithaca, N.Y.: Cornell Univ. Press, 1996), 141–50; E. Hornung, *The Ancient Egyptian Books of the Afterlife* (Ithaca, N.Y.: Cornell Univ. Press, 1999); J. H. Taylor, *Death and the Afterlife in Ancient Egypt* (Chicago: Univ. of Chicago Press, 2001); M. Müller, "Afterlife," in *The Oxford Encyclopedia of Ancient Egypt*, ed. D. B. Redford (New York: Oxford Univ. Press, 2001), 1:32–37.

A-106. Taylor, *Death and the Afterlife*, 46–91.

A-107. E. Otto, *Das altägyptische Mundöffnungsritual* (Ägyptologische Abhandlungen 3; Wiesbaden: Harrassowitz, 1960); J. C. Goyon, *Rituels funéraires de l'ancienne Égypte : le rituel de l'embaument, le rituel de l'ouverture de la bouche, les livres de respiration* (Paris: Éditions du Cerf, 1972); *AEL*, 2:120.

A-108. Taylor, *Death and the Afterlife*, 190–92.

A-109. J. Zandee, *Death as an Enemy according to Ancient Egyptian Conceptions* (Studies in the History of Religions 5; Leiden: Brill, 1960); P. S. Johnston, "Death in Israel and Egypt: A Theological Reflection," in *The Old Testament in Its World*, ed. R. P. Gordon and J. C. de Moor (OTS 52; Leiden: Brill, 2005), 100–104.

A-110. *CANE*, 1886–88; D. Katz, *The Image of the Netherworld in the Sumerian Sources* (Bethesda, Md.: CDL, 2003).

A-111. George, *Epic of Gilgamesh*, 187. See also the description in Ishtar's Descent to the Netherworld in Foster, *Before the Muses*, 499.

A-112. *ANET*, 110.

A-113. Aharoni, *Macmillan Bible Atlas*, 52; MacDonald, *"East of the Jordan,"* 171–83; Routledge, *Moab*, 48–57.

A-114. See also the Moabite Stone, COS, 2.23; Routledge, *Moab*, 41–48, 133–53.

A-115. *ANET*, 282.

A-116. Ibid., 287.

A-117. See P. M. Michèle Daviau and P.-E. Dion, "Moab Comes to Life," *BAR* 28/1 (2002): 38–49, 63.

A-118. *KTU*, 1.14 I:26–27. See also COS, 1.86.

A-119. D. W. Baker, *Joel, Obadiah, Malachi* (NIVAC; Grand Rapids: Zondervan, 2006), 44. On mourning in general in Israelite society, see R. N. Boyce, *The Cry to God in the Old Testament* (SBLDS 103; Atlanta: Scholars, 1988); G. A. Anderson, *A Time to Mourn, A Time to Dance: The Expression of Grief and Joy in Israelite Religion* (University Park: Pennsylvania State Univ. Press, 1991); P. W. Ferris Jr., *The Genre of Communal Lament in the Bible and the Ancient Near East* (SBLDS 127; Atlanta: Scholars, 1992).

A-120. COS, 1.86. See also *AEL*, 2:206.

A-121. Ibid., 1.86.

A-122. Dalley, *Myths from Mesopotamia*, 91–92.

A-123. Ibid., 93. Special mourning garments are also worn in Egypt, see *AEL*, 3:132.

A-124. E.g., *ANET*, 455–63; COS, 1.118–19, 166; S. N. Kramer, "The Temple in Sumerian Literature," in *Temple in Society*, ed. M. V. Fox (Winona Lake, Ind.: Eisenbrauns, 1988), 1–16.

A-125. *AEL*, 1:152.

A-126. Ibid., 3:5.

A-127. *SSS*, I, 2.

A-128. See *ANET*, 283.

A-129. Ibid., 285.

A-130. *NBD*[2], 295–99; K. A. Kitchen, "Egypt, History of (Chronology)," *ABD*, 2:325–31; A. Spalinger, "Egypt, History of (Dyn. 21–26)," *ABD*, 2:358–60.

A-131. Rainey and Notley, *Sacred Bridge*, 42.

A-132. Aharoni, *Macmillan Bible Atlas*, 11.

A-133. COS, 1.45.

A-134. *AEL*, 3:95

A-135. Jacob and Jacob, "Flora," 2:815.

A-136. Pers. trans.; *ANET*, 320.

A-137. King and Stage, *Life*, 148–52; Jacob and Jacob, "Flora," 2:815.

A-138. H. T. Wright, "Mesopotamia, History of (Chronology)," *ABD*, 4:721.

A-139. *AEL*, 1:207.

A-140. Ibid., 2:172.

A-141. *CAD*, 8, 473–75.

A-142. Ibid., 7, 254.

A-143. *AEL*, 1:153.

A-144. Del Olmo Lete, *Dictionary*, 688.

A-145. Younger, "Recent Study on Sargon II," 313–18.

A-146. *ANET*, 286.

A-147. Ibid.

A-148. *NEAEHL*, 1:100.

A-149. Amiran, "Water Supply," 75–78.

A-150. See map in Watts, *Isaiah 1–33*, 283.

A-151. COS, 2.28; pers. trans. See also K. L. Younger Jr., "The Siloam Tunnel Inscription: An Integrated Reading," *UF* 26 (1994): 543–56.

A-152. Grayson, *Early First Millennium*, 2:247.

A-153. Ibid.

A-154. See King and Stager, *Life*, 233–39; Hasel, *Military Practice*, 51–93.

A-155. COS, 1.166.

A-156. *ANET*, 445.

A-157. Cf. T. Hiebert, "Theophany in the OT," *ABD*, 6:505–11.

A-158. J. Niehaus, *God at Sinai: Covenant and Theophany in the Bible and Ancient Near East* (Grand Rapids: Zondervan, 1995), 125–36.

A-159. D. D. Luckenbill, *The Annals of Sennacherib* (OIP 2; Chicago: Univ. of Chicago Press, 1924), 45; *CAD*, 13, 246.

A-160. COS, 1.102.

A-161. Ibid., 1.103.

A-162. Budge and King, *Annals*, 42.

A-163. COS, 1.86.

A-164. T. G. H. James, "Egypt: The Twenty-Fifth and Twenty-Sixth Dynasties," in *CAH*, III[2], 2, 682–89.

A-165. *CAH*, III², 1, 576–77; Grayson, "Assyria: Tiglath-pileser III," 2:89; Spalinger, "Egypt, History of (Dyn. 21–26)," *ABD*, 2:359–60.
A-166. H. R. Hall, *Catalogue of Egyptian Scarabs, etc. in the British Museum* I (London: British Museum, 1913), numbers 2775, 2776; James, "Egypt," 693.
A-167. James, "Egypt," 693.
A-168. Wiseman, *Vassal-Treaties*, 38; cf. Nissinen, *References to Prophecy*, 156.
A-169. Nissinen, *References to Prophecy*, 111, 120–50; see also 156, 160–61.
A-170. *COS*, 3.80.
A-171. Day, "Baal (Deity)," *ABD*, 1:546; del Olmo Lete, *Dictionary*, 788.
A-172. Lambert, *Babylonian Wisdom Literature*, 53; see *CAD*, 17/I, 52, 55.
A-173. *CAD*, 17/I, 55–56.
A-174. Ibid., 57.
A-175. See R. E. Averbeck, "Sumer, the Bible, and Comparative Method: Historiography and Temple Building," in Chavalas and Younger, ed., *Mesopotamia and the Bible*, 120.
A-176. Roaf, *Cultural Atlas*, 104–7; Bienkowski and Millard, *Dictionary*, 327–28; J. H. Walton, "The Mesopotamian Background of the Tower of Babel Account and Its Implications," *BBR* 5 (1995): 155–75.
A-177. Hurowitz, *I Have Built*, 335–36.
A-178. Ibid., 66.
A-179. Borger, *Inschriften Asrhaddons*, 5; translation Hurowitz, *I Have Built*, 245.
A-180. See King and Stager, *Life*, 247–51.
A-181. *COS*, 2.119B; pers. trans.
A-182. King and Stager, *Life*, 247–51; see D. Ussishkin, *The Renewed Archaeological Excavations at Lachish*, 5 vols. (Tel Aviv: Tel Aviv Univ. Press, 2004); P. J. King, "Why Lachish Matters: A Major Site Gets the Publication It Deserves," *BAR* 31/4 (2005): 36–47.
A-183. There is also a suggestion that there were two campaigns by Sennacherib and that vestiges of both are found in the Bible. See W. Shea, "Jerusalem Under Siege: Did Sennacherib Attack Twice?" *BAR* 25/6 (1999): 36–44, 64.
A-184. On this genre in Sumerian literature, see W. W. Hallo, "Individual Prayer in Sumerian: The Continuity of a Tradition," in Hallo, *Essays*, 75–80. Another text identified as a "letter to god" is rather an account of a conquest, being a different literary genre; N. Naʾaman, "Sennacherib's 'Letter to God' on his Campaign to Judah," in *Ancient Israel and Its Neighbors: Interaction and Counteraction: Collected Essays: Volume 1*, ed. N. Naʾaman (Winona Lake, Ind.: Eisenbrauns, 2005), 135–52, originally *BASOR* 214 (1974): 25–39.
A-185. See a similar lament by the king of Sidon; *COS*, 2.57.
A-186. Ibid., 1.164.
A-187. Hallo, "Individual Prayer," 75.
A-188. See Holloway, *Aššur is King*, 80–216.
A-189. Moran, *Amarna Letters*. More broadly, see B. U. Schipper, *Israel und Ägypten in der Königszeit: Die kulturellen Kontakte von Salomo bis zum Fall Jerusalems* (OBO 170; Göttingen: Vandenhoeck & Ruprecht, 1999).
A-190. For treaties, see *ANET*, 199–206, 529–41; *COS*, 2.17–18, 82, 127–29. For discussion, see Holloway, *Aššur is King*, 217–319; *CANE*, 964–65.
A-191. Holloway, *Aššur is King*, 338–88.
A-192. *CANE*, 1380–81.
A-193. Oppenheim, *Ancient Mesopotamia*, 93.
A-194. N. Yoffee, *Explaining Trade in Ancient Western Asia* (MANE, 2/2; Malibu: Undena, 1981); J. G. Dercksen, ed., *Trade and Finance in Ancient Mesopotamia: Proceedings of the First MOS Symposium (Leiden 1977)* (MOS Studies, 1; Leiden: Nederlands Instituut voor het Nabije Oosten, 1999); Nemet-Nejat, *Daily Life*, 269–81.
A-195. For maps from several periods, see Roaf, *Cultural Atlas of Mesopotamia*, 34, 79, 98, 113; *CANE*, 1373–497; M. T. Larsen, *The Old Assyrian City-state and its Colonies* (Mesopotamia 4; Copenhagen: Akademisk Forlag, 1976); B. G. Wood, *The Sociology of Pottery in Ancient Palestine: The Ceramic Industry and the Diffusion of Ceramic Style in the Bronze and Iron Ages* (JSOTSup, 103; Sheffield: Sheffield Academic Press, 1990); M. Elate, "Phoenician Overland Trade within the Mesopotamian Empires," in M. Cogan and I. Ephʾal, *Ah Assyria*, 21–35; T. E. Levy, ed., *The Archaeology of Society in the Holy Land* (New York: Facts on File, 1995); Schipper, *Israel und Ägypten*, 35–83, 159–85, 247–65.
A-196. D. Dorsey, *Roads and Highways of Ancient Israel* (Baltimore: Johns Hopkins Univ. Press, 1991); Oppenheim, *Ancient Mesopotamia*, 119.
A-197. *CAD*, 6, 231–232.
A-198. *ANET*, 82; *CAD*, 6, 107; pers. trans.
A-199. A paved street is noted in EB III Beth-Yerah, D. Ussishkin, "Beth Yerah," *RB* 75 (1968): 267.
A-200. *ARM*, 2.78 (*CAD*, 6, 107–8); pers. trans.
A-201. *CAD*, 6, 232.
A-202. Grayson, *Assyrian Rulers*, 2:8.
A-203. Ibid., 2:13.
A-204. *CAD*, 6, 108; K. Kessler, "'Royal Roads' and Other Questions of the Neo-Assyrian Communication System" in Parpola and Whiting, *Assyria 1995*, 129–36.
A-205. Wiseman, *Vassal-Treaties*, 54.
A-206. See Kramer, *The Sumerians*, 115–16; G. Farber-Flügge, *Der Mythos "Inanna und Enki" unter besonderer Berücksichtigung der Liste der me* (Studia Pohl 10; Rome: Pontifical Biblical Institute, 1973), 116–213; idem., "ME," in *RlA*,7, 610–613; Berlejung, *Die Theologie der Bilder*, 20–30.
A-207. *COS*, 1.161.
A-208. *ANEP*, 561; Lurker, *Illustrated Dictionary*, 78; E. Teeter, *The Presentation of Maat: Ritual and Legitimacy in Ancient Egypt* (SAOC 57; Chi-

cago: Oriental Institute of the Univ. of Chicago, 1997).

A-209. *ANEP*, 639.

A-210. *ANET*, 213.

A-211. *AEL*, 2:125.

A-212. See S. G. F. Brandon, *Creation Myths of the Ancient Near East* (London: Hodder & Stoughton, 1963); R. J. Clifford, *Creation Accounts in the Ancient Near East and in the Bible* (CBQMS 26; Washington, D.C.: Catholic Biblical Association, 1994); R. S. Hess and D. T. Tsumura, *I Studied Inscriptions from before the Flood: Ancient Near Eastern, Literary, and Linguistic Approaches to Genesis 1–11* (SBTS 4; Winona Lake, Ind.: Eisenbrauns, 1994), especially the introduction, 27–44.

A-213. *AEL*, 2:96.

A-214. Ibid., 3:112.

A-215. COS, 1.15. In 1.14 he is called "father of the gods ... who begot himself by himself."

A-216. Ibid.

A-217. V. H. Matthews and D. C. Benjamin, *Old Testament Parallels: Law and Stories from the Ancient Near East*, rev. ed. (New York: Paulist, 1997), 8; J. D. Currid, *Ancient Egypt and the Old Testament* (Grand Rapids: Baker, 1997), 57–59, where Atum is the actor. On expectoration as a creation means, see also *ANET*, 3.

A-218. L. Oakes and L. Gahlin, *Ancient Egypt* (New York: Barnes and Noble, 2003), 301.

A-219. COS, 1.111.

A-220. Ibid.

A-221. Ibid., 1.157.

A-222. *ANET*, 100.

A-223. COS, 1.86

A-224. See Walton, *Ancient Near Eastern Thought*, 97–99.

A-225. COS, 1.111; T. Jacobsen, "The Battle Between Marduk and Tiamat," *JAOS* 88 (1968): 104–8.

A-226. Ibid. See a seal inscription showing Ishtar in her warrior's regalia, B. N. Porter, "The Anxiety of Multiplicity: Concepts of Divinity as One and Many in Ancient Assyria," in *One God or Many? Concepts of Divinity in the Ancient World* , ed. B. N. Porter (Chebeague, Me.: Casco Bay Assyriological Institute, 2000), 244.

A-227. *CAD*, 8, 52.

A-228. Moran, *Amarna Letters*, 107.

A-229. See Lurker, *Illustrated Dictionary*, 101; van der Toorn, *Dictionary*, 701–2.

A-230. COS, 1.86.

A-231. Ibid.; van der Toorn, *Dictionary*, 37–38.

A-232. J. Leclant, "Anat," *Lexikon der Ägyptologie* I (1973), 253–58; van der Toorn, *Dictionary*, 38–40.

A-233. M. Lind, *Yahweh Is a Warrior: The Theology of Warfare in Ancient Israel* (Scottdale, Pa.: Herald, 1980); S.-M. Kang, *Divine War in the Old Testament and in the Ancient Near East* (BZAW 177; Berlin: de Gruyter, 1989); T. Longman III and D. G. Reid, *God Is a Warrior* (Grand Rapids: Zondervan, 1995).

A-234. A. George, *House Most High: The Temples of Ancient Mesopotamia* (Mesopotamian Civilizations 5; Winona Lake, Ind.: Eisenbrauns, 1993), 139–40.

A-235. Borger, *Die Inschriften Asarhaddons*, 13; B. Landsberger, *Brief des Bischofs von Esagila an König Asarhaddon* (Amsterdam: Noord-Hollandische Uitg. Mij., 1965), 20–27; van de Mieroop, "Revenge, Assyrian Style," 3–21, especially 17; idem, "A Tale of Two Cities: Nineveh and Babylon," in *Nineveh: Papers of the XLIXe Rencontre Assyriologique Internationale London 7–11 July 2003*, ed. D. Collon and A. George (London: British School of Archaeology in Iraq, 2005), 1–7; see J. Milgrom, *Leviticus 1–16* (AB; New York: Doubleday, 1991), 350; J. A. Brinkman, "Through a Glass Darkly: Esarhaddon's Retrospects on the Downfall of Babylon," *JAOS* 103 (1983): 35–42; G. Frame, *Babylonia 689–627 B.C.: A Political History* (Uitgaven van het Nederlands Historisch-Archaeologisch Instituut te Istanbul 69; Istanbul: Nederlands Historisch-Archaeologisch Instituut, 1992), 52–63.

A-236. H. Tadmor, B. Landsberger, S. Parpola, "The Sin of Sargon and Sennacherib's Last Will," *State Archives of Assyria Bulletin* 3/1 (1989): 3–51; Longman, *Fictional Akkadian Autobiography*, 231–33 (text), 117–18 (discussion); A. M. Weaver, "The 'Sin of Sargon' and Esarhaddon's Reconception of Sennacherib: A Study in Divine Will, Human Politics and Royal Ideology," in Collon and George, ed., *Nineveh*, 1:61–66.

A-237. J. A. Brinkman, *Prelude to Empire: Babylonian Society and Politics, 747–626* B.C. (Occasional Publications of the Babylonian Fund, 7: Philadelphia: The Univ. Museum, 1984), 67–84; Frame, *Babylonia 689–627 B.C*, 64–101; B. N. Porter, *Images, Power, and Politics: Figurative Aspects of Esarhaddon's Babylonian Policy* (Philadelphia: American Philosophical Society, 1993); Nissinen and Parpola, "Marduk's Return," 213.

A-238. M. Nissinen, *Prophets and Prophecy in the Ancient Near East* (SBLWAW 12; Atlanta: Society of Biblical Literature, 2003), 157.

A-239. See O. Negbi, *Canaanite Gods in Metal: An Archaeological Study of Ancient Syro-Palestinian Figurines* (Tel Aviv: Tel Aviv Univ., 1976); Keel and Uehlinger, *Gods, Goddesses*; C. Uehlinger, "Anthropomorphic Cult Statuary in Iron Age Palestine and the Search for Yahweh's Cult Images," in van der Toorn, ed., *Image and the Book*, 97–155.

A-240. See 4 Kingdoms 18:34 LXX; M. Anbar, "*Kai pou eisin hoi theoi tēs chōra Samareias*, 'et où sont les dieux du pays de Samarie,'" *BN* 51 (1990): 7–8.

A-241. COS, 2.118D. For a picture of captured deities being transported away, see *ANEP*, 538. See A. Spycket, *La statuaire du Proche-Orient ancien* (Leiden: Brill, 1981).

A-242. H. Niehr, "In Search of YHWH's Cult Statue in the First Temple," in van der Toorn, ed., *The*

Image and the Book, 73–95, especially 79; Uehlinger, "Anthropomorphic Cult Statuary," 125; B. Becking, "Assyrian Evidence for Iconic Polytheism in Ancient Israel," ibid., 157–71; regarding Yahweh representations, see Sass, "Pre-Exilic Hebrew Seals," 234; B. B. Schmid, "The Aniconic Tradition: On Reading Images and Viewing Texts," in *The Triumph of Elohim: From Yahwisms to Judaisms*, ed. D. V. Edelman (Grand Rapids: Eerdmans, 1996), 75–105; D. V. Edelman, "Tracking Observance of the Aniconic Tradition through Numismatics," in ibid., 185–225. For an opposing view, see, e.g., S. Timm, "Die Eroberung Samarias aus assyrisch-babylonischer Sicht," *WO* 20/21 (1989/1990): 77.

A-243. T. Mettinger, "The Veto on Images and the Aniconic God in Israel," in *Religious Symbols and Their Functions*, ed. H. Biezais (Stockholm: Almqvist & Wiksell, 1979), 15–29; S. Olyan, *Asherah and the Cult of Yahweh in Israel* (Atlanta: Scholars Press, 1988); M. Smith, *The Early History of God*, 2nd ed. (San Francisco: Harper & Row, 2002); idem, *The Origins of Biblical Monotheism* (Oxford: Oxford Univ. Press, 2001).

A-244. T. N. D. Mettinger, "Israelite Aniconism: Developments and Origins," in van der Toorn, ed., *The Image and the Book*, 173.

A-245. Keel and Uehlinger, *Gods, Goddesses*, 294–309.

A-246. C. Uehlinger, "Gab es eine joschijanische Kultreform? Plädoyer für ein begründetes Minimum," in *Jeremia und die "deuteronomistische Bewegung*, ed. W. Gross (BBB 98; Weinheim: Beltz Athenäum, 1995), 65–67; Mettinger, "Israelite Aniconism," 178–79.

A-247. *COS*, 1.124.

A-248. M. Boyce, *Zoroastrians: Their Religious Beliefs and Practices* (London: Routledge & Kegan Paul, 1979), 19–20; Yamauchi, *Persia and the Bible*, 395–466.

A-249. Boyce, *Zoroastrians*, 50–53; idem., *A History of Zoroastrianism* (Leiden: Brill, 1982), 2, 41–43; M. Mallowan, "Cyrus the Great (558–529 B.C.)," in *The Median and Achaemenian Periods: Vol. 2, Cambridge History of Iran*, ed. I. Gershevitch (Cambridge: Cambridge Univ. Press, 1985), 416. Denying this early an appearance of worship, see Yamauchi, *Persia and the Bible*, 419–30.

A-250. See I. T. Abusch, *Babylonian Witchcraft Literature: Case Studies* (BJS 132; Atlanta: Scholars, 1987); W. Farber, "Witchcraft, Magic, and Divination in Ancient Mesopotamia," in *CANE*, 1895–909; G. Cunningham, *"Deliver Me from Evil": Mesopotamian Incantations 2500–1200 B.C.* (Rome: Pontifical Biblical Institute, 1997); T. Abusch and K. van der Toorn, ed. *Mesopotamian Magic: Textual, Historical and Interpretative Perspectives* (Groningen: Styx, 1999); M.-L. Thomsen, "Witchcraft and Magic in Ancient Mesopotamia," in *Biblical and Pagan Societies*, ed. F. H. Cryer (Philadelphia: Univ. of Pennsylvania Press, 2001), 1–91; T. Abusch, *Mesopotamian Witchcraft: Toward a History and Understanding of Babylonian Witchcraft Beliefs and Literature* (Leiden: Brill, 2002).

A-251. E.g., J. Baines, "Society, Morality, and Religious Practice," in Shafer, *Religion in Ancient Egypt*, 164–72; R. K. Ritner, *The Mechanics of Ancient Egyptian Magical Practice* (Chicago: Oriental Institute of the Univ. of Chicago, 1993); Meeks and Favard-Meeks, *Daily Life*, 187–98; G. Pinch, *Magic in Ancient Egypt* (Austin: Univ. of Texas Press, 1994); J. F. Borghouts, "Witchcraft, Magic, and Divination in Ancient Egypt," in *CANE*, 1775–85.

A-252. *COS*, 1.94; see del Olmo Lete, *Canaanite Religion*, 360–78; J.-M. de Tarragon, "Witchcraft, Magic, and Divination in Canaan and Ancient Israel," in *CANE*, 2071–81.

A-253. Bienkowski and Millard, *Dictionary*, 186–87. Even allegations of witchcraft needed to be investigated, according to the Code of Hammurabi (Richardson, *Hammurabi's Law*, 43).

A-254. For a listing of comparisons between the servant of the Lord and the ideal royalty of Isa. 11 and 61–62, see J. H. Walton, "The Imagery of the Substitute King Ritual in Isaiah's Fourth Servant Song," *JBL* 122 (2003): 742.

A-255. As one of his exploits, Tiglath-pileser I tells of releasing captured kings (*CAD*, 12, 293).

A-256. See comment on 42:7.

A-257. Sin-shar-ishkun chosen by the gods for kingship, *CAD*, 11/II, 22; Seux, *Épithètes royales*, 188.

A-258. Kings needed to undertake irrigation projects to supply water for crop growth, Oppenheim, *Ancient Mesopotamia*, 84–85; Saggs, *Might*, 131–32; *CAD*, 17/III, 95–96; O. Borowski, "Irrigation," *OEANE*, 3, 1–184. See Sennacherib making improvements to Nineveh, including waterworks, Luckenbill, *Annals*, 96, 98.

A-259. S. Parpola, *Letters from Assyrian and Babylonian Scholars* (SAA X; Helsinki: Helsinki University Press, 1993), 12.

A-260. Ibid., 287.

A-261. Ibid., 288; Walton, "Imagery," 738; see J. Bottéro, "The Substitute King and his Fate," in Bottéro, *Mesopotamia*, 151 ("in order to save them").

A-262. Parpola, *Letters from Assyrian and Babylonian Scholars*, 352:17–19.

A-263. *CAD*, 4, 162–164.

A-264. Ibid., 4, 170.

A-265. Moran, *Amarna Letters*, 219, 306; *CAD*, 4, 164–65.

A-266. J. M. Hadley, "Two Pithoi from Kuntillet ʿAjrud," *VT* 37 (1987): 187; P. D. Miller Jr., "El, the Creator of the Earth," *BASOR* 239 (1980): 45.

A-267. *ANET*, 380.

A-268. See Leick, *Sex and Eroticism*, especially 30–41.

A-269. See Wilkinson, *Complete Gods and Goddesses*, 141.

A-270. Ibid., 115–17.

A-271. Dalley, *Myths*, 32.
A-272. Ibid., 113.
A-273. COS, 1.111.
A-274. Ibid., 1.88.
A-275. *AEL*, 1:37.
A-276. E. A. W. Budge, *The Book of the Dead: The Hieroglyphic Transcript of the Papyrus Ani* (New Hyde Park, N.Y.: University Books, 1960), 461.
A-277. *AEL*, 3:179.
A-278. J. L. Foster, *Hymns, Prayers, and Songs: An Anthology of Ancient Egyptian Lyric Poetry* (SBLWAW 8; Atlanta: Scholars, 1995), 77.
A-279. Lambert, *Babylonian Wisdom Literature*, 86; *CAD*, 11/II, 185.
A-280. Nemet-Nejat, *Daily Life*, 143–44.
A-281. Hornung, *Ancient Egyptian Books*; Hornung and Bryan, *Quest for Immortality*.
A-282. S. Sauneron, *The Priests of Ancient Egypt*, new ed. (Ithaca, N.Y.: Cornell Univ. Press, 2000), 108–9.
A-283. *AEL*, 2:122.
A-284. T. J. Lewis, *Cults of the Dead in Ancient Israel and Ugarit* (HSM 39; Atlanta: Scholars, 1989), 2. See Alster, *Death in Mesopotamia*.
A-285. *CAD*, 8, 427.
A-286. Ibid., 8, 425; see 426–27 where oil, water, wine, and beer are also poured out.
A-287. Lewis, *Cults of the Dead*, 5–97. An alternative interpretation of the Ugaritic material reflecting burial practice rather than ancestor veneration is presented by B. B. Schmidt, *Israel's Beneficent Dead: Ancestor Cult and Necromancy in Ancient Israelite Religion and Tradition* (Winona Lake, Ind.: Eisenbrauns, 1996), 47–122.
A-288. C. F. A. Schaeffer, *The Cuneiform Texts from Ras Shamra-Ugarit* (London: Oxford Univ. Press, 1939), 50; Lewis, *Cults of the Dead*, 97–98.
A-289. R. E. Cooley, "Gathered to His People: A Study of a Dothan Family Tomb," in *The Living and Active Word of God: Studies in Honor of Samuel J. Schultz*, ed. M. Inch and R. Youngblood (Winona Lake, Ind.: Eisenbrauns, 1983), 50–52; Lewis, *Cults of the Dead*, 179–80; Johnston, *Shades of Sheol*, 62.
A-290. See Lewis, *Cults of the Dead*, 99–181; Schmidt, *Israel's Beneficent Dead*, 132–293; King and Stager, *Life*, 376–80.
A-291. Van der Toorn, *Family Religion*, 107, from W. G. Lambert, "A Further Attempt at the Babylonian 'Man and his God,'" in *Language, Literature, and History: Studies presented to Erica Reiner*, ed. F. Rochberg-Halton (AOS 67; New Haven, Conn.: American Oriental Society, 1987), 192.
A-292. *AEL*, 1:17.
A-293. *ANET*, 627.
A-294. Van der Toorn, *Family Religion*, 106–7.
A-295. *ANET*, 627.
A-296. Moran, *Amarna Letters*, 195–96, n. 1.
A-297. *AEL*, 1:64; see also 106, 126, 175, etc.
A-298. Ibid., 2:111.
A-299. COS, 1.149.
A-300. S. N. Kramer, "Dilmun, the Land of the Living," *BASOR* 96 (1944): 18–24; idem, *Enki and Ninhursag*; N. Sarna, *Understanding Genesis* (New York: Schocken, 1966), 24–25.
A-301. T. Jacobsen, *The Harps That Once*, 185–86.
A-302. *ANET*, 38–40.
A-303. Kramer, *Enki and Ninhursag*; idem, *Sumerians*, 147–49.
A-304. Alster, "Dilmun, Bahrain," 52–74; Batto, "Paradise Reexamined," 33–66.
A-305. See J. Baines, "Society, Morality," in Shafer, *Religion in Ancient Egypt*, 147–49.

We want to hear from you. Please send your comments about this book to us in care of zreview@zondervan.com. Thank you.

ZONDERVAN.com/
AUTHORTRACKER
follow your favorite authors